Dragon Days

Other Tactics Manual Supplements from Posterity Press:

The Last Hundred Yards: The NCO's Contribution to Warfare
One More Bridge to Cross: Lowering the Cost of War
Phantom Soldier: The Enemy's Answer to U.S. Firepower
The Tiger's Way: A U.S. Private's Best Chance for Survival
Tactics of the Crescent Moon: Militant Muslim Combat Methods
Militant Tricks: Battlefield Ruses of the Islamic Militant
Terrorist Trail: Backtracking the Foreign Fighter

DRAGON DAYS

TIME FOR "UNCONVENTIONAL" TACTICS

ILLUSTRATED

H. JOHN POOLE

FOREWORD BY

MAJ.GEN. RAY L. SMITH USMC (RET.)

POSTERITY PRESS

Published by Posterity Press
P.O. Box 5360, Emerald Isle, NC 28594
(www.posteritypress.org)

Cataloging-in-Publication Data
Poole, H. John, 1943-
Dragon Days.
Includes bibliography and index.
1. Infantry drill and tactics.
2. Military art and science.
3. Military history.
I. Title. ISBN: 978-0-9638695-4-8 2007 355'.42
Library of Congress Control Number: 2007930932

Edited by Dr. Mary Beth Poole
Proofread by William E. Harris

First printing, United States of America, October 2007

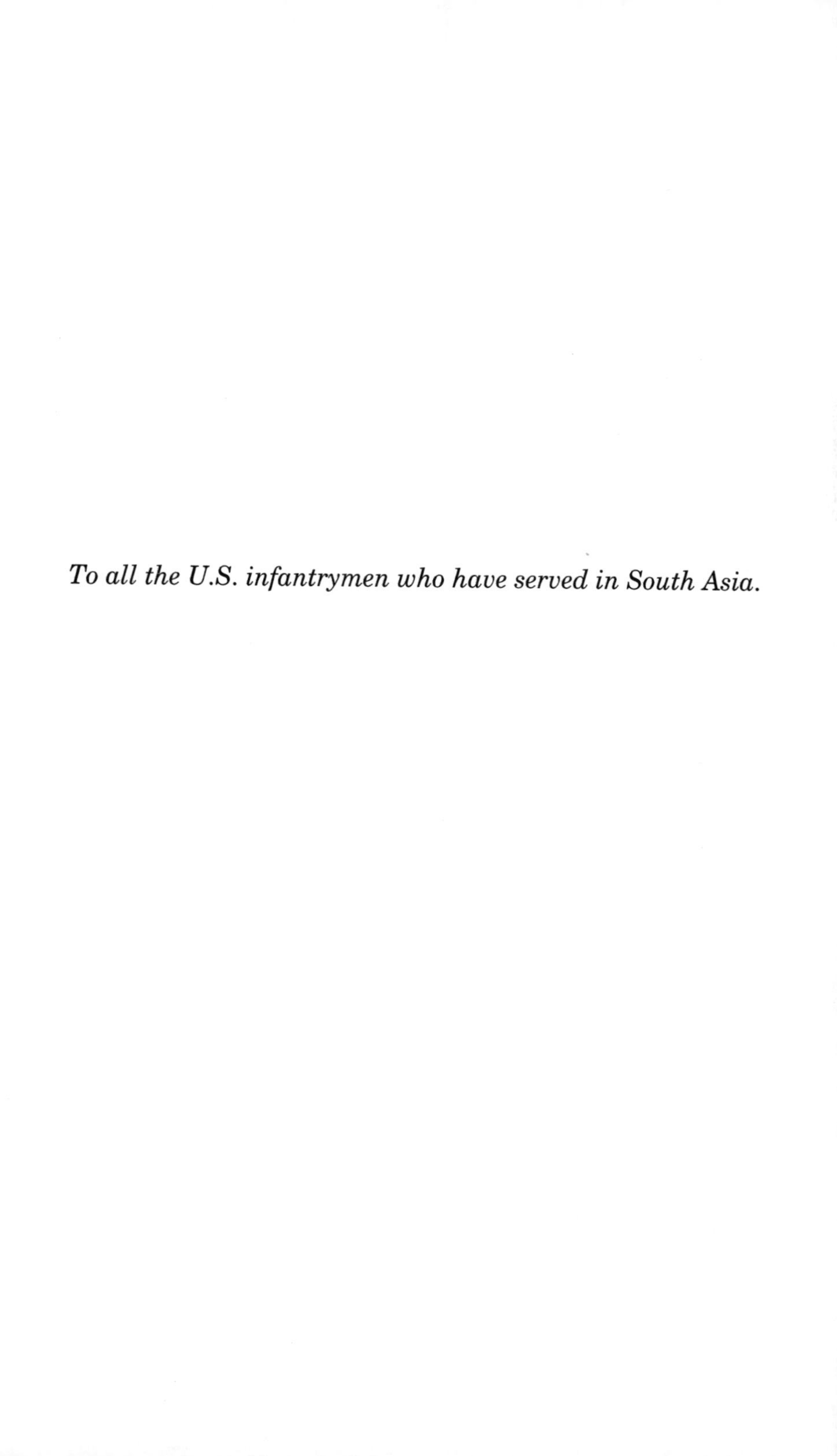

To all the U.S. infantrymen who have served in South Asia.

Disclaimer:

For the sake of spacing and aesthetics, this work's subtitle had to be condensed. Unconventional warfare (UW) is an extremely broad subject. It typically encompasses every aspect of espionage, guerrilla warfare, and escape / evasion. Over the last 60 years, many unseemly activities have been attributed to UW, and rationalized through UW. The author does not endorse any of them. All that might possibly be perceived as overbearing or subversive behavior by the United States of America has been intentionally omitted from these pages. In a world increasingly shaped by media coverage and public opinion, such things will prove counterproductive. They and all espionage should be carefully avoided by the U.S. military. The edge in all future conflicts will go to the side that fights in the most ethical manner. There is nothing inherently immoral about "behind-enemy-lines" reconnaissance, guerrilla warfare, and escape / evasion. This work contains UW procedures for those kinds of initiatives. It is hoped that they will help American Marines, soldiers, sailors, airmen, Coast Guardsmen, and police to now turn the tide in the so-called "War on Terror."

Contents

List of Illustrations ix
Foreword xv
Preface xvii
Introduction xxiii
Acknowledgments xxxi

Part One: Return of the Dragon

Chapter 1: *The Sino-Islamist Connection* 3
Chapter 2: *Burma, Thailand, and Malaysia* 25
Chapter 3: *Southern Philippines and Indonesia* 37
Chapter 4: *Cambodia and Laos* 65
Chapter 5: *Nepal and Bangladesh* 79
Chapter 6: *India and Sri Lanka* 91
Chapter 7: *Pakistan and Afghanistan* 107

Part Two: A Viable Containment Strategy

Chapter 8: *What Hasn't Worked in the Past* 145
Chapter 9: *The Law Enforcement Dimension* 157
Chapter 10: *A Thorough Investigation* 163
Chapter 11: *Pursuit and Arrest* 175
Chapter 12: *The Sting* 183
Chapter 13: *The Only Defense Is Unconventional* 191

Part Three: Prerequisite Unconventional Warfare Skills

Chapter 14: *Finding an Enemy Weakness* 199
Chapter 15: *Obscure Approach* 215
Chapter 16: *Disguising the Attack* 237
Chapter 17: *Precluding a Counterstroke* 249
Chapter 18: *Rural Escape and Evasion* 281

Chapter 19: *Enhancing Rural Terrain* 303
Chapter 20: *Urban Escape and Evasion* 327
Chapter 21: *Enhancing Urban Terrain* 345

Afterword 367
Notes 375
Glossary 419
Bibliography 429
About the Author 449
Name Index 451

Illustrations

Maps

Chapter 1: *The Sino-Islamist Connection*

1.1: Eastern Oil Route from Africa 5
1.2: The Malay Peninsula Bottleneck 9
1.3: China 10

Chapter 2: *Burma, Thailand, and Malaysia*

2.1: The New Irrawaddy Conduit 31
2.2: Old Burma Road 32
2.3: Towns and Boundaries in Northwest Burma 33
2.4: "Golden-Triangle" Buffer 34

Chapter 3: *Southern Philippines and Indonesia*

3.1: Philippine Island Chain 39
3.2: Indonesia 45
3.3: Sulawesi 56

Chapter 4: *Cambodia and Laos*

4.1: Once China's Closest Ally in Southeast Asia 67
4.2: Laos 75

Chapter 5: *Nepal and Bangladesh*

5.1: The Jewel of South Asia 80
5.2: The Road between Lhasa and Kathmandu 81
5.3: Easy Access to the Bay of Bengal 83

Chapter 6: *India and Sri Lanka*

6.1: Indian Subcontinent 93
6.2: Communist Insurgency "Corridor" 94
6.3: Naxalite-Targeted Areas as of August 2006 95
6.4: Sri Lanka 99

Chapter 7: *Pakistan and Afghanistan*

7.1: The Afghan Provinces 113
7.2: Area of Strategic Significance to the PRC 117
7.3: Chinese Transportation Hub 121
7.4: The Way through Jammu-Kashmir to Afghanistan 131
7.5: Karakoram Highway 132
7.6: The Two Reinforcement Routes from China 134
7.7: Close-Up of Chitral Region 135
7.8: Close-Up of Pamir Region 138-139

Chapter 19: *Enhancing Rural Terrain*

19.1: U.S. Guerrilla-Prepared Hides 315
19.2: U.S. Guerrilla-Prepared Conduits 318

Chapter 20: *Urban Escape and Evasion*

20.1: From Citadel's SW Corner to Phu Cam Canal 330
20.2: Up Phu Cam's Runoff Ditch Feeders to the Ridge 333

Chapter 21: *Enhancing Urban Terrain*

21.1: The Citadel's Walls and Many Gates 347

Figures

Chapter 7: *Pakistan and Afghanistan*

7.1: U.S. Army's Strategic Studies Institute Table 114-116

Chapter 8: *What Hasn't Worked in the Past*

8.1: GIs Now Spend Too Much Time on Defense 148

Chapter 10: *A Thorough Investigation*

10.1: The Most Common Type of Hidden Evidence 168
10.2: Crime Scene Search Patterns 171
10.3: Most Indoor Searches Require the Zone Method 173

Chapter 11: *Pursuit and Arrest*

11.1: POW Procedures Still Apply 179
11.2: All Suspects Are Presumed Innocent 181

Chapter 14: *Finding an Enemy Weakness*

14.1: *Al-Qaeda's* Strongpoint Defense in Waziristans 203
14.2: Fort Affords Visibility & Fire at Base of All Walls 204
14.3: Eastern Sappers Crawl through Barbed Wire 209
14.4: UW Guerrilla Course for Reconnoitering 210-211

Chapter 15: *Obscure Approach*

15.1: UW Guerrilla Instruction for Approach March 216-217
15.2: Mounds Provide a Horizon to Foes at Their Base 217
15.3: Lighter Backgrounds Create "False Horizons" 218
15.4: The Enemy's Position Looms 219
15.5: What's Really of Interest Is on the Inside 220
15.6: There's Only One Safe Way to Find Out What It Is 221
15.7: Probable Gaps in Enemy Lines 222
15.8: Sentries Have Limitations 223
15.9: Distracters to a Sentry's Night Vision 225
15.10: Distracters to a Sentry's Hearing 226
15.11: Distracters to a Sentry's Attention 227
15.12: Distracters to a Sentry's Ability to Act 229
15.13: Time to Go 230
15.14: The East-Asian Stalking Approach 231
15.15: Penetration Sequence for Objective without Wire 232
15.16: Getting In through a Vacant Watershed Ditch 233
15.17: Getting In through Undefended Wet Ground 234
15.18: Getting In through Uncleared Vegetation 235

Chapter 16: *Disguising the Attack*

16.1: Much Depends on the Lowly Bush 239
16.2: UW Guerrilla Course for Silent Rural Attack 239-240
16.3: Most Forward Movement Must Be by Crawling 240
16.4: Camouflage Netting May Help near Enemy Sentry 241
16.5: There Are Several Ways to Silently Cross Wire 242
16.6: Even Russians Climb Trees 243
16.7: Urban Combat Requires Structure Climbing 244
16.8: UW Guerrilla Course for Silent Urban Attack 245-246
16.9: Passing an Asian Sentry Is More of a Chore 246

Chapter 17: *Precluding the Counterstroke*

17.1: UW Guerrilla Instruction for Noisy Attack 251
17.2: The Inevitable Trip Flare 251
17.3: American UW Noisy-Assault Specialist 258
17.4: Mission Is to Retrieve Intelligence from Bunker 260
17.5: Squads Crawl up Parallel Covered Lanes 261
17.6: The Enemy's Lines from Up Close 261
17.7: Each Squad Must Make Its Own Breach 262
17.8: Bangalores Blown When Artillery Barrage Hits 263
17.9: Lead Man Carries M-79 and Shoots Only Forward 264
17.10: Others with Rifles Shoot Only to Side and Down 265
17.11: Target of the Subsequent Attack 266
17:12: Flying Columns Stalk the Target 268
17.13: Shooters Know Fire Sectors at Limit of Advance 270
17.14: Shooters Crawl Up and Silently Dispatch Sentries 271
17.15: Center Team Retrieves Intelligence from Bunker 273
17:16: Columns Leave the Same Way They Came In 274
17.17: Columns Converge on Bunker from All Directions 276
17.18: All Sentries Grenaded at Once 277
17.19: Bunker Blown to Resemble Lucky Artillery Hit 278

Chapter 18: *Rural Escape and Evasion*

18.1: UW Instruction for Rural Escape/Evasion 286-287
18.2: U.S. Infantrymen Get No E&E Training 287
18.3: Even Russians Learn How to Hide in Plain Sight 289

18.4: The Eventual Encirclement 294
18.5: Exfiltration Is Not That Hard 295
18.6: Five Hide in Tree As One Diverts at Hollow Stump 297
18.7: Five Hide under Roots As One Diverts at Stream 298
18.8: Best After-Dark Back-Up Is Fake Mortar Attack 300
18.9: Non-Firing Rush Away from Fused Firecrackers 301

Chapter 19: *Enhancing Rural Terrain*

19.1: Hiding Places beneath the Hummocks on Iwo Jima 306
19.2: Main Tunnel beneath Bottom Tier of Huge Rooms 306
19.3: More Than Just a Bomb Shelter on Luzon in 1945 307
19.4: Korean Hill Covered with Escape Chambers 308
19.5: Secret Exit by Trapdoor to Sealed Tunnel 308
19.6: UW Instruction on How to Enhance Rural Terrain 312
19.7: Certain Species of Trees Have Spreading Roots 313
19.8: One-Man Escape Chamber from Scratch 313
19.9: Spider Hole Preparation 316
19.10: Taking Advantage of Every Fold in the Ground 316
19.11: Five Hide in Bramble as One Diverts at Hole 322
19.12: All Six at Hidden Depression in Fake Minefield 323
19.13: "Flash-Bang" Maze to Break Contact 325

Chapter 20: *Urban Escape and Evasion*

20.1: Storm Drains and Sewers 334
20.2: Crawl-Spaces beneath Houses 334
20.3: Breezeways between Buildings 335
20.4: Basements 336
20.5: Ventilation Ducts 336
20.6: Eaves 337
20.7: Roofs and Attics 338
20.8: UW Instruction for Urban Escape/Evasion 339
20.9: Naturally Existing Escape Routes at U.S. Outpost 341
20.10: Secretly Leaving the Outpost Building 342
20.11: Remotely Set Fire-and-Firecracker Diversion 343

Chapter 21: *Enhancing Urban Terrain*

21.1: UW Instruction on How to Enhance Urban Terrain 353
21.2: Storm Drain Feeder Branches Can Be Widened 353
21.3: Removable Back to Obvious Shelter 356
21.4: The Beginnings of a Fake Wall 357
21.5: Exfiltration Lanes from CAP Platoon Outpost 358
21.6: U.S. Guerrilla-Option Urban Hides 359
21.7: U.S. Guerrilla-Option Urban Conduits 360
21.8: Strings of American Safe Houses 361
21.9: With Secret Safe Room, GIs Need Not Depart 362
21.10: Today's GIs Need Training in UW 366

Afterword

A.1: Infantry Company Training Facilitator 371

Foreword

In *Dragon Days,* John Poole attempts two seemingly disjointed studies back to back. The first is to see what, if any, strategic link may exist between the Peoples Republic of China (PRC) and the most prominent Muslim militant movements. The second is to show how tactically to limit the expansionist progress of either. Strategy and tactics are seldom discussed in the same breath. Yet, Poole has discovered evidence of a PRC strategy that is only visible through easily ignored details. This strategy involves the destabilization of free nations to garner not only their natural resources, but also the shipping lanes back to China. Whether or not this hypothesis is adequately supported, Poole's solution to it has tremendous applicability to the wars in Iraq, Afghanistan, and wherever else U.S. troops may find themselves in future years. Just as Iraq and Afghanistan have become 4th Generation Warfare (4GW) counterguerrilla exercises, so too will most 21st Century deployments. That's the enemy's best, and perhaps only, way to win.

Poole reasons that to beat guerrillas, U.S. infantrymen and special operators must learn to fight like guerrillas. All will additionally need advanced Escape and Evasion (E&E) training. Those two skill sets comprise a full two-thirds of what is generally considered to be "unconventional warfare" (UW). GIs trained in UW could simply "slip away" whenever surrounded. This would give them the capability of anchoring isolated Combined Action Platoons (those with one squad each of U.S. troops, local police, and indigenous soldiers). Presently, a detachment of Americans in such a predicament would have to be saved through heavy bombardment. With that bombardment would unavoidably come collateral damage and the "loss of hearts and minds" that has so often led to defeat in the past. If its members were additionally trained in police procedure, they could function as foreign aid workers in the law enforcement sector instead of unwelcome occupiers.

Though the new threat is most visible through a strategic assessment, its solution lies in good enough small-unit tactics to counter the expansionists' local effort. Overt power projection by the United States will only make things worse. This is the lesson of Vietnam, Beirut, and Somalia. Standoff surveillance and firepower may still appear to preserve U.S. lives, but they no longer suffice to win wars. U.S. service personnel know their job to be risky. What they demand in return for their sacrifice is the assurance that their lives will not be spent on a losing effort. With UW and police training, Americas finest could easily weather the additional danger of a tactics-oriented strategy. More importantly, they might collectively manage a reversal to the downward trend in world stability that more conventional, "centralized" approaches have so far failed to achieve.

I therefore recommend this book highly to all U.S. infantrymen and special operators. The "tactical techniques" of UW are new to the literature and not covered by any government manual. They should serve as a welcome supplement to the mostly conventional skills that those who must ultimately win the War on Terror already have.

M.Gen. Ray L. Smith USMC (Ret.)

Preface

Somebody or something has been destabilizing much of South Asia, the Middle East, Africa, and the Middle Americas. On 30 April 2007, the U.S. State Department finally acknowledged the possibility of a global insurgency. It admitted that the annual number of terrorist attacks had risen to 20,000, some 25% more than the previous year.[1] America's leaders now have a choice. They can continue to exact revenge on the structureless umbrella organization that ostensibly perpetrated 9/11 despite this statistical monument to the futility of such an approach. Or, they can step back for a moment to consider which nation or nations might have something to gain from America's overriding obsession with *al-Qaeda*. No past or imagined Muslim caliphate ever came close to encompassing one third of the areas now under duress.[2]

The U.S. military has become proficient enough at "conventional" warfare that no enemy nation would want to confront America directly. It would attack instead through proxy-applied "unconventional" warfare. It would also take advantage of the bureaucratic ineptitude for which America's defense agencies have recently been called to account. While democracy provides the most freedom, it is not necessarily the most expedient form of government. Throughout Asia, America's leaders are better known for assigning blame than for enough follow-up to actually fix a serious problem. That's why any "hidden instigator" could so easily pursue an expansionist agenda.

Most Americans claim to believe in God. Those who regularly attend church are well aware of the very real, ongoing struggle between good and evil. The personification of evil would like nothing better than a war between the world's two largest religions. Thus, one must take all this talk about the "worldwide Islamic threat" with a grain of salt. The threat is not from Islam, *per se;* it is from that religion's fringe element. By simply providing more basic services to oppressed Muslim populations, the West could eventually isolate their radical fundamentalists. Aerial bombing does little to provide local security. That's why it has been so ineffective in Iraq and Afghanistan. It also encourages response in kind by another means of delivery. Local security can only be provided by tiny contingents of U.S. infantrymen who assist each village/neighborhood's detachment of indigenous police and soldiers.

Any street cop knows that a prisoner will say anything to "cut a deal" or "mess with his jailer's mind." Thus, the whole idea of gaining "valuable intelligence" through the extended interrogations of suspected *al-Qaeda* operatives is, at best, naive. Again, it may have done more to inflame anti-Western sentiment than to preclude future attack.

Assuming the above-mentioned problems are resolved, the United States may finally be able to win an unconventional war. Of course, it must additionally determine if there are any hidden sponsors of its opposition. At one time or other, *al-Qaeda* has been assisted by the following nationally sanctioned entities: (1) Saudi *Wahhabis;* (2) Pakistani Inter-Service Intelligence (ISI); (3) the Sudanese ruling party (Muslim Brotherhood); (4) Iranian Revolutionary Guard *(Sepah);* and (5) Lebanese *Hezbollah*. While Iran may be a contender for the title of "hidden instigator" of international terrorism, it remains a developing nation with limited global influence. War by proxy has become so popular in the Far East that a more powerful, non-Muslim country may well be involved. That more powerful country would have something to gain from the West's preoccupation with Muslim extremism.

In 2000, shortly after the mistaken bombing of the Chinese embassy in Belgrade, a retired U.S. serviceman and his wife visited Beijing on the first leg of a trip through China. After learning that Tibet was on their itinerary, a government "tour guide" made an angry call over his cell phone. Upon returning from Tibet, the two Americans were almost kidnapped twice in five days—(1) first on the way to their hotel in Guilin, and (2) again while trying to board their Yangtse River cruise boat at Chongqing.[3] That type of thing does not happen in a country that is truly friendly with the United States.

If there is a "clash of cultures" going on, it is more probably between those who believe in God and those who don't. The latter would have too little fear of evil. Within the group of believers would be all Hindus, Buddhists, and members of the three Abrahamic religions. Within the nonbeliever group would be animists and atheists.

Only five to ten percent of all Mainland Chinese attest to any religious affiliation at all. Most who do, must practice their faiths in secret. The People's Republic of China (PRC) has formally declared itself an atheistic state.[4] Its ruling (Communist) party is all-powerful by doctrine and only allows micromanaged "hybrid" churches to operate inside its borders. For example, the head of the Chinese Catholic Patriotic Association is not the Pope in Rome but rather the Party itself.[5] While Hanoi regularly offers mainstream Christian services at its city center, Beijing does not.[6] Unlike Vietnam, the PRC remains on the U.S. government's list of religious-freedom violators. It routinely demolishes any nongovernment "house church" it finds operating on its soil.[7]

As the PRC is obviously threatened by mainstream religion, it may also be capable of more serious repression. It has supported anti-Christian cleansing in both Laos and Burma, and persecuted millions of its own Christians. Considered instruments of Western "infiltration," many of its religious leaders end up in *gulags*.[8] While the most brutal of these labor camps *(laogai)* are near the Russian border,[9] others are now springing up on the outskirts of Beijing.[10] Many of their occupants have had no trial. China's judiciary system is also closely monitored by the Party, and cases are often decided in advance. Those who have been "re-educated" in the *laogai* become "new people."[11] So while much of the government rhetoric may now be the same as in the West, what still happens on the Chinese mainland has little resemblance to Western society. Communist China must therefore be considered (along with its Communist allies) as a significant contributor to any ideological confrontation with the West.

The PRC, of course, denies all this and maintains a massive media network and U.S. lobby to quickly rebut any such evidence (or bury it in disinformation). The Chinese military—People's Liberation Army (PLA)—has five main branches: (1) Ground Forces; (2) Navy; (3) Air Force; (4) Second Artillery Corps (ballistic missiles); and (5) the new "Information Warfare" organization.[12] To fully appreciate the threat, Americans must therefore reacquaint themselves with China's background. In 1999, a well-respected European historian (endorsed by Agence France-Presse) estimated the death toll from Mao's various programs to be as follows:

(1) "Rural Purges" (1946-49) two to five million,
(2) "Urban Purges" (1950-57) one million,
(3) "Great Leap Forward" (1959-1961) 20-43 million,
(4) "Cultural Revolution" (1966-1976) two to seven million,
(5) "Labor Camps" (ongoing) 20 million.[13]

A study done for the U.S. Congress in 1971 came up with only slightly lesser totals.[14] The most thorough analysis estimates 9.2 million deaths from all causes during the relatively recent Cultural Revolution.[15] Thus, China's only political party has been so far responsible (through mass relocation, repression, famine, executions, and forced labor) for the deaths of 45-78 million of its own citizens. As late as 2000, survivors of the "Cultural Revolution" were still risking imprisonment or worse to apprise U.S. tourists of the horrors of an "uncivilized" nation.[16] From 1966 to 1976, almost 200,000 intellectuals had to move from China's cities to remote parts of its countryside. Forced to live in caves and lacking the survival skills of a rural peasant, many died.[17]

It was almost 15 years after *entente* with America, fall of the Gang of Four, Mao's death, and the reforms of Deng Xiaoping,[18] that Tiananmen Square occurred in 1989. That crackdown on democratic aspiration left 5,000-10,000 killed and 50,000-60,000 imprisoned throughout China.[19] To now say that the Chinese Communist Party has somehow morphed into a benevolent committee of anti-terrorists is nothing short of ridiculous. As late as January 2007, PBS's *China from the Inside* reported all village elections rigged and an "election process that made the Communist Party more secure."[20] Though much has been made of China's recent shift toward a market economy, every enterprise must still contain a Communist Party cell.[21] Thus, the People's Republic of China remains to this day a totalitarian state that routinely supports rogue Marxist and Islamist regimes.

Thus, one has to wonder about the extent of China's overseas ambitions. Minimally, it wants access to every region's natural resources and clear shipping lanes home. Only yet to be determined is how much force it is willing to use. The prestigious International Crisis Group in Brussels made the following charge in late June 2007: Beijing has "a vested interest in the continuation of low-level security. It keeps the other investors out. . . . There is (on the part of the Chinese) an almost total disregard for the human-rights implications of their investments."[22] While this particular charge was made in the context of Sudan, it almost certainly applies to other regions of the world.

If China has been instigating global discord for financial or ideological reasons, then the "War on Terror" has been misnamed and that misnaming has already led to considerable error. It should more rightly be called the "Pivotal Stage in the Global Struggle for Human Rights" and only privately considered to be a new Cold War with China. In the world's few remaining Communist countries, the military "awe" with which America answered 9/11 does little to promote cooperation. There is no "Axis of Evil," *per se,* only regimes with less respect for human rights than others. The word "evil" can be applied to any action that might offend God. While combating evil abroad, the U.S. must remember that there is only one thing strong enough to defeat that particular malady—namely, "good." It must further try not to do anything itself that might offend God. Within this context, it is easier to see why any large explosion (by whatever delivery vehicle) or interrogation excess (for whichever reason) will simply exacerbate the problem. That's because the ultimate enemy is not some country or movement, but evil itself.[23] It can only be defeated through widely dispersed and well-structured love. Until the U.S. military learns how successfully to apply minimal force, it will be unable to curtail the current epidemic of insurgencies.

H. JOHN POOLE

Introduction

The Seldom-Mentioned Other Player in the "War on Terror"

Might the PRC be secretly backing the Islamist factions at war with the West? That it has its own problems with Islamic separatists does not rule out this possibility. Through a unique military heritage, its leaders thoroughly understand the ways of deception. One of their favorite ploys is to let someone else do their fighting. The only evidence of a Sino-Islamist coalition might then be PRC benefits from Islamist activities. Since the days of Sun Tzu, the Chinese have preceded every attack with a diversion. The sixth of their famous 36 Stratagems translates, "Make a clamor or feint to the east while attacking from the west."[1] Well, making a clamor in the Middle East and then consolidating the Western Pacific would also qualify. To pursue this hypothesis, one must view the problems in Iraq and Palestine as a possible diversion to what China really wants elsewhere. It clearly wants Africa's natural resources. That has been adequately proven by the hordes of Chinese contract workers in places like Sudan, Eritrea, Djibouti, Nigeria, Angola, and Zimbabwe.[2] But China also wants Taiwan and a way for its oil tankers to bypass the Straits of Malacca. For those reasons, the focus of this book will be on South Asia.

Some say that the Chinese government has been too polite toward the United States of late to be secretly pursuing an anti-American foreign policy. How that government feels about the West's favorite crusade should have been adequately demonstrated at Tiananmen Square in June 1989. Just before the turn of the century, two active-duty Chinese colonels produced a treatise entitled *Unrestricted Warfare* through the PLA Literature and Arts Publishing House. From a nation in which all information is closely monitored and infantry techniques (football play equivalents) protected like nuclear secrets, such a treatise should have evoked a little suspicion. Yet, a FBIS (Foreign Broadcast and Information Service of the Central

Intelligence Agency [CIA]) translation was soon available over several U.S. military internet circles. In an introductory note, the FBIS arrogantly (and also insightfully) asserted that the article "proposes tactics for developing countries, in particular China, to compensate for their 'military inferiority' vis-a-vis the United States during a high-tech war."[3] The FBIS was obviously using the term "tactics" in its broadest sense, for the treatise never once described a small-unit tactical maneuver. Instead, it used the roundabout philosophical format for which Communist writing is so famous to vaguely discuss some of the technological alternatives to open warfare.[4] One must carefully assess what is too easily obtainable from China. More likely, those alternatives (like "cyberwar") were intended to distract Western planners from what they would really need to thwart a less sophisticated main attack. (Chinese infantry manuals show the "front-door" human wave to be a diversion, and a concurrent "back-door" infiltration to be the main attack.[5]) To stop infiltration, American planners will need more tactically skilled (or "light") infantrymen. In the hands of every prospective terrorist worldwide, the ideas in *Unrestricted Warfare* could also create a more concrete diversion. Particularly disturbing are its 20 direct references to Osama bin Laden. One such reference comes close to suggesting another way to attack a previous target. If "plays on words" were not so common in East-Asian Communist writing,[6] its phraseology might pass as coincidence.

> [I]f all terrorists confined their operations simply to the traditional approach of bombings, kidnappings, assassinations, and plane hijackings, this would represent less than the maximum degree of terror [p. 54]. . . .
>
> . . . Whether it be the intrusions of hackers, a major explosion at the World Trade Center, or a bombing attack by bin Laden, all of these greatly exceed the frequency band widths understood by the American military [p. 144].[7]
>
> — PLA Lit. and Arts Pub. House, February 1999

A few months after this treatise appeared, China's latent animosity toward the West began to boil over. In May 1999, the PRC's Belgrade embassy was mistakenly bombed by a NATO (North Atlantic Treaty Organization) warplane. Though China loudly objected, its temporary shelving of plans for a Yangtse River Dam was its only warlike reaction. But the extent to which its hostility had been rekindled was soon evident. In April 2001, a U.S. reconnaissance plane was lucky to make it to Hainan Island after being intentionally bumped by a Chinese fighter jet over international waters. After detaining the crew of 20 American men and women for days, the Chinese finally agreed to release them.[8] It took several more months of "negotiations" and an exorbitant fine before the U.S. finally got permission to bring home its plane in pieces.[9]

That China has since come close to completing the Yangtse River Dam only proves that it has no plans for a "conventional" war with the West. Unfortunately, there are other kinds of war, to include "unconventional ones by proxy." If China is now in league with (or manipulating) the Islamists, its global strategy will almost certainly include extra-low-intensity attacks in all four 4th-Generation Warfare (4GW) arenas: (1) martial/combat; (2) political/media; (3) economic/infrastructure; and (4) psychological/religion. A more recent (and obscure) article from a Chinese military magazine may more succinctly describe the plan.

> China's "comprehensive warfare" strategy wears down [an] enemy using non-military means. . . .
>
> . . . [Chinese] National Defense University Senior Col. Meng Xiansheng . . . defined the term as "the means of defeating enemies without waging a war through deploying a wide range of political, economic, cultural, diplomatic and military tactics."
>
> [Col.] Meng said "comprehensive warfare" advocates the use of non-violent means in handling state-to-state disputes, . . . but [it] also fits with China's grand strategy of "peaceful development."[10]
>
> —*Geostrategy-Direct,* 2 August 2006

All martial endeavors by the PRC will almost certainly follow its most unique and successful option—the Maoist guerrilla method. Its military may continue to improve in more conventional areas, but its principal tool will be "guerrilla war by proxy" that masquerades as "an integral part of a locally grown insurgency." The Chinese have lately been pushing the "Maoization" of their military.[11] At the same time, they have been removing Mao from their history books.[12] That unlikely dichotomy may mean they have just classified their most promising strategy. As U.S. forces learned from human-wave attacks in the early 1950's, the Chinese will follow through on any feint that is not properly defensed. To combat China's rarely defeated guerrilla method, the U.S. will have to become much more proficient at counterinsurgency than it has demonstrated in Vietnam, Iraq, and Afghanistan. The first step in that transformation must necessarily be giving every U.S. rifleman some training as a guerrilla. Until he learns how to think and fight like a guerrilla, he will be unable to stop guerrillas. Like his Far-Eastern counterparts, he will then be proficient in both conventional and unconventional warfare. Within Asia (and most of the rest of the world), unconventional warfare has now become the norm.

A Brief History of Islamic Revolution in Asia

Aside from struggles against discrimination in Central Asia and colonial rule in South Asia, one of the region's longest running Islamic rebellions occurred in the southern Philippines. The term "Moro" derives from the Spanish word "Moor" and was applied to all Filipino Muslims who primarily inhabited the Sulu Archipelago and Mindanao during the Philippine-American War. As that war immediately followed the Spanish-American War, most Americans are unaware of its details. Much of the trouble subsided after three years (1899-1902), but Muslim resistance continued in the southern Philippines until 1913. That resistance was called the Moro Rebellion.[13]

Since that time, there have been Islamic separatist movements in Indonesia, Malaysia, southern Thailand, Bangladesh, India, Pakistan, Afghanistan, and China. In these and other locations, there have also been a number of factions with *sharia* law and a new caliphate as their goal. Unable to differentiate one from the other, America has linked all members of both groups to the "War on Terror." Its preoccupation with Muslim extremism provides any non-Muslim expansionist nation with a perfect way to screen its initiatives. The most powerful—China—bears the most watching. It has a revolutionary government that is culturally predisposed toward political and military deception. It has defended every radical Islamic regime to be investigated by the U.N. Yet, the U.S. continues to base its foreign policy on the unrealistic expectation that China will resist all Islamic revolutionary activity around the globe.[14]

Within China's closest Communist ally, there is a claim. It is that "Americans are easy to fool."[15] The extent to which that claim is true is not nearly as important as the extent to which it has shaped Chinese foreign policy.

A Brief History of Chinese-Supported Revolution in Asia

After China's rape of Tibet, few Asia-watchers still doubt its instigation of the Maoist uprising in Nepal. At one time or another, China has trained and equipped guerrillas to fight in Cambodia, Laos, Thailand, Malaysia, and Burma.[16] Most famous was its support of the Cambodian Khmer Rouge during the late 1970's. However, it also assisted the North Vietnamese/Viet Cong in the late 1960's,[17] Chinese Malay rebels in the late 1950's,[18] and Korean-peninsula and Viet Minh forces in the early 1950's.[19] Its revolutionary government considers insurgency to be an integral part of regional growth.

The Research Method

Within Part One of this book is an assessment of China's current degree of subversion in the countries of South and Southeast Asia. Respected news sources provide the research medium. East Asians are "bottom-up," holistic thinkers. That's why so many of their strategic initiatives have escaped the attention of Western leaders. By traditionally solving problems from the "top down," those Western leaders neither delve into sufficient detail, nor see beyond the sums of various parts. Instead they focus on major categories and attempt grandiose reforms. Inventors of the famous 36 Stratagems of deception, the Chinese have had little trouble looking benign from a Western perspective.

To see what, if anything, the Chinese have been up to in South Asia, one must look at the same kinds of detail in many nations. In the case of proxy-applied 4GW, some of that detail must necessarily be political, economic, and psychological. Thus, the first few chapters combine a smattering of all three with battlefield tactics. Considered as a whole, they should reveal how much Chinese subversion has so far occurred against the backdrop of Muslim or other types of extremism.

As most of the unrest has been "low in intensity," any military aspect of its solution must be nearly invisible. Parts Two and Three of this work investigate which types of law enforcement and unconventional warfare (UW) techniques might help U.S. service members to perform such a mission. Their end goal must be to limit what has now become a worldwide epidemic of Chinese and Islamist expansionism. The author (like most U.S. service personnel) has never personally waged UW, so Part Three will necessarily be somewhat "visionary" in nature. It will be based on how three widely recognized UW experts prepare guerrillas: (1) the *ninjas* whose individual training regimen helped them to fight better-armed Samurai; (2) the North Vietnamese who trained the Viet Cong; and (3) the Light Infantry Training Guidance Bureau of China's closest ally. From their combined experience, a subject matter chart has been developed for each chapter. Its carefully documented contents should move what would have otherwise been guesswork into the realm of research. There are those in America who claim to be counterguerrilla experts, though the U.S. military has never succeeded against world-class guerrillas. There are those in America who have peripherally studied rural escape/evasion. But those who know something about fighting like a guerrilla or urban escape/evasion are few and generally unable to be heard. It is hoped that this work will add to the body of knowledge on how most morally to wage UW, and in the process help America to win the so-called War on Terror.

Limitations to the Research Method

Any thread of evidence linking the Chinese to global discord will necessarily be tenuous or the U.S. government would have long since acknowledged its existence. That can mean only one of two things—either it has been well hidden or unfairly extracted from a more hopeful context. The world is a complicated place. Seasoned U.S. strategists warn against too simplistic an approach to its problems. To show what might be occurring, this book has intentionally focused on a single thread in a veritable maze of other threads. To totally embrace that thread as being the entire truth would be a mistake. More polarization between nations will do little to promote world peace. Any overzealous military reaction would virtually preclude its possibility. Though the Chinese dragon is believed to be real and lethal, it is nevertheless subliminal. It therefore requires a subliminal solution. The army-oriented regimes in the PRC and its most proficient Communist ally literally feed off any overtly militaristic initiative of the U.S. That's how they justify their expansionist policies.

America's Future Responsibility to the World

Low-intensity warfare is like high-intensity police work. There is the same overriding need to protect bystanders. And there is the same requirement to physically apprehend perpetrators. The only real difference is that a low-intensity warrior must be able to disappear whenever badly outnumbered. So doing is not cowardice, but simply common sense. Unfortunately, even "tactical withdrawal" is not part of the U.S. military *mantra*. For that military to now "project freedom" around the world, its *mantra* must change. Blind obedience to rank must give way to decentralized control and enlisted initiative. Those who are commissioned or otherwise senior must delegate tactical training and operations authority to junior noncommissioned officers (NCOs). The dismounted rifle squad has been the key to short-range combat for quite some time. America needs some "truly-light" infantrymen (under the Eastern definition)—those with enough skill to escape encirclement without the help of supporting arms. To senior U.S. commanders who have yet to realize this, history may not be overly kind. For by failing at their counterinsurgency mission, they will also have let down their organization, their country, and ultimately their Creator. Late in life (about 2004), Pope John Paul II proclaimed, "America is still the world's best hope." If the evidence in Part One is, per chance, a fair sampling of the whole, then the United States of America may be the world's only hope.

Acknowledgments

Many organizations and individuals have tried hard to provide U.S. leaders with foreign policy instruments that might better preserve the physical safety and human rights of everyone around the world. This work presents—in some detail—a way to thwart the current epidemic of Chinese and Islamist expansionism without having to resort to open warfare. To the extent that it might help to promote freedom and peace simultaneously, it is the doing of the Holy Spirit.

Part One

Return of the Dragon

"All that is necessary for the triumph of evil
is that good men do nothing."
— Edmund Burke

(Source: www.quotationspage.com/quotes/Edmund_Burke)

1 The Sino-Islamic Connection

- Why has China always sided with rogue Muslim regimes?
- What evidence is there of an anti-Western coalition?

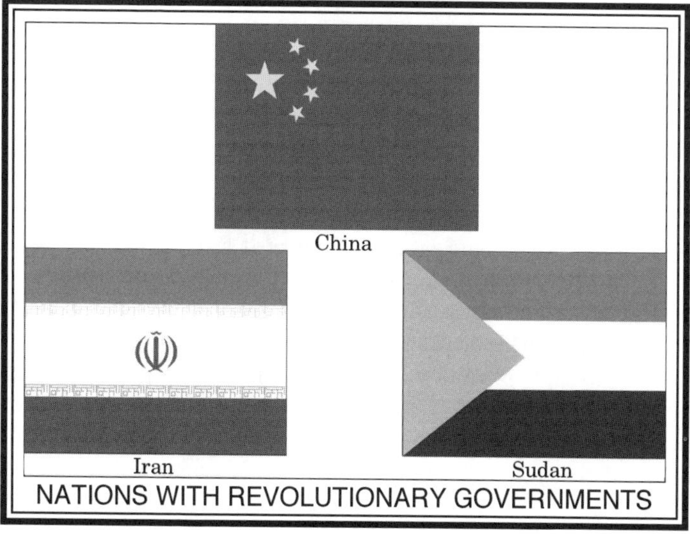

NATIONS WITH REVOLUTIONARY GOVERNMENTS

(Source: Corel Gallery Clipart—Flag, Corel #19C006, #19G006, #19G009)

Not Everyone Shares the Same Vision of Progress

It's only natural to assume that every country wants peace. Unfortunately, the "absence of armed conflict" no longer denotes peace. A competing nation can also be ruined through political, economic, or psychological sabotage. That's why all four arenas are involved in 4th-Generation Warfare (4GW).[1]

Of the potential threats to America, Communist China has been near the top of the list since 1950. While it is now experimenting with a new type of economy, its political agenda hasn't changed all that much. It still has a choke hold on Tibet, is obviously behind the

Nepalese uprising, and routinely returns hundreds of refugees to incarceration or death in an allied nation.[2] Its government remains "revolutionary"—one that considers rebellion to be a prerequisite of regional growth.[3] Only two other governments in the world undeniably qualify as revolutionary. They are Iran and Sudan. One is led by radical Shiites, and the other by radical Sunnis (the Muslim Brotherhood).[4] Thus, one wonders to what extent all three countries might be cooperating despite their religious differences. After all, China does now need the oil and oil conduits that are largely controlled by Islamic regimes. (See Map 1.1.) In return, those that are rogue might be receiving protection in the U.N. But to objectively pursue such an inflammatory train of thought, one must first acknowledge that any conclusions will be hypothetical.

An Ominous Development in Lebanon

Israeli leaders have been less hesitant than their U.S counterparts to acknowledge a problem with China. They are painfully aware that the PRC maintains diplomatic relations with the Palestinian National Authority.[5] The U.N. bunker that was "mistakenly" bombed by Israeli planes just inside Lebanon in July 2006 had a Chinese observer inside.[6] On 19 September, China announced an increase to the 182 U.N. "peacekeepers" it had sent to Lebanon at the start of the year. The new total will be close to 1,000.[7] All of this came amidst claims by *Hezbollah* chieftain Nasrallah that the U.N. forces and Lebanese Army would do nothing to deplete his new arsenal of 20,000 rockets and missiles. The anti-ship missiles in that arsenal are of Chinese design.[8]

Without having tracked U.N. progress in Sudan, one might not see the parallels with Lebanon. Since early 2006, several thousand Chinese "peacekeepers" have been stationed in Waw—a town equidistant from Darfur, the Sudanese oil fields, and the uranium-rich eastern Congo. Waw has long been the training site for Sudanese-sponsored militiamen.[9]

If *Hezbollah's* defense line had been more easily breached by Israel's well-supported armor in July 2006, one might not suspect East-Asian construction advice. But China and its neighbor both have embassies in Beirut, and there is a limit to how much Muslim irregulars can accomplish with Iranian sponsorship. Just as German designers had tested new aircraft during the Spanish Civil

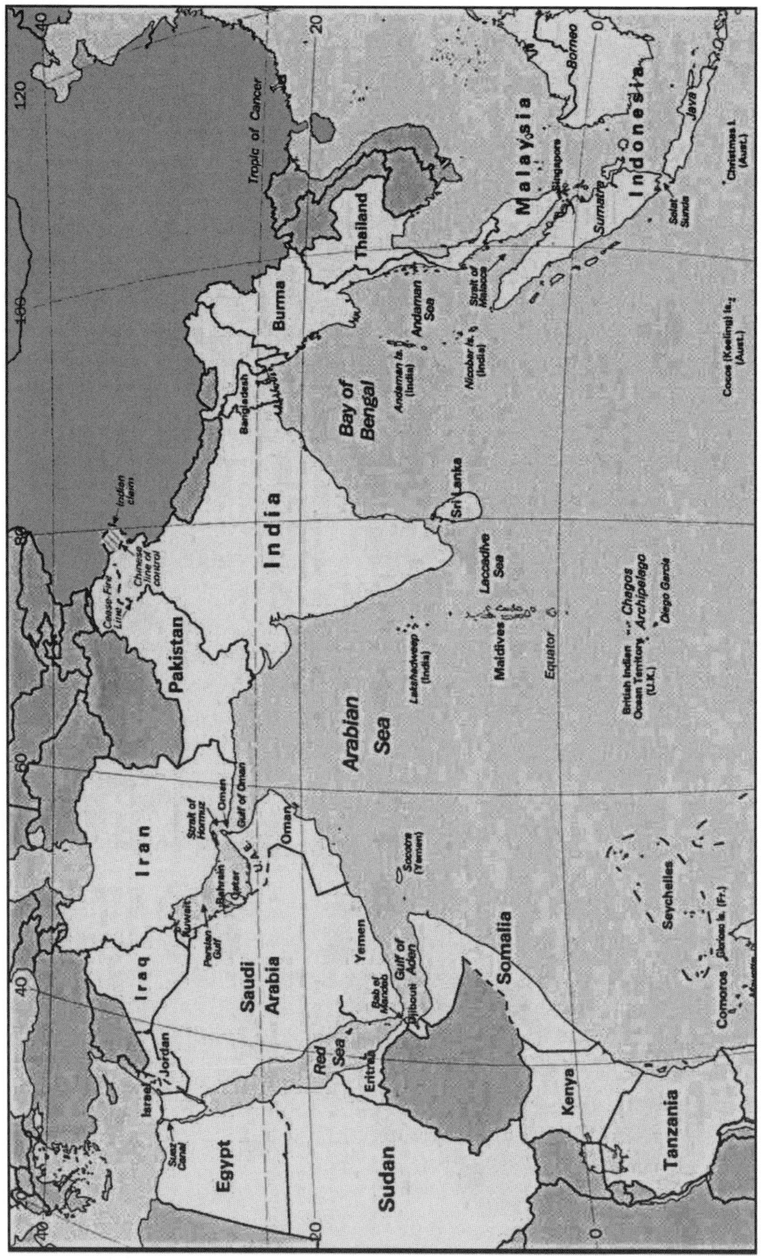

Map 1.1: Eastern Oil Route from Africa

(Source: Courtesy of General Libraries, University of Texas at Austin, from their website for map designator "indian_ocean_area_1993.pdf")

War, Communist tacticians may have been looking for new ways to stop a "high-tech" Westernized force in southern Lebanon. The most obvious of those ways would be the "remote-control killing of modern tanks" from a below-ground strongpoint defense.[10] With Chinese help, Iran had just developed a 333-mm rocket that could be fired remotely.

> Industry sources said the [Iranian] effort, reportedly aided by China, was designed to turn the Fajr-3 [possible misprint] into a more mobile and accurate system. . . .
>
> An earlier version of the Fajr-5 [rocket], which contains a high-explosive warhead, was supplied to Hizbullah in Lebanon. . . .
>
> Each battery contains a command post vehicle, with each launcher equipped with a mission computer and capable of being fired via remote control from a distance of one kilometer.[11]
>
> — *Geostrategy-Direct,* 31 May 2006

By early 2007, *Hezbollah* was already building a sequel to its defense line—this time behind the Litani river and out of sight of the U.N. It was from this area that it had fired its long-range missiles during the Israeli incursion of 2006. *Hezbollah's* leaders have made no secret of transporting heavy weaponry into the region.[12]

Hezbollah, Sepah, and *al-Qaeda* Are Already Cooperating

The Iranian Revolutionary Guard *(Sepah)* and its Lebanese offspring *(Hezbollah)* have been cooperating with *al-Qaeda* for a long time. In November 2006, London's prestigious *Telegraph* reported that Iranian President Ahmadinejad wanted his own candidate as *al-Qaeda's* number three man.[13] Shortly after 9/11, something even more shocking surfaced. The much-respected *DEBKAfile* (an Israeli intelligence bulletin) reported a *Sepah* leader in charge of an *al-Qaeda* region. One wonders if that same *Sepah* leader may have overseen *al-Qaeda* activity in Iraq.

> Intelligence sources point out that [Osama] bin Laden's retreat . . . does not impair the functioning of his al-Qaeda network. . . .

> . . . [His] Gulf-Middle East command [is] under the Tehran-based former Hezbollah hostage-taker Imad Mughniyeh.[14]
>
> – Israeli Intell. Periodical, 28 September 2001

While fundamentalist Shiites and Sunnis have opposing ideologies and sometimes even contest the same territory, their Salafist roots permit them to work together against a common foe.[15] This unfortunate paradox holds true for both Iraq and Afghanistan. It shows where *al-Qaeda* gets much of its apparent strength.

> Gen. Jack Keane, a retired four-star general who advises senior U.S. defense officials on Iraq, said Iran is so intent on pushing the United States out of the country that it is now aiding all enemy factions.
>
> "They are assisting all of our opponents—the Shi'ite militia, the Sunni insurgents and al Qaeda," Gen. Keane, who travels regularly to Iraq, said Monday during a conference at the American Enterprise Institute.[16]
>
> – *Washington Times,* 11 July 2007

In late April 2007, weapons of recent Iranian manufacture were found in possession of the Taliban in Afghanistan. In June, more were intercepted *en route* to the Taliban.[17] While such a union may seem improbable, a mutual ally might have easily facilitated it. Alliances of convenience are more common in the Muslim world—sometimes between factions that have just been at each other's throats.

How the Sino-Islamist Coordination May Be Occurring

Over the years, Sudan and *al-Qaeda* have both tried to consolidate radical Muslim factions. Sudan did so through the Islamic National Front (INF), and *al-Qaeda* through the World Islamic Front for the Jihad against Jews and Crusaders (WIFJ).[18] During the early 1990's, the INF convened some 40 Islamist parties, movements, and organizations under the guise of a Popular Arab and Islamic Conference (PAIC).[19] It and the Saudi-dominated Organization of Islamic Conference (OIC) provided a way for Islamist leaders to discretely confer.[20]

The Non-Aligned Movement (NAM) may now be the vehicle through which China is planning to influence the action. After all, the Peoples Republic of China was at one time a member of that organization.[21] During the period 11-16 September 2006, a NAM conference took place in Havana. In attendance were Chinese "observers,"[22] delegates from China's Communist neighbor,[23] and the presidents of Iran, Venezuela, and Chinese-bolstered Zimbabwe.[24] Just two weeks earlier, the supreme leaders of Venezuela and China's neighbor had been in Beijing on the same day (28 August).[25] One did not need too active an imagination to smell PRC orchestration in Havana. At that summit, Cuba was awarded NAM's rotating presidency, and Iran chosen to chair the G15.[26] (The latter posting is of particular interest because Iran was not previously a member.) Both terms of office are for three years.

What China Needs

As the world's second largest consumer of oil, China is now struggling to find ample supplies for its growing economy and military. Traditionally distrustful of the West, it prefers to get that oil from an ally. That's why it has befriended Iran and established such a large presence in Sudan, Angola, Nigeria, and other parts of Africa.[27] While China prefers doing business with a well-established Marxist or Islamist regime, it is also comfortable wherever there is an ongoing Communist or Islamic uprising.

China will need a safe way to get that oil home. (Refer back to Map 1.1.) There are too many pro-Western nations between Africa and East Asia to make an overland pipeline feasible. For now, China must depend on sending it by sea around the congested tip of the Malay Peninsula. (See Map 1.2.) Any Communist or Islamist uprisings (or regime changes) along the approaches to the Straits of Malacca would be to her benefit. They would limit Western interference with her port facilities and naval bases. While any proof of Chinese instigation of these uprisings would be circumstantial, enough such proof might serve as an adequate warning to the West.

> China is constructing a new naval base . . . at the Pakistani port of Gwadar, building bases in Myanmar [Burma], and expanding its facilities on . . . Hainan, and the Spratley and Parcel Islands [all in the South China Sea]. China has also

Map 1.2: The Malay Peninsula Bottleneck

(Source: Courtesy of General Libraries, University of Texas at Austin, from their website for map designator "southest_asia_ref_2002.pdf")

Map 1.3: China

(Source: Courtesy of General Libraries, University of Texas a Austin, from their website for map designator "china_rel01.pdf")

signed a military agreement with Cambodia, strengthened its ties with Bangladesh, and is considering a . . . $20-billion-dollar canal in Thailand [across the narrowest part of the Malay Peninsula] (Gertz, "China Builds Up Strategic Sea Lanes," *Washington Times,* 18 Jan. 2005).[28]

— *U.S. Naval Institute Proceedings,* October 2006

The above report ostensibly deals with China's "String of Pearl's" strategy to keep the sea lanes open from its African and Middle Eastern oil sources to the northern end of the South China Sea. But, upon closer examination, one can see that much more is involved.

Bangladesh and Burma are too far outside the normal sea lanes. (Refer back to Map 1.1.) The "String of Pearls" has also to do with how China will bypass the Straits of Malacca in case of war.

The Story at Gwadar

Two things are happening at Gwadar, Pakistan. A Chinese naval presence near the Straits of Hormuz will provide protection to China-bound oil tankers (and a possible impediment to others). From Gwadar, oil can also be piped or otherwise transported overland to China.[29] (See Map 1.3.)

> The construction Gwadar deep-sea port is just one component of a . . . plan which includes building a network of roads [and railroads]. . . . This network of roads connects with China through the Indus Highway. . . . China . . . [is] developing extensive road and rail links from Central Asia and the Chinese province of Sinkiang [Xinjiang] to the Arabian Sea coast.
>
> The [Pakistani] Government has initiated several projects, with majority financial and technical assistance from China, to develop Gwadar's strategic location. . . . The new port will also encompass conversion facilities to allow for the movement of natural gas as a part of plans for a termination point for the Turkmenistan-Afghanistan-Pakistan natural gas pipeline. . . . [A] coastal highway connecting Gwadar to Karachi . . . will be completely financed by the Chinese. Gwadar will serve as a port of entry for oil and gas to be transported by land to the western regions of China. China has been promised sovereign guarantees for use of the ports [Niazi, Assoc. for Asian Research, "Gwadar: China's Naval Outpost on the Indian Ocean"].
>
> The significance of Gwadar is great to . . . China. . . . China, with permission from Pakistan, will also be able to dock naval ships in or around Gwadar.[30]

China's Malaya Peninsula Bypass Plan Is Multifaceted

If China only had one or two ways to bypass the Straits of Malacca, no one would see any problem. But, as subsequent chapters will show, it must have close to a dozen. The most promising is a transportation corridor through Burma (Myanmar) to Kunming. The oil will be shipped up the Irrawaddy River to Bhamo (only 12 hours from the Chinese border) and then loaded on trucks or trains. At some point, a Chinese rail line might stretch all the way to Myanmar's rail head at Lashio.[31] As Lashio is also the terminus of the old Burma Road, a rail (or pipe) line could then be easy to build into China.

Then there is the railway from Jinghong in southern Yunnan Province through Laos to Thailand's deep-sea port at Laem Chabang, near Bangkok.[32] (Refer back to Map 1.3.) It could haul the oil that had just been transported across the Malay Peninsula from Kantang, Thailand's Andaman Sea port, or any of Malaysia's western ports. Most spectacular is the PRC's long-term plan for a canal across the Thai Isthmus of Kra. (Refer back to Map 1.2.)

Far to the north, China is helping build a second road through Nepal to India. When combined with the existing road from Lhasa to Kathmandu, China will have yet another overland route to the Bay of Bengal.[33] It has already far exceeded any projected need for tourist transportation to Tibet. In April 2006, China completed a new railroad from Golmud City in Qinghai Province to Lhasa.[34] It plans to build three more rail lines to and from one of the most remote regions on earth.[35]

It should come as less of a surprise then that southern Thailand has been subjected to an Islamist uprising since 2004,[36] and Nepal and northern India to long-standing Communist insurgencies. Calcutta already has a Communist form of government, as does its parent state.[37] Circumstantial or not, the evidence of Chinese revolutionary expansion is growing.

How China Distributes Its Revolutionary Wherewithal

When China's neighbor to the south conducted its first nuclear explosion in early October 2006, China joined other members of the U.N. Security Council in condemning the act and agreeing to sanctions. Those sanctions would be aimed at limiting the proliferation of weapons of mass destruction. The U.N. resolution specifically called for the following: (1) a ban on all exports and imports of material to make nuclear weapons or ballistic missiles; (2) a limited embargo on major military hardware, like tanks, warships, aircraft, and missiles; (3) a freeze on the foreign assets of any person or company supporting that country's weapons program; and (4) inspection of all cargo coming in and out of that country. While the U.S. wanted military force authorized in the search of its ships on the high seas, other Security Council members blocked the clause. China's U.N. ambassador additionally stipulated that his nation "would not participate in the cargo inspections program that the resolution theoretically mandated."[38]

So, while a signatory of the U.N. document, China had no official responsibility to check overland shipments for military contraband. As the American press converged on the disconnect, Chinese leaders did what they do best—waffle just enough to appease the West. An article in a Chinese newspaper attested to an "increase in border inspections" as a result of the nuclear test. Yet, the amount of space dedicated to the article (about one-twentieth of a page) spoke volumes. Later that day, an ABC news crew traveled to the most heavily used border crossing—a train and truck bridge over the frontier river. After watching for hours, it reported only cursory inspections of truck-borne cargo.[39]

Then came more proof of Chinese collusion with its neighbor. On 20 October, all the major U.S. television (TV) networks reported that the neighbor's leader had informed a Chinese emissary that "he was sorry" for the test. In a place where hard-line rhetoric and "saving face" are all-important, such an admission would only be to exploit Western gullibility. Four days later, China denied that Tang Jiaxuan—their "State Councilor"—had ever received such an apology. True to its tradition of warning-laced double-talk, it further stipulated that its emissary was told that its neighbor had "no plans currently to carry out a second nuclear test." Then, the Chinese State Councilor made the mistake of adding his own telling footnote: "But, if it faces pressure, it reserves the right to take further action."[40]

While the tiny subterranean detonation may have been from a partial misfire, it could also have been from a device small enough to fit on the end of a missile. While that nation has a few bulldozers, pharmaceuticals, and office machines available for export, it only has three major sources of income. Those sources are drugs, missiles, and foreign aid. It's the world's third largest producer of opium.[41] It has sold missiles and missile components to countries that are mostly Marxist or Islamist. The list includes Iran, Syria, Sudan,

Pakistan, Burma, Indonesia, Angola, the Democratic Republic of the Congo, and Zimbabwe. While it most certainly acquired much of its nuclear technology from Pakistan,[42] it may have gotten the rest from China. It was China, after all, that had helped Pakistan with nuclear weapon development from 1990 to 1997.[43] In July 2007, China's neighbor finally lived up to its six-month-old promise to shut down its best-known nuclear reactor in return for fuel oil, food, and having its foreign assets unfrozen. That the reactor "was nearing the end of its useful life anyway" prompted warnings that the West was once again being "hoodwinked."[44]

China uses this same neighbor as a go-between for more controversial types of military aid. As late as January 2007, Britain's prestigious *Telegraph* reported it helping Iran with both missile and nuclear technology. Four years earlier, Japan's *Sankei Shimbun* had said it was trying to sell Taepodong-2 missiles to Iran and then jointly develop nuclear warheads.[45] In mid-September 2007, Israeli war planes bombed a cache of "nuclear components" from the PRC's go-between in Syria just west of where the Euphrates enters Iraq. Before the cache was destroyed, Israeli commandos seized physical proof the "nuclear material" had come from the go-between.[46]

China uses several nations to distribute its less sophisticated weaponry. Chinese-government-owned firms have sold missile-related items directly to the neighbor mentioned, Iran, and Pakistan. Those countries further disseminate things like anti-air or anti-ship missiles. That only one is Communist doesn't seem to bother the Chinese. Perhaps that's because Islamist nations have more access to Muslim movements. It was, after all, a limited number of handheld anti-aircraft missiles that drove the Russians from Afghanistan. To a free-enterprise-minded American, trade or technical assistance from a Chinese-government-owned company poses no threat. While the full delivery network of Chinese conventional munitions is beyond the scope of this book, some hints of its extent are available. The PRC has sold a wide variety of conventional arms directly to its neighbor, Pakistan, and several other Middle Eastern or North African countries. Among that neighbor's best subsequent customers were Pakistan, Sudan, Iran, Syria, Burma, and Indonesia.[47]

Direct Chinese Aid to Radical Islamic Factions?

Only occasionally have PRC-owned firms risked shipping arms

directly to Islamic militants. On 3 May 2006, Israeli customs officials discovered night-vision devices and sniper telescopes in a Chinese shipping container bound for the Gaza Strip. On 8 November, a Chinese vessel containing 63 tons of explosives and detonators was intercepted near the Straits of Malacca bound for Yemen. Its final recipient was not reported.[48]

To maintain deniability, China would let someone else train Islamic militants in the finer points of guerrilla warfare. While a growing number of Chinese "peacekeeping" contingents are suspected of "secondary missions,"[49] they couldn't get enough accomplished alone. Who would be better qualified to provide that kind of assistance than the neighbor already identified? Its 100,000-man Light Infantry Training Guidance Bureau specializes in unconventional warfare instruction.[50] Perhaps, that's what China gets in return for all the fuel and food it routinely pumps into an otherwise-failed state.[51] (China also keeps Zimbabwe afloat but for other reasons.[52]) There is now proof that the neighbor provided military advisers to Lebanese *Hezbollah*.[53] There is also evidence that *Hezbollah* has been active in the Iraqi insurgency. In July 2007, the U.S. Command admitted to catching *Hezbollah's* "Special Operations Chief"—Ali Musa Daqduq—in Iraq. In addition to training Iraqi proxy militias for Iran's Quds Force, Daqduq had orchestrated the sophisticated raid on a U.S. base at Karbala in January.[54]

The Other Chinese Link to Iraq

PRC military leaders are well aware of their superiority at short range over Westernized forces and are more than willing to openly brag about it in person.[55] Nine months after the U.S. invasion of Iraq, one made the mistake of bragging about it in print. His remarks constitute a rare Chinese fingerprint on what was to come. During Japan's occupation of China, the term "Sparrow Warfare" was applied by the Chinese to a variant of the Maoist-guerrilla method.[56]

> It was called sparrow warfare because, first, it was used diffusely, like the flight of sparrows in the sky; and because, second, it was used flexibly by guerrillas or militiamen, operating in threes or fives, appearing and disappearing unexpectedly and wounding, killing, depleting and wearing out the enemy forces.[57]

Sparrow Warfare was often combined with land-mine warfare, tunnel warfare, sabotage warfare, and riverine warfare.[58] Here is what the Chinese Army had to say in 2003 about the U.S. invasion of Iraq.

> The U.S. is the No. 1 military power in the world and its best-equipped troops are good at fighting long-range wars, which are overwhelmingly in their favor. But, after Iraq falls into the hands of U.S. troops, the mechanized U.S. troops [are] finding themselves incapable of fighting "sparrow warfare" against Iraqi guerrillas.
>
> Sporadic attacks by anti-U.S. fighters are taking [a] heavy toll upon the U.S. troops. Today anti-U.S. armed forces may fire a few rockets here, and lay an ambush somewhere else, . . . and then they disappear. . . .
>
> It is obvious that the people who started the Iraqi War tended to oversimplify the war in Iraq, thinking that they could gulp down the country without the slightest effort. They did not expect that it was easy to gulp down the country, but difficult to digest. Now hundreds of thousands of U.S. soldiers are acting as policemen in Iraq, but it is of not much help to the Iraqi security situation and the sporadic attacks launched by Iraqis are numerous, and even safety for the U.N. personnel in Baghdad cannot be guaranteed. The U.S. is now in a dilema *[sic]*. Of course, it would be very reluctant to cough up what it has gained in the war, but on the other hand, the increasing number of U.S. casualties has resulted in anti-war protests at home. . . .
>
> Let the people of each country . . . manage their own affairs free from outside interference. Trying to impose one's own political model or values onto other countries can only be the daydream of those who style themselves as the Savior.[59]
>
> — *People's Liberation Army Daily,* November 2003

The Masking of Chinese Expansionism

China has tried every possible trick to pursue its strategic goals around the globe. It has placed "peacekeepers" in southern Lebanon and nine of the U.N.'s African missions.[60] Its embassies routinely help Chinese intelligence and military personnel to enter foreign countries.[61] Many of the Chinese Patriotic Catholic Association's so-called "missionaries" are in actuality spies.[62] Totalitarian China has gone so far as to send "election observers" and "election planners" to Africa.[63] To further obscure its self-serving goals on that continent, it has flooded several nations with hundreds of thousands of contract laborers. While most ostensibly work on petroleum and transportation projects, some undoubtedly have a more "revolutionary" purpose. In early November 2006, China went invited the leaders of every African nation to Beijing for an "economic summit." In return for support in the U.N. on the Taiwan issue, the African nations were offered commerce and aid. Of the world's 192 governments, only 29 from small countries still give Taiwan diplomatic recognition.[64]

As Chapter 4 will show, China has been using its own, overqualified version of a "Peace Corps" to watch for U.S. meddling in the more remote areas of south Asia. It is now so confident of the West's trust in its new, more charming *persona,* that it plans to send a full 40% of its top students abroad to graduate school.[65] From a nation of over a billion people, that could create a fairly sizable number of temporary residents in many countries. Not of all those residents will be trying to develop a better understanding of democracy.

How China May Have Capitalized on One Islamic Uprising

Within Africa, China's biggest objective has been oil. To determine how it has used Islamic insurgency to pursue that objective, one must find an example. History records its promotion of Communist revolution in southern Africa to acquire Angolan and Mozambican oil. But one needs a more recent example in the continent's volatile center to prove the Islamic sequel.

In southern Nigeria, the Movement for the Emancipation of the Niger Delta (MEND) has cut the flow of oil from America's fifth largest source in half. Because there has been open warfare between Muslims and Christians in Nigeria's north, MEND is often associated with *al-Qaeda*. But what has oil to do with *sharia?* MEND has primarily gone after Western oil interests. It has kidnapped U.S. workers and destroyed U.S. facilities. While its jailed leader is a professed admirer of Osama bin Laden, its members are non-Muslim. In a 2007 *National Geographic,* its fighters are pictured with brand new Yamaha outboard motors and Eastern-bloc weapons.[66] One could reasonably conclude that MEND is being supported by someone. Westerners have dangerously assumed that its benefactor is Islamist.

> MEND emerged independent of either the Wahhabi Shari'ah movement in northern Nigeria or the Nigerian Taliban that first appeared in Yobe state in December 2003. . . . Its members are mainly Catholics, though Asari [its jailed leader] is an exception.[67]
>
> — Project for the Research of Islamist Movements

Should the big American oil companies find that operating in Nigeria is too risky, Chinese oil companies are set to move in according to ABC News.[68] Thus, the PRC's roundabout way of assuming control over a region starts to take shape. Against a backdrop of Islamic revolution, it discourages Western development through pseudo-Islamic guerrilla proxies and then establishes its own economic parameters. As many Americans equate capitalism with democracy, they might fail to notice that the following companies are just a few of the known extensions of the PLA: (1) Hutchinson Whampoa Ltd. (port facilities); (2) China Ocean Shipping Company (container ships); and (3) China National Electronics Import and Export Company (telecommunications networks).[69] As China needs South Asian oil, it may very well be attempting the same type of ruse in that theater.

The Possibility of a Sino-Islamist Coalition

Some of America's best thinkers have concluded that the existence of Islamic separatists in Xinjiang Province makes a Sino-Islamist coalition impossible. If China had a Western heritage and were in the Western World, they would be correct. But it hasn't, and it isn't. In the Eastern World, such dichotomies are common. A few examples will help to make the point.

While Pakistan publicly discourages the Taliban's use of its territory, it privately condones that use.[70] Where the Taliban is helped, so too is *al-Qaeda*. Thus, while Pakistan still occasionally runs military operations against *al-Qaeda* operatives, it still indirectly supports their cause.

Iran also purports to contest *al-Qaeda*. It and Pakistan have traditionally vied for the right to decide what type of Islamic state Afghanistan would become. Yet, Iran still harbors Osama bin Laden's family and many of his top advisers.[71]

While Gulbuddin Hekmatyar is theoretically allied with the Taliban,[72] he also has strong ties with Iran.[73] That's the way things are done in this part of the world. Combatants will often have a dog in both sides of a fight so that the unexpected entrant can glean valuable intelligence and sabotage pivotal initiatives. That China has a large military force in its part of occupied Kashmir points to a possible interest it has in exploiting (or even instigating) that region's unrest.

Has China Manipulated Both Western and Muslim Worlds?

China now has a way to expand its empire without having to do any of the actual fighting. Its insidious method not only obeys the teachings of Sun Tzu, but also approximates 4GW. A closer—somewhat abbreviated—look at the three Colonels' dual disclosure may reveal China's future strategy.

> One of China's [future] strategies is . . . to defeat an enemy without a military conflict using "comprehensive warfare." . . .
>
> Meng [Col. Meng Xiansheng] said "comprehensive warfare" . . . offer[s] another way of interpreting [solving] . . . the cross-Taiwan Strait and Sino-U.S. crises. . . .
>
> The concept follows the publication in 1999 of a book by two PLA air force senior colonels. . . .
>
> The book revealed that China's military plans to use all forms of warfare, including terrorism and terrorist-related tactics to prevail.[74]
>
> — *Geostrategy-Direct,* 2 August 2006

If atheistic China needed South Asia, the Middle East, and Africa for an oil conduit, it would not hesitate to play fundamentalist Muslims off against fundamentalist Christians. By so doing, it could solve two problems at once. To manipulate the Muslim world, it would infiltrate *al-Qaeda* with Chinese operatives posing as Muslim separatists. Since the Soviet-Afghan War, there have been Maoist *mujahideen* leaders.[75] Prior to America's invasion of Afghanistan, one of its intelligence reports admitted to the following: "China's military provided training to the Taliban militia and its *al-Qaeda* supporters." When Pakistani troops cornered *al-Qaeda* leaders in the Waziristans in 2004, they found Uighur fighters from China's Xinjiang Province.[76] Since 2001, more than just Chinese weapons have entered Afghanistan. There will be more about that in a later chapter.

Like Pakistan, China May Condone *al-Qaeda* Activity

Pakistan has officially disallowed any *al-Qaeda* training facility within its borders, yet it still permits a 200-acre *Lashkar-e-Toiba (LET)* camp near Lahore.[77] *LET* has been linked to *al-Qaeda* training for years.[78] Instead of rebanning *LET* and its Wahhabi parent in 2003,[79] Pakistan just shifted them to a "watch list."[80]

Why couldn't some of the camps in western China be used for training foreign fighters? In November 2006, an Islamic website featured a videotaped view of such a camp. In it, Saudi trainees promised to help their Iraqi brethren.[81]

China has experienced strings of Muslim uprisings in several of its western provinces since 1821.[82] Yet, according to three highly credible sources (including a U.S. Army War College study), the PRC was still willing to train Uighurs to fight the Russians in Afghanistan.[83] Some of those Uighurs came home to push for a Muslim state. Others stayed abroad. In Afghanistan, there were Uighur fighters in *al-Qaeda's* elite 055 Brigade until 2001. That brigade was largely comprised of non-Afghans, and hundreds were deployed around the globe to anchor local guerrilla movements.[84] Might some of those "Uighurs" have really been PRC agents? Was their job to train brigade members in the finer points of Maoist guerrilla warfare and thus spread "growth-enhancing" revolution around the globe (train the trainers)?

It is far more likely that *al-Qaeda* has been infiltrated by the Chinese government than the other way around. According to a U.S. Army study, Osama bin Laden has never made much of an attempt to train fighters for Xinjiang.[85] There is no evidence of Arabs going to China, but the Western Chinese have been making frequent trips to Afghanistan and Pakistan.[86] Uighurs would have more logically fit in with the multi-ethnic Northern Alliance, but most ended up with the Taliban.[87] Throughout Asia, opposites hold great promise. Why, then, are so many Americans willing to accept China's self-professed friendship in the War on Terror? The answer must lie in U.S. foreign policy and the various factors that drive it.

Too Much of the Same Kind of Smoke

Most Americans aren't aware that China has progressively purchased or leased land and port facilities at both ends of the Panama Canal. Hutchinson Whampoa Ltd. now controls many of the docks in Balboa and Christobal, as well as many of the former U.S. military installations. Any part of the following may be included: (1) Albrook Air Field; (2) Rodman Naval Air Station; (3) Fort Clayton; (4) Fort Sherman; (5) Corozal and Corundu intelligence facilities; (6) Special Forces jungle training center; and (7) the former underground headquarters of U.S. Southern Command at Quarry Heights.[88] Like many other Chinese companies, Hutchinson Whampoa is an extension of the PLA.[89] Thus, the Chinese military has been given a way to slow the reinforcement of the U.S. Pacific Fleet and a place from which to control the land bridge between North and South America.

In November 2006, U.S. leaders barely blinked an eye when their long-time Socialist nemesis—Daniel Ortega (of the Sandinista National Liberation Front)—won the election in Nicaragua. What happened next was more than a coincidence. With Chinese money and people, Nicaragua was suddenly planning to build an alternate canal across its part of the isthmus. Three months later, the president of Venezuela nationalized Western oil company holdings.[90] One of two things was happening. Either the PRC wanted to ship oil west from Venezuela or export something east into the Caribbean. Might that something be all the wherewithal and expertise for a regional revolution? There were disturbing indications that the world's three existing revolutionary governments were about to be joined by a fourth—Venezuela.[91] While Chavez has befriended Iran and allowed *Hezbollah* to operate from Venezuela's Isla de Margarita,[92] his government more closely parallels the Chinese model. His million-man military reserve lacks the ideological sponsorship/monitoring of an Iranian-Revolutionary-Guard or Sudanese-Popular-Defense-Force equivalent.

But any further study of Western Hemisphere problems must

wait. First, each of South Asia's six subregions must be carefully analyzed. It is from this part of the world that the most effective form of guerrilla warfare springs.

A U.S. Reply That Is Neither Conciliatory Nor Militaristic

The world situation is clearly deteriorating. America's leaders can continue to blame structureless *al-Qaeda,* or they can look for a more robust instigator. To control Africa and South Asia, China has subtly milked two of America's favorite crusades—democracy and trade. Its "unity" governments have turned into one-party dictatorships, and its oil network has far surpassed any contingency requirement. As both initiatives are "peaceful," China must only rely on its technologically expanding military to discourage Western intervention.

The U.S. has had a "one-China" policy and no diplomatic relations with Taiwan since the 1970's.[93] The PRC considers Taiwan to be its 23rd province.[94] Its National People's Congress has already decided "to use force as a last resort" if that province ever tries to secede.[95] In February 2000, the Chinese government issued a White Paper that threatened invasion if Taiwan were to "indefinitely postpone negotiations on reunification."[96] When Taiwan planned a referendum in March 2004 on whether to deploy an anti-missile defense system, both the U.S. and PRC objected. They were worried that the referendum might be interpreted as a move toward independence.[97] When the system was finally voted upon, less than 50% of the eligible Taiwanese electorate participated, thereby nullifying the procedure.[98] Should PLA hawks ever think the U.S. incapable of responding to an invasion of Taiwan, they might do something to trigger one. For an effective naval response, America would depend heavily on its surveillance of adjacent seas from space.[99] On 11 January 2007, China used one of its ballistic missiles to destroy a weather satellite that had been traveling at the same altitude as U.S. spy satellites.[100]

Most probably, Taiwan will fall into the Chinese Co-Prosperity Sphere without a shot being fired. As America's trade imbalance and foreign debt continue to grow, it will become more susceptible to Chinese blackmail. By January 2007, China held between $330 and $660 billion of America's debt with that total projected to reach $1.3

trillion by 2012.[101] If China's Washington lobby were additionally to arrange a wide assortment of tiny concessions, there is no telling what might happen. Openly disdainful of anything small, America's "big-picture" leaders might not notice the cumulative danger. Most have yet to realize that it was near-naked, *ninja*-like saboteurs who ultimately defeated the U.S. military machine in Vietnam. At some point, those leaders might conclude that Taiwan would be better off going the way of Hong Kong and Macau.

China's current method of expansion is so deceptive and low in profile that it should never lead to a large-scale military confrontation with the West. Just showing what it has accomplished so far in South Asia will take many chapters of carefully researched detail. In effect, the PRC has a hidden aspect to its overall strategy that is only apparent through little things. The extent to which that aspect mirrors the whole is well beyond the purview of this book. The reader is simply warned not to confuse the two. In most locations, this "obscure initiative" has been largely masked by a concurrent Islamic uprising.

2 Malaysia, Thailand, and Burma

- How close are Burma's (Myanmar's) ties to China?
- What's the story behind the recent coup in Thailand?

The Center of Islamic Influence at Kuala Lumpur

(Source: DA Pam 550-45, cover)

Malaysia—a Good Place to Start

An in-depth look at Sino-Islamic cooperation in South Asia would logically start at the Muslim end of the Malay Peninsula. The mostly Chinese "Communist Party of Malaysia" (CPM) anchored that country's anti-Japanese resistance during WWII and then became affiliated with the PRC. In June 1948, following attacks by CPM's armed wing—the Malayan Races Liberation Army (MLRA), the British administrators of the Federation of Malaya declared an emergency. For support, the MLRA turned to the half million Chinese "squatters" who inhabited the middle ground between the cities and interior.[1] As its soldiers were well uniformed and fairly proficient,[2] some foreign power must have been providing covert assistance. In 1951, the British moved those squatters into 400 new villages and began to dismantle the Communist apparatus through a series of sweeps. By 1960, the MLRA had been forced into the border region of southern Thailand, and an independent Federation of Malaysia was planned.[3] The greatest threat to that federation would come from its neighbor to the south—Indonesia.

> That country's [Indonesia's] President, Sukarno, vilified the new federation as "neocolonialist." . . . A strategy of infiltration was implemented as Indonesian troops landed in . . . the peninsula. . . .
>
> Violence broke out within hours of the proclamation of the Federation of Malaysia on September 16 (1963). . . . Sukarno hoped the infiltrators would spark a popular revolt against the government. . . .
>
> International attempts to bring Indonesia and Malaysia together failed in 1964; [then] Britain, New Zealand, and Australia sent troops and other military aid in accordance with their defense arrangements to help the Malaysian Armed Forces. . . .
>
> Sukarno was forced to step down from power following an abortive left-wing coup on September 30, 1965. . . . On August 11, 1966 a peace treaty between Malaysia and Indonesia ended the hostilities.[4]
>
> — Dept. of the Army Pamphlet 550-45

Malaysia's Current Relationship with China

China established very close "political and military relations" with longtime Prime Minister Mahathir Mohammed of Malaysia. Critical of U.S. efforts to promote democracy and human rights, Mahathir moved toward authoritarian rule. He was also quite anti-Semetic. Like China, Malaysia soon became a staunch supporter of the Palestinian cause and established diplomatic relations with the Palestinian Liberation Organization (PLO). Having retired on 31 October 2003, Mahathir remains vocal in the Malaysian media. His replacement is Abdullah Ahmad Badawi. Though having served as chairman of both the OIC and the Non-Aligned Movement, Badawi is believed to be more moderate. His main thrust has been to limit internal corruption. Thus, Malaysia's policy toward Islamist movements and other nations many not have changed much. China Ocean Shipping Company (COSCO)—the "Merchant Marine Arm of the PLA"—remains a major presence at Malaysia's main harbor (Port Klang) near the Straits of Malacca.[5]

More on Malaysia's Government and Possible Intentions

The *CIA World Factbook* lists Malaysia as a "constitutional monarchy." Its position of king is rotated every five years among the hereditary rulers of nine states. Its prime minister is the product of parliamentary and regional elections every five years. While Malaysia's population is varied, its government is decidedly Muslim. Malaysia has some of the toughest censorship laws in the world. Its authorities exert substantial control over the media, and they often impose restrictions in the name of national security. They are trying to insulate the largely-Muslim population from what they consider to be harmful Western influences. Malaysia's news and entertainment are both subject to censorship. While state-owned Radio Television Malaysia (RTM) operates two TV networks and many of the country's radio services, there are also a few private stations. Newspapers must renew their publication licenses annually, and the country's "Home Minister" can suspend or revoke publishing permits. Malaysia's only news agency—Bernama—is state run. While the country has no external threats to speak of, it maintains a sizable military. As of 2005, service in that military became obligatory for all males at age 18. Almost 250,000 Malaysian males now reach that age annually.[6]

Spots Where Islamic Radicals Might Still Train in Malaysia

An extremist Filipino organization—the Moro National Liberation Front (MNLF)—was born on Malaysian soil about 1968. In the remote regions of Malaysian Borneo, Islamist factions might still train without the central government's knowledge. That's because Malaysian Sarawak and Sabah share the immense and heavily jungled island of Borneo with Indonesian Kalimantan and independent Brunei. At the very end of the Sulu Archipelago, easternmost Sabah lies a scant 30 miles from Philippine territory. Through mostly Muslim, Malaysia still has Islamist factions (those that oppose a secular state). It banned the *Al-Arqam* movement (with ties to the Egyptian Muslim Brotherhood) but now has the *Al-Maunah* movement. In July 2000, the latter went so far as to raid two Malaysian army bases to obtain weapons. *Al-Qaeda* affiliate—Indonesian *Jemaah Islamiyah (JI)*—also maintains a presence in Malaysia. That's where its founders—Sungkar and Ba'asyir—fled in 1985.[7]

Malaysian Support for Thai Rebels

There is no evidence that the Malaysian government has sponsored subversion in the upper Malay Peninsula. However, Thailand has accused Malaysia of harboring militants who cross the porous border to avoid capture. Thailand's three southernmost provinces were ruled as a Malay-speaking sultanate until Thai annexation in 1902. As a result of religious discrimination, an armed separatist rebellion smoldered there until the early 1980's. Since 2004, that smoke has become a fire. By October 2006, it had killed 1,700 people. There appears no direct link between *al-Qaeda* and this uprising, but southern Thailand undoubtedly falls within "Mantiqi 1"—the first of *JI's* three operational areas. As early as 1969, Muslim separatist fighters from the Philippines were training at camps in Peninsular Malaysia near the Thai border.[8]

The Tactics of Islamic Insurgency in Thailand

Muslim discontent in southern Thailand flared up in January 2004 when 30 militants launched a coordinated attack against a weapons arsenal. Since then, most of the violence has been relegated to the provinces of Pattani, Yala, and Narathiwat. It has consisted of bombings, drive-by shootings, arson attacks, and assassinations.[9] On 2 April 2005, there was a string of simultaneous explosions outside this Muslim-dominated area. They occurred at an international airport, French-owned supermarket, and hotel.[10] In July 2005, two gunmen shot a Buddhist cloth vendor and then cut off his head. Shortly thereafter, 60 insurgents launched a coordinated attack against the capital of Yala province. First, there were daylight bombings and shootings. Then, after plunging Yala city into complete darkness by destroying its electrical transformers, the rebels targeted two convenience stores, a restaurant, a railway station, and an area near a hotel.[11] (Muslim extremists will often attack several places at once to keep the main objective from being reinforced.) The main objective in this case was probably the train station. In February 2006, a remotely controlled bomb went off under a truck passing a meeting of village officials at the district office.[12] Some six months later, Muslim extremists disrupted rail service in southern Thailand.[13]

While the targeting of Buddhists in a predominantly Muslim region has tended to divide the two faiths, this uprising does not appear to be faith oriented. Muslims who worked for the government have also been killed as informants.[14] Places of worship have not yet been targeted.

This is not the first time that Thailand has experienced rebellion. It had Communist rebels during the Vietnamese War.[15] The decades-old Muslim rebellion fizzled out in the 1980's, only to be reborn in 2001 under younger leadership.[16] So far, the government has tried military action,[17] bipartisan commissions,[18] and public works projects.[19] An overly enthusiastic military response early on may have sparked further violence. In the Tak Bai incident of October 2004, 80 Muslim men died of suffocation while in government custody.[20]

After the September 2006 coup, a former Communist guerrilla fighter was chosen as interim president.[21] There was also a media ban on any bad news from the southern provinces.[22] While there are rumors of Middle Eastern or *Jemaah Islamiyah* sponsorship of the violence,[23] there may also be also be a hidden instigator.

Thailand's New Muslim Prime Minister

Gen. Sondhi Boonyaratkalin—a Muslim in a country dominated by Buddhists—seized power from Prime Minister Thaksin Shinawatra in a bloodless coup in Thailand on 20 September 2006.[24] One of the first things he did was to restrict the media and ban all political party meetings.[25] On 18 October, his choice for prime minister—Surayud Chulanont—constituted a radical change from Thailand's previous policy toward Muslim separatists. Instead of using force, that prime minister planned to talk with them. His declaration came a day after two more Muslim separatist attacks—one against an Army outpost. As of 14 February 2007, the new government's conciliatory approach, with promises of autonomy and economic aid for the southern provinces, hadn't worked. Four days later, guerrillas of undisclosed identity attacked and burned one of Thailand's biggest rubber warehouses. Somewhere in southern Thailand, that warehouse had held some 400 tons of the valuable substance.[26] Uprisings of strictly ethnic origins normally target churches and public gatherings; they do not go after rail and rubber infrastructure. Thailand is one of those countries in which one would expect a hidden Communist element. After all, the North Vietnamese did chase the Khmer Rouge to the Thai border in 1979.[27] Southern Thailand is more than just predominantly Muslim, it is also part of the Isthmus of Kra—a place of great strategic importance to China.

Something Similar Is Occurring in Burma (Myanmar)

Burma has become a powerful military dictatorship with no apparent foe other than its own people. The Karin tribe provides its only real source of internal opposition. Yet, by garnering a full half of the national budget, its military junta has built one of the largest armies in Southeast Asia. On construction projects, it regularly uses forced laborers who can suffer death for an infraction. Plastered around its old capital of Mandalay are red and yellow signs proclaiming the power of the "State." While Burma's Communist party is no longer very active, it's government has been Socialist since 1962.[28] With the military coup of 1989, the Socialist police state became a military police state. Aung San Suu Kyi's opposition party won 83% of the parliamentary seats in 1990, but the military quickly invalidated the election. Now Burma's leader holds the title of "Chairman of the State Peace and Development Council." As with Africa's Marxist and Islamist regimes, China has fully defended the Burmese junta's repressive rule in the U.N.[29] In return, that junta may have allowed China to reestablish its old transportation link with the Indian Ocean. Early in WWII, much of China's war materiel had to come overland from Calcutta or Chittagong. (See Maps 2.1, 2.2, and 2.3.) Its tortuous route was as follows: (1) by rail to Ledo; (2) by truck to Myitkyina, Bhamo, and Wanting (down

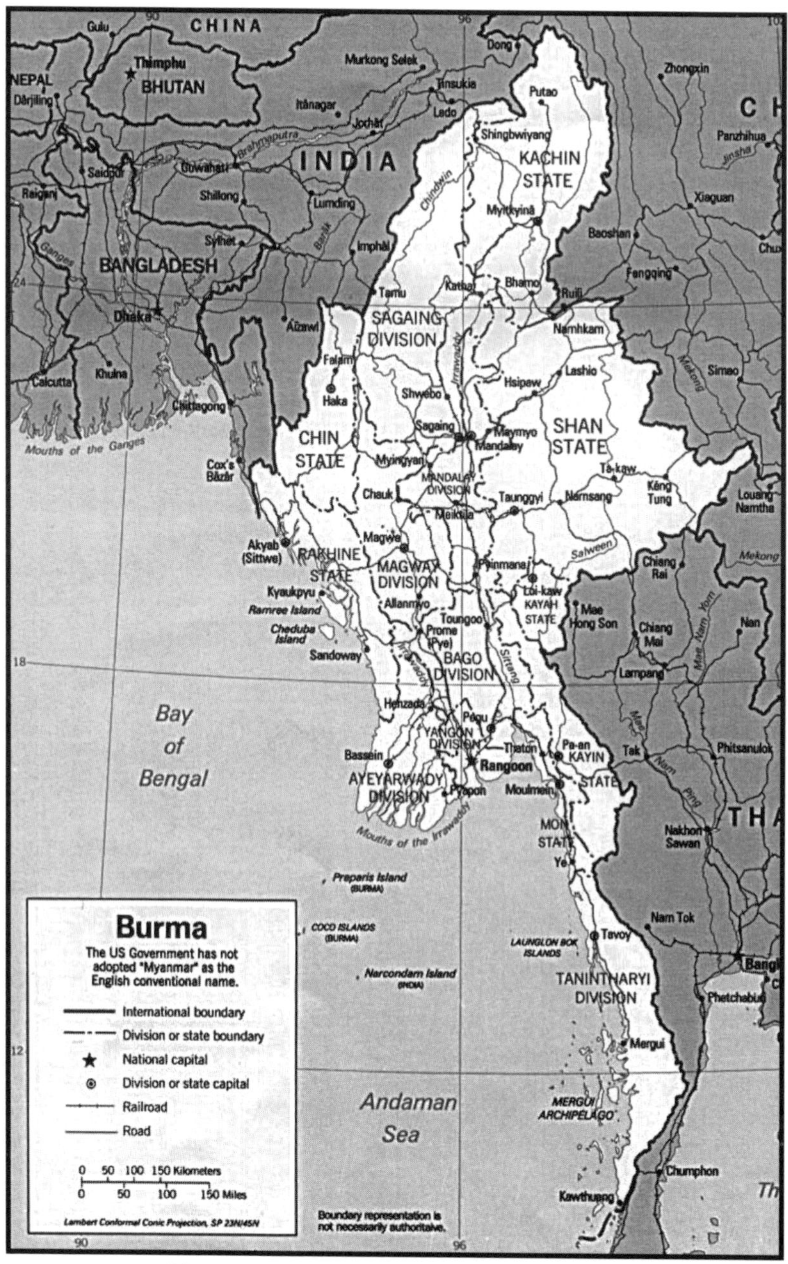

Map 2.1: The New Irrawaddy Conduit
(Source: Courtesy of General Libraries, University of Texas at Austin, from their website for map designator "burma_pol_96.pdf")

Ledo and Stillwell Roads); and (3) by truck to Baoshan, Xiaguan, Chuxiong, and finally Kunming (up the Burma Road).[30] Later in the war, some materiel made it by boat to Mandalay and then by train to the Burma Road entrance at Lashio.

China has been shipping its oil past Mandalay to Bhamo while it extended its railroad to Lashio. (See Figure 2.4.) Based on the date of the following news story, that rail link may now be nearly complete.

> Chinese construction crews are building a railway from Kunming, the capital of Yunnan, southwest to Mangshi,

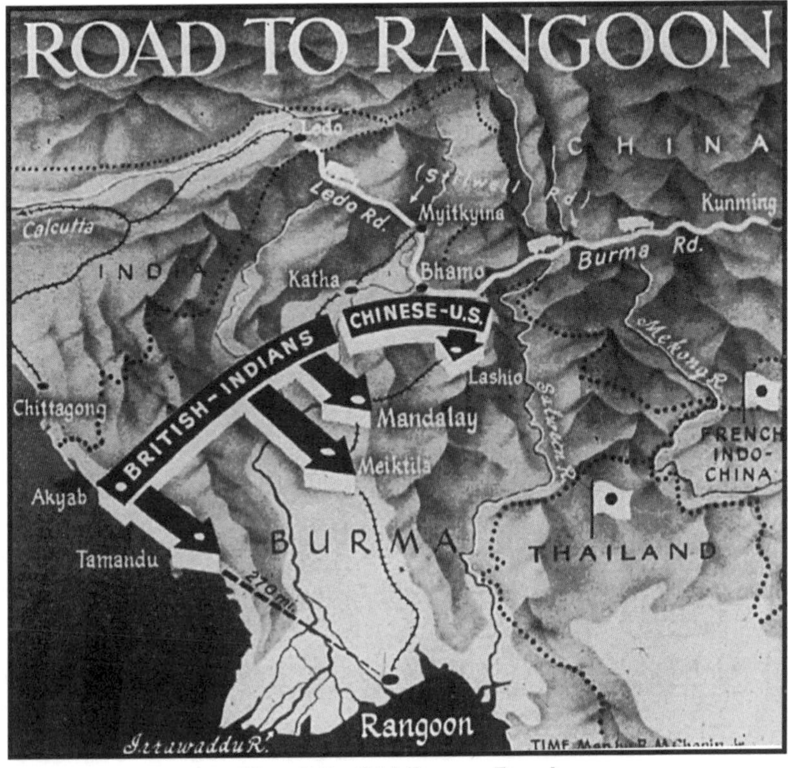

Map 2.2: Old Burma Road
(Source: Courtesy of *Time Magazine*, as republished by NIC Changlang District Unit, India, © n.d.)

> the capital of Dehong Dai [Province]. People in Chinese Ruili—a busy cosmopolitan border town astride roads to Bhamo . . . and Lashio—expect the railway to arrive from Mangshi within a few years. That will leave the Chinese and Myanmar railways only 145 km apart.[31]
>
> — *Asia Times*, 23 September 2004

China's Renewed Interest in the Irrawaddy

As southern and central Burma are almost entirely flat, the Irrawaddy is navigable for much of the way to the Chinese border. The Burmese government only holds sway over 11 of its 14 administrative parts.[32] It marginally controls those along the Irrawaddy River

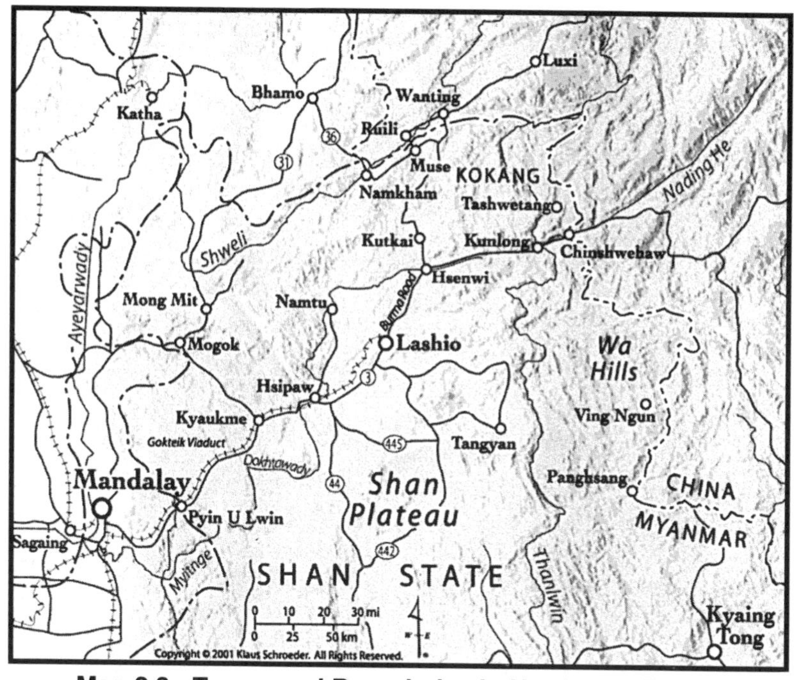

Map 2.3: Towns and Boundaries in Northwest Burma
(Source: School of Oriental and African Studies, Univ. of London, from mercury.soas.ac.uk/wadict/wa_maps.html,© n.d. by Klaus Schroeder)

Map 2.4: "Golden-Triangle" Buffer
(Source: "The Opium Kings," Frontline, © 1998 by PBS and WGBH/Frontline)

to Mandalay, but not the river bank north of there into Sagaing Division and Kachin State, nor the first leg of old Burma Road through Shan State.[33] (See Map 2.1.) Thus, China would need alliances with local warlords to safely transport its African oil beyond Mandalay. Currently enjoying a cease fire with the Burmese junta is the New Democratic Army (NDA) of Northeast Kachin State and the Kachin Defense Army (KDA) of Northern Shan State. Also operating in the Kokang region of Northern Shan State—directly atop the old Burma

Road—is a remnant of the old Nationalist Chinese Army. Having also signed a cease fire with the junta in 1989, it now calls itself the Myanmar National Democracy Alliance Army (MNDAA).[34] As the old Burma Road runs just north of the most active part of the heroin-producing Golden Triangle,[35] the West would be hard pressed to interdict it in time of war. (See Map 2.4.)

There Is Relatively Little Islamist Activity in Burma

Burma is one of the countries that Azzam—the founder of al-Qaeda—wanted returned to the Islamic fold.[36] While somewhere between four and ten percent of the Burmese population are Muslim,[37] most live either in the cities or in Arakan State. That state directly abuts the Bay of Bengal at the narrow border with Bangladesh. Those in the Arakan Mountains are called Rohingiya Muslims. They and the Islamic Party *(Mahaz-e Islami)* of Myanmar are *al-Qaeda* affiliated.[38] Rohingiya Muslim fighters are being trained by an *al-Qaeda* affiliate from Bangladesh, but their influence on Myanmar as a whole has been limited.[39]

> Banned Bangladeshi Islamic extremist outfit Harkat-ul Jehad-al Islami (HUJAI) . . . is imparting training to similar extremist groups from Myanmar. . . .
>
> . . . HUJAI . . . has been declared a terrorist outfit by the U.S. State Department for its al-Qaeda and Taliban connections. . . .
>
> The HUJAI has been imparting arms training to Islamic extremist outfits like those belonging to the Rohingiya Muslims of Arakan mountains in Myanmar.[40]
>
> — *Hindustan Times* (Delhi), 2 September 2004

One reputable researcher equates *Harkat-ul Jehad-al Islami* (HIJAI) with Pakistani *Harakat-ul-Jihad-i-Islami (HUJI).* He claims that Karachi's Madrasa Khalid bin Walid is the "command headquarters of Karachi Muslims fighting the military regime in Burma."[41]

For the heaviest Islamist activity in Southeast Asia, one must look at *JI's* principal theater of operations—the Southern Philippines and Indonesia.

3 Southern Philippines and Indonesia

- Are there still Communist guerrillas in the Philippines?
- Does Indonesia support the Islamic rebels in Thailand?

Mindanao Has Both Communist and Islamic Guerrillas

(Source: DA Pam 550-72, p. 57)

The Philippines' Long History of Insurgency

Muslim influence over parts of the Philippines predates the onset of Spanish rule in 1565. The Islamic sultanates of the Sulu Archipelago and Mindanao were subsequently able to resist the Spanish penetration and Christianization of their areas.[1] (See Map 3.1.) In 1892, their non-Muslim northern brethren grew tired of Spanish oppression and revolted. At the end of the Spanish-American War in 1898, U.S. troops inherited this anti-colonialist sentiment. Then, they were forced to fight in the very costly (almost 5,000 American fatalities) and largely guerrilla Philippine-American War.[2] Since that time, Filipinos have used guerrilla tactics to resist both Japanese occupation and internal abuse. Among their most famous uprisings was that of the Huks. Organized in 1942 by Communist Luis Taruc, the Huks quickly extended their control over much of Luzon. At the end of WWII, Luzon's tenant farmers rebelled against their landlords, and the Huk Rebellion ensued. That Taruc's forces became known as the People's Liberation Army (PLA[P]) may indicate some link to their namesake. They soon extended their revolt to the Visayan Islands and Mindanao. By 1951, the Huk Rebellion had been largely defused through military pressure and economic reform. Three years later, Taruc unceremoniously surrendered.[3]

With varied population and piecemeal geography, the Philippine Islands have always been volatile. In the late 1960's, several Communist and Islamic elements became restive. First, there was a remnant of the PLA(P), then another small "People's Army" connected to what was left of the pro-Soviet Communist Party of the Philippines (CPP). But most troublesome was the New People's Army (NPA)—the armed wing of a pro-Chinese faction of the "regenerated" Marxist Leninist CPP (CPP-ML).[4]

In 1968, the founder of CPP-ML adopted the Maoist strategy of a "people's democratic revolution." His NPA was soon in control of large portions of Isabela Province in northern Luzon. About that same time, a surprisingly leftist Moro National Liberation Front (MNLF) was organized on Malaysian soil. Soon, the MNLF began to receive support from Middle Eastern Islamic states, most notably Libya.[5] Well accustomed to internal discord, the Philippines' president soon became worried about too much "foreign involvement." Though not quite sure of what happening, he perceived more of a threat from the Communist countries than from any other variety. It would appear that some of his problems may have been Communist inspired and Muslim led.

> In response to what he perceived as . . . an active conspiracy on the part of leftist elements to overthrow the government, President Ferdinand E. Marcos declared martial law on September 21, 1972.[6]
>
> — Dept. of the Army Pamphlet 550-72

Marcos also mentioned the growth of violence between

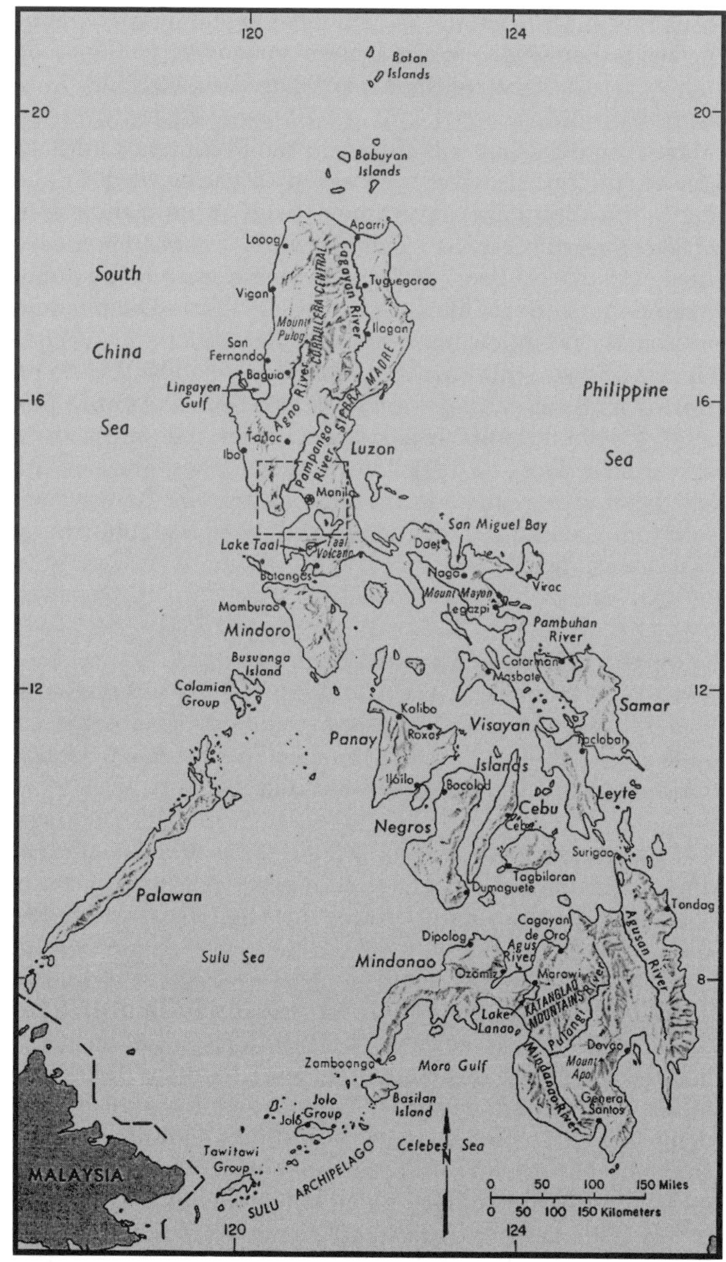

Map 3.1: Philippine Island Chain

(Source: DA Pam 550-72, p. 62)

> Muslims and Christians on Mindanao and the Sulu Archipelago as being encouraged by foreign powers.[7]
>
> — Dept. of the Army Pamphlet 550-72

Marcos' martial law was to last in the Philippines until 1981. Shortly thereafter, the U.S. was asked to vacate its bases. For 20 years, the Philippine government tried on its own to rein in its various guerrilla groups. Then in 2002, it asked for American military assistance. Soon, Philippine troops were being supplied and trained by U.S. soldiers. One of their first accomplishments was the ouster of Islamic militants from Basilan island in the Sulu Archipelago. Then, thinking that *Abu Sayyaf* had shifted its headquarters from Basilan, they went after Jolo island. As of 15 February 2007, 7,000 Philippine troops with U.S. Special Forces advisers were sweeping Jolo. A week later, despite all of the operations against Islamic extremists in the south, President Arroyo's advisers said that Communist insurgents still posed a greater threat to the country as a whole.[8]

More on the Filipinos' Islamic Heritage

The Philippines is one of those countries that Azzam—the founder of *al-Qaeda*—wanted back in the Islamic fold.[9] Below is a synopsis of the Muslim history of that country.

> Bangsamoro was originally home to the Muslim sultanates of Mindanao. . . . These sultanates resisted Spanish colonial rule, and were therefore not fully integrated with the rest of the islands. . . .
>
> Two decades after the Philippines reclaimed its independence from the U.S., the area was claimed by the Moro National Liberation Front [MNLF], who intended it to become the "Moro homeland" separate from the Republic of the Philippines. However, claims were suspended due to a peace agreement in 1996. Currently, the Moro Islamic Liberation Front (MILF) seeks to establish an independent Islamic state in this area.
>
> In 1990, the Autonomous Region in Muslim Mindanao was created to act as a homeland for Moros. However, only

the provinces within the Sulu Archipelago (excluding the city of Isabela) and the provinces of Lanao del Sur and Maguindanao (excluding Cotabato) are currently included.[10]

Al-Qaeda's Link to Filipino Extremists

In 1988, Osama bin Laden sent his brother-in-law—Muhammad Jamal (or Abdul Rahman) Khalifa—to the Philippines to recruit fighters for the Afghan-Soviet War. With help from the Middle East, Indonesia and Malaysia, the Mindanao Independence Movement (MIM) and the Union of Islamic Forces and Organizations (UIFO) had already existed since 1969. Many of their fighters had been trained at camps in Sabbah and Peninsular Malaysia. Three years later, MIM was mysteriously replaced by the leftist MNLF. In 1982, the MILF split off from the MNLF and first operated as an exile group in Pakistan. As both organizations became hard pressed by Philippine government forces in 1991, bin Laden's brother-in-law stepped back into the picture. Soon, with a fresh infusion of *al-Qaeda* cash and Afghan veterans, the *Abu Sayyaf Group (ASG)* was born. Ramzi Ahmed Yousef—the now imprisoned 1993 World Trade Center bomber—turned up in the Philippines about the same time, claiming to be Osama bin Laden's emissary. One source claims that the *ASG* was bin Laden's direct contribution to the Philippine *jihad*. It further asserts that *al-Qaeda* relinquished control of the group four years later. Still, one could say that all three organizations—the MNLF, MILF, and *ASG*—are still affiliated with *al-Qaeda*. While the MILF is ostensibly separatist (wanting to sever all ties with the Philippine government), *ASG* prefers to attack Western interests. Also an offshoot of MNLF, *ASG* has bombed churches, murdered missionaries, and kidnapped Americans. While all three organizations are formidable, a collocated *al-Qaeda* headquarters element may have planned the assassination of U.S. leaders and downing of U.S. planes.[11]

Osama's brother-in-law (Khalifa) was to leave the Philippines, and Ramzi Yousef become *al-Qaeda's* chief operative and organizer there. He was closely affiliated with the Sunni extremist organization *Sipah-i-Sahaba Pakistan (SSP,* later renamed *Milat-e-Islamia Pakistan [MIP]). SSP's* militant offshoot—*Lashkar-i-Jhangvi (LEJ)*—has been likened to *al-Qaeda's* "delta force." In Peshwar,

Yousef met *ASG's* founder and then traveled to the Philippines to instruct its members in bomb making. He went on to train *ASG* terrorists in the Madin camp on Basilan. As early as 1994, Yousef (alias Najy Awaita Haddad) and his chief deputy (Abdul Hakim Ali Hashim Murad, alias Abdul Hakim) were hatching a plot in the Philippines to crash an explosive-laden plane into the Pentagon.[12] (There will be more proof of that shortly.)

The extent to which *al-Qaeda* subsequently influenced world events from its Philippine location is truly amazing. Besides relief-oriented Non-Government Organizations (NGO's), it had several front companies in Manila. One could almost conclude that it had set up an alternate headquarters in the Philippines.[13] From that headquarters, it also orchestrated regional activity.

> At the military level, foreign instructors imparted specialized training to MILF and foreign Islamist members at Camp Abubakar [overrun on Mindanao in 2000]. . . .
>
> . . . Using the Philippines as a base, al-Qaeda penetrated several Islamist groups in Malaysia, Indonesia, and Singapore. . . .
>
> . . . [I]t built a pan-Islamic network linking the key Islamist groups in the region; this was accomplished by first infiltrating . . . (JI), initially an Indonesian Islamist group in the 1990's. Thereafter it developed . . . [JI] a pan-Asian network extending from Malaysia to Japan. . . .
>
> . . . JI was formed by [Abdullah] Sungkar after meeting Osama in Afghanistan.[14]
>
> — Gunaratna, *Inside al-Qaeda*

A Troubling Series of Coincidences

Some of the 9/11 bombers may have traveled to China before their dreadful deed. Within the details of the official 9/11 Commission Report lies the proof. In late December 1999, Riduan Isamuddin (alias Hambali) provided help in Kuala Lumpur to four people whom 9/11 mastermind Khalid Sheikh Mohammed had just trained in Karachi. That help consisted of lodging and airline reservations. Three of those four people were Tawfiq bin Attash (alias Khallad, who would later help to bomb the U.S.S. Cole), and future

9/11 hijackers Nawaf al Hazmi and Khalid al Mihdhar. On 31 December, Khallad flew from Kuala Lumpur to Bangkok, on to Hong Kong (part of the PRC since 1997), and then back to Kuala Lumpur a day later. It is known that Hamzi and Mihdhar accompanied Khallad as far as Bangkok and then returned to Kuala Lumpur. Thus, they probably accompanied him to Hong Kong as well. On 5 January 2000, Hambali again hosted Mohammed and hijackers Mihdhar and Hamzi in Kuala Lumpur at an Indonesian *Jemaah Islamiya* operative's apartment. At that time, Hambali commanded the *JI* region that included mainland Malaysia and its environs. According to the commander of another of *JI's* regions, Hambali (now in U.S. custody) also handled all *JI* liaison with *al-Qaeda.*[15]

> On January 5, 2000, al-Qaeda's Malaysian cell hosted . . . two of the 9/11 hijackers.[16]
>
> — Gunaratna, *Inside al-Qaeda*

If not for Operation (Oplan) Bojinka (Ramzi Yousef's now five-year-old explosive-laden-plane plot), one could attribute that Kuala Lumpur meeting to coincidence. But a U.S. court later convicted Yousef and two co-conspirators of planning Operation (Oplan) Bojinka, so its second and third phases are a matter of public record.

> The first [of Oplan Bojinka's three phases] refers to a plot to destroy 11 [America-bound U.S.] airliners . . . , the second . . . a plan to kill Pope John Paul II . . . , and the third . . . a plan to crash a plane into the CIA headquarters . . . and other buildings. . . .
>
> The money handed down to the plotters originated from al-Qaeda. . . . Philippine authorities say that Operation Bojinka was developed by Ramzi Yousef and Khalid Sheikh Mohammed while they were in Manila, Philippines in 1994 and early 1995.
>
> Phase [three] . . . involved Abdul Hakim Murad either renting, buying, or hijacking a small airplane. . . . The airplane would be filled with explosives. He would then crash it into the CIA headquarters in Langley, Virginia. There were alternate plans to hijack a 12th commercial airliner and use that instead of the small aircraft. . . .
>
> A report from the Philippines to the United States on

> January 20, 1995 stated, "What the subject has in his mind is that he will board any American commercial aircraft pretending to be an ordinary passenger. Then he will hijack said aircraft, control its cockpit and dive it at the CIA headquarters."
>
> Another plot the men were cooking up would have involved [the] hijacking of more airplanes. The Sears Tower (Chicago, Illinois), the Pentagon (Arlington County, Virginia), the Washington Capitol (Washington, D.C.), the White House (Washington, D.C.), the Transamerica Tower (San Francisco, California), and the World Trade Center (New York, New York) would be the likely targets.[17]

Hambali was also in on Operation Bojinka. So, while 9/11 was executed by people from the Middle East, it appears to have been planned in the Far East. After 9/11, Hambali took refuge with his Chinese-Malaysian "wife" in pro-Chinese Cambodia.[18] Any further research into the possibility of other-nation involvement with 9/11 must be left up to the U.S. intelligence community. This chapter has primarily to do with insurgency in the Philippines.

Mindanao's Current Problems

Though nearly a fourth of Mindanao's 18 million residents are Muslim, Catholic missionaries claim that much of its current trouble has nothing to do with religion. They identify oil as the catalyst. (See Map 3.2.)

> The discovery of large deposits of oil and natural gas in Liguasan Marsh near Pikit has drawn foreign oil corporations into a joint venture with the Philippine oil company to develop the area. This is where the confrontation is now occurring.[19]
>
> — *Maryknoll Magazine,* January/February 2004

There are several factions actively contesting government forces on Mindanao. In the extreme southwestern Zamboang del Sur region, it is the Communist NPA. The *Abu Sayyaf* also operates there. In Kadpawan (at the south end of the main part of the

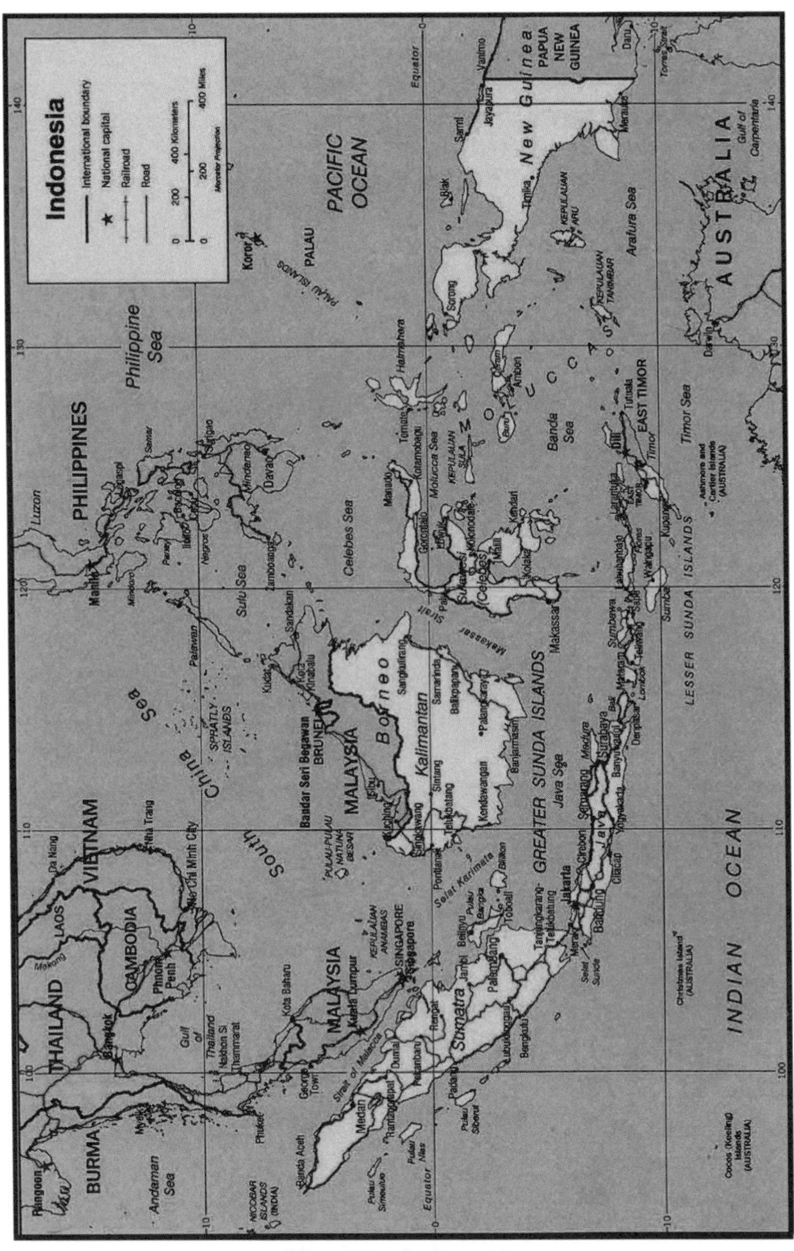

Map 3.2: Indonesia

(Source: Courtesy of General Libraries, University of Texas at Austin, from their website for map designator "indonesia_pol_2002.pdf")

island), the MILF controls an almost autonomous Muslim region next to the oil-rich Liguasan Marsh. As of February 2004, more than 100,000 people had been displaced by the fighting.[20]

More about the NPA

Formed in March 1969 with the stated goal of overthrowing the Philippine government through protracted guerrilla warfare, the NPA is a Maoist group. By 1983, it had 6,000-10,000 fighters and little apparent support from outside sources. It was active in about half of the country's 73 provinces, to include eastern Mindanao, Samar, and Luzon.

The NPA has more recently targeted the following: (1) Philippine security forces, (2) government officials, (3) local infrastructure, (4) businesses that won't pay "revolutionary taxes," and (5) politicians who object to extortion. Opposing any U.S. military presence in the Philippines, it attacked U.S. military interests killing several American service personnel before the U.S. base closures in 1992. In December 2005, the NPA publicly expressed its intent to target U.S. personnel if they were discovered in NPA operating areas. As of April 2006, it was still estimated to have 9,000 fighters.[21]

That the NPA has now extended its operations into Muslim controlled southwestern Mindanao seems a bit strange. Normally, guerrilla factions of divergent ideologies would give each other more elbow room.

MNLF's Current Activities

By 1983, the MNLF had been reduced from a force of 50,000-60,000 fighters to one of 10,000-15,000. As the main draw for dissatisfied Muslims, the MNLF only operates in the southern Philippines.[22]

The MNLF made a surprise appearance on Jolo Island in the Sulu Archipelago in April 2007. In the midst of a well-orchestrated and largely bloodless push by U.S.-advised Philippine forces on supposedly *Abu Sayyaf* refuge, it was the MNLF who put up a fight.[23] The obvious implication was that the *Abu Sayyaf* and MNLF were now combined.

An Update on *Abu Sayyaf*

Founded on Basilan Island, the *ASG* also goes by the name of *Harakat al Islamiyya*. While primarily operating in the provinces of the Sulu Archipelago (Basilan, Sulu, and Tawi-Tawi), it is now on Mindanao's Zamboanga peninsula and has run a few operations as far north as Manila. (Refer back to Map 3.1.) While the *ASG* is largely supported by Middle Eastern Islamist factions, it also receives funding from Indonesia's *JI* (a known *al-Qaeda* affiliate). *JI* has even helped to train *ASG's* 200-500 fighters. As of March 2005, *JI* was providing *ASG* with money for underwater-explosives training.[24] While *Abu Sayyaf's* intentions appear more anti-Western than Muslim separatist, its love of extortion makes it difficult to tell.

> Abu Sayyaf is known more for its kidnap-for-ransom schemes—including many involving Americans and Western tourists—and conducting deadly raids against Christian towns.
>
> More recently, Abu Sayyaf has been accused of more spectacular explosive attacks, including the almost simultaneous bombings in Manila and two southern cities Feb. 14 [2005] that killed eight people and wounded more than 100. Those attacks came a year after a bomb blew up on a ferry in Manila Bay, killing 116 people in the Philippine's worst terrorist strike.[25]
>
> — Associated Press, 18 March 2005

What the MILF Has Been Up To Lately

Despite a two year cease-fire and peace negotiations, MILF fighters attacked Philippine government troops in Maguindanao (a province in south-central Mindanao) in January 2005. After days of fighting with the combined forces of MILF, *Abu Sofia,* and *Abu Sayyaf,* government troops resorted to 105mm howitzer barrages. Thousands of civilians had to leave their homes to avoid the danger. This incident, along with a 2003 Davao airport bombing that the government blamed on "rogue MILF" elements,[26] raised speculation that the peace negotiations were at an end. The MILF denies any ties with *JI*, though it is believed to have provided *JI* with training facilities. Some MILF camps may have even served as *JI* staging areas for Indonesian attacks.

The MILF denies any connection with *al-Qaeda,* though it admits to sending about 600 volunteers to *al-Qaeda* training camps in Afghanistan, and hearing about money bin Laden sent to the Moro region. For a while, *Abu Sayyaf* leader—Khadaffy Janjalani—was believed to be hiding in MILF-controlled territory.[27]

A new round of fighting between the MILF and provincial militia backed by Philippine troops occurred in Maguindanao Province between 28 June and 6 July 2006. It began after Governor Ampatuan blamed the MILF for a 23 June bomb attack on his motorcade that killed five in his entourage.[28]

The MILF's degree of cooperation with *Abu Sayyaf* became more apparent in July 2007. A combined force ambushed 14 Filipino Marines who had been looking for a kidnapped priest and beheaded all but four.[29]

The PRC's Interest in the Philippines

As 2006 drew to a close, China was actively courting the Philippine government with huge sums of money.

> In the Philippines, China is . . . offering an extraordinary package of $2 billion in loans each year for the next three years.[30]
>
> — *New York Times,* 18 September 2006

According to the Jamestown Foundation, the PRC wants three things in return: (1) an end to the dispute over its Spratley Island base, (2) oil exploration and drilling rights, and (3) the continued absence of U.S. bases.[31]

While exploration companies have so far found very little petroleum under the Spratleys, they are still believed to be sitting atop huge reserves of oil and natural gas.[32] So, China has more of an interest in this string of islets and reefs than just control of the South China Sea. (Refer back to Map 3.2.) Of the hundred Spratleys, China only occupies seven, while Vietnam has physical possession of 27, the Philippines eight, Malaysia seven, and

Taiwan one.[33] In 1988, China sank three of Vietnam's ships and then drove its troops off Fiery Cross Reef. In February 1992, the National People's Congress of China claimed sovereignty over all of the Spratleys and authorized the Chinese Navy to "evict trespassers."[34] In 1995, China took over Philippine-owned Mischief Reef.[35] Since then, it has dredged the reef's entrance to create a harbor for large ships. It has also heavily fortified that harbor from attack.[36]

In 1974, Chinese troops evicted what was then South Vietnam from some of the Parcels—the other island chain in the South China Sea.[37] On Woody Island, it has since built port facilities, ammunition bunkers, fuel tanks, gun emplacements, and a runway long enough for its largest aircraft.[38]

U.S. military intelligence personnel say that what has happened to the Spratleys and Parcels is part of "China's 'outward expansion' to move forward on its 'island chain strategy' . . . to control all the territory in an arc stretching from Japan to Indonesia."[39]

As of January 2007, hundreds of U.S. Special Forces personnel were training Filipino troops in counterinsurgency on Mindanao. Unfortunately, their only targets appear to be Muslim. *Abu Sayyaf* leader Abu Sulaiman was killed that month after a U.S. bounty was placed on his capture.[40] As in Nigeria, the real threat may be low-level Communist subversion. U.S. oil companies may find themselves under attack by pseudo-Islamic guerrillas while Chinese oil companies wait to take over. Most likely to attempt such a ruse would be the NPA's "out-of-place" Zamboanga contingent. China's objectives in Indonesia are less obvious but very possibly more sinister.

Indonesia Is No Stranger to Communism Either

Indonesia has had a Communist party since the early 1920's. Thus, it has long been fertile ground for PRC meddling. As in Malaysia, China would like access to whatever oil and natural gas may lie beneath Indonesia's widely dispersed land masses and territorial waters. It also wants to keep the Straits of Malacca open to its oil tankers from the Middle East and Africa. Those straits are bounded on the east by Malaysia and on the west by the Indonesian Sumatra. In 1956, there was a short-lived Communist uprising on Sumatra.[41]

In the 1960's, Indonesian President Sukarno tried to balance the often-opposing influences of his military, Islam, and Communism. Tensions between the powerful Communist Party of Indonesia *(Partai Komunis Indonesia* or *PKI)* and the military culminated in an abortive coup on 30 September 1965, in which six generals were murdered. A countercoup by Maj.Gen. Suharto led to a violent anti-Communist purge. When Indonesia's military rule finally ended in 1998, one of the first things its new president—Abdurrahman Wahid—did was to establish closer ties with China. In 2001, Abdurrahman was impeached after Amien Rais, the chairman of Indonesia's new parliament, posted 40,000 troops outside his office. It was Amien who had led the reform movement that forced Suharto to resign in 1998. As leader of *Muhammadiyah,* one of the biggest Muslim organizations in Indonesia, he had gotten Abdurrahman elected in the first place. In Indonesia's first-ever direct elections in 2004, Susilo Bambang Yudhoyono became president. He is known to favor more foreign investment.[42] Amien is still very vocal in the Indonesian media.

Like the Philippines, Indonesia has now been included in the PRC's regional "charm offensive." China's apparent goal is to offset U.S. influence in the area.[43] Besides petroleum and Taiwan's isolation, it may have a more sinister motive. Indonesia's 17,500 islands are so diversely spread and governed as to offer a perfect refuge for revolutionaries. As in Africa in the 1960's and 1970's,[44] the PRC has been bringing many of the region's residents back to China for education. "Education in what?" is the question.

Between 2002 and 2004, the number of Cambodians in Chinese institutions of higher learning increased by 20 percent and the number of Indonesians by 50 percent. Concurrently, most Southeast Asian governments (including Cambodia) were cutting all links with Taiwan, whether formal or informal. They had effectively demonstrated a willingness to isolate any perceived threat to the PRC.[45]

China has, after all, been assisting Indonesia militarily. According to the International Institute for Strategic Studies, it entered into a strategic partnership with Indonesia in July 2005. Part of that partnership involved technological assistance on short-range-missile construction. As there was a U.S. arms embargo on Indonesia at the time, much more than missiles may have been arranged.[46] Back-to-back opinion pieces in a well-respected newspaper help to describe the present dynamic.

[C]laims that the Indonesian military is fighting terrorism doesn't make it so. The Indonesian police, no longer part of the military, is the body fighting terrorism in Indonesia.

The military engages in and fosters terrorism and the violation of human rights. Witness . . . the killing of two Americans in Papua [New Guinea] to try to increase the army's bribes . . . , the army-supported militia reign of terror in East Timor [an independent country], the terrorist bombings and beheadings in Central Sulawesi and the Malukus [Molucca islands], and the bloody persecution of Papuans for exercising free speech.

[The U.S.] Congress imposed the ban on military sales to pressure the Indonesian Army to stop its blatant and continued violation of the human rights of innocent Indonesians (and Americans). There was no reason to lift the ban, for the military has not reformed.[47]

—*Internat. Herald Tribune* letter, 9 January 2006

It is difficult to see how U.S. aid to the Indonesian military supports democracy or opposes terrorism in the region. . . . By waiving restrictions on such assistance last November, the State Department abandoned its best leverage to press for reform.

The recalcitrance and corruption of the military remains a major roadblock to democratic advances in Indonesia. A number of initiatives to bring the military under civilian control remain stalled. . . .

The military plans to reinsert itself into communities throughout Indonesia under the pretense of fighting [international] terrorism. Its links to radical Muslim groups are well documented. Generals and other senior officials responsible for terror campaigns in East Timor and elsewhere have largely escaped prosecution and entirely escaped punishment.

American weapons and training will only embolden the Indonesian military, not encourage reform. An end to military impunity would be an important step to ending terror.[48]

— *Internat. Herald Tribune* letter, 9 January 2006

Do Regional Rebels Still Train in Indonesia?

There is now hard evidence that Indonesian Army "volunteers" participated in Malaysia's Maoist insurgency in the early 1960's.[49] For years, history only recorded that *PKI* members did so.[50] (Refer back to Map 3.2.) Now it appears that participants in Thailand's current Muslim insurgency may have been trained in Indonesia as well.

> While the Thai government goes to great lengths to state that the insurgency in Southern Thailand is solely a domestic affair, there is evidence that a growing number of Indonesians are involved. In late-2005, the Thai government began to acknowledge that a number of Barisan Revolusi Nasional (BRN-C) militants, one of the two key insurgent groups in southern Thailand, had been trained in Indonesia. . . . Additionally, both Thai officials and the media began to discuss a group known as the Runda Kumpulan Kecil (RKK) *(Bangkok Post,* 24 November 2005). Yet RKK is unlikely to be a separate group altogether, but rather a name for BRN-C militants who received some training in Indonesia; mostly, it seems, while studying there. The RKK simply translates as "small group tactics." . . .
>
> A growing number of insurgent suspects do seem to have ties to Indonesia. The 17 suspects arrested in connection with the October 16, 2005 killing of a monk all claimed to be part of the RKK and police asserted that they were trained in Bandung, Indonesia. . . . [T]he group that had decapitated an army commando in early January was trained by Islamic scholars who studied in Indonesia. Likewise, three men suspected of participating in an ambush on a commando unit in Yala on January 2 said that they had received training in guerrilla tactics from the RKK in Indonesia *(The Nation,* 10 January [2006]). . . .
>
> Thai officials have expressed concern that a handful of Indonesian operatives are also becoming directly involved in the insurgency.
>
> Regardless of Thai denials, the Thai insurgency is becoming increasingly internationalized. Since late-2005, both the deputy prime minister and the commander of the Royal Thai Army have traveled to Indonesia to discuss

> counter-terrorism cooperation, and the Indonesians agreed to monitor links between the southern Thais and the Free Aceh Movement (GAM) *(Bangkok Post,* 29 November and 17 December 2005). There is still no evidence that Jemaah Islamiya has conducted the training.[51]
>
> — Jamestown Foundation, 11 July 2006

As implied by its title, the BRN-C once had close ties to the Communist Party of Malaysia.[52] Like the Philippines' MNLF, the BRN-C is an Islamist party with leftist roots.

Indonesia's Half-Hearted Tries to Control Militant Activity

Indonesia has tried to control some of its militant Islamic elements; but, like Pakistan, it has interfered too little with others.

> Indonesia, says Rohan Gunaratna, an expert on terrorism and author of a recent book on al-Qaeda *[Inside al-Qaeda],* "is the only place in the world where radicals tied to al-Qaeda aren't being hunted down." Adds a Western intelligence source in Jakarta: "The country's like an aircraft carrier from which terrorists can safely launch attacks throughout the region."
>
> Not surprisingly, Ba'asyir's, and JI's apparent untouchable status has set off alarm bells in Washington.[53]
>
> — *Time,* Asia edition, 23 September 2002

Though founded in Indonesia by spiritual leader Ba'asyir, *JI* was obviously allied with *al-Qaeda* by 1991. From 1996 to 2001, 400-600 Indonesians trained at Camps Bushra, Abubaker, and Hudaibie (Hudabiya) in the Philippines. Inside Abubakar, Camp Hudaibie was only for foreign fighters. *Al-Qaeda's* first reported training camp in Indonesia was on the tiny island of Panthbharat. In 2001, it also has a small camp at Poso, Central Sulawesi.[54]

JI's More Recent Activities

JI is an extremist group that initially claimed to seek an Islamic caliphate spanning Indonesia, Malaysia, southern Thailand, Singapore, Brunei, and the southern Philippines.[55] It now targets Westerners and Western interests throughout the region.

> Jemaah Islamiyah has been blamed for a string of attacks in Southeast Asia starting in 1999. Major strikes include the Aug. 5, 2003, bombing of the J.W. Marriott hotel in the Indonesian capital, Jakarta, which killed 12 people, and the Oct. 12, 2002, bombings on Bali island that killed 202, mostly foreign tourists.[56]
>
> — Associated Press, 18 March 2005

In the autumn of 2004, *JI* generated a second Bali bombing and an explosion outside the Australian Embassy in Jakarta. Unfortunately, *JI's* terror campaign against Westerners has not been limited to Indonesia. In June 2003, authorities disrupted a *JI* plan to attack several Western embassies and tourist sites in Thailand. In December 2001, Singaporean authorities uncovered a *JI* plot to attack the U.S., Israeli, British, and Australian diplomatic facilities in Singapore. *JI* is also to blame for the coordinated destruction of Christian churches in Indonesia in December 2000 and the bombings of several targets in Manila the same month.[57]

JI May Be More Than Just an *al-Qaeda* Affiliate

Though based in Indonesia, *JI* has divided Southeast Asia into regions, and long operated throughout those regions. Its principal training center was on Mindanao (Camp Hudabiya). Nasir bin Abas, the Malaysian-born *JI* operative (who upon capture turned informant) claims to have taught at Camp Hudabiya. He also claims to have commanded the *JI* region containing Sulawesi and the Southern Philippines from somewhere in the Philippines' Sulu Archipelago.[58] He was the person who said that the commander of *JI's* Malay Peninsula region—Hambali—had been its principal liaison with *al-Qaeda*.[59] But *JI* also had a liaison office in Karachi, Pakistan.[60] Because Hambali and *al-Qaeda* both wanted to globalize the *jihad* and attack Western interests, the prestigious Jamestown Foundation strongly implies that Hambali was instead *al-Qaeda's* principal operative inside *JI's* top leadership echelon.[61] Gunaratna, the region's *al-Qaeda* authority, clearly stipulates that

JI had been infiltrated by *al-Qaeda* since its inception. *JI* was, after all, formed by Abdullah Sungkar right after meeting Osama bin Laden in Afghanistan.[62]

JI furnished operatives for *al-Qaeda's* 2001 plot to use airliners to attack targets in the United States of America.[63] At present, it may provide *al-Qaeda* with both regional headquarters and expeditionary strike force.[64] Thus, one wonders if *JI* might now be more of an *al-Qaeda* arm or extension. If any of *al-Qaeda's* high-level operatives in the Philippines had to flee south for protection, they may now be part of *JI's* top-leadership echelon. Though fully capable of its own fund raising, it still receives financial, ideological, and logistical support from Middle Eastern contacts, non-governmental organizations, and other sources.[65]

Why Has *JI* So Much Influence over Indonesia?

JI and affiliated rebel groups may be to Indonesia, what *Jamiat Ulema-e-Islam (JUI)* and the Taliban are to Pakistan. While both parties have supported rebel groups in neighboring countries, they are still legal at home. Most would agree that it is the ISI that has ultimately protected Taliban interests inside Pakistan. Some say that it is all or part of the Indonesian Army that secretly condones *JI's* armed affiliates.[66] Might the two Asian countries be using proxies to pursue similar strategic goals?

After being charged with conspiracy in the first Bali bombing, the head of *JI*—Abu Bakar Ba'asyir—was fully exonerated by the Indonesian Supreme Court in September 2006. Like Pakistan, Indonesia appears to support the West's "War on Terror." It has conducted a "Deradicalization Program" and jailed hundreds of supposed militants. Yet, *JI* is relatively unaffected. In early 2006, some of its most radical members split off to form *Tanzim Qaedat al-Jihad*.[67] Like Pakistan with its heady Interservice Intelligence (ISI), Indonesia may have an agency (or military branch) that it can't or won't control. Considering its pro-active past, all or part of the Indonesian Army is the most likely candidate.[68]

Al-Qaeda Training Camps on Sulawesi?

Indonesia is a widely dispersed oceanic nation. Its central gov-

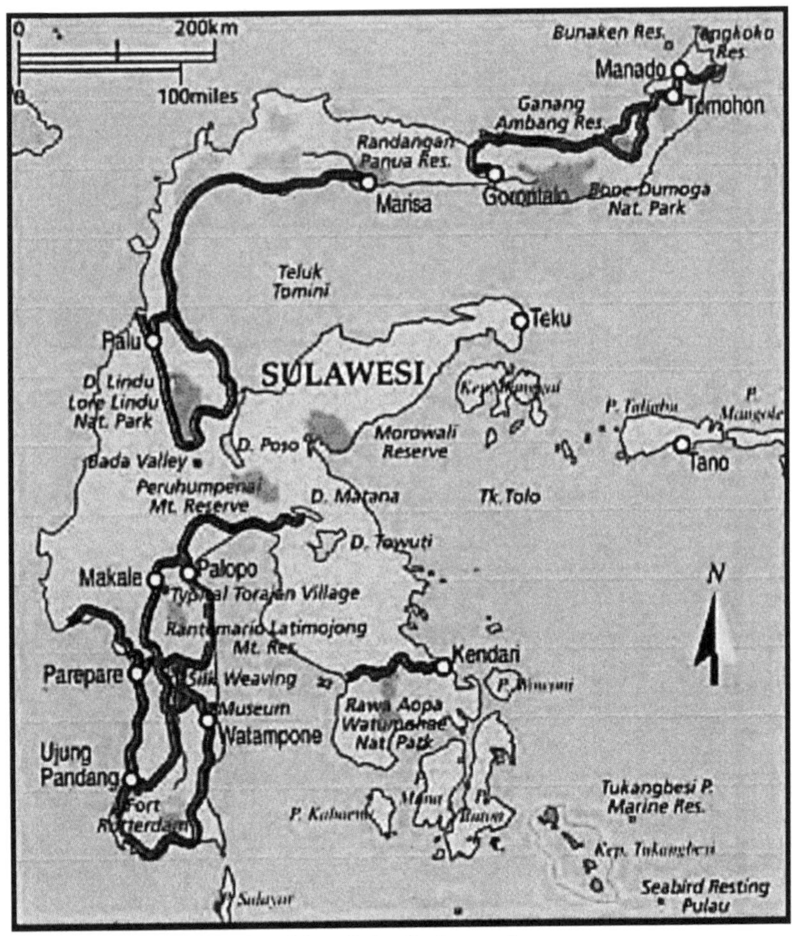

Map 3.3: Sulawesi
(Source: Asia Travel, from map designator "asiatravel.com/ujungmap.html," © n.d.)

ernment holds little sway over what happens in the more remote locations. Sulawesi, the biggest of Indonesia's Celebes Islands, is a scant 300 miles south of the Philippines' island of Mindanao. (See Map 3.3.) From Sulawesi's northernmost point (the ports of Manado and Bitung), a string of closely spaced islets connect the two.

Simply by island hopping, one could travel between them. As late as 2004, there were fully operational jungle training camps with *al-Qaeda* instructors on Sulawesi.

> One man from Luwu, South Sulawesi . . . testified that he had taken part in a three-day military training session in June 2001 in the forest outside Suli, a subdistrict of Luwu. . . . Another of the Makassar bombers testified that he had taken part in a one-month explosives training course in 2001 on the shores of Lake Towuti in the district of North Luwu (Interrogation deposition of Ilham Riadi, 15 January 2003).
>
> More rigorous training was conducted at a camp set up in Pendolo in Pamona Selatan, on the shores of Lake Poso in 2001. Used by JI, Mujahidin KOMPAK, and Laskar Jundullah, it was designed to replicate the military academy at JI's Camp Hudaibiyah [Hudabiya] in Mindanao, but had shorter courses. . . .
>
> One suspect, Jusuf Galan, reportedly told police that he had received military training in a camp in the Poso area in July 2001. Agus Dwikarna's arrest in Manila in March 2002 led to press reports, based on Western and Philippines intelligence sources, that dozens of men from the Philippines and Malaysia and "scores from other parts of the world, including the Middle East, Europe and North Africa" [had] trained in the jungles outside Poso city in late 2000. . . . Hendropriyono, Indonesia's intelligence chief, said in December 2001 that he was told by the Spanish the camp was in Kapompa village, Tojo subdistrict, to the east of Poso, and suggested it was dismantled after 11 September 2001 (Pontoh, "Dari Sintuwu Maroso ke Sintuwu Molonco," *Pantau,* March 2002).
>
> Later, videotapes seized at the Jakarta home of a freelance German-Egyptian photo-journalist, Reda Seyam, confirmed that a camp with some foreign instructors had been operating in Poso. . . .
>
> A recent account of the Poso camp, based on Indonesian intelligence sources, notes that Parlindungan Siregar, an Indonesian with ties to the al-Qaeda cell in Spain, went to Poso in October 2000, about the same time that Mujahidin KOMPAK sent its first team there (Conboy, *Intel*

> [Jakarta 2003], 224, 225). . . . In May 2001, according to this account, Siregar accompanied the head of the Spanish al-Qaeda cell, Imad Eddris Barakat Yarkas, to Poso. As a result of his visit, Yarkas agreed to arrange funding for an international training camp (Conboy, *Intel* (Jakarta 2003), 224, 225). A video either made or edited by Reda Seyam shows a training camp with about twenty Indonesians running an obstacle course, learning how to move in the jungle at night, and crossing a rope bridge with their weapons (mostly sticks carved to look like rifles). The instructor is an Indonesian with a South Sulawesi accent. The end of the video shifts to a night ceremony where the instructor hands out real weapons to about 60 young men. It appears to be the prelude to an attack, also documented on the video, on the village of Tangkura, Poso Pesisir subdistrict, which was burned to the ground in late November 2001.[69]
>
> —*Internat. Crisis Grp. Asia Rpt.,* 3 February 2004

Al-Qaeda's Newest Headquarters and Safe Area?

Over the years, *al-Qaeda's* tiny nucleus has harbored in Sudan, Afghanistan, and Pakistan. Various members have taken refuge in Somalia, Kashmir, Lebanon, Iran, and possibly China. Somewhere in the Southwestern Pacific may be another harbor site in development. If Islamist leaders are moving south out of the Philippines, *al-Qaeda* may have shifted its training and operations center to Indonesia. In all four directions from Sulawesi, there has been trouble: (1) the Moluccas to the east; (2) Java, Bali, and East Timor to the south; (3) Mindanao and the Sulu Archipelago to the north; and to a lesser extent (4) Borneo to the west.

As of February 2007, Indonesian authorities were trying to arrest *JI* cell members in Poso, Sulawesi. Some of those cell members were reportedly fleeing to Java to join Noordin Mohamed Top (Nurdin Nur Thop)—the leader of *JI's* most radical wing (Thoifah Muqatilah).[70] But it is another *JI* splinter group—*Komite Aksi Penanggulangan Akibat Krisis (KOMPAK)*—that has been behind much of the violence on Sulawesi.[71] While the island's north is largely Christian, its south is Muslim. In the two years before the 2001 Malino Peace Accord, as many as a thousand people may have died there in sectarian fighting.[72]

An *al-Qaeda* Presence at *JI's* Headquarters on Java?

It was no coincidence that many of *JI's* members on Sulawesi fled to Java. Though *JI's* precursor—the Ngruki Network—had its roots in the early Islamic uprisings, it was established by *al-Qaeda* affiliates Sungkar and Ba'asyir in 1971 near Solo, Java. *JI,* itself, was not officially founded until 1993 in Malaysia, where Sungkar and Ba'asyir had been forced to flee. While *JI's* principal goal was an Islamic government in Indonesia, its overall goal was an Islamic state that would stretch from southern Thailand, through the Malay Peninsula, across the Indonesian archipelago, and into the southern Philippines.[73] *JI* has been linked to acts of terror as far north as Manila.[74] In a letter to regional *jihadist* leaders dated 3 August 1998 and authenticated by Indonesian intelligence, Sungkar and Ba'asyir stated that they were acting on Osama bin Laden's behalf to advance "the Muslim Global *Jihad.*"[75]

While *JI* remains to this day more of an societal umbrella than an organization, it has divided its proposed caliphate into operational areas.[76] "Mantiqi 1" covers Malaysia and its environs and is additionally responsible for *JI's* overall finances and economic development; "Mantiqi 2" contains most of Indonesia and is responsible for *JI's* recruitment and organizational development; and "Mantiqui 3" includes the Philippines and Sulawesi and is responsible for *JI's* military training and arms supply.[77]

During a congress of Indonesian extremists in Yogyakarta, Java, on 5-7 August 2000, some of *JI's* senior members formed a "strategic guidance" council. With Ba'asyir at its head, the *Majelis Mujahidin Indonesia (MMI)* now contains representatives from many of the militant groups throughout Indonesia. As such, it can loosely coordinate their actions and still maintain enough distance.[78]

Perhaps the most violent of the Islamic extremist groups on Java is *Laskar Jihad.* It is known to have sent thousands of *jihadists* to the Moluccas and Sulawesi to fight Christians. That it also includes several hundred foreign extremists is more than worrisome. *Lashkar Jihad's* parent body, the *Ahl al-Sunna W'al Jamaah,* is a Wahhabi group headquartered in a small village north of Yogyakarta.[80] *JI's* senior leadership is composed almost entirely of Afghan War alumni. For recruits, *JI* depends on no fewer than five fundamentalist *madrasas* throughout Java,[81] one in Sabah (Malaysia),[82] and who knows how many elsewhere.

Traveling to Sulawesi and Parts of Java Can Be Risky

About 200 miles east of Sulawesi and half way to New Guinea lie the Molucca (Malaku) Islands and Indonesia's Malaku Province. A ferry *en route* from that province to Manado, Sulawesi, sank in July 2000.[83] It was carrying mostly Christian refugees from the sectarian violence in Malaku Province. One might consider this an unfortunate accident, if not for what happened four years later. In the summer of 2004, *al-Qaeda* affiliate *Abu Sayyaf* intentionally scuttled a ferry boat near Manila with great loss of life and little remorse.[84]

In late December 2006, a plane with three Americans aboard mysteriously crashed on the way from Java to Manado, Sulawesi. It was only a male tourist and his daughters, but terrorists don't need much of an excuse to make a statement.[85]

In March 2007, a commercial jet carrying two dozen Australian diplomats crashed and burned while landing at Yogyakarta.[86] One of two things was happening: (1) Indonesia's two biggest airlines were no good at flying Westerners to places frequented by *JI's* leaders, or (2) *JI* was discouraging any further Western scrutiny over those places. With *JI* so closely affiliated with *al-Qaeda,* the latter would portend a very long and difficult "War on Terror" in the southern Philippines. Generally, only an official agency can get close enough to an airliner to fool with it. That suggests involvement by part of the Indonesian establishment.

More about *al-Qaeda* on Sulawesi

The other group fighting on Sulawesi—*Laskar Jundullah*—was Ujung Pandang based (the city at the island's south end). With close ties to Osama bin Laden and *al-Qaeda,* it operated the jungle training center near Poso that hosted *jihadists* from all over the world.[87] All the *Laskars* appear to take some direction from *JI's "MMI."* A reliable source claims *Laskar Jundullah* and *Laskar Mujahideen* were specifically created by *JI* to engage in sectarian conflict.[88] It goes on to say that *Laskar Jihad* has links to *JI* but gets its recruits from a *madrasa* in Yogyakarta.[89] To complicate matters, Pakistani *SSP* (the parent of *Lashkar-i-Jhangvi)* is known to have branches in 17 foreign countries, one of which is likely to be Indonesia.[90]

Like *al-Qaeda, JI* follows *Wahhabi* doctrine and principally targets Western interests. After the Malino Accord, several of *JI's* senior leaders moved to Poso. As of February 2007, one of its most radical—Hasanuddin—had been captured and was on trial in Jakarta. Among other things, he stood accused of beheading three Christian school girls in October 2005. He is said to have trained in MILF-controlled territory on Mindanao before moving to Poso in 2002.[91] While the Indonesian government is looking for 29 more Islamic radicals on Sulawesi, observers fear that this will not be enough to control the region's *jihadist* rebound.[92]

MMI has close ties with Indonesia's Islamist political parties.[93] Like Pakistan with its religious parties that support the Taliban and Hekmatyar, Indonesia will probably allow the *MMI (*and most of *JI)* to continue to operate. For whatever reason, the Islamic separatist factions on Sumatra have not welcomed *MMI*.[94]

The Same Media Game As in Pakistan?

To date, Pakistan has helped America to kill or capture several successors to *al-Qaeda's* top "operations officer" post. That *al-Qaeda* is a bottom-up umbrella organization and largely structureless has never seemed to bother anyone. In essence, it can operate just fine without any continuity at that position.

In mid-June 2007, Indonesian police captured Abu Dujana. Though only the commander of a *JI* battalion thought to be its special forces,[95] he was mistakenly labeled by normally reliable *Newsweek* as its overall commander and chief.[96] Thus, Americans became further convinced that the War on Terror was going well in the Western Pacific. Like *al-Qaeda, JI* is largely structureless. Government-protected Ba'asyir is its *de facto* chief, and names like "Thop" crop up far more often in the research than "Dujana."

The Possible Link between China and *al-Qaeda's* Affiliate

One cannot help but notice the similarity between PRC and *JI* strategies in the South China Sea region. China is pursuing an "'island chain strategy' . . . to control all the territory in an arc stretching from Japan to Indonesia."[97] *JI* is after an Islamic state that stretches in the west from southern Thailand to Sumatra and

Singapore, and in the east from the southern Philippines through all of Borneo and Indonesia.[98] In the first chapter, it was shown how the PRC may have used Uighur look-alikes to infiltrate *al-Qaeda* in Pakistan and Afghanistan. Why couldn't the PRC have infiltrated *JI* the same way? Though now Indonesian, *JI* was created in Malaysia. Malaysia's population is 23.7% ethnic Chinese.[99] The Filipino MNLF was also born on Malaysian soil.[100] At first, it was leftist as well as Muslim.[101] In fact, it was created as the Communist NPA was taking over northern Luzon.[102] Soon thereafter, Ferdinand Marcos became so fearful of foreign-nation-fomented leftist conspiracy that he declared martial law.[103] Might this be the first good look at what would become the PRC's strategy to mask expansionist activity with Islamic discord? Such a ruse would perfectly mesh with China's famous 36 Stratagems.

JI was not created until 1993, a full eight years after Ba'asyir and Sungkar fled to Malaysia.[104] The two then directed all *JI* operations from exile for five more years (until the end of the Suharto regime in 1998). About the time Ba'asyir returned to Malaysia (1999), Sungkar died of natural causes. In 2002, the U.S. government asked Indonesia to extradite Ba'asyir. That President Megawati Sukarnoputri refused to do so may mean that Ba'asyir enjoys high-level connections beyond Indonesia. This would help to explain why his conviction for treason and bombing was overturned by Indonesia's Supreme Court on 21 December 2006. Undoubtedly aware of so-far-undisclosed 9/11 details, Ba'asyir is no master of East-Asian double-talk. By trying to divert attention from what he knows, he may have unintentionally dropped a few hints. He claims that 9/11 was made to look like a Muslim attack by another country or countries (specifically America and Israel). He also claims that *JI* doesn't exist.[105]

Indonesia's mixed allegiances have more to do with oil than *sharia*. There were Indonesia-China Energy Forums on Bali in 2002 and in Shanghai four years later. Over 20 million ethnic Chinese now live in Indonesia (the largest such population outside of China), so *JI* and the Indonesian Army would not be hard for PRC operatives to infiltrate.[106] On 17 August 2007, the Chinese *People's Daily* unwisely chose military terminology to admit that "Indonesia has a strategic location within easy reach of 3 billion people in the Asia Pacific region." Though trying not to, it also hinted at its other strategic interest—what lies next to southern Sumatra.

The Communists and Islamists need not be full partners in a regional conspiracy. The latter may simply have been manipulated by the former. A widespread Islamist uprising would adequately screen the smattering of subversion China would need to secure the region's petroleum reserves and shipping lanes. Sulawesi just happens to be sitting atop the biggest (almost 100 trillion cubic feet) of two natural-gas deposits in the southwestern Pacific.[107] The Spratleys are just north of the other (80 trillion cubic feet).[108] China has already demonstrated its interest in the Spratleys. Why now would *al-Qaeda* have the only interest in Sulawesi? Here, the aspiring superpower and Islamist movement are most assuredly (albeit circumstantially) linked. Following the same train of thought, why is it so hard for U.S. leaders to believe that China has a vested interest in what happens in Iraq? Iraq and Iran have the second and third largest oil reserves in the world.[109] But that carefully obscured link is best substantiated by continuing to show what the Chinese have managed to so-far accomplish in South Asia.

One whole side of Malacca Straits' oil-shipping bottleneck is formed by the Indonesian island of Sumatra. When asked by *Frontline World* how order was maintained after the tidal wave in Aceh Province, its Indonesian Army commander recently said that he had followed the Chinese model.[110] To the northeast on the Asian mainland, the Chinese tiger is more clearly visible.

4 Cambodia and Laos

- Is Cambodia still a Chinese ally?
- What has been happening in Laos?

America Once Supported the Khmer Rouge

(Source: DA Pam 550-32, p. 141)

China's Influence over Modern Cambodian History

The PRC provided both arms and military trainers to the infamous Khmer Rouge before and after that faction's takeover of Cambodia in 1975.[1] (See Map 4.1.) Then, between 1.5 and 2 million Cambodians died from execution, forced hardships, or starvation under Pol Pot's regime. All the "mass relocation, forced labor, and psychological reprogramming in an attempt to achieve an ultracollectivist agrarian utopia" just happened to coincide with the end of China's Cultural Revolution.[2] Pol Pot's method was almost identical.

When North Vietnamese troops invaded Cambodia in 1978 to end the slaughter of what it called "enemies of the Revolution," the U.S. objected and China subsequently attacked Vietnam north of Hanoi.[3] While North Vietnamese militiamen were blunting the Chinese attack, NVA regulars drove the Khmer Rouge quickly from the Cambodian battlefield. Then, they reoccupied most of Cambodia to limit the amount of civil strife. In 1991, the Paris Peace Accords mandated democratic elections and a cease fire in Cambodia. Factional fighting in 1997 ended the first coalition government, but another election in 1998 led to the formation of another coalition government and slightly more political stability. The remnants of the Khmer Rouge surrendered in 1999. A few of its leaders are still awaiting trial by a U.N.-sponsored tribunal for crimes against humanity.[4] The Cambodian government has been only partially supportive of this endeavor.

Cambodia's elections in 2003 were relatively peaceful, but the new coalition government took a full year to form.[5] That government still contains remnants of the Khmer Rouge. Thus, one suspects a continuing PRC presence as well. This chapter will attempt to confirm that suspicion.

> In 1975, under the mantle of "liberation," Pol Pot's peasant army of Maoist guerrillas swept into Phnom Penh and immediately imposed their puritanical vision of a classless, agrarian society. Urbanites . . . were herded out into rice paddies to sweat in extreme privation alongside rural "base people." Intellectuals . . . were systematically eliminated.
>
> In 1979, invading Vietnamese troops sent the Khmer Rouge fleeing to remote jungles, yet even now several reconstituted ex-Khmer Rouge cadres, including Prime Minister Hun Sen, retain a grip on politics and business.[6]
>
> — *Christian Science Monitor,* 11 December 2006

The Ruling Party in Cambodia

As the coalition's majority party provides the prime minister,[7] one might think Hun Sen to be nothing more than a popular member of the Cambodian People's Party.[8] That he has ruled the country since before the start of U.N.-mandated elections suggests a much different profile.

Hun Sen, one of the world's longest-serving prime ministers, has been in power . . . since 1985. . . .
He was reelected by parliament in July 2004 after nearly

Map 4.1: Once China's Closest Ally in Southeast Asia
(Source: Courtesy of General Libraries, University of Texas at Austin, from their website for map designator "cambodia_rel_97.pdf")

> a year of political stalemate. His Cambodian People's Party (CPP) won general elections in 2003, but without enough seats for it to rule alone.
>
> It finally struck a deal with the royalist Funcinpec party, headed by Prince Norodom Ranariddh, in June 2004.
>
> . . . [S]ome Western countries have said his rule has become increasingly authoritarian.
>
> Born in 1952, Hun Sen joined the Communist Party in the late 1960's and, for a time, was a member of the Khmer Rouge. He has denied accusations that he was once a top official within the movement, saying he was only an ordinary soldier.[9]
>
> – *BBC Country Profile,* updated 1 January 2006

It was through a bloody coup that Hun Sen seized power from his co-prime minister in 1997. In 2003, he also did some fanning of anti-Thai sentiments.[10] Thus, Hun Sen's record deserves a closer look.

> During Pol Pot's tyrannical regime . . . , Hun Sen fled to Vietnam to join troops opposed to the Khmer Rouge.
>
> When Vietnam installed a new government in Cambodia in 1979, he returned as minister of foreign affairs, becoming prime minister in 1985 at the age of 33.
>
> He refused to cede power in 1993, when the Funcinpec party headed by Prince Norodom Ranariddh won the election, but acquiesced to a coalition government with the prince as first prime minister and Hun Sen himself as second prime minister.
>
> In 1997 . . . Hun Sen's supporters ousted Prince Ranariddh and forced him to temporarily leave the country.[11]
>
> – BBC News, 15 July 2004

Too Close a Resemblance to Mugabe of Zimbabwe

Students of African history will remember how Robert Mugabe of the Chinese backed Zimbabwe African National Union (ZANU) won the U.N.-brokered elections of 1980 in Rhodesia.[12]

Since then, Zimbabwe has had a multi-party parliamentary

democracy that routinely reelects Mugabe.[13] A Maoist land reform in Zimbabwe in 2006 led to 700,000 people being evicted from their homes.[14] Something similar happened in Cambodia the same year. Again, the resemblance to the forced migration of city dwellers during China's Cultural Revolution comes to mind.

> Human rights activists have warned that forced evictions in Cambodia's capital Phnom Penh are spiralling out of control.
>
> People are being moved to new sites out of the city
> In recent weeks, thousands of people have been removed from their homes, and thousands more are set to follow [them] . . . .
>
> The official line is that the evictions are necessary for the development of the city. . . .
>
> Meanwhile the former slum dwellers are finding life difficult in resettlement sites outside Phnom Penh which have no running water, . . . electricity or sewage. . . .
>
> "They use the word development as a pretext for evictions," claimed Phal Sithol, a member of the commune council for another riverside community.
>
> "They say we're living on someone else's land, but we've been here since 1991, and the property developers didn't come until this year so how can that be the case?"[15]
>
> — BBC News, 29 September 2006

Cambodia's Official Stance on the Atrocities

In July 2006, the U.N.-sponsored court to look into the Khmer Rouge atrocities was belatedly starting to convene. There was every indication that its efforts would be short-lived and its findings watered down.

> A team of Cambodian and foreign judges are beginning the long process of bringing former Khmer Rouge leaders to trial. . . .
>
> "They will discuss the milestones and critical activities for year one," said tribunal spokesman Reach Sambath.
>
> Investigations will begin next week, with trials starting in 2007. . . .

> Many people had begun to fear that the trials would never get off the ground.
>
> Since Cambodia first asked the United Nations for help in 1997, the government has been reluctant to commit resources, and foreign donors have provided much of the funding.[16]
>
> — BBC News, 4 July 2006

Present-day Cambodians speak of the Khmer Rouge as having never left. By not fully acknowledging Pol Pot's atrocities, the current regime may be giving indications of future policy. In a 79-page textbook for 9th graders published by the Cambodian Ministry of Education in 2000, the Khmer Rouge era rated just two sentences.[17]

Further Evidence of Public Duress in Cambodia

On a trip to Seam Reap in 2003, a U.S. tourist noticed how Cambodian citizens boarded a plane to Phnom Penh as if ordered to do so under the muzzle of a gun (all at once and in perfect unison).[18] In Cambodia's "democracy," there may be a little too much "top-down" leadership.

> Since New Year's Eve, three prominent human rights activists have been arrested and jailed pending trial for defaming the government. They have joined two others facing similar charges.
>
> Several activists and government critics have left the country rather than risk arrest. The leader of the main opposition party [Sam Rainsy] is in self-imposed exile—and has recently been sentenced to 18 months in prison for defaming the leaders of the governing coalition.
>
> Human rights groups and diplomats alike say they are increasingly worried about the situation. . . .
>
> It was the second round of arrests of government critics in recent months. . . .
>
> Defamation is a criminal offence in Cambodia, a legacy of the United Nations transitional regime in the early 1990's. Critics say it was a law for exceptional circumstances that should have been replaced by now. . . .

At the same time, China has become the biggest investor in Cambodia, and asks few questions about human rights issues.[19]

— BBC News, 7 January 2006

China's Principal Interest in Cambodia

Exploitable reserves of oil and natural gas were discovered beneath Cambodia's territorial waters in 2005.[20] In August 2006 (after an extensive seismic survey and test drilling), U.S. oil giant Chevron divulged their immense size.[21] The Cambodian government's share alone of the projected oil and gas revenues will be $1 billion a year. China has been vying hard for offshore drilling rights. Cambodia only has two small seaports on the Gulf of Thailand—Kampong Saom and Krong Koah Kong. At one, a massive new port facility is being constructed.[22] Yet to be ascertained, but probably no surprise, is who is funding the project. China is, by far, Cambodia's biggest import partner.[23]

There's Something Funny Going On in this Whole Region

With only minor border disputes and no apparent threat, Cambodia has recently enhanced its ability to make war. Like Malaysia, it has just made military service mandatory for all of its young males. The Cambodian conscription law of October 2006 requires all males between 18-30 to serve 18 months in the military. Indonesia, Burma, and Laos have had military conscription for several years.[24]

China Wants the Port of Kampong Saom (Sihanoukville)

If the PRC's interest in overland oil conduits holds true for its offshore drilling sites in Cambodia, it will want a road from the closest port through Laos into southern China. To conclude such an arrangement, it would need better port facilities, bridges across the Mekong at Phnom Penh, and a road north from there.

In the dense humidity of northern Cambodia, where

> canoes are the common mode of transportation, a foreman from a Chinese construction company directs local laborers to haul stones to the ramp of a nearly completed bridge. . .
>
> Nearby, engineers from the China Shanghai Construction Group have sunk more than a dozen concrete pylons across a tributary of the mighty Mekong River, a technical feat that will help knit together a 1,200-mile route from the southern Chinese city of Kunming through Laos to the Cambodian port of Sihanoukville on the Gulf of Thailand.[25]
>
> — *New York Times,* 18 September 2006

Chinese Military Aid to Cambodia

One would think that Hun Sen would be pro-Vietnamese and therefore greatly suspicious of the Chinese. But many years have passed since he first came to power. Of late, he has cultivated much closer ties with China.[26] Those ties have been indicated by more than just trade and infrastructure assistance.

> China's Prime Minister Wen Jiabao has promised $600m . . . in aid and loans to Cambodia, much of it earmarked for the construction of dams and bridges.
>
> Mr. Wen agreed the deal with Cambodian leader Hun Sen at the end of his visit. . . .
>
> The aid deal is one of several recent signs that China is strengthening its ties with Cambodia, analysts say.
>
> In September, Beijing gave six naval patrol vessels to Cambodia. . . .
>
> In recent years, China has also given millions of dollars of aid to the country, struck trade agreements with it and invested heavily in its clothing industry.
>
> Hun Sen has, in turn, described China as Cambodia's "most trustworthy friend" . . .
>
> Analysts say China is keen to strengthen ties with southeast Asian countries that have sea ports that can serve Beijing's growing hunger for oil from the Gulf.
>
> Cambodia hopes its closer ties to China will help it counter the influence of its rival, neighbouring Vietnam, analysts say.

> Hun Sen spent years fighting the Khmer Rouge, Cambodia's Beijing-backed government, but since their overthrow and his rise to power, he has tried to repair relations with China.[27]
>
> — BBC News, 8 April 2006

Within the details of China's foreign assistance package to Cambodia lies its grand strategy for the region. Most disturbing is its building of a "fiber-optic network." The Peoples Republic of China also constructed such a network in Afghanistan—for the Taliban.[28] As will be demonstrated later, such a network has great military significance.

> The [Chinese] money will help pay for two major bridges near the capital, Phnom Penh, that will link to a network of roads; a hydropower plant; and a fiber-optic network.[29]
>
> – *New York Times,* 18 September 2006

China's Ultimate Objective in Cambodia

The above-mentioned assistance was not the PRC's first to Cambodia. Its previous package contained funding for the rest of the overland oil conduit.

> Chinese Premier Wen Jiabao pledged Sunday that his country will provide Cambodia with 100 million yuan (about $12.38 million) in loans and grants for the country's infrastructure development. . . .
>
> The package—50 million yuan in loans and 50 million yuan in grants—will be used for road construction in eastern parts of Cambodia linking the country with Laos.[30]
>
> —*Asian Economic News,* 12 December 2005

Hun Sen Not Pro-Western

Despite an infectious smile, Hun Sen appears little interested in befriending the West or instituting true democracy. Nor is he particularly worried about human rights.

> Cambodia's Prime Minister Hun Sen has launched a scathing attack on a U.N. envoy who criticised the government's record on human rights.
>
> Yash Ghai said on Tuesday that Cambodia's government was not committed to human rights, and power had been too centralised around "one individual". . .
>
> Mr. Ghai, a Kenyan lawyer, completed a 10-day fact-finding tour of Cambodia on Tuesday. . . .
>
> "I have been quite struck by the enormous centralisation of power, not in the government but in one individual," he added.
>
> "I have talked to judges, so many people, politicians, and everyone is so scared."[31]
>
> — BBC News, 29 March 2006

Hun Sen is badly in need of funding for his regime. Before his oil can get to China, it must first pass through Laos.

Laos' Communist Government Is Now an Ally of China

At the end of Vietnam War, the Communist Pathet Lao took over Laos. That country became the Lao People's Democratic Republic. While its government has decentralized a little control and permitted some free enterprise since 1986, it remains one of the world's few Communist states.[32] Since 2002, a few independent candidates have been allowed to run for office, but only one political faction—the Communist Lao People's Revolutionary Party (LPRP)—is legal. It presently holds 113 of the 115 seats in the National Assembly. In Laos, slandering the state, distorting party policies, and spreading false rumors are all criminal offenses.[33]

Less developed than its neighbors, Laos has relatively primitive infrastructure. It has no railroads, a rudimentary road system, and limited telecommunications.[34]

Laos has no oil of its own,[35] but it is strategically located between China and two of that country's biggest sources of oil. To bring petroleum overland from the southern Andaman Sea or Gulf of Thailand, China would need a better transportation network within Laos. It plans to build a railway from Jinghong in southern Yunnan Province through Laos to Thailand's deep-sea port at Laem Chabang near

Bangkok.[36] (See Map 4.2.) It also plans a third bridge across the Mekong River. That bridge will permit a road link between Laos' landlocked southwest and Thailand.[37]

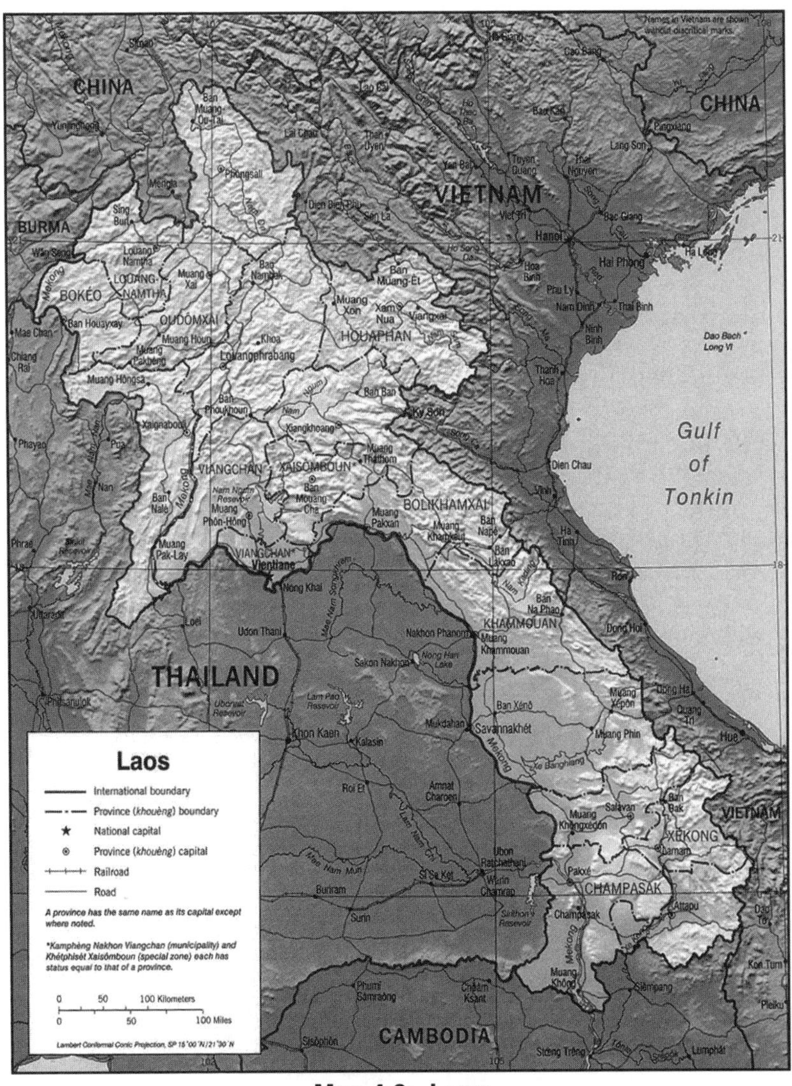

Map 4.2: Laos

(Source: Courtesy of General Libraries, University of Texas at Austin, from their website for map designator "laos_rel_2003.pdf")

> Chinese Commerce Minister . . . told Thai Commerce Minister Krirk-krai Jirapaet on Saturday that China is ready . . . to construct a third bridge across the Mekong River linking northern Thailand, Laos, and southern China.[38]
>
> — *Asian Economic News,* 20 November 2006

According to *Time Magazine,* Chinese engineers are also "blasting the rapids and reefs in the upper Mekong so that large boats can take Chinese-manufactured goods to markets in Southeast Asia."[39] Most likely, those barges will be carrying oil on the return trip. By allowing bigger loads and skirting Thailand, the Mekong would make almost as good a conduit as Burma's Irrawaddy. The Mekong also runs through the Golden Triangle in western Laos.

Laos' Only Resource and the Protection It Provides

Like North Korea,[40] *Hezbollah,*[41] and the Taliban,[42] China may see drug trafficking as a way to fund foreign programs while undermining Western society. If the Laotian government were to be profiting from what goes on at its western border, it would have no reason to stop it. With China, pro-Chinese Burma and Cambodia, and nonexpansionist Vietnam as neighbors, Laos would not need much of a national defense force. The drug lord armies alone would be enough to discourage any Western invasion.

> Laos is one of the world's least developed countries; the Lao People's Armed Forces are small, poorly funded, and ineffectively resourced; there is little political will to allocate sparse funding to the military, and the armed forces' gradual degradation is likely to continue; the massive drug production and trafficking industry centered in the Golden Triangle makes Laos an important narcotics transit country, and armed Wa and Chinese smugglers are active on the Lao-Burma border.[43]
>
> — *CIA World Fact Book,* 19 December 2006

Any potentially embarrassing arrangement requires a good front. The PRC grows much of its food in Laos. As of October

2006, it had thousands of agricultural workers there. To get all that produce home, it had to refurbish parts of the Laotian transportation system.[44] Those roads were undoubtedly used for more than just melons. The CIA's *World Factbook* describes China as a "major transshipment point for heroin produced in the Golden Triangle."[45]

Further Discouraging Western Influence

China has done everything possible to limit Western influence in Laos. It was there that the PRC first deployed volunteer "aid workers." That those aid workers had to speak English suggests a secondary mission.

> Recruiting has begun for young volunteers for six-month tours of aid service in Laos, China's first youth volunteer project abroad. The volunteers should be healthy Chinese citizens between 20 and 40, fluent in English and holding at least a bachelor's degree.[46]
>
> — *People's Daily* (China), 29 March 2002

No More Discord within Laos

Communist regimes tend not to worry much about human rights issues. Within Laos, any public dissent is dealt with harshly by the authorities.[47] A former U.S. ally—the Christian Hmong—resisted for a while but have been unable to do much since 1990.[48] The remaining Hmong now suffer abuses so severe as to border on genocide.[49]

> The country's human rights record has come under scrutiny. Laos denies accusations of abuses by the military against the ethnic minority Hmong.[50]
>
> — BBC News, *Country Profile*

In terms of U.S. foreign policy, the Hmong may have suffered the same political fate as the Chinese Uighurs. Since 2002, America's most dedicated Vietnam War allies have been treated as terrorists and refused refuge.[51]

Far to the west of Laos, several long-smoldering Communist revolutions have flared up in recent years. While most have yet to succeed, there are exceptions on the Indian subcontinent.

5 Nepal and Bangladesh

- What evidence is there of Chinese involvement in Nepal?
- What role does Bangladesh play in the Islamic uprising?

IN THE SHADOW OF A HUNGRY NEIGHBOR

(Source: DA Pam 550-35, p. 105)

The "Political Phase" of Nepal's Guerrilla War

In early November 2006, Nepalese Maoist rebels signed the "most hopeful" of three peace accords since 2001. (See Map 5.1.) They would be allowed to help govern the country after "locking up" their weapons.[1] Sadly, this was no one-sided surrender of arms.

> The deal calls for the rebels and government forces to be confined to their bases with their weapons locked up under U.N. supervision.[2]
>
> — *Christian Science Monitor,* 10 November 2006

This agreement and an interim parliament containing 73 Maoists were to lay the ground work for the election of a Constituent Assembly in June 2007. Still, confining Nepalese forces to their

Map 5.1: The Jewel of South Asia

(Source: Courtesy of General Libraries, University of Texas at Austin, from their website for map designator "nepal_rel_1990.pdf")

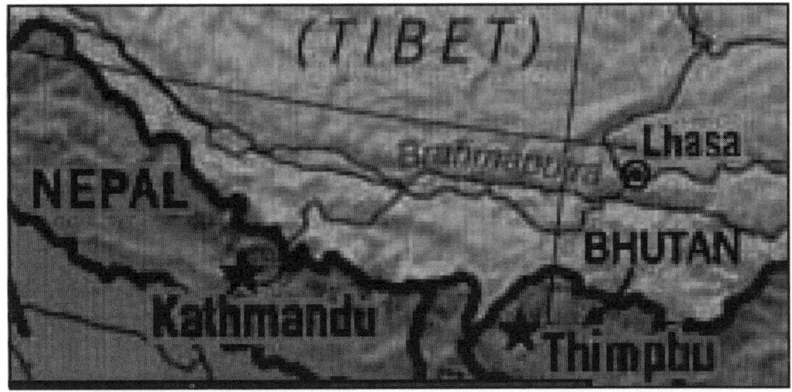

Map 5.2: The Road between Lhasa and Kathmandu
(Source: Courtesy of General Libraries, University of Texas at Austin, from their website for map designator "china_rel01.pdf")

barracks does little to provide the local security that a fair election demands.[3] Pranchanda, the rebel leader, had dropped his calls for a "Communist republic" and now seemed ready to accept a multiparty democracy.[4] If similar episodes in southern Africa are any indication, his ultimate goal is a "single-party" democracy.

No one really knows how many people and weapons the Maoists had, and Nepal is right next to Chinese-controlled Tibet. (See Map 5.2.) Thus, the whole plan may work about as well as the offer of amnesty and surrender of weapons in Fallujah.

Only time will tell whether the new political phase of this Maoist struggle will produce anything more than another defeat for the West. As the Nepalese people had no real justification for an uprising, one cannot help but suspect PRC meddling. In July 2006, Pranchanda objected to the prime minister's request for U.N. involvement.[5] And the "Fierce One's" bragging and continued excesses tend to suggest a larger unseen presence.

> Pranchanda . . . proclaimed that even countries arrogant with power [i.e., Western] would be forced to study Nepal's 21st-Century revolution, a mix of armed uprising and nonviolent protests. . . .

> . . . Despite the accord, their [the Maoists'] excesses, in the form of abductions, [combatant] recruiting, and forced labor, continue.[6]
>
> — *Christian Science Monitor,* 5 December 2006

Here "recruiting and forced labor" mean the induction of under-age soldiers into the Maoist army. Already in control of 75% of the country, the Maoists had firmly established their own courts and other governance and taxation systems in most outlying areas.[7] The parallels to the "alternative governance systems" of Nasrallah and al-Sadr are striking.

Pranchanda's Threats Continue

When the Nepalese government tried to appoint a few foreign ambassadors without the Maoists' approval in late December 2006, Pranchanda warned of a nationwide strike.[8] This was no idle threat. Back when the security forces could leave their barracks, his "strike" of April 2006 got out of hand and subsequently led to 19 days of mayhem and an equal number of deaths.[9]

On 3 May 2006, the Communists in Nepal's government brashly demanded the immediate dissolution of its monarchy. Unhappy with delays in the parliamentary elections that were to have decided the monarchy's fate, Pranchanda threatened mass protests.[10] Only the most naive of U.S. leaders could still doubt the insidious and lethal nature of his takeover method, or which nation was ultimately behind it. The "Fierce One" is not arriving at all of these strange demands on his own. Their timing and effect have so far been too consistent to come from a local "freedom movement." A mere 300 miles to the south of Nepal lies the Bay of Bengal and Indian Ocean. Within that context, Pranchanda's degree of success is much less a mystery.

Nepal's Southern Neighbors Have Had Similar Problems

Only 70 miles of sovereign Indian territory separate Nepal from Bangladesh. It is precisely there—at the Nepalese border town of Naksalbari (Naxalbari)—that India's now-rampant Communist uprising took root in 1967.[11] (Refer back to Map 5.1 and forward to Map 6.3.) Four years later, a rebellion caused East Pakistan to break away from West Pakistan, and Bangladesh to be born. While

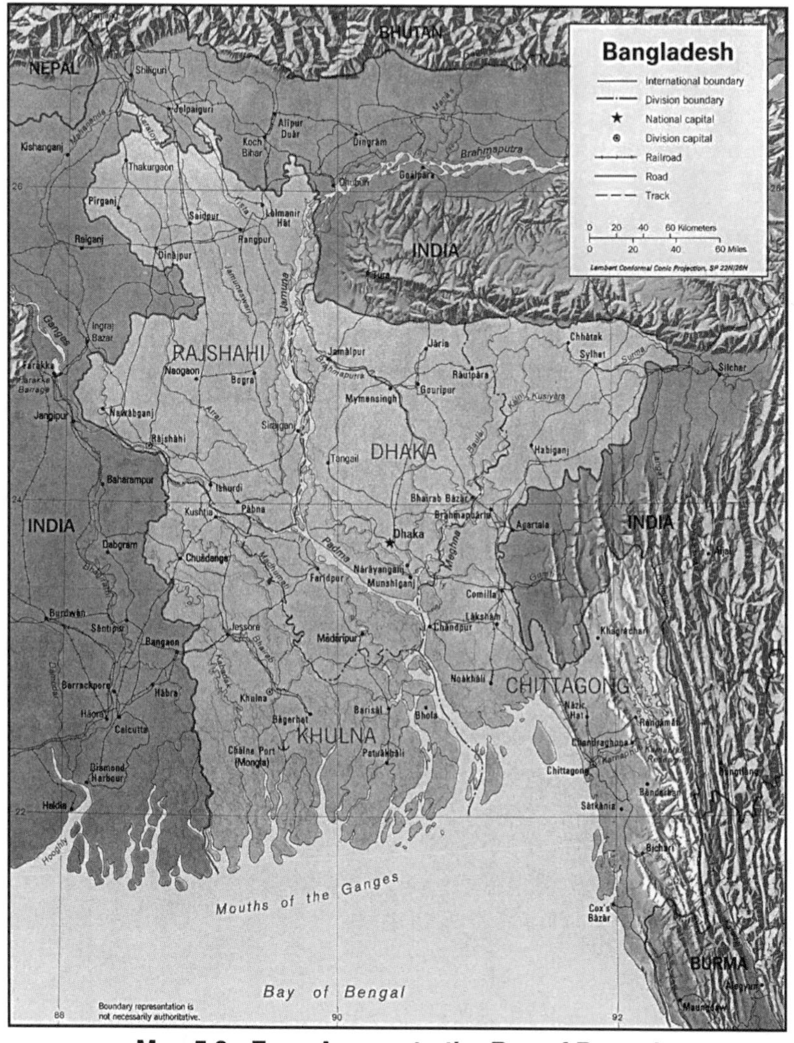

Map 5.3: Easy Access to the Bay of Bengal
(Source: Courtesy of General Libraries, University of Texas at Austin, from their website for map designator "bangladesh_rel_1996.pdf")

its people were Muslim, its first ruling party—the Awami League[12]—was decidedly pro-Communist. (This will become more apparent as the chapter progresses.) To take control of the government in 2001, the more moderate Bangladesh National Party (BNP) had to form a coalition with *Jamaat-e-Islami (JeI).*[13] *JeI* was initially awarded only 18 seats in Parliament,[14] but its influence has since grown.

> Jamaat-e-Islami's power to project an Islamist agenda has grown considerably now that it controls several powerful ministries, as well as a host of welfare organizations, schools, and madrasas. The party also owns a staggering array of businesses.[15]
>
> — *Christian Science Monitor,* 30 October 2006

With the Islamists' power in the ruling coalition steadily growing, one would expect only isolated dissatisfaction from fringe Muslim factions. Yet, during the summer of 2006, Bangladesh suffered a rash of highly visible bombings. During one 30-minute period in August, no fewer than 300 to 500 tiny explosives were detonated in several cities. Though roughly 400 other bombings had occurred since 1999, these were different. Their devices contained no shrapnel and were obviously intended only to send a warning.[16]

As had happened in Nepal in April 2006,[17] a Bangladeshi "alliance of opposition parties" then organized a strike in November 2006 to immobilize the country's transportation system.[18] While that alliance professed to want "electoral reform" in the January 2007 elections,[19] its method spoke of a goal more sinister. With the BNP and *JeI* in power, one might expect all evidence of criminal behavior to point toward the Awami League. But as is too often the case in Sun Tzu's backyard, it didn't.

The Plot Thickens

A few months after the rash of tiny explosions, Bangladesh's first-ever suicide bombers appeared on the scene to kill several lawyers and judges.[20]

> An Islamic militant group claimed responsibility for the attacks, and subsequent arrests revealed that several sus-

> pects were former members of Jamaat-e-Islami's student wing.[21]
>
> — *Christian Science Monitor,* 30 October 2006

Either *JeI* was growing weary of slowly amassing power as a coalition partner, or a third party was discrediting the Bangladeshi regime to increase public support for an alternate system of governance. The Maoists had already developed such a system in Nepal.[22] Only one regional power would find access to the Indian Ocean through Nepal strategically advantageous. Only to naive Westerners are its intentions legitimate.

JeI's Background

JeI has become Bangladesh's largest religious party.[23] If it is anything like its Pakistani namesake, it would prefer an Islamic state over the existing "moderate Muslim democracy."[24] (Any current link between the two is doubtful.)

Traditionally at odds in Bangladesh are the BNP and Awami League—its two main political factions. Since forming a coalition with *JeI* in 2002, the BNP has ruled. Prior to that time, the Awami League was in power.[25]

Which Islamic Radicals Are Active in Bangladesh?

An Awami League rally was attacked in 2004 by the most radical of the Islamist factions. This is the same faction that has been exporting unrest to Burma.

> Banned Bangladeshi Islamic extremist outfit Harkat-ul Jehad-al Islami (HUJAI), which is suspected to be behind recent attack on Awami League leader Sheikh Hasina's rally, has camps running in different parts of that country and is imparting training to similar extremist groups from Myanmar and India, a media report said.
>
> A five-part article in prominent Bangladeshi newspaper Prothom Alo has reported that HUJAI, which has been declared a terrorist outfit by the U.S. State Department for

> its Al Qaeda and Taliban connections, has established an active network through 'madrasas' (religious seminaries) and local NGOs to carry out its activities.
>
> The HUJAI has been imparting arms training to Islamic extremist outfits like those belonging to the Rohingiya Muslims of Arakan mountains in Myanmar and some Indian organisations.
>
> The areas, where the newspaper sent reporters to investigate the camps, are Bandarban, Naikhangchari, Ukhia, Dailpara, Chandgaon and Khatunganj among others in Cox Bazar and Chittagong district of southeastern Bangladesh.
>
> Quoting police officials in Cox Bazar, the article said the HUJAI activists, who were at one point operating openly, were now known to be based in these camps many of which were located on the Naikhangchari No Man's Land [at the Bangladesh-Burma border].
>
> The central Command Headquarters of ULFA and northeastern insurgent outfits like NLFT and NDFB are based in these areas [all are Assamese separatist groups based in Bangladesh].[26]
>
> —*Hindustan Times* (Delhi), 1 September 2004

One reputable source equates *Harakat ul-Jihad al-Islami (HUJAI)* with Pakistani *Harakat ul-Jihad i-Islami (HUJI)*. If they are the same, then the Bangladeshis have given refuge to a real troublemaker. *HUJI* has been heavily involved in the Afghan and Kashmiri fighting since the 1980's. Closely affiliated with *al-Qaeda*, it may even qualify as an operating arm. Reportedly headquartered in Chittagong, *HUJI* (or its Bangladeshi branch, *HUJIBD)* is supposed to have six training camps spread across in the southern, coastal part of the country. Of course, it is just one of many radical Islamic factions in Bangladesh. As of 2005, thousands of militants from some 40 groups controlled large portions of the country under the auspices of ruling coalition partner *JeI*.[27]

Though over a thousand people were killed in political violence from October 2001 to February 2005 in Bangladesh, this is far less than would have died from an all-out Islamic rebellion. Of the 34 major bomb blasts, eight have targeted the Awami League, nine were aimed at cultural functions, and five have hit religious shrines.[28]

Thus, any sole perpetrator has set no clear pattern. And one sees *HUJAI* (or *HUJIBD*) exporting more revolution to nearby countries than it applies at home. Thus, much of the chaos may come from another source—a source for which internal discord offers a welcome smoke screen.

The Common Thread in a Confused Situation

Before East Pakistan broke away from West Pakistan in 1971, the National Awami Party (NAP) was regarded by many as the front organization of the Communist Party of Pakistan (CPP). Hasan Nasir—the NAP Office Secretary—was a card-carrying member of the CPP's politburo.[29] It had been the eastern chapters of the NAP and CPP that had sparked the rebellion that led to the new nation's birth. The NAP chapters were pro-Chinese,[30] and so were those of the CPP.

> In 1966 the Sino-Soviet split reached the [Communist Party of Pakistan] CPP. In East Pakistan, a pro-Chinese group broke away. . . .
>
> At the 4th party congress in Dhaka (1968) a decision was taken [made] that a separate communist party should be constituted for East Pakistan. Thus the Communist Party of East Pakistan was founded. The CPEP later became the Communist Party of Bangladesh [CPB].[31]

The CPP had tried but not succeeded to foment revolution in Pakistan in 1951.[32] And the CPB had much to do with East Pakistan's breakaway rebellion some 20 years later.

> The Party [CPB] played a vital role in the 1969 uprising and also during the nationwide upheaval that followed it including the non co-operation movement of 1971. The CPB also actively participated in the nine-months-long armed struggle for independence of Bangladesh in 1971. A "Special Guerrilla Force" under the direct command of CPB-NAP-BSU [a CPB faction] fought against the Pakistani army. Communists . . . also took . . . part in the other segments of the armed resistance . . . and the new Bangladesh Army.

> Moni Singh, the ex-President of CPB, was elected a member of the Advisory Council of the Provisional Government of Bangladesh.[33]

At first, the Communist Party of Bangladesh was allowed by the Bangladeshi government to work legally and openly. Then it fell on hard times.

> On August 15 1975 President Sheikh Mujib was assassinated by a section of the army which ultimately brought the country under a rightist military rule. During the following 15 years, in spite of several changes of government, change from military to civil political rule and vice versa, real power always remained in the hands of the army. . . . During these struggles the Party and its newspaper were banned several times and leaders and activists killed, arrested or forced to go underground. Democracy [their right to operate in the open] was finally restored in 1991.[34]

The Long-Standing Ties between CPB and Awami League

In the provincial elections of 1954 in East Pakistan, the CPP supported the Awami League's United Front. Overall, the Front won 223 of the 310 seats, and 27 CPP members were elected. When the CPP was later banned,[35] the formation of a front organization (like the NAP) would have been likely. After all, the Awami League did serve as the principal catalyst for the 1971 rebellion of independence.[36]

Since 1991, most of Bangladesh's Communist and Socialist factions have operated under the protective umbrella of the Awami League's alliance.

> [The Awami League's] decision to participate in 1986 parliamentary elections . . . [subsequently] left [it] at the head of an eight-party alliance whose membership . . . included the Bangladesh Communist Party, the Bangladesh Krishak Sramik Awami League, . . . the National Awami Party, [and] the Samajbadi Dal (Socialist Party). . . .
>
> . . . [I]n the late 1980's it [the Awami League] contin-

> ued to advocate many of the socialist policies of the early 1970's.[37]
>
> — *Library of Congress Country Study,* 1988

The Communist Threat Still Lurks

Within Bangladesh, the Communist Party is now given considerable leeway. Any Vietnam veteran will cringe at the current extent of its reach and objectives.

> The CPB has organizations in 60 out of the 64 districts and 275 out of 520 sub-districts in Bangladesh. . . .
>
> . . . Party members and activists are working in trade unions and mass organizations of agricultural workers, peasants, women, students, youth, children, teachers, doctors, lawyers, professionals, indigenous national minorities and aboriginal . . . organizations, etc. . . . [T]he Party is capable of mobilizing several hundreds of thousands of people through its influence in these mass organizations. . . .
>
> The CPB is working with a strategy of bringing about a "revolutionary democratic transformation of society and state" with the ultimate goal of socialism-communism. . . .
>
> . . . [The] CPB is working to build up [a] united movement with . . . the Awami League.[38]

There was to have been a parliamentary election in Bangladesh on 22 January 2007. It had to be "postponed" after the CPB/Awami Alliance claimed the election commission was biased. That claim led to weeks of strikes, other anti-government protests, and the election commissioners quitting.[39]

While some of the events in Bangladesh may resemble those in Iraq and Afghanistan, they are more likely to be Communist inspired than part of a worldwide *al-Qaeda* conspiracy. To discredit the ruling BNP/*JeI* coalition and enlist more lawyers and judges, CPB could have copied the Islamist's suicide-bombing tactic to gain more control over the Awami League. As will be evident from the next chapter, suicide bombing is not strictly a Muslim tactic.

China has recently been strengthening its ties with Bangladesh. It has already helped to upgrade Chittagong's port facilities with the end goal of establishing a Chinese naval presence. Besides being Tibet's outlet to the Indian Ocean, Chittagong is supposedly a part of the PRC's sea-lane-protection "string of pearls" strategy.[40] But it is no secret that China is also trying to establish another overland oil conduit through Bangladesh.[41] Wherever a revolutionary Communist government has strategic interests, one should not be too surprised to find some stage of Communist revolution.

There was a short-lived Communist insurgency in Bangladesh in 1975—about the same time as the military take-over.[42] What is happening now is most probably a better-prepared and less obvious (4GW) sequel to that insurgency. The Indian state just to the west of Bangladesh already has a Communist government. And China has already upgraded the port facilities in its capital city.[43]

6 India and Sri Lanka

- Who does India blame for the Mumbai train bombings?
- Which Sri Lankan factions have had Maoist influence?

ALL IS NOT AS CALM AS IT SEEMS

(Source: Dept. of the Army Pamphlet 550-21 [1985], p. 87)

The Extent of Religious Discord in India

Since the horrific "post-Separation" blood letting of 1947, there have been many incidents of localized fighting between Muslims and Hindus in India. One of the most recent examples occurred in the far western state of Gujarat in February 2002. After 58 Hindu pilgrims/activists died in a train fire, almost 1,000 Muslims and 250 more Hindus were killed in the ensuing riots.[1] (See Map 6.1.)

In July 2006, several crowded trains were bombed simultaneously in Mumbai. The trail of evidence led back to an extremist group headquartered in Karachi, Pakistan—*Lashkar-e-Toiba (LET,* alias *Khairun Naas).* While *LET* had previously been active in Kashmir, it was shifting its attention to central India. In December 2001, some of its people actually assaulted the Indian Parliament building in New Delhi.[2] Since then, it and its Indian subsidiaries—*Lashkar-e-Qahar (LEQ)* and Students Islamic Movement of India (SIMI)—have been causing trouble as far east as the states of Andhra Pradesh and Tamil Nadu.[3] It may be no coincidence that Andhra Pradesh is also the end of a string of states that have been host to a Nepalese-like Communist uprising.[4] Both corridors lead to Sri Lanka, the island nation just off India's southeast coast. It too has had a long-smoldering Maoist insurrection that reignited in 2006.[5] (See Map 6.2.) In the late 1970's, Rhodesia came under a similar "pincer-type" attack from Soviet-backed rebels from Botswana and Chinese-backed rebels from Mozambique.[6]

When three bombs were detonated in Malegaon (one of India's few predominantly Muslim cities) in September 2006, authorities suspected a ruse. They thought that Muslims might have been bombing Muslims to provoke an anti-Hindu response.[7] They should have also considered which third party might have something to gain from a nationwide diversion.

India's Steadily Growing Communist Insurgency

In 1967, a leftist faction of the Communist Party of India-Marxist [CPI-M] launched a peasant uprising in the little town of Naxalbari near the Nepalese border. Since that time, India has been plagued by the same thing that has all but destroyed its tiny northern neighbor—a mushrooming Maoist insurgency.[8] Now most serious in the states of Bihar, Jharkhand, Chhattisgarh, and Andhra Pradesh, that insurgency has mostly raged along the mineral-rich (and hilly) "tribal corridor" that stretches all the way down the east coast of India.[9] The northern leg of the Kathmandu-Calcutta highway has already fallen into the most heavily affected region and large portions of Orissa (to the southwest of Calcutta) have also been targeted.[10] (See Map 6.3.) Not like the separatist movement in Assam,[11] this is a well-organized rural insurrection by a homegrown party or foreign proxy bent on moving into the cities and taking over the entire country. So far, the violence has included train hijackings, truck bombings, jailbreaks, politician assassinations, and protester beheadings.[12] As of mid-August 2006, it had so intensified as to include coordinated attacks against police stations, paramilitary bases, and refugee camps. Apparently interested in isolating the whole region and altering its political make-up, the insurgents were attacking lone targets by the hundreds. Wherever government-

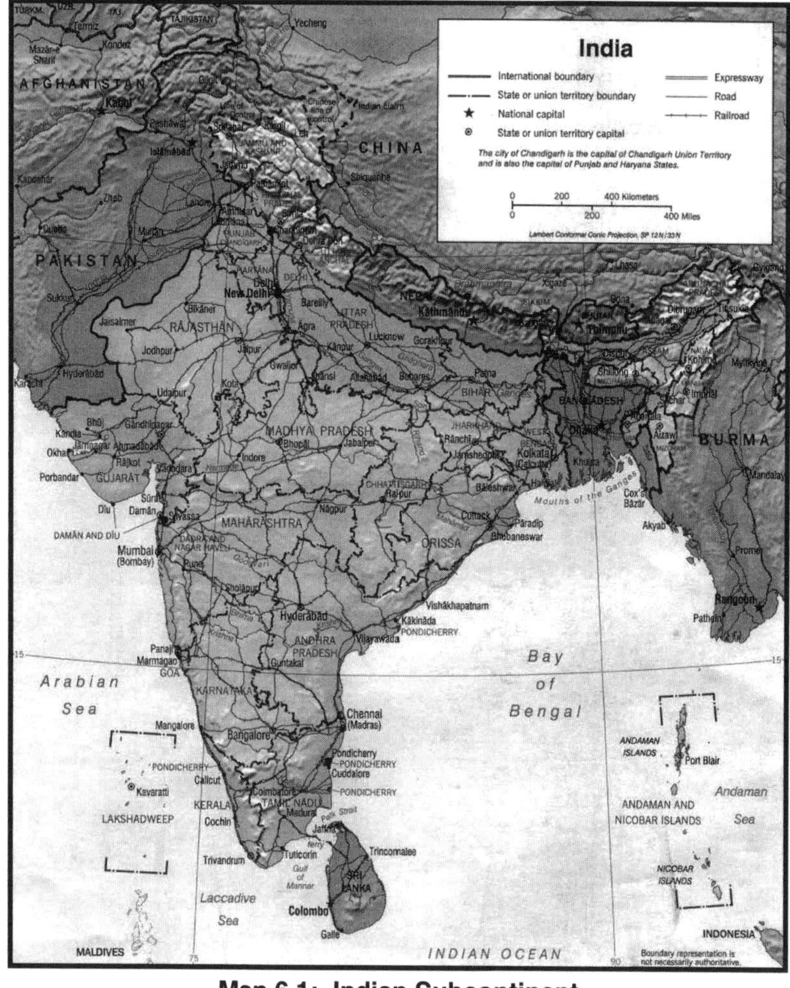

Map 6.1: Indian Subcontinent

(Source: Courtesy of General Libraries, University of Texas at Austin, from their website for map designator "india_rel01.pdf")

Map 6.2: Communist-Insurgency "Corridor"

(Source: Courtesy of General Libraries, University of Texas at Austin, from their website for map designator "india_rel01.pdf")

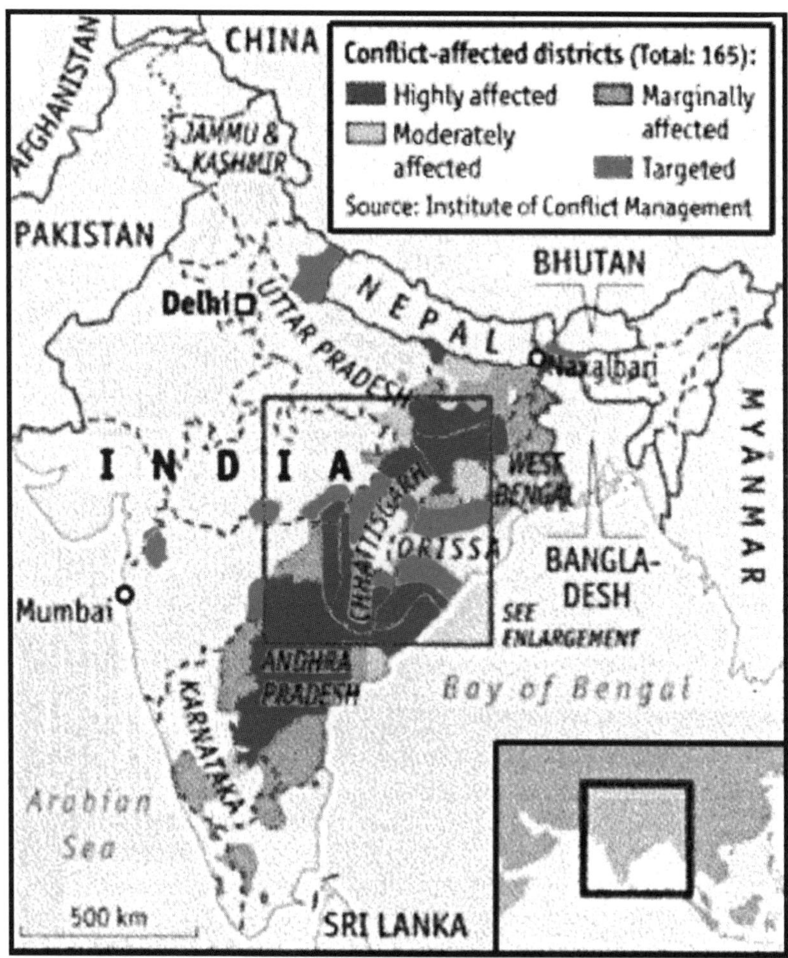

Map 6.3: Naxalite-Targeted Areas as of August 2006
(Source: Institute of Conflict Management, from "A Spectre Haunting India," *The Economist*, 17 August 2006, © 2006)

provided basic services were missing, Naxalite committees were more than happy to fill the void. Within the tribal areas, officials already estimate that half of the citizenry support the insurrection by choice or coercion. A state politician of tribal heritage says that the Naxalites have "collapsed the social, economic and traditional administrative structure."[13]

> India's Maoist insurgents, also called Naxalites, have expanded their area of operations from just four states 10 years ago to half of India's 28 states today. In 165 districts, they claim to run parallel "People's" governments. . . .
>
> Prime Minister Manmohan Singh turned heads recently by calling the Naxalites, "The single biggest internal security challenge ever faced by his country." . . .
>
> . . . [The] rural insurgency is slowly . . . spreading . . . in what analysts see as a . . . plan to extend their red corridor—called the "Compact Revolutionary Zone"—throughout India. Their ultimate stated goal is to capture India's cities and overthrow Parliament. . . .
>
> . . . Rebels attack in large numbers—much like the Maoists of Nepal, with whom they're suspected to have links.[14]
>
> – *Christian Science Monitor,* 22 August 2006

> The Red Corridor held by Naxals stretches across the swath of forest lands from Andhra Pradesh in South India to Maharashtra, Chhattisgarh, Orissa, West Bengal, Jharkhand and Bihar and is expanding.
>
> The past few years has *[sic]* seen the insurgents spreading Naxal influence from 76 districts in nine states to 118 Districts in 12 States. The Communist Party of India (Maoists) was formed on September 21, 2004 through the merger of two prominent naxalite outfits—the People's War Group (PWG) and the Maoists Communists Center (MCC). The military resources of these guerrilla movements have been now combined as People's Guerrilla Army (PGA) forming the cutting edge of the Naxal movement.[15]

The Naxalites Have Already Achieved a Major Victory

Calcutta (Kolkata) constitutes the government seat for the Indian state of West Bengal. West Bengal has been ruled for over 30 years by the CPI-M dominated Left Front. It therefore has the world's longest-running democratically-elected Communist government.[16] Though the Naxalites have since broken away from the CPI-M, they nevertheless helped that Communist government to take power.

> Over the 1960's and 1970's, . . . a violent Marxist-Maoist movement—the Naxalites—damaged much of . . . [Kolkata's] infrastructure. . . . Kolkata has been a strong base of Indian communism . . . for three decades now.[17]

Who Might Be Sponsoring the Naxalites?

China fought a border war with India in 1962. With the ground seized in that war, it was able to build a western connection (China National Highway G219) between its provinces of Tibet and Xinjiang.[18] Though Xinjiang administers Aksai Chin (and many Chinese troops are stationed there), India still claims it to be part of its state of Jammu-Kashmir.[19] Thus, China has already demonstrated its lack of regard for Indian sovereignty. Even if it didn't want access to the Indian Ocean, it would still be the most likely candidate for Naxalite sponsor.

> In the 1960's, they [the Naxalites] won the approval of Beijing, but China has since denounced the guerrillas. . . . With a force of 15,000 soldiers, it [the CPI-M] controls an estimated fifth of India's forests. The eventual aim is to capture the Indian state [take over its government].[20]
>
> — *The Guardian* (UK), 16 October 2006

As late as 1998, the Indian government listed Communist China as its leading security threat.[21]

India's Detached, Eastern Segment

The part of India that lies east of Bangladesh looks like Burma. It is home to Assam separatists and militant Muslim groups.

> Bangladeshi Islamic extremist outfit Harkat-ul Jehad-al Islami (HUJAI) . . . is imparting training to similar extremist groups from . . . India . . .
>
> The HUJAI has been imparting arms training to Islamic extremist outfits like those belonging to . . . some Indian organisations.[22]
>
> — *Hindustan Times* (Delhi), 1 September 2004

Due South Is Sri Lanka

Sri Lanka's formal title is the Democratic Socialist Republic of Sri Lanka. While it presently has what appears to be a democratically elected parliament and president, it also has a decidedly Marxist (and Maoist) past. Thus, one would minimally expect an authoritarian regime. Mahinda Rajapakse has been president since 19 November 2005. He is both the chief of state and head of that regime. Ratnasiri Wickremanayake holds only the ceremonial title of prime minister.[23]

While Sri Lanka still has many political parties, some are more powerful than others. The ruling United People's Freedom Alliance (UPFA) contains the Sri Lanka Freedom Party (SLFP) and *Janatha Vimukthi Perumuna (JVP).* In the last election of April 2004, the UPFA won 105 of the 225 parliamentary seats. Therefore, though a Marxist party with a heavily checkered past, the *JVP* is now the second-largest partner in Sri Lanka's current coalition government.[24]

The *JVP's* Origins

The *JVP* started out as an underground militant movement. Founded in 1965, it wanted to lead a Socialist revolution in Sri Lanka. There were four other leftist political parties at that time: (1) the *Lanka Sama Samaja Party (LSSP*, established in 1935); (2) the Communist Party of Sri Lanka (CP, a breakaway from the LSSP); (3) the *Mahajana Eksath Peramuna (MEP);* and (4) the CP-Chinese faction.[25] In the 2004 elections, all but the last were still viable and captured two seats apiece.[26]

In the early days, the CP-Chinese faction was led by Premalal Kumarasiri. The founder of *JVP*—Wijeweera—came into contact with Kumarasiri and joined the Chinese faction's staff. Wijeweera felt that the "Old Left" hadn't produced any professional revolutionaries; they had never made a meaningful effort to educate the masses on Marxism. He and others decided in mid-1966 to launch a new party that would be explicitly revolutionary in character. Not entirely peaceful, that party's method was to lead to an armed uprising.[27]

Between 1967 and 1970, the fledgling *JVP* expanded quickly, gaining control of the student Socialist movement at a number of universities and winning recruits and sympathizers within the armed forces. Some of the latter provided the sketches of police sta-

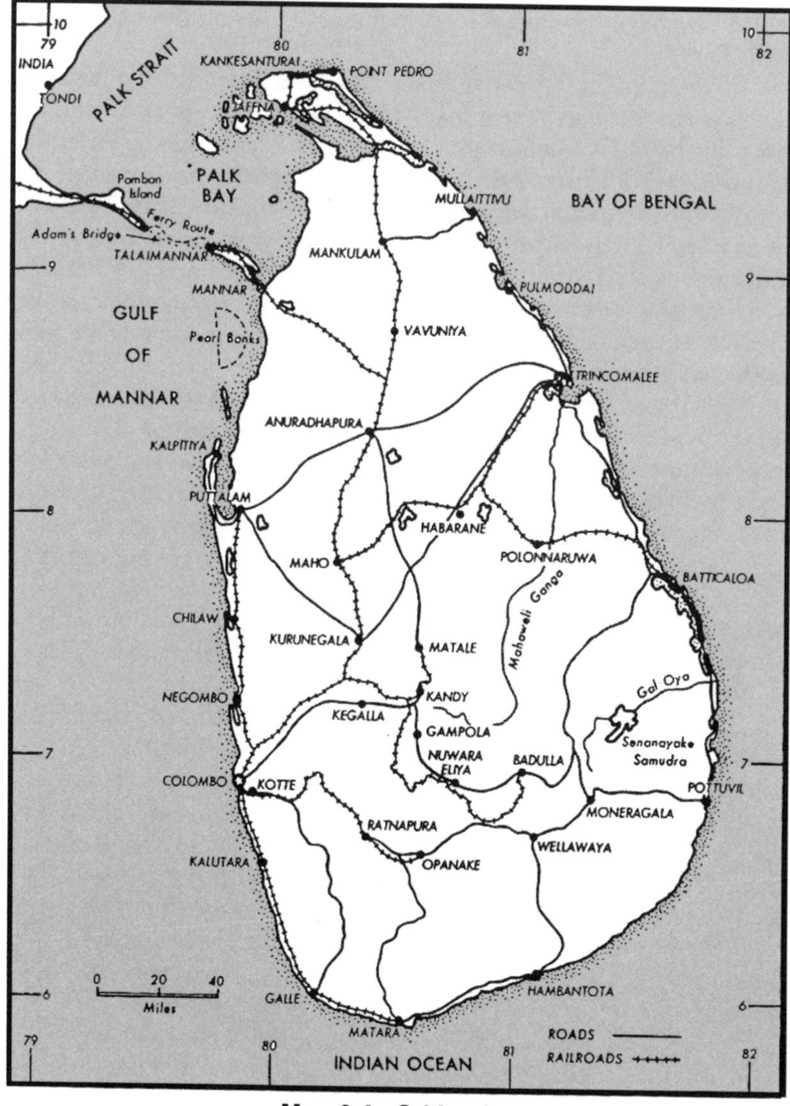

Map 6.4: Sri Lanka
(Source: DA Pam 550-96, p. 17)

tions, airports, and military facilities that would lead to the revolt's initial success. Wijeweera opened "education camps" in several remote areas along the south and southwest coasts. These camps provided training in Marxism-Leninism and basic military skills. While developing secret cells and regional commands, Wijeweera's group also began to take a more public role during the elections of 1970.[28]

In the politically tolerant atmosphere of the next few months, the new Sri Lankan government attempted to win over a wide variety of unorthodox leftist groups. The *JVP* took this opportunity to intensify both its public campaign and private preparations for revolt. Though relatively few in number, its members hoped to immobilize the government through selective kidnapping and simultaneous strikes against the island's security forces. To obtain weapons, they primarily relied on raids against police stations and army encampments. They were able to manufacture their own explosive devices.[29]

The armed uprising began on 5 April 1971. With Indian assistance, Sri Lankan forces were able to regain control of all but the most remote areas in a couple of weeks. Amnesties were eventually awarded, and the *JVP* was allowed to resume political activities in 1977. It even appeared to embrace the heretofore rejected concept of parliamentary democracy. In the elections of 1982, the charismatic leader of the *JVP*—Rohana Wijeweera—ran for president but lost. After riots a year later, the government—fearing a Communist coup—again banned both the *JVP* and CP from all political activity.[30]

Next came the post-1987 revolt of the *JVP*. Cleverly exploiting the arrival of the Indian Peace Keeping Force and the nationalist sentiment of the Sinhala majority, the *JVP* was soon back in business. It began by terrorizing regime agencies and any segment of society that was opposed to its thinking. In the process, it nearly brought the State to its knees. Organized in cells of three people each, the *JVP* was based around Matara in the south. For two years, it killed hundreds (if not thousands) of people and virtually crippled the country with violently-enforced *hartals* (general strikes). Government forces were able finally to capture and kill Wijeweera and his deputy in November 1989 at Colombo. By early 1990, they had slain or imprisoned the remaining *JVP* "politburo" and detained an estimated 7,000 *JVP* members.[31]

The *JVP* Today

The *JVP,* alias People's Liberation Front, remains a Socialist party. Though having mounted an armed insurrection in April 1971 and again in 1987-1989, it is currently part of the ruling coalition. As of January 2007, Somawansa Amarasinghe was the leader of *JVP.*[32]

Comrade Somawansa Amarasinghe is the only surviving politburo member in Sri Lanka. In the early 1990's, he led the party from exile. In 1994, the government had to lift the "emergency" to calm the people's agitation. At that point, the *JVP* was again allowed to enter into mainstream politics. It has since won more seats in each successive election. The *JVP,* for the first time in its history, is now part of the Sri Lankan government.[33]

Singapore-based regional-terrorism expert Rohan Gunaratna felt compelled in 1995 to publish a book about the *JVP*. The question mark at the end of its title—*Sri Lanka: The Lost Revolution?*—infers an ongoing effort by the Sri Lankan Marxists to take over. This inference was bolstered by Gunaratna's last-chapter title—"Where Will It All End?" That the *JVP* is now relatively peaceful should not bring much comfort. "Politicizing" was, after all, part of Mao's guerrilla method. And the island of Sri Lanka is strategically situated. Against the backdrop of Tamil separatism, who in the West would notice its loss?

Deja Vu

As in Calcutta and Nepal, the Communist revolution in Sri Lanka has simply moved into the political arena of 4GW. Like its shy Bangladeshi sister, it has currently become almost invisible against the backdrop of other public disturbance. In Sri Lanka, that disturbance has come from the little-understood and much-demeaned Tamil Tigers.

The History of the Tamil Uprising

The Tamil people have controlled southeastern India since ancient times. The Indian state of Tamil Nadu was home to four Tamil kingdoms. The most powerful of these kingdoms was the

Chola Empire. At one time, it stretched as far as Bengal, Sri Lanka, coastal Burma, the Andaman and Nicobar Islands, Sumatra, Java, and Malaya. Unlike other parts of India, the traditionally Tamil homelands were never conquered by the ruling Mughals.[34]

Even before Ceylon's independence from Britain in 1948, there were Maoist rumblings in its minority Tamil community.[35] In 1949, all Tamil plantation workers of Indian descent were disenfranchised by the acting government. Between 1956 and 1958, hundreds of Tamils of every description were killed in anti-Tamil riots.[36]

In 1976, the Liberation Tigers of Tamil Eelam (LTTE, alias Ellalan Force or Tamil Tigers), was founded in response to active discrimination from the largely Sinhanese government.[37] A year later, hundreds more of their ethnicity were killed in anti-Tamil riots.[38] Hoping to establish an independent Tamil state on Sri Lanka's north and east side, the LTTE began an armed rebellion in 1983. This, in turn, led to more large riots in Colombo, Sri Lanka's capital.[39]

The LTTE relied on a Maoist guerrilla strategy that included terrorist tactics. Many of its fighters were sent to southeastern India for further training. In mid-1987, India intervened in the conflict by air-dropping supplies to the Tamils. It did so to prevent what it considered to be "harsh treatment and starvation of the Tamil population in the Jaffna Peninsula caused by an economic blockade by Colombo." Under an accord of 29 July 1987, the Sri Lankan government made a number of concessions to Tamil demands. These included the delegation of power to the provinces, and the merger—subject to later referendum—of those in the north and east. India agreed to establish order in the north and east with an Indian Peace Keeping Force (IPKF) and to cease assisting Tamil insurgents. Within weeks, however, the LTTE declared its intent to continue the struggle for an independent Tamil Eelam and refused to disarm. Soon the IPKF found itself engaged in a bloody police action against the LTTE. It was then that the *JVP*, which had been relatively quiet since the 1971 insurrection, began to reassert itself.[40]

Next, the LTTE targeted key personnel in the countryside and senior Sri Lankan political and military leaders in Colombo and other urban centers. It also went after rival Tamil groups and figures. Over the years, it has managed to assassinate the heads of two governments: (1) Prime Minister Rajiv Gandhi of India in 1991; and (2) President Premadasa of Sri Lanka in 1993.[41] In what came to resemble a civil war, there were intermittent peace talks, Tamil bombing attacks, and government pushes into Tamil-controlled territory between 1987 and 2002. Most Tamils of Indian descent were granted citizenship in 1988.[42] Feeling bogged down, the Indian peacekeepers left Sri Lanka two years later.[43]

In response to government death squads (and probable torture) in the late 1980's, the Tamil Tigers became obsessed with internal security. Once a member, a Tamil Tiger was not allowed to leave the organization. Many carried cyanide capsules.[44] Political assassinations and bombings became commonplace before the cease-fire in 2002. The LTTE is most notorious for its cadre of suicide bombers, the Black Tigers.[45]

Sri Lanka's Ethnic Make-Up

Today, Sri Lanka's Tamil community represents only 8.5% of the total. The rest are 73.8% Sinhalese and 7.2% Moors. In terms of religious affiliation, Sri Lanka's overall population is 69.1% Buddhist, 7.6% Muslim, 7.1% Hindu, and 6.2% Christian.[46]

The Current Escalation of Violence

Since mid-2005, the cease fire between the Tamil Tigers and Sri Lankan government has badly eroded. In April 2006, the Tigers were blamed for explosions and rioting in Trincomalee, on the northeastern coast. Then, after a suicide bomber attacked the main military compound in Colombo, the military launched air strikes on Tamil Tiger targets. In May, Sri Lankan army forces entered the Tamil homeland on the Jaffna Peninsula. Shortly thereafter, seaborne Tamil Tigers attacked a naval convoy near its principal city. A month later, a fully loaded government bus detonated a mine in Anuradhapura district. By this time, land and sea battles were raging between government forces and Tamil rebels across a wide expanse. In August, the two clashed in the northeast in the worst fighting since the 2002 ceasefire.[47] Two months later, the Tigers dealt the Sri Lankan army a major blow by destroying four T-55 tanks, eight armored vehicles, and 130 men in a two hour battle on the Jaffna peninsula.[48] Within five days, a suicide truck bomber had driven into a bus convoy of naval personnel near its largest urban center, killing 90 and wounding another 150.[49] The LTTE also attacked a naval base in Galle, a southern town frequented by tourists. After weeks of heavy fighting in January 2007, the Sri Lankan military claimed it captured the Tamil Tiger stronghold of Vakarai, on the eastern side of the island.[50]

Before the latest trouble, LTTE was estimated to have 8,000 to 10,000 armed combatants, with a core of 3,000 to 6,000 trained fighters. Headquartered in northern Sri Lanka (probably Jaffna), it controlled portions of the northern and eastern coastal areas of the country. There, it had set up a comprehensive administrative system.[51]

Of late, LTTE leader Velupillai Prabhakaran has established an extensive network of checkpoints and informants to keep track of any outsiders who enter his area of control.[52] There are some indications that the Tamil Tigers may now be forcing children to join their ranks.[53]

A Good Possibility of Communist Meddling

India's Naxalite Communist insurgency stretches all the way down its east coast into Andhra Pradesh—the state just above Tamil Nadu and Sri Lanka. Thus, one can reasonably assume that Sri Lanka may be experiencing some of the same Communist pressure. According to BBC News, there was a strange occurrence during its last presidential election. In November 2005, an LTTE-enforced voting boycott in the areas under its control led to a narrow victory by an SLFP candidate—Mahinda Rajapakse. It is the SLFP with which the Socialist *JVP* is so closely allied in the ruling alliance.[54] Either the LTTE had made a mistake, or a third party was pulling the strings.

That the Tamils and *JVP* both have Maoist roots should be noted. Until just recently, Sri Lanka was not known to have any petroleum reserves.[55] On 30 January 2007, its government offered the rights to an "oil block" to India. That block is in Mannar, near the Kavery basin. In return, India's National Rail System is to set up a 160 kilometer train route from Colombo to Matara.[56] Where oil rights are concerned, the Chinese oil companies cannot be far behind.

Sri Lanka is strategically located between the Arabian Sea and Bay of Bengal. With seaborne separatists in the north and an increasingly Marxist government at Colombo, it might be more likely to entertain a full-time Chinese naval presence. Colombo would be an ideal resting place for Chinese oil tankers *en route* to and from Africa. On the other side of India lies a much more obvious affiliate of the PRC.

7 Pakistan and Afghanistan

- Does Pakistan still support the Taliban?
- Has China any strategic interest in Afghanistan?

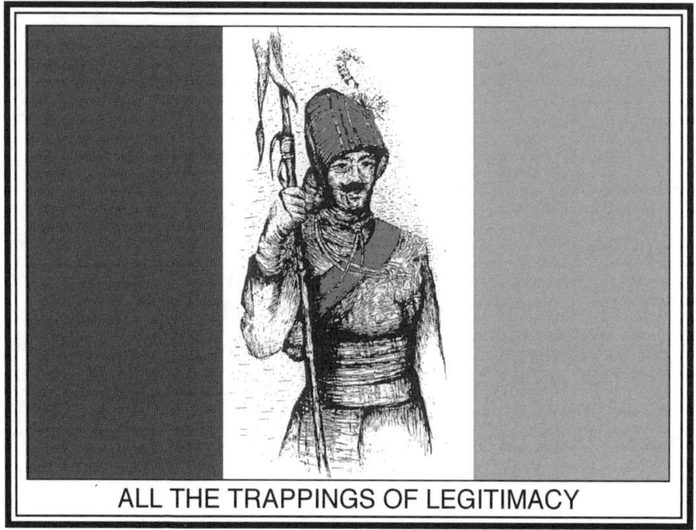

ALL THE TRAPPINGS OF LEGITIMACY

(Source: Dept. of the Army Pamphlet 550-21 [1985], p. 503)

Musharraf's Deal with the Taliban

On 10 September 2006, a Pakistani religious political party—the *Jamiat Ulema-e-Islam (JUI)*—brokered a deal between its government and the Taliban in North Waziristan.[1] In return for a promise to evict foreign fighters and prevent cross-border raids, the militants were given back confiscated arms, detained personnel, and effective control of the area.[2] To more easily influence the nearly autonomous Federally Administered Tribal Areas (FATA), Northwest Frontier Province (NWFP), and Baluchistan, President Musharraf had—in effect—formed a political alliance with the Taliban. It had been the *JUI*—with the help of Pakistan's Interior Ministry and ISI [Interservice Intelligence][3] —that had initially used its *madrasas* to spawn the Taliban in 1994.[4] While its breakaway "Fazlur Rehman" faction *(JUI/F)* still provides the Taliban with money, men, and arms,[5] its parent denies any direct link. *JUI* does, however, admit to still supporting the Taliban ideologically.[6] As of 2004, Mullah Omar was most often associated with the "*JUI*-Taliban stronghold" at Karachi's Binori Mosque.[7] Since February 2005, *JUI* has supposedly broken ranks with its other partners in the fundamentalist Muslim coalition—the *Muttahida-Majlis-e Amal (MMA).*[8] One of those partners is *JUI/F.*[9]

It's not hard to see what had happened with the September 2006 deal. To survive politically, Musharraf had enlisted the help of the main political force in NWFP and Baluchistan.[10] When asked why he had let up on *al-Qaeda* and the Taliban, he said something about preempting the enemy with tribal reconciliation. By January 2007, the pact had failed, carving out a sanctuary from which militants could launch their raids. NATO and Afghan officials soon noticed a spike in the number of cross-border attacks. Late in February 2007, Vice President Cheney went to Pakistan to show Musharraf proof of *al-Qaeda* training camps springing up in the Waziristans. By this time, the cross border raids had increased fivefold. But the visit did little good. In late March, Musharraf renewed the peace accord with Waziristan's tribal leaders.[11] The president of Pakistan had a good reason for his conciliatory stance.

> Analysts predict that Musharraf will need JUI to bring in votes in those [border] regions during the presidential election of 2007.[12]
>
> — *Christian Science Monitor,* 27 September 2006

The Pakistani government cut a similar deal with tribal leaders in South Waziristan in 2004. The area quickly became a vacuum that was quickly filled by Taliban.[13] According to PBS's *Frontline*, no fewer than 100 tribal elders were assassinated over the next two years due to an insufficient government presence. The Taliban "rearmed while the Pakistani government did nothing to stop them." As of January 2007, that government had not arrested any high-level Taliban official, and its ISI appeared to be still assisting Taliban forces.[14]

Musharraf relieved a few ISI leaders after 9/11 but left those of Pakistan's religious parties alone. He did nothing to stop the flow of Taliban reinforcements into Afghanistan. After Tora Bora, what was left of the Taliban was allowed to escape south into the Waziristans. A key player in all of this was a former *mujahideen* commander by the name of Jalaluddin Haqqani. While fighting the Russians, his area of operations had been just south of the Parrot's Beak around Khost—right where *al-Qaeda* had many of its training camps.[15] Haqqani has since become the Taliban's director of operations against U.S. and NATO forces. He has additionally been credited with introducing suicide bombers to the struggle.[16] Two Pakistani factions are known to be producing suicide bombers. One is the ISI's new proxy—*Lashkar-e-Toiba (LET* or Khairun Nas).[17] The other is *Lashkar-i-Jhangvi (LJ)*. Sometimes called *al-Qaeda's* "delta force," *LJ* may be too anti-Shiite to suit *al-Qaeda's* Salafist leaders.

LET openly trains near Lahore and *LJ* does so in Karachi.[18] As late as 2004, Karachi's Binori Mosque was still described as a "*JUI*-Taliban stronghold."[19] As of January 2007, the Taliban's principal reinforcement/resupply route remained relatively free of Pakistani government inspection at the principal Afghan border crossing north of Quetta. As late as the previous spring, anyone without identification papers could bribe the Frontier Constabulary at Chaman's "Friend Gate" (probably the same crossing) for as little as fifteen cents. For about $1.50, he could hop on the back of a motorcycle and avoid the occasional random search.[20]

When Musharraf authorized force to evict Muslim militants from Islamabad's Red Mosque in July 2007, it was the Taliban that declared an end to the peace pact in the Waziristans.[21] By evicting militants from his government center, Musharraf was again hoping to convince the West that he didn't tolerate extremist enclaves anywhere in his country. Seldom do appearances in a Communist capital match what goes on elsewhere either.

Another Perspective on Musharraf

President Musharraf is an enigma. Former U.S. CENTCOM commanders have touted his value to the War on Terror. His ambassador claims he is the only U.S. ally in the region. President Musharraf has even written a book—for the U.S. market—attesting to his friendship. Yet, his closest neighbors (Afghanistan and India) still say that the terrorist trail leads back to Pakistan. In February 2006, President Karzai personally delivered to Musharraf a list of known Taliban sites within Pakistan (to include leader addresses). Though that list had been carefully derived from NATO and Afghan intelligence, Pakistan's president was insulted by the effort. In July, India called off negotiations with Pakistan after finding that its ISI had orchestrated the deadly Mumbai train explosions. Four months later, a captured Taliban spokesman told interrogators that Mullah Mohammed Omar was hiding in Quetta under the protection of the ISI. He also claimed the Taliban, with the help of the ISI, was responsible for more than 100 suicide attacks within Afghanistan.[22] Thus, two completely different impressions of Musharraf emerge. The following statement from a former Pakistani prime minister helps to explain the dichotomy.

> To some, the disquieting pattern of the link between Pakistan and terrorist plots against the west may seem irrelevant and coincidental. To me, the pattern is a consequence of the west allowing Pakistani military regimes to suppress the democratic aspirations of the people of Pakistan, as long as their dictators ostensibly support the political goals of the international community.
>
> In the late 1970's the democratically elected government of Pakistan was toppled by a coup led by the army chief General Zia ul-Haq. At first, the international community demanded a restoration of democracy. But after the Soviet invasion of Afghanistan, these demands subsided as the U.S. saw an opportunity to hobble the Soviet Union. The U.S. funneled aid for the fundamentalist mujahideen through Pakistan, specifically through the military intelligence agencies Zia had created to cement his iron rule.
>
> This alliance converted my homeland from a peaceful nation into a violent society of weapons, heroin addiction and a radicalised interpretation of Islam, and the diversion of resources to the military devastated Pakistani society. As the government relinquished its responsibility in education, health, housing and social services, people looked elsewhere for support. The clearest manifestation of this was the spread of political madrasas. They became the breeding ground for hatred, extremism, militancy and terrorism. Once the Soviets left Afghanistan, the [W]est abandoned

> democracy there. Pakistan and Afghanistan became the sources of a political and religious extremist movement that morphed into the Taliban and al-Qaeda.
>
> The new Pakistani dictator, General Pervez Musharraf, has played the [W]est like a fiddle, dispensing occasional support in the war on terror to keep America and Britain off his back as he proceeded to arrest and exile opposition leaders, decimate political parties, pressure the press and set back human and women's rights by a generation. His regime, claiming sections of the frontier are ungovernable, has relinquished responsibility to the Taliban and al-Qaeda. During both of my tenures as prime minister, my government enforced the writ of the state there through the civil administration and paramilitary troops.
>
> The Musharraf dictatorship doles out ostensible support in the war on terror to keep it in the good graces of Washington, while it presides over a society that fuels and empowers militants at the expense of moderates.[23]
>
> — Benazir Bhutto, 16 August 2006

Someone is not telling the whole truth. With regard to the Taliban, it is more likely to be Musharraf than Karzai.

The Recent Strengthening of Pakistan's Ties with China

Since Pakistan's birth as an independent nation, it and China have gotten along well. In 1963, Pakistan happily ceded part of occupied Kashmir to China. Some 25 years later, it and China built the Karakoram Highway that now connects the two countries "over the roof of the world." In March 2007, it and China celebrated the opening of the port of Gwadar in Balochistan Province. To more easily ship home its Persian Gulf oil, China had bankrolled the entire building of the port. It further "plans to put billions [of dollars] more into railways, roads, and pipelines linking Gwadar to China." Pakistan stands to earn $60 billion a year in transit fees alone. Without the normal U.S. strings attached (human rights, democracy, and counterterrorism), this much money could bring Pakistan even further into the Chinese camp.[24] With suspicions rising that Pakistan is once again backing the removal of Afghanistan's infidel occupiers, this might present a major problem for the West.

On 13 August 2007, the PRC's *People's Daily* complained that Musharraf had "bungled" the removal of his Chief Justice. It apparently wanted no obstacles to Gen. Musharraf's plan to remain in office past the two terms authorized by the Pakistani constitution. It further decried the "calls for democracy" that protestors had made after entering the streets.[25]

The Part of Afghan History That Is Not Being Discussed

History records China helping the West to defeat the Russian occupation of Afghanistan in the late 1980's.[26] (See Map 7.1.) The PRC did so mostly with munitions sent to the *mujahideen* via Pakistan. As Pakistan endorsed the birth of *al-Qaeda* and spawned the Taliban,[27] it is not unreasonable to conclude that one or more of its allies may have continued to support them. This would be particularly true of any neighbor requiring overland oil conduits from the Middle East. (See Map 7.2.) A table from the U.S. Army's Strategic Studies Institute provides a detailed account of the interaction between China and the Taliban before the U.S. invasion of Afghanistan.[28] (See Figure 7.1.) That is not the only proof of collusion.

> A Taliban military commander stated in a published interview in October that China was secretly assisting the Islamic militia. . . .
>
> Haqqani said Taliban fighters were prepared to conduct a long guerrilla war against the United States.[29]
>
> — *Washington Times,* 12 April 2002

> In their final days, the Taliban themselves boasted that they had a strategic pact with China. Last October, the powerful Taliban commander Maulvi Jalaluddin Haqqani told reporters that China was "extending support and cooperation to the Taliban, but the shape of the cooperation cannot be disclosed." . . .
>
> What is clear is that the vast majority of the weapons captured by U.S. and allied forces since the fall of the Taliban last November have been Chinese made, say Afghan military chiefs.[30]
>
> — *Christian Science Monitor,* 23 August 2002

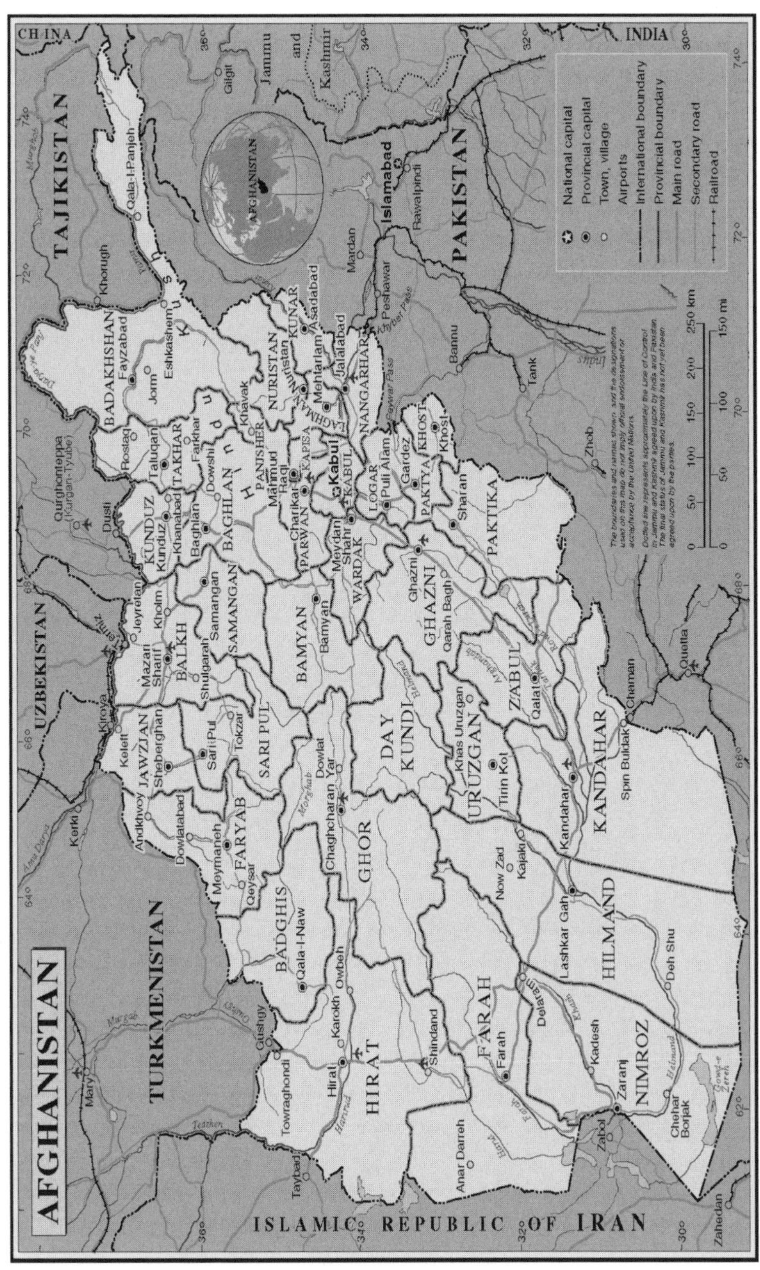

Map 7.1: The Afghan Provinces

(Source: Courtesy of the United Nations, Department of Peacekeeping, Cartographic Section, Map No. 3958 Rev. 5, October 2005, © n.d.)

YEAR	KEY DEVELOPMENTS
December 1998	- Following the escalation of separatist violence in Xinjiang in 1998, contact facilitated by Pakistan between China and Taliban at Beijing's request. Five senior Chinese diplomats held talks in Kabul with the Taliban's Deputy Chairman Mullah Muhammad Hassan, Interior Minister Mullah Abdur Razzaq, and Deputy Foreign Minister Abdurrahman Zayef and obtained their assurance that the Taliban would not allow Afghan territory to be used against China. The Taliban also transferred two unexploded U.S. Tomahawk cruise missiles to China for $20 million each. In return, the Chinese agreed to: • start direct flights between Kabul and Urumuqi; • open formal trade ties; • increase Chinese food aid to Afghanistan; • institutionalize military-to-military contacts; and • provide arms and spares for Taliban's aging military equipment.
October 1999	- Annual felicitations conveyed by Mullah Omar (via Radio Shariat) on the occasion of China's National Day from 1999.
November 2000	- A delegation from the Ministry of State Security-run think tank, China Institute of Contemporary International Relations, visited Kabul and Kandahar.
December 2000	- A delegation led by China's ambassador to Pakistan, Lu Shulin, met with Mullah Omar, following the Taliban's plea to veto U.S.-Russian moves to tighten U.N. Security Council sanctions (including travel restrictions against Taliban officials).
2000	- China's Huawei Technologies Co., also accused of helping Iraq to upgrade its military communications system, signed a deal to install 12,000 fixed-line telephones in Kandahar. - Another Chinese telecom firm, ZTE, agreed to install 5,000 telephone lines in Kabul after Pakistan provided a counter-guarantee for the project.

Figure 7.1: U.S. Army's Strategic Studies Institute Table

(Source: *Dragon on Terrorism*, by Mohan Malik, Strategic Studies Institute, U. S. Army War College, Carlisle, PA, October 2002)

2001	- China started the repair work on Afghanistan's power grid, damaged by years of war. Repair and expansion work on the Kajaki Dam in Helmand, Dahla Dam in Kandahar and the Breshna-Kot Dam in Nangarhar began. - The Dongfeng Agricultural Machinery Company was hired to add 16.5 MW to power generation. Work was still in progress when the site was bombed in November 2001. - The Chinese were involved in refurbishing the Herat Cement Plant. - By late 2001, China had become the biggest investor in Afghanistan, with "legitimate" investments running to several tens of millions of dollars.
July 2001	- A Taliban delegation, led by their Commercial Attaché to Pakistan, spent a week in China as guests of the government. The Chinese Commerce Ministry facilitated their interaction with some Chinese industrialists and businessmen. - Chinese Foreign Minister Tang Jiaxuan met with a Taliban delegation whilst visiting Pakistan, and agreed to consider the Taliban's position on U.N. sanctions against Afghanistan.
August 2001	- Osama bin Laden called for cultivating closer Taliban-China ties to reduce U.S. influence.
September 2001	- A new protocol on Sino-Taliban commercial relations was inked on September 11: the day of the World Trade Center attacks.
October 2001	- A Taliban military commander, Maulvi Jalaluddin Haqqani, told a Pakistani newspaper that China had maintained contacts with the Islamic militia even after U.S. air strikes had begun, and that Beijing was "also extending support and cooperation to the Taliban, but the shape of this cooperation cannot be disclosed." China's government described the commander's statement as a "fabrication." - U.S. intelligence reported that China continued to supply arms (including Chinese-made SA-7 shoulder-fired missiles) to *al-Qaeda* terrorists after September 11.

Figure 7.1 (Cont.): U.S. Army's Strategic Studies Institute Table

(Source: *Dragon on Terrorism*, by Mohan Malik, Strategic Studies Institute, U. S. Army War College, Carlisle, PA, October 2002)

December 2001	- Indian media reported that the Indian Government was considering deporting 185 Chinese telecom experts working at Huawei Company's Bangalore office, who were suspected of developing telecom surveillance equipment for the Taliban. China's ambassador to India issued a denial. - Defense Secretary Donald Rumsfeld said Alliance forces near Tora Bora had "captured a good deal of Chinese ammunition." The Chinese Foreign Ministry spokesman said he had "no idea" what Rumsfeld was referring to. - U.S. officials acknowledged that a few Chinese passport-holders were discovered among the fighters in Afgha

SOURCE: A. Rashid, "Taliban temptation," *Far Eastern Economic Review* [hereafter *FEER*], March 11, 1999; R. Chattoapdhyay, "China's Taliban Connection," *Bharat Rakshak Monitor, Vol. 4, No. 3, November-December 2001; T. S. Sahay,* "Taliban-China deal puzzles diplomats," *Rediff.com*, February 12, 1999; "Bin Ladin Calls for Taliban-China Good Relations to Reduce US Influence," *Ausaf* (Pakistan), August 14, 2001, trans. in FBIS; AFP, "China paid Laden for access to Cruise missiles," March 9, 2001; J. Pomfret, "China Strengthens Ties With Taliban by Signing Economic Deal," *Washington Post*, September 13, 2001; M. Hasan, "Taliban team to visit China to boost," *The Nation*, July 4, 2001; D. Murphy and S. V. Lawrence, "Beijing Hopes to gain from US raids," *FEER*, October 4, 2001; D. Bristow, "China flirts with an independent pro-active Afghan policy," *Central Asia Analyst*, January 3, 2001; "China Firm Trades with Taliban," *FEER*, March 15, 2001; C. McLeod, "China–Taliban Deal Signed on Attack Day," *Washington Times*, September 14, 2001, p. 1; J. Iyengar, "Chinese geeks to be deported for Taliban links," *Economic Times* (India), December 10, 2001, p.1; B. Gertz and R. Scarborough "Chinese help Taliban," and "China-*al-Qaeda* nexus," *Washington Times*, November 23, December 21, 2001, p. 8; "China sold arms to *al-Qaeda* after Sept 11," December 22, 2001, *http://headlines.sify.com/399news4.html*; B. Gertz, "China-Made Artillery Seized In Afghanistan," *Washington Times*, April 12, 2002, p. 1; "China denounced ties with Taliban," and "Anti-terrorism stance reiterated," *Beijing Review*, September 27, 2001 and November 1, 2001, p. 5.

Figure 7.1 (Cont.): U.S. Army's Strategic Studies Institute Table

(Source: Dragon on Terrorism, by Mohan Malik, Strategic Studies Institute, U. S. Army War College, Carlisle, PA, October 2002)

Unfortunately, the PRC's support of the Taliban was not limited to equipment. It also provided training. Such training would have helped the Taliban to better defend itself. It would have also permitted the PRC to infiltrate *al-Qaeda.*

> China's military provided training for Afghanistan's Taliban militia and its al-Qaeda supporters, according to a U.S. intelligence report. . . .

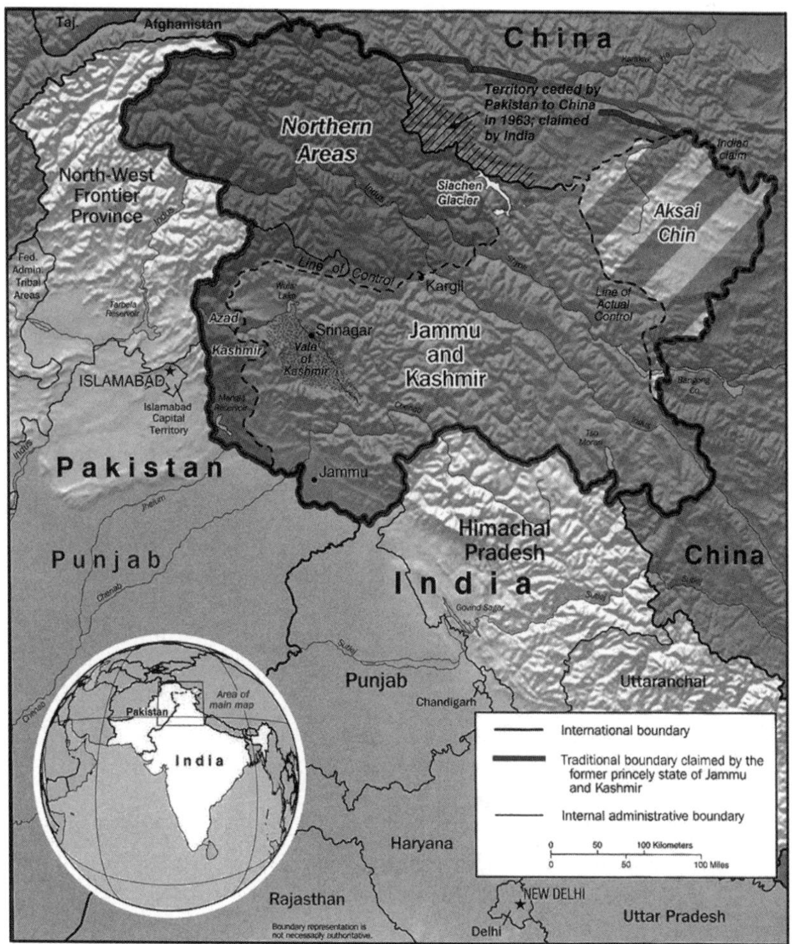

Map 7.2: Area of Strategic Significance to the PRC
(Source: Courtesy of General Libraries, University of Texas at Austin, from their website, for map designator "kashmir_region_2004.pdf.")

> The training of the Taliban forces took place before September 11. It was carried out in cooperation with Pakistan's ISI intelligence service, defense officials told us. . . .
>
> U.S. intelligence officials do not know why the Chinese provided the military training to Islamic radicals. But some analysts believe it was an attempt to gain influence over the Taliban and al-Qaeda.[31]
>
> – *Washington Times,* 21 June 2002

Just the Tip of the Iceberg

This was no last-minute try to protect the Taliban from invasion. China had been bettering the Taliban's defense systems for years.

> The first target in Afghanistan for U.S. airpower was the Taliban air defense system. B-2 bombers and F-14 Tomcats dropped precision guided weapons on . . . a Chinese-made fiber-optic military communications network.
>
> Although China officially denied that it installed the fiber-optic air defense network inside Afghanistan, the Pentagon is certain that China sold the military system to the Taliban. . . .
>
> "A fiber optic based 'phone' system can do a lot more than carry commercial traffic," noted one U.S. defense analyst who requested that he not be identified. . . .
>
> The military command network in Afghanistan is described by Pentagon analysts as similar to the fiber-optic air defense system installed in Iraq by China. . . .
>
> The fiber-optic network in Afghanistan has more than just a common thread with the Iraqi air defense system. The Chinese company CEIEC that built and installed the new system for the Taliban is also a known arms manufacturer, owned and operated by the People's Liberation Army. According to an official Defense Intelligence Agency (DIA) document, CEIEC is the prime maker of electronics for the Chinese army. The DIA documents state that virtually all CEIEC products are military in nature, including "cryptographic system," "mine detection equipment," "fiber and laser optics," "communications technology" and "radars."[32]
>
> – Newsmax.com, 20 October 2001

What China Wanted in Return

China was not doing all of this out of sheer kindness. It wanted things in return. One was an Afghan transportation corridor to the Iranian oil fields. Another was information about U.S. weaponry. Shortly after 9/11, it was reported that PRC had purchased unexploded U.S. cruise missiles from *al-Qaeda* in 1998 . . . to "reverse engineer" them. That report was confirmed on 29 November 2001.[33]

Then Came the Chinese "Volunteers"

The most glaring example of PRC manpower support occurred just before the U.S. invasion of Afghanistan. While only one reliable source provides details, others confirm the event.[34] *Al-Qaeda* could not have managed Uighur convoys from China without the PRC's knowledge. (Refer back to Map 1.3 and see Map 7.3.)

> Before even the launching of the major U.S. military offensive in Afghanistan, long Chinese convoys were carrying armed Chinese Muslim *servicemen* through northwest China into Afghanistan, according to DEBKAfile's intelligence experts [italics added].
>
> They were sent in to fight alongside the ruling Taliban and Osama bin Laden's al-Qaeda. Their number is estimated [to be] . . . between 5,000 and 15,000. Our sources report another three convoys are behind the first 3,000 [troops], who crossed the frontier Friday, October 5.
>
> They are entering Afghanistan along the ancient Krakoram [Karakoram] Road to the Afghan-Pakistani border, through the Kulik Pass of Little Pamir, which is situated in one of the highest and most remote regions of the world.
>
> Beijing is deploying this force in two places:
>
> A. Whakyir, the Kirgyz tribal encampment near the Little Pamir-Tadjik frontier, opposite the swelling concentration of U.S. and Russian Special Forces and air strength.
>
> The Chinese have brought with them Kirgyz fundamentalist militants from the Ferghana Valley of Central Asia, as interpreters.
>
> From Whakyir, the Chinese generals believe, with Bin Laden's and the Taliban's tacticians, they will be able to

> block off the movement of the U.S.-led force from its rallying point in Dzhartygumbez, Tadjikistan, no more than 35 miles from Little Pamir, into the mountains of Hindu Kush.
>
> B. Jalalabad in north Afghanistan, at the foot of the Hindu Kush range.
>
> DEBKAfile's Chinese sources reveal that, immediately after the terrorist strikes in the United States on September 11, the Chinese intelligence service, MSS, handed in to the defense ministry in Beijing their estimation that the United States would go to war to overthrow the Taliban regime, for the sake of which it would sign a pact with Russia. The Chinese leadership viewed this eventuality as the most significant shift in the global balance since the 1962 Chinese-Russian feud, with dangerous implications for China's world standing and its interests in Central and Southwest Asia. They decided it must be counteracted. . . .
>
> According to DEBKAfile's Far East experts, the removal of substantial U.S. military strength from the Pacific Rim [to the Persian Gulf Region] opened the way for Chinese intervention in Afghanistan and its effort to slow down the US-Russian advance.[35]
>
> — Israeli Intell. Periodical, 6 October 2001

A follow-up article suggests that these Chinese "reinforcements" were sent directly to *al-Qaeda*.

> DEBKAfile was the first publication to reveal that China had sent thousands of armed men into Afghanistan in support of Osama bin Laden and the Taliban. . . .
>
> DEBKAfile continued to run with the story through different stages of the Afghanistan War.
>
> Follow-ups, verified by other media, appeared on October 20 and November 15. In the first, we reported 15 Chinese fighters found dead in Kandahar. They were part of an escort convoy for one of bin Laden's senior lieutenants, Basir al-Masri, commander of the Arab contingents in Jalalabad, which came under U.S. bombing as it left Kandahar.
>
> In the second, David Chater of Sky television attested to the presence of Chinese fighting alongside the Taliban and al Qaeda in the battles of Konduz [Kunduz] and Khanabad in northern Afghanistan.

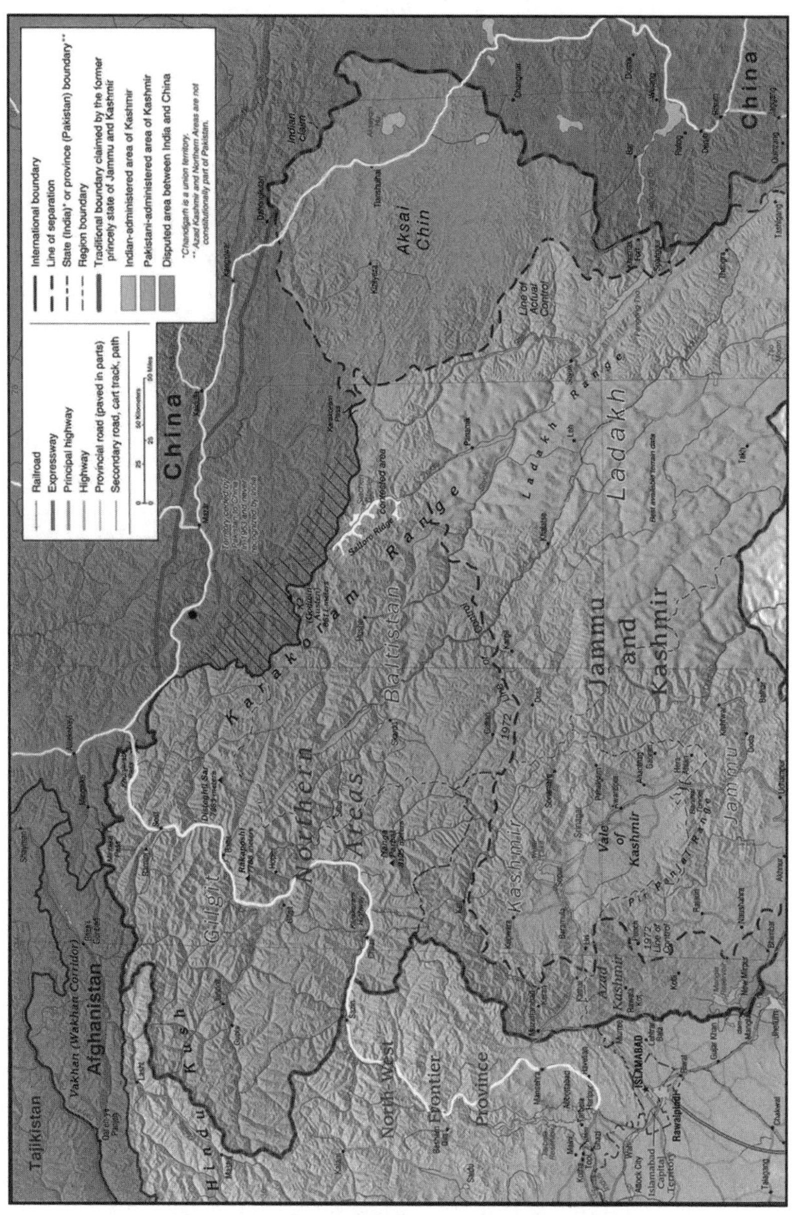

Map 7.3: Chinese Transportation Hub

(Source: Courtesy of General Libraries, University of Texas at Austin, from their website, for map designator "kashmir_disputed_2003.pdf.")

> Now comes the CNN report, which confirms that Beijing sent to bin Laden, not only men but also quantities of weapons.[36]
>
> — Israeli Intell. Periodical, 17 December 2001

The Uighur Heritage

In 1949, the Communist Party of China (CPC) sent out the PLA to annex several entire regions around periphery of China. One was "East Turkestan." From 1933 to 1934, this area had been home to the First East Turkestan Republic. Since 1944, it had constituted the Second East Turkestan Republic. After CPC annexation, it was to be administered as the "Xinjiang Uyghur Autonomous Region." To offset the understandable resentment of the area's predominantly Muslim population, the PRC has since massively resettled it with Han Chinese.[37]

China has no intention of returning independence to a place so rich in oil, gas, and uranium deposits. As the precursor to Tibet's rape, the PLA's control over this region will undoubtedly continue to be brutal.

> East Turkestan maintained a measure of independence until the early 1950's, when Mao's victorious rebel armies turned to the peripheries and began securing Chinese borders, capturing Manchuria, Inner Mongolia, Tibet and East Turkestan. It is the country's [PRC's] largest province, estimated to have approximately 40 million residents, as well as large deposits of oil, gas and uranium. The native Uighurs resisted Chinese occupation until the 1960's, but failed to win support from neighboring Muslim states because of their fractured tribal nature. . . .
>
> China has pursued political support for its actions in Xinjiang for several years now. . . . As in Tibet, Chinese resettlement policies have resulted in a sharp rise of Han Chinese among the population. . . . China maintains strict supervision over the region. . . . Human rights activists claim that during 1997 and the later part of 1996, some 1,000 Uighurs were executed and more than 10,000 were incarcerated for political reasons.[38]
>
> — Center for Defense Info. (D.C.), December 2002

For decades, Uighur dissatisfaction over Chinese occupation translated into an occasional riot or demonstration. After Tiananmen Square, any public disorder involving Uighurs was violently squashed. In April 1990, five Uighurs were killed in riots near Kashgar, and the region was put under martial law. Shortly thereafter, 22 people were killed in riots at Baaren. One source says the cause of those riots was the Communist banning of mosque construction. The violent dispersal of a public prayer service in Baaren led to local citizens taking over the town and government forces taking it back by aerial bombardment and ground assault. In 1995, the province experienced sabotage of railroad tracks and oil fields. The following year, approximately 5,000 Uighurs were arrested after a series of attacks on Chinese interests. An arrest of Uighur dissidents in Yining in 1997 led to a protest in which 3,000-5,000 people were arrested and hundreds more may have been shot. During the subsequent crackdown, as many as a half million Uighurs may have fled their homes and several armed resistance movements taken root. Though now labeled a terrorist group by the U.S. (after intense Chinese lobbying), the East Turkestan Islamic Movement (ETIM) remains separatist in nature. Many say the designation was to gain Chinese support for the Iraq war, but the *Washington Post* claims it was in return for Chinese regulations limiting the export of missile technology.[39]

> The East Turkestan Islamic Movement (ETIM) is a separatist Muslim group. . . . [It wants] separation from China and the creation of an independent state called East Turkestan. . . .
>
> . . . While China has portrayed its battle with ETIM as part of a worldwide struggle against international terrorism, the group's global reach and links to al Qaeda are [widely] disputed. . . .
>
> [C]ritics claim the U.S. decision to recognize ETIM as a terrorist group was a political move, designed to appease China during U.N. Security Council negotiations over a resolution on Iraq. Human rights groups have accused China of [inhumanely] repressing Xinjiang's native Uighur population. . . . Until recently, the United States had accused China of using the war against terrorism as an excuse to clamp down on political dissent in the region, and castigated the Chinese military for human rights violations against

> Uighur nationalists. ETIM leader Hahsan Mahsum has denied any connections between al-Qaeda and his group.[40]
> — Center for Defense Info. (D.C.), December 2002

Some Unanswered Questions about the Chinese Convoy

If all the Chinese fighters spotted by DEBKAfile contacts were Uighur, why did they need Islamic translators? And why, after the U.S. invasion, did China immediately demand that all ethnic Chinese captives be returned? Estimates of the number captured in Afghanistan vary from 22 to 300.

> A Chinese official complained Monday that the United States is holding 300 captured Chinese Muslim extremists in Afghanistan, whom China wants returned.[41]
> — *Chicago Tribune,* 28 May 2002

The "volunteer" ploy is nothing new to Korean War veterans. Many faced 10 divisions of Chinese volunteers at the Chosin Reservoir. The DEBKAfile article did, after all, specifically refer to Chinese "servicemen."

The Chinese Support Did Not End with the U.S. Invasion

There is also proof the Chinese government has continued to aid the Taliban since its defeat in December 2001. Much of that aid has come in the form of what ultimately beat the Russians.

> Evidence of Chinese military backing for the Taliban continues to surface. Late last month, U.S. Army Special Forces troops found 30 HN-5's, the designation for Chinese-made SA-7's surface-to-air missiles, in southeastern Afghanistan.
>
> Other intelligence reports indicated the Chinese shipped missiles to the Taliban after September 11. China's government has denied supporting al-Qaeda and the Taliban.[42]
> — *Washington Times,* 21 June 2002

> On a stroll through some bunkers, he [an Afghan Border Se-

> curity Force officer] picks through antiaircraft weapons left behind by the Taliban. "Whatever we have now is Chinese. Rockets, missiles, they're all Chinese," says Daud. He picks up a Chinese shoulder-fired antiaircraft rocket launcher.[43]
>
> — *Christian Science Monitor*, 23 August 2002

China's Direct Support of *al-Qaeda*

Proof of the PRC's military aid to the Taliban does not necessarily mean it was supporting *al-Qaeda* as well. Unfortunately, there is almost as much evidence of the latter.

> Pentagon officials aboard the plane taking U.S. defense secretary Donald Rumsfeld to Brussels, revealed that large quantities of Chinese-manufactured ammo were discovered in the Tora Bora cave hideouts of al Qaeda.
>
> They were speaking to CNN's senior defense correspondent James McIntyre, who ran the story with close-up shots of the cache.[44]
>
> — Israeli Intell. Periodical, 17 December 2001

What if China has been supplying *al-Qaeda* with surface-to-air missiles since the U.S. invasion of Afghanistan? Would U.S. leaders see those kinds of arms as a threat to the Western occupation?

> To blunt U.S. air superiority, al Qaeda forces are attempting to acquire surface-to-air missiles in China. . . .
>
> In Kunar Province, Afghan intelligence sources say that their reports were compiled this week, after Afghan spies, pretending to be Islamic radicals, infiltrated the two al Qaeda camps in Pakistan. The report concludes that China itself may be involved in supporting the camps, either by tacitly allowing [Chinese Muslims] . . . to join al Qaeda, or overtly offering to provide al Qaeda with antiaircraft missiles. . . .
>
> Osama's top lieutenant, Ayman Zawahiri, is now thought to be directing operations from al Qaeda's newly built base in the village of Shah Salim, about 30 miles west of the Pakistani city of Chitral, near the border of Afghanistan's Kunar Province. The other base is in the Pakistani village

of Murkushi on the Chinese border, about 90 miles north of the Pakistani city of Gilgit.[45]

— *Christian Science Monitor,* 9 August 2002

U.S. intelligence agencies stated in classified reports last year that China continued to supply arms to al Qaeda terrorists after the September 11 attacks. A week after the attacks, Beijing supplied a shipment of Chinese-made SA-7 shoulder-fired missiles to Osama bin Laden's terror network, according to senior U.S. officials.[46]

— *Washington Times,* 12 April 2002

U.S. intelligence reported that China continued to supply arms (including Chinese-made SA-7 shoulder-fired missiles) to al-Qaeda terrorists after September 11.[47]

— U.S.Army Strategic Studies Inst., October 2002

Other sophisticated equipment can be of great help in confronting a "high-tech" army. What if China also sent some of that?

Pakistani forces recovered an unmanned drone aircraft and seized 21 militants in a raid on suspected al-Qaeda hideouts in the tribal areas near Afghanistan. . . .

Militants used the Chinese-made vehicle to spy on security forces in the rugged area, where Pakistani soldiers have battled Islamic militants for more than a year, Lieutenant General Safdar Hussain told reporters. . . .

"The terrorists used the RPV (remotely piloted vehicle) to check the position of security forces and attack them," the general said, adding that the drone was capable of carrying weapons.[48]

— Agence France-Press, 13 September 2005

And, there are indications that China has been providing *al-Qaeda* with training as well.

China trained . . . al-Qaeda fighters says U.S. Intel.[49]

— *Washington Times* journalist, 22 June 2002

Most disturbing is reliable evidence that *al-Qaeda's* first website was developed in southern China.[50]

The Exaggeration of Xinjiang's Terrorist Problem

What appears to be true in a totalitarian Asian nation is often not. Since the time of Sun Tzu, Chinese leaders have understood how to deceive foreign counterparts who were bent on reconciliation. The PRC has had much less trouble controlling Xinjiang's separatist movement than it publicly admits. This has been confirmed by more than one reliable source.[51] Westerners must start asking themselves why.

> [T]he facts show that "terrorism" in Xinjiang has been subsiding significantly since the late 1990's (Mackerras, "Why Terrorism Bypasses China's Far West," *Asia Times,* 23 April 2004). . . . In short, underscoring Eastern Turkestan Terrorism does not necessarily reflect the reality but it does reflect China's changing interests (such as winning U.S. support [and confidence] in the worldwide fight against terrorism).
>
> Because, in spite of its repeated statements, Beijing firmly controls Xinjiang and does not perceive any real, serious or immediate "terrorist" threat to its national security in the northwest. . . . Similarly, Islamic radicalism in Xinjiang appears to be marginal at best and does not propagate terrorism. . . . The bottom line is that Beijing has been trying to manipulate public opinion–at home and abroad . . . to influence foreign governments (primarily the United States) (Kurlantzick, "China's Dubious Role in the War on Terror," *Current History,* December 2003, 432-438). . . . Having monopolized political and military power in Xinjiang, Beijing must be aware that Uyghur activism and Islamic radicalism . . . do not constitute a real threat to China's social cohesion and economic stability, let alone to its national security and territorial integrity. Yet, the Chinese have . . . frequently exaggerated their threat. . . . [B]y depicting [this] national separatism and religious radicalism as . . . linked to global "terrorism," . . . Beijing can . . . scare potential external supporters. . . . This has opened the door for the PRC to join the U.S.-led international crusade against terrorism and, moreover, to gain unexpected sympathy [and trust].[52]
>
> — *China and Eurasia Forum Quarterly,* 2006

China Would Have to Carefully Hide Any Afghan Meddling

Afghanistan's strategic location has been adequately demonstrated by the number of times it has been invaded by competing world powers. China did not buy into the idea that U.S. bases a few hundred miles from her border in Central Asia would help to defeat Islamic fundamentalism. That's why the Shanghai Cooperation Organization (SCO) was formed. At a July 2005 summit, all six members—China, Russia, Kazakhstan, Kyrgyzstan, Tajikistan, and Uzbekistan—called on Washington to set a date for the military withdrawal of its forces from the region.[53]

If the PRC wanted the North Atlantic Treaty Organization (NATO) out of Afghanistan, it would now use Bamian Province as its center of operations. Lying less than 100 miles west of Kabul, this province is adequately remote and home to the Hazaras. Descended from Mongol invaders, the Hazaras are more Oriental in appearance than other Afghans.[54] From Bamian City, Chinese "special operators/tactical trainers" could deploy southward to help the Pakistani-supported Taliban or in other directions to help the Iranian-sponsored Northern Alliance (Afghanistan's ruling faction). The side controlling the thin land bridge to China would be the most logical recipient, but China might have a more sinister plan. Over the years, it has provided military assistance to both Iran and Pakistan.[55] Might the PRC be playing both sides against the middle to increase the level of violence and thus hasten Western withdrawal?

Besides obscure military training, China would have its standard array of "quasi-humanitarian" fronts. With no possibility of a Chinese "peacekeeping force," it would turn to pipeline, road, bridge, irrigation, and dam building initiatives. Each would require Chinese security personnel. Since 2004, China Railway Shisiju Group Corporation has been constructing a road linking Pakistan with Kabul through Jalalabad. In late summer of 2006, that same company started an extension from Kabul westward through Wardak Province into Bamian City. (Refer back to Map 7.1.) Chinese workers were attacked at another road project in Kunduz Province (near the border of Tajikistan) in June 2004. As of August 2006, Chinese companies had built or were in the process of building some 485 kilometers of roads.[56]

Any Chinese infiltration of Afghanistan would not be restricted to road crews. Agreeing to write off that country's debt in 2004, the PRC additionally pledged to rebuild a major irrigation project near Kabul. That project includes at least one dam.[57]

Inside Kabul, the Chinese embassy is only about 300 yards from the offices of President Karzai and his intelligence service. There is also a Chinese restaurant next to the U.S. embassy.[58]

Not Many Chinese Separatists in Bamian

After revolting against the Taliban in August of 1998, 10,0000 Hazara civilians were massacred at Mazar-e-Sharif.[59] As Shiites, the Hazaras are now trying to rebuilt Bamian infrastructure with Iranian help. That help will soon produce a Herat-to-Bamian road to complement the Chinese-built Bamian-to Peshwar road.[60] Together, those roads will greatly facilitate travel between Iran's oil fields and Pakistan's transportation links to China.

Descended from Huns, Uighurs are Sunni and pro-Taliban.[61] Though the Taliban is now resurgent throughout Afghanistan (64% of its residents report local Taliban activity on 7 December 2006),[62] there is little chance that the Chinese immigrants to Bamian are Uighur. Thus, one cannot help but recognize the all-too-familiar indications of Chinese expansion.

The Trouble in Jammu/Kashmir May Not Be Coincidental

A closer look at the foreign-occupied Indian state of Jammu-Kashmir reveals some unsettling coincidences. The Chinese control the Aksai Chin portion. The Pakistanis control Azad Kashmir and the Northern Areas. They ceded the Trans-Karakoram Tract (along the northern frontier of Gilgit-Baltistan agency) to the PRC in 1963. It was in those Northern Areas that the Taliban reinforcement route and *al-Qaeda* base camp were reported in 2001 and 2002, respectively. (Refer back to Map 7.4.)

Might the transport of oil somehow pertain to the ongoing dispute in Jammu-Kashmir? (Refer back to Map 7.2.) Shortly after partition in 1947, Pakistan seized the northern portion of the Indian state of Jammu-Kashmir.[63] China invaded Tibet in 1951 but did not secure it until 1959.[64] Then, to facilitate travel between Tibet and Xinjiang Province, it built an unauthorized road (China National

Highway G219) through the eastern portion of Jammu-Kashmir. India objected and was defeated in the Sino-Indian Border War of 1962.[65] A year later, Pakistan ceded the Trans-Karakoram Tract of its occupied Northern Areas to China. Then, in 1965 and again in 1999, India had to fight two more wars with Pakistan over Kashmir.[66]

China had demonstrated a willingness to use force to extend its trade routes to the west. Its position on Afghanistan in the 1980's indicated no change to that strategic plan. Might a direct route from Peshwar across Afghanistan to Herat now complete that plan?

The Karakoram Highway

In 1986, the PRC and Pakistan completed the Karakoram Highway. In two years, it would be the way most Chinese arms were shipped to the Afghan *mujahideen*.[67] (See Maps 7.4 and 7.5.)

> The Karakoram Highway . . . is the highest paved international road in the world. It connects China and Pakistan across the Karakoram mountain range, through the Khunjerab Pass. . . . It connects China's Xinjiang region with Pakistan's Northern Areas [occupied India]. . . .
>
> The Karakoram Highway . . . was built by the governments of Pakistan and China, and was completed in 1986, after 20 years of construction.[68]

Such a highway would also permit the sending of volunteers into Afghanistan through Pakistan's Northern Areas (occupied Jammu-Kashmir) and North-West Frontier Province.

> They [the Chinese troops] are entering Afghanistan along the ancient Krakoram [Karakoram] Road to the Afghan-Pakistani border, through the Kulik Pass of Little Pamir.[69]
>
> — Israeli Intell. Periodical, 6 October 2001

> The other *[al-Qaeda]* base is in the Pakistani village of Murkushi on the Chinese border, about 90 miles north of the Pakistani city of Gilgit [both within occupied Jammu-Kashmir].[70]
>
> — *Christian Science Monitor*, 9 August 2002

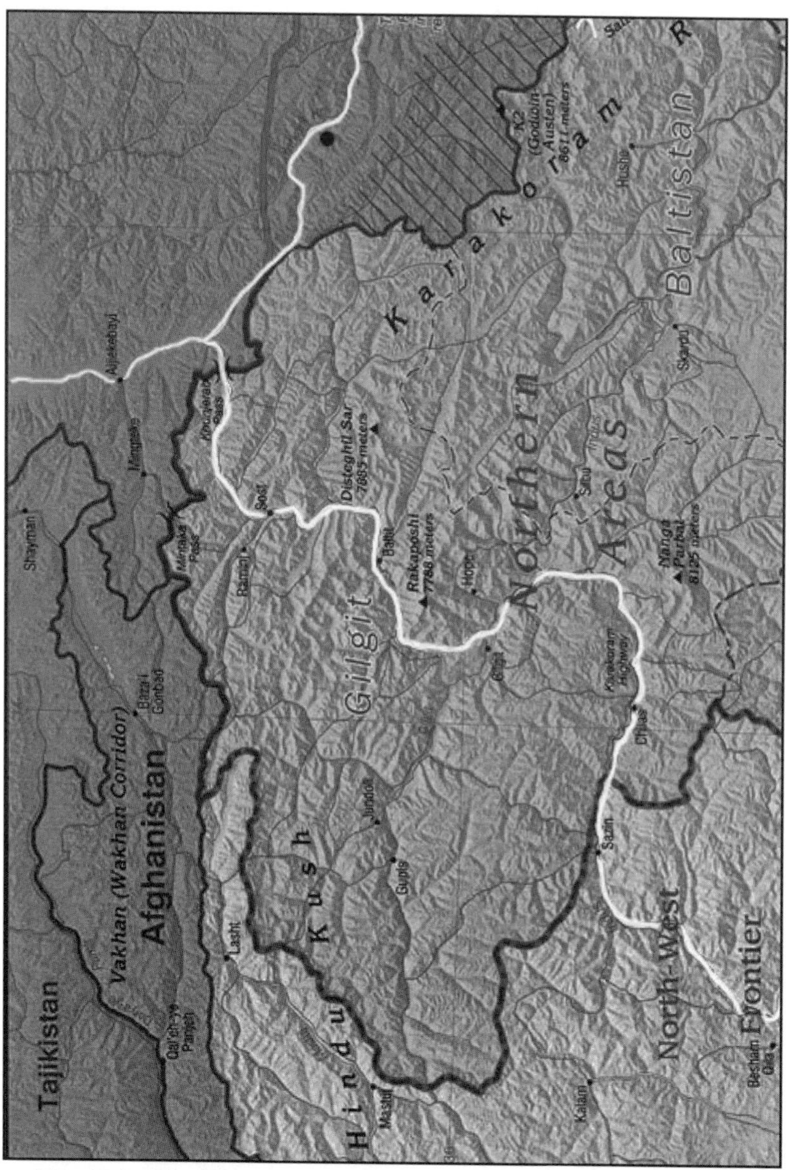

Map 7.4: The Way through Jammu-Kashmir to Afghanistan

(Source: Courtesy of General Libraries, University of Texas at Austin, from their website, for map designator "kashmir_disputed_2003.pdf.")

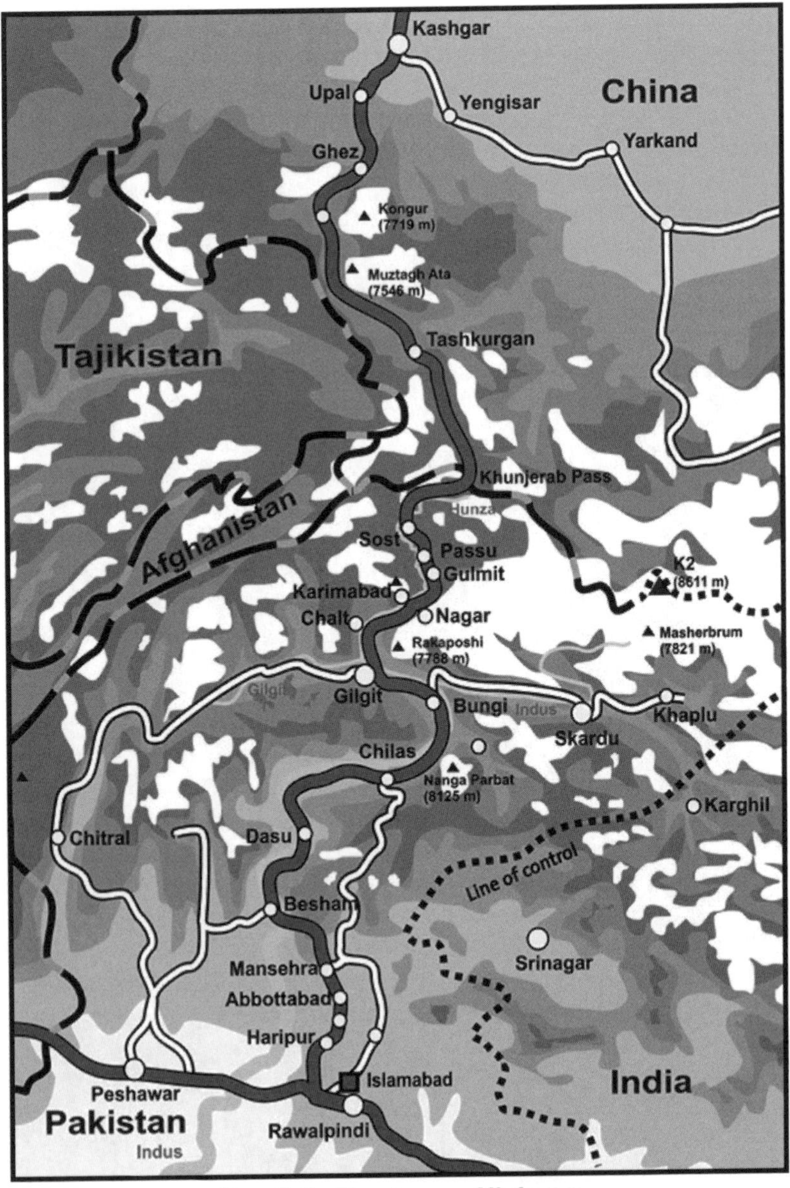

Map 7.5: Karakoram Highway

(Source: Courtesy of Wikipedia Commons and Beschreibung, Quelle, und Libenz, created by de:Benutzer;Grag, © n.d.)

The Precise Route of the Chinese Convoy

While the exact location of "Kulik Pass" cannot be determined, that of other landmarks can. "Little Pamir" is an area in the Afghan corridor south of Tajikistan. The Chinese convoys could have taken one of two routes. They may have left the Karakoram Highway north of Tashkurgan to enter Tajikistan at the Kulma Pass. The road then goes to Murgab, across Najzatash Pass to Alichur, and through Khargush pass to the Tajik-Afghan border. It subsequently follows that border to Lyangar, Ishkashim, and then on to the central part of Afghanistan. Farther along that road are Faizabad, Kunduz, and Khanabad (where the Chinese volunteers are known to have fought). (See Map 7.6.) This is probably the route taken by the Chinese convoy, because Kulik Pass is somewhere on the way to Lyangar.

> The road to China passes through the Kulik Pass of Little Pamir, with three wayside stations at Whakyir, Langar [Lyangar] and Whakan [Wakhan].[71]
>
> — Israeli Intell. Periodical, 28 September 2001

Passing through Tajik territory would have posed very little problem for the Chinese convoy. Tajikistan is friendly to the PRC. In the autumn of 2006, the two countries held joint military maneuvers.[72]

To keep from crossing Tajik territory, other Chinese convoys may have driven past Tashkurgan and then into the Pakistani occupied Northern Areas of Jammu-Kashmir through the Khunjerab Pass. For all practical purposes, this area is now part of Pakistan. At this point, the Karakoram Highway connects easily to Chitral and the ancient Afghan invasion route through the Kunar Valley. The Afghan extension of the Kunar valley road leads right to Jalalabad—the other destination of the Chinese reinforcements. (See Maps 7.7 and 7.8.)

Strange Goings-On in the Pamirs

The narrow strip of Afghan territory that stretches all the way to China is called the Wakhan Corridor. While often thought to be under Northern Alliance control, it may have other occupants.

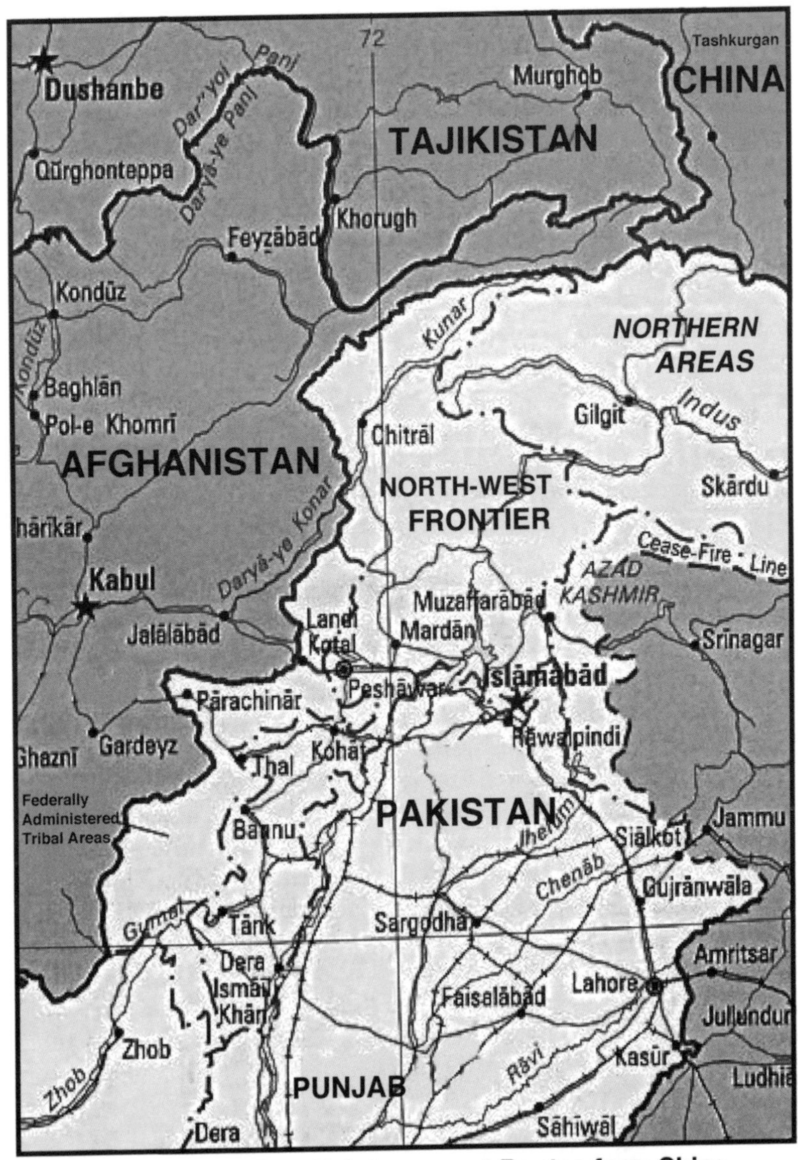

Map 7.6: The Two Reinforcement Routes from China
(Source: Courtesy of General Libraries, University of Texas at Austin, from their website, for map designator "pakistan_pol_1996.pdf")

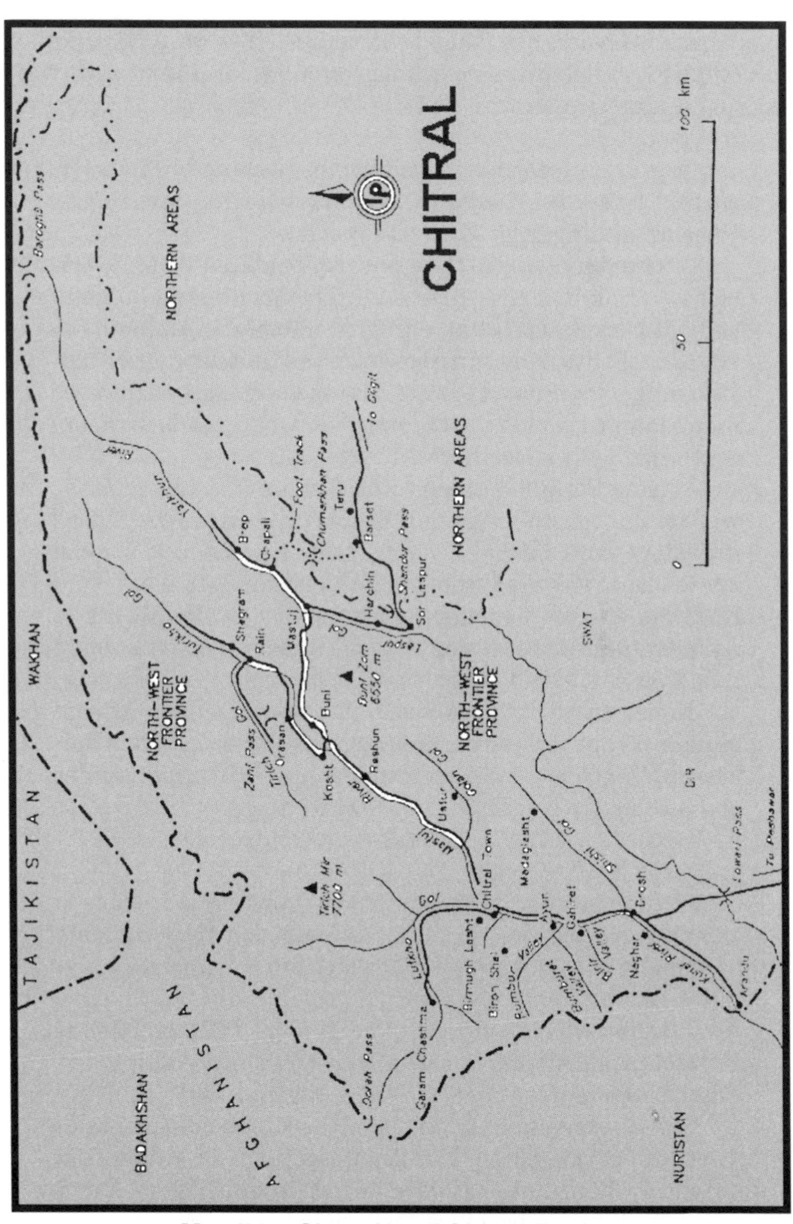

Map 7.7: Close-Up of Chitral Region

(Source: Courtesy of Pakistan and Karakoram Highway and Loney Planet, from Kyber Gateway map designator "chitraldistrict.gif," © 2005 by Loney Planet Publications)

Within that corridor lies the tail-end of the Pamir mountains. In a region sometimes called "Little Pamir" or the "Top of the World," there have been other unusual occurrences. (See Map 7.8.) Both of the following articles were written before the Chinese convoys were spotted in the region.

> It is . . . impossible to confirm his [Osama bin Laden's] current location. The Pamir scenario was first revealed by Russian intelligence. . . .
>
> . . . The bunker is in the sparsely populated Wakhan corridor—a Silk Road detour travelled by Marco Polo. Technically, it is in Badakhshan province, a finger of Afghanistan advancing between southern Tajkistan and northern Pakistan in the direction of China. The area—a high-altitude no man's land with peaks averaging 5,800 meters—is in theory controlled by the Northern Alliance. . . .
>
> During the jihad against the Soviets, the Little Pamir was totally controlled by the Red Army. The Soviets used it to store their intercontinental ballistic missiles. Osama knew about the area and the bunker through a bunch of Kazakhs and Kyrgyz who fought alongside the jihadis in the mid-1980's. But it was almost 10 years before he would take over the whole area.
>
> Northern Alliance sources confirm that the underground bunker complex is huge, and meant to be totally self-sufficient. There is a kind of extension near the Tajik border and a connection to a way out toward Xinjiang.[73]
>
> — *Asia Times on Line*, 4 October 2001

> If there is a part of the world that is still inaccessible to any but a special breed of mountain goats, it is the forbidding panhandle of Afghanistan's Pamir Mountain area known as Little Pamir.
>
> It is here that Osama bin Laden plans to make his last stand against American and allied forces, according to the intelligence sources of *DEBKA-Net-Weekly*.
>
> The approximate locations of his bases are known to American strategists. But reaching them is a daunting prospect. The basic U.S. intelligence working proposition is that winkling [drawing] the master terrorist out of his lair will not be achieved by going in with guns blazing and

cannons booming. Neither will it be served by propping up the Northern Alliance of the Afghan opposition, or even by ousting the Taliban rulers in Kabul. Bin Laden will still elude them [the Americans].

Therefore, the United States has posted a small force of Special Forces commandos–mostly Seals and Delta units–in the Tadjik center of Dzhartygumbez, no more than 35 miles from the Little Pamir panhandle, sending small squads in with orders to avoid engagements but searching for any clues to bin Laden's whereabouts. Some have already skirmished with outlying al-Qaida patrols and sentries scattered around the mountain valleys.

The U.S. crack troops are escorted by Russian elite forces intelligence officers–armed with maps of a Little Pamir site the Soviet Union occupied and abandoned in 1993–Russian troops permanently posted in Tadjikistan, and Tadjik mountain guides familiar with the smuggling trails between Russia, Afghanistan and China.

The Americans hope to cut the Pamir panhandle off, bottle bin Laden up in his retreat and then move in to capture him before the cruel mountain winter sets in. The first snow has already begun to fall. . . .

The few roads follow ancient caravan routes through mountain passes to China's northwestern Xinjiang province (formerly known as Chinese Turkestan) and south into Afghanistan's Hindu Kush of which the Pamirs are an extension.

The road to China passes through the Kulik Pass of Little Pamir, with three wayside stations at Whakyir, Langar [Lyangar] and Whakan [Wakhan]. At Whakyir, the main Afghan-China route branches north heading into Tadjikistan and reaching Dzhartygumbez, where the U.S. anti-terrorist force has set up its forward base. . . .

In 1993, the Russians abandoned the site and bin Laden took over. . . .

The retreat is self-supporting. The Russians left behind functioning electricity. Bin Laden and his handful of close aides, having laid in essential stores for many years, live off the land. His citadel has three fortresses: a set of chambers buried in the mountains south of the Sari Qul Valley; a

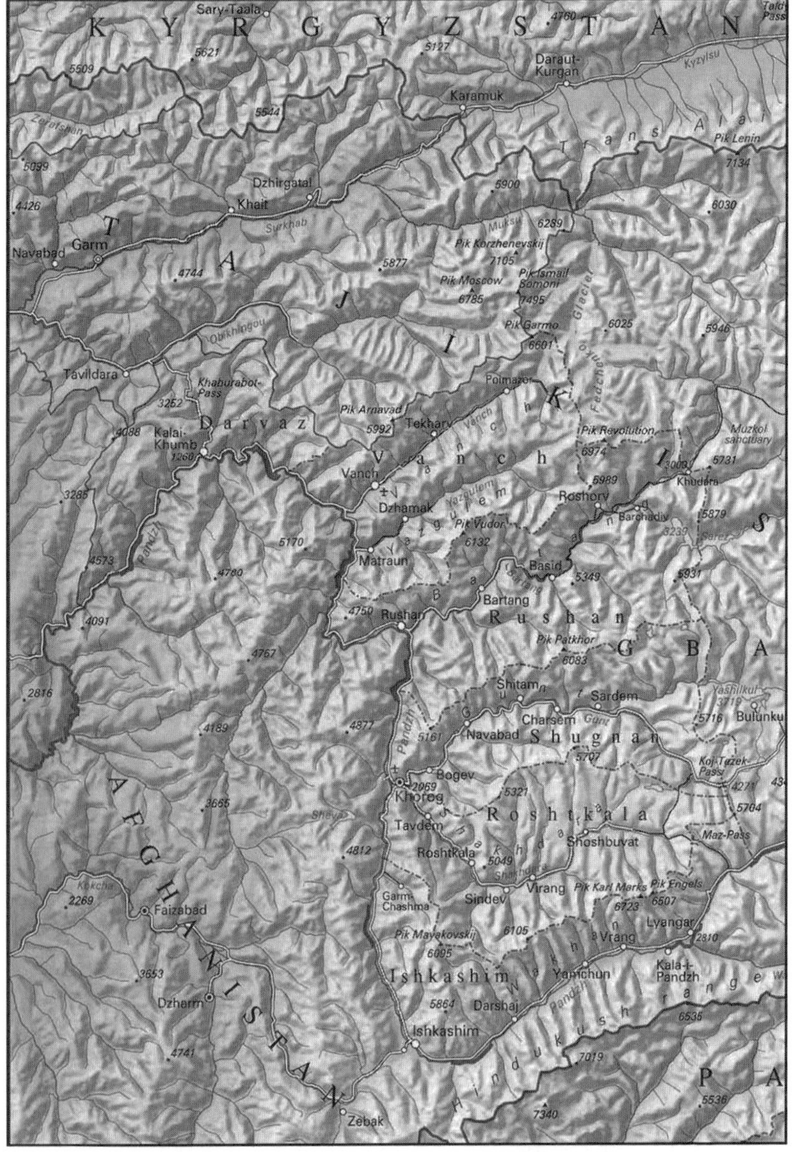

Map 7.8 (Left Side): Close-Up of Pamir Region

(Source: Courtesy of Markus Hauser and www.pamirs.org, from map designator "pamir-gr.jpg," © n.d. by Markus Hauser)

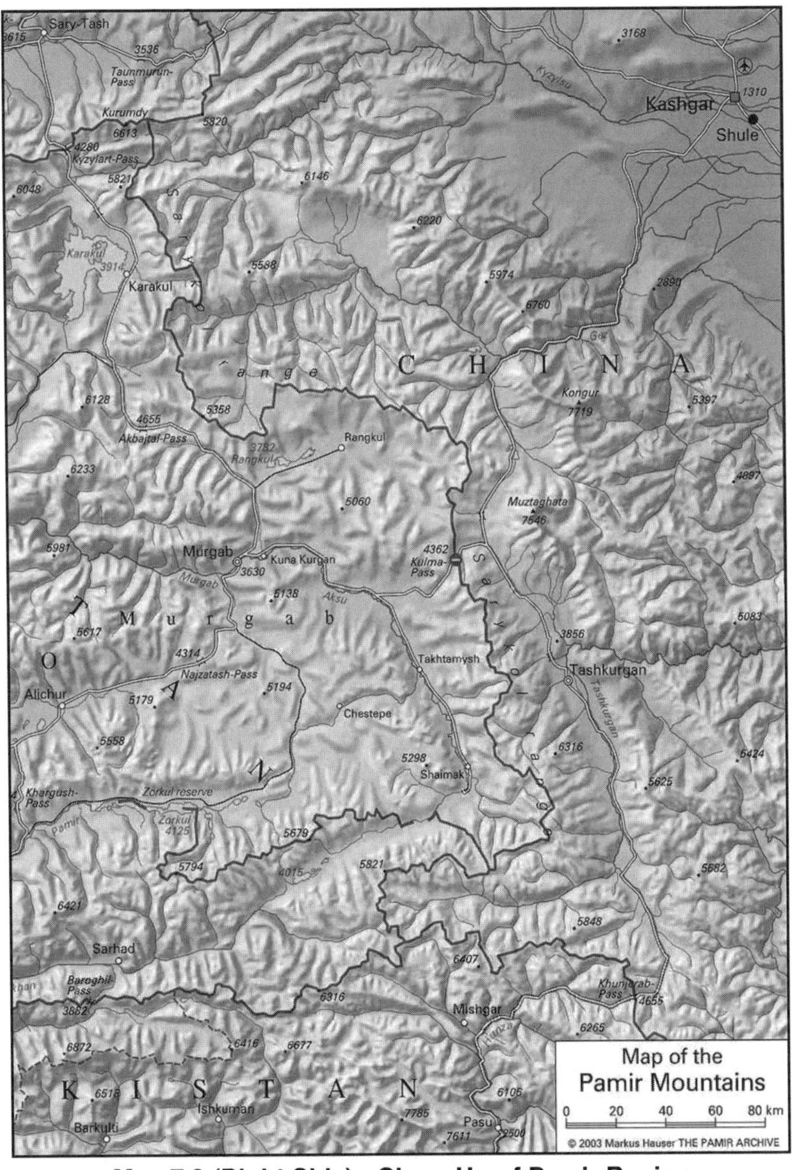

Map 7.8 (Right Side): Close-Up of Pamir Region

(Source: Courtesy of Markus Hauser and www.pamirs.org, from map designator "pamir-gr.jpg," © n.d. by Markus Hauser)

> site on the Tadjik frontier north of Buzai Gumabad; and a fort carved out of the mountains northeast of Wakhyir, the wayside station to China.
>
> He is protected by a number of outer defensive rings. Under 200 close followers occupy his main retreat; some 2,500-3,000 al-Qaida partisans, his eyes and ears, are distributed at key points of Little Pamir's mountain valleys; local fundamentalists, a wild lot whom no conqueror ever tamed, are the third ring, and, in the last resort, he can count on the ardent Moslem Uygar [Uighur] militants and ethnic Kazaks in Chinese Xinjiang.
>
> A cardinal problem for the United States in keeping bin Laden caged is China's refusal to cooperate in its war on terror. While the Russians have strung 25-30,000 troops along their frontier with Afghanistan, the Afghan-Chinese frontier into Xinjiang is wide open. Bin Laden can look forward to a helping hand there from the local Muslim radicals, over whom Beijing, in any case, has little control. China also appears to be ready to withdraw from the Bishbek Protocol signed last April by China, Russia, Kazakhstan, Tadjikistan and Kyrgizia setting up a combined multinational Rapid Reaction Collective Security Force to combat Islamic terrorist unrest in their territories, and headquartered in Bishbek, capital of Kyrgistan.[74]
>
> — Israeli Intell. Periodical, 28 September 2001

As the second of these articles was written a full week before the Chinese "volunteer" convoys were spotted in Little Pamir, one wonders if one or more might have been heading for bin Laden's hideout. What would have been their mission?

Why Was bin Laden's Lair So Near the Chinese Border?

One can almost see a pattern in Osama bin Laden's string of hideouts. The are positioned all along the ancient invasion route from China. He has been reported near the Chinese frontier northeast of Chilgit in occupied Jammu-Kashmir, inside the narrow Afghan corridor to China, and near Chitral where the invasion route enters the Kunar Valley of central Afghanistan. Whether or not China is actually supporting him, his actions seem to be somehow linked with

Chinese expansionism. Perhaps both threats should be handled at once. In this part of the world, the enemy of one's enemy is not necessarily one's friend.

The Paradoxical Revelation of June 2007

On 7 June 2007, America's former Anti-Terrorism Czar asserted that Iran's war by proxy had shifted from Iraq to Afghanistan.[75] He said the sophisticated EFPs (explosively formed projectiles) recently discovered in Afghanistan,[76] were associated with arms convoys from Iran.[77] Two of those convoys had just been intercepted by NATO forces and confirmed to have come from the Iranian Revolutionary Guard. Those convoys were carrying explosives and RPG rounds.[78] (The EFPs in Iraq are of Iranian origin.[79])

The report surprised students of the region. In the absence of a foreign occupier, Iran and Pakistan have always vied with each other over Afghanistan's future. Iran's principal proxy was the Northern Alliance,[80] and Pakistan's main player was the Taliban. Even during the Soviet-Afghan War, there was only limited cooperation between their respective *mujahideen* factions. Yet, the evidence of Iran now supporting the Taliban was conclusive.

One of three things had happened: (1) radical Sunni and Shiite factions had set a new precedent in their level of cooperation; (2) the Iranian arms were intended for Hekmatyar (though officially allied with the Taliban,[81] he has strong ties to Iran.[82]); or (3) a third, more powerful "behind-the-scenes" player had directed two of its less compatible minions to cooperate. In September, the answer came. U.S. military personnel were worried that Iran was sending munitions it had gotten from China to Afghanistan.[83]

Some Unpleasant Conclusions

Due to the wartime inaccessibility of the Malacca Straits, the PRC has been trying since its inception to establish overland oil routes to the Middle East through South Asia. To do so initially, it invaded one country (Tibet), fought a war with another (India), and encouraged a third (Pakistan) to seize territory belonging to the second. Its ties with Iran were strengthened by the fall of the Shah, and those with Pakistan by the rise of the Islamist dictators. Its only real impediment was Afghanistan, so it vehemently objected to the Russian takeover. In 1986, it built a road to Pakistan through Pakistani-occupied Indian territory. After the Russians were evicted from Afghanistan, it supported the Taliban and built roads there. Since the emergence of the pro-Iranian Karzai regime, the PRC has worked on an oil conduit from Herat to Peshwar through Bamian and on another to China through Tajikistan. That's because its investment in Iran's energy sector is expected to exceed 100 billion by 2030. The Tajik pipelines alone will carry 5% of the world's dwindling energy reserves to market.[84] Fearing that Karzai might become too pro-Western, China has continued to support the Taliban.

Previous chapters have described China's other, more recent attempts to bypass the Straits of Malacca. Within the framework of road, railway, and canal building, has appeared the unmistakable trend of nearby insurrection. The most glaring examples are in Nepal, India, and Thailand. While the insurrection in southern Thailand is ostensibly Islamic, the Chinese-backed Malayan Races Liberation Army did retreat to the same area years ago.

Despite repeated denials from the Chinese lobby, the Red Dragon is very obviously still on the prowl throughout south and southeast Asia. *Terrorist Trail* revealed a similar trend in Africa, and there is no shortage of evidence of this syndrome in the Western Hemisphere. To keep from being isolated on the world stage, America must find some way to "peacefully" limit the expansion of China's Co-Prosperity Sphere. That will take more than just tougher diplomacy.

How "Peacefully" to Contain the Dragon

To contain the Chinese dragon and its Islamist counterpart, U.S. military leaders must depart their comfort zone. As much as they might like the control associated with waging a conventional war, they must finally admit that another such war is unlikely to happen. As in Vietnam, Iraq, and Afghanistan, they will be facing other nation proxies masquerading as local rebels. Insurgency is a bottom-up problem that requires a bottom-up solution. That means smaller units doing more things. One of the most useful of those things in a 4GW context is establishing local security without alienating the public. That takes a way of operating that very closely resembles police work.

Part Two

A Viable Containment Strategy

"To subdue the enemy without fighting is the acme of skill."
— Sun Tzu

(Source: Constantine Menges, *China: The Gathering Threat* [Nashmville, TN: Nelson Current, 2005], p. 10)

8 What Hasn't Worked in the Past

- Why can't the U.S. military beat guerrillas more easily?
- How could China capitalize on this deficiency?

THE FUTILITY OF CURSORY SWEEPS & CORDONS

(Source: FMFM 6-4 [1978], p. 247)

What to Do about the Chinese and Islamist Expansion

From Part One's many details, one can see that the Chinese tiger and Islamist lion are both on the prowl throughout South Asia. Whether they are knowingly cooperating is not that important. Both types of revolution are growing, and both use the same methodologies. Any solution must therefore be predicated on a thorough understanding of the Maoist method and the evolution of small-unit tactics. Then, by looking at how well the West's counterinsurgency initiatives have fared in the past, one should be able to come up with better solutions for the future.

The Record of Western-Style Counterguerrilla Operations

Most Western tries to defeat guerrillas have followed the Western mind-set— "top-down" solutions for everything. That guerrillas constitute a "bottom up" problem has never been of much concern. Easy to see coming (and for guerrillas to evade), there have been four Western strategies: (1) battalion-sized sweeps; (2) regiment-sized cordons; (3) division-sized civil-affairs programs; and (4) corps-sized intelligence gathering. Seldom has any real effort been made to ensure local security, understand the Eastern thought process, or copy the insurgent's tactics. The effort has routinely been long on firepower and short on maneuver. A few of the West's counterguerrilla initiatives have succeeded through enough meanness to overcome its tactical indifference, but most have simply been lost and then blamed on extenuating circumstances. To make the point, some of the largest counterguerrilla campaigns of the 20th Century will be briefly considered. As Mao has become the recognized authority on guerrilla warfare, most of these campaigns involved Maoist tactics. In almost every case, the rebels were greatly outnumbered by Western forces.

At the turn of the 19th Century, the much-vaunted British army had all it could handle with the Boer militia in southern Africa. While the Boers were good at stalking and infiltration on offense, and alternately manning parts of hidden trenchlines on defense, their tactics were relatively simple. Their only standoff capability was from long-range rifle and artillery fire. After their avenues of resupply were severed, the Boers shifted to guerrilla warfare. To beat them, the British put Boer families in concentration camps and built barbed-wire-enclosed blockhouses along the major routes of communication.[1] Lacking the tactics and firepower to successfully assault those blockhouses, most Boer guerrillas finally opted for conjugal visits.

By 1900, American troops were embroiled a largely guerrilla Philippine-American War. Though short lived, it was to take almost 5,000 U.S. lives.[2] In part, it was fought in the Islamic areas of the Sulu Archipelago.[3] After WWI, U.S. Marine detachments successfully outposted towns in Haiti and Nicaragua during the counterguerrilla "Banana Wars."

With the end of WWII, there was a spike in the numbers of guerrilla uprisings. As almost all were Communist inspired/supported, many have been associated with the birth of the PRC. First, there was the Filipino Huk Rebellion. Economic reform played as big a role as military pressure in defusing it by 1951.[4]

About the same time, the British encountered a Communist insurrection in Malaya. First, they moved many of the half million Chinese "squatters" into 400 carefully monitored villages. Then, they conducted sweeps that forced remnants of the MLRA into southern Thailand.[5] Their most effective strategy may have been dispatching tiny tracker teams after each terrorist incident. Within the confines of the Malay Peninsula jungle, those teams could sufficiently chastise the perpetrators without disturbing the people.[6]

Then, there were the Viet Minh. How they were able secretly to build a 600-mile road from their Chinese supply depot into Dien Bien Phu in 1954 still boggles the Western mind. They did it from the "bottom up" with thousands of shovel-wielding and tree-limb-tying coolies.[7] In essence, the French had tried the old-British-blockhouse routine against someone who knew something about tactics. (By this time, most Eastern armies had acknowledged the advances in tactical technique by the loser of WWI.) Then, in inimitable Asian fashion, the Viet Minh simply tunneled close enough to the French positions to run squad-sized "stormtrooper" assaults.[8]

The early 1960's saw a rash of Communist uprisings throughout Southeast Asia and Africa. Veterans of the Vietnam War remember cursory sweeps, grandiose cordons, and a whole lot of defending. (See Figure 8.1.) During those sweeps and cordons, most of the enemy escaped. They did so by hiding beneath the sweeps (below ground) or exfiltrating the cordons. Early in the war, friendly farmers were moved into fortified villages. Then, for a while, existing villages were protected by Marine Combined Action Platoons (CAPs). Without the distraction of an officer in charge, each depended solely on the cooperation between an American rifle squad and its local counterpart. At least one of the U.S. squad leaders was assassinated,[9] but there is no record of any CAP platoon ever being overrun. Nor did this brilliant experiment in community service ever end in atrocity. As had Carlson's Raiders in WWII, the CAP platoons simply established too much of a precedent for a "top-down" bureaucracy to tolerate. Systems that primarily aspire toward 2nd-Generation [firepower-dominated] Warfare (2GW) are largely predicated on everyone doing the same kinds of things. Anything different—however useful—tends to go away.

After China and Russia went their separate ways, Africa became heavily contested by their guerrilla proxies. Soon to become that continent's most effective counterguerrilla fighters were the Selous Scouts of Rhodesia. Well aware of the disastrous record of the Portuguese in Angola and Mozambique, the Scouts decided to do something different. Through the political pressure to take minimal casualties and the economic pressure to use the "latest" equipment, the Portuguese had become obsessed with "force protection" and motorized columns. From the guerrillas' perspective, they were simply passive and road-bound. So, the Selous Scouts did almost the opposite—sending tiny assault teams far afield on foot. Because those teams had been well schooled in unconventional warfare, few were lost. Over six years of existence, the Selous Scouts suffered only 40 of their own people killed while directly or indirectly accounting for two thirds of all guerrilla casualties.[10] Those

Figure 8.1: GIs Now Spend Too Much Time on Defense

(Source: FM 5-103 [1985], p. 4-5)

Scouts started out as trackers and ended up as undercover guerrillas (in "pseudo-operations"). Their fight with the Communist proxies was eventually lost, but not through insufficient tactics or initiative. Their government's apartheid policy made it too hard to capture the hearts and minds of people oppressed by colonialists. Plus, the Scouts had never heard of 4GW. Their tactics were so lethal that their foes easily claimed atrocity.

While U.S. history books seldom admit it, southern Africa was essentially ceded to Chinese and Russian proxies at the end of Mao's "Cultural Revolution" (in the late 1970's). No one seemed to connect the Red Guards that ZANLA (Zimbabwe African National Liberation Army) talked about in its account of the Selous Scouts' Nyadzonya/Pungwe incident with Mao's Revolution.[11] Through a cursory attempt at "top-down" democracy, the U.N. and Britain did not impart enough learning and security at the village/neighborhood level to permit a fair election. Unable to deal with the lies and threats of local commissars, the people in each place voted for Communist candidates. While most of the countries in southern Africa today are theoretically democratic, most have only one viable party. Zimbabwe has become almost totally dependent on China.[12]

While America's fate in Iraq and Afghanistan has yet to be fully ascertained, one can safely venture a few observations. Most of the sweeps and cordons in both locations have failed to meet expectations. Within a 4GW urban setting, they easily do more harm than good. They destroy infrastructure, intimidate residents, and fuel political opposition. Early on, there were more productive initiatives from individual American units in both theaters. Many tried—with limited resources—to rebuild local infrastructure or provide basic services. A few even dismounted their vehicles to outpost towns and neighborhoods. Unfortunately, all still had to endure the vast reams of uninterpreted intelligence from headquarters.

By 2007 on Jolo in the southwestern Philippines, a U.S. Special Forces contingent had successfully combined training and advisory duties with local aid projects. A new coastal road and mobile clinics made Jolo's Muslim population more welcoming than it had been during the occupation of the Philippine-American War.[13]

Within the connecting threads of those examples must lie a more viable counterguerrilla strategy than what Western armies can generally manage. Perhaps, by critically analyzing their four traditional strategies, one can zero in on which threads to pursue.

Intelligence Gathering

As in Vietnam, most battlefield intelligence in Iraq and Afghanistan is collected electronically by higher headquarters and then fed—without much interpretation—directly to the field battalions. From the standpoint of the enemy's tactics, thought process, and deception, it is raw data. No attempt has been made to weed out enemy disinformation. With all of the advances in electronic intelligence gathering, each battalion now has to deal with a virtual flood of conflicting information. Its one hastily trained intelligence officer can do little more than sort varieties. As a noninfantryman, he or she generally has no prior knowledge of Eastern infantry tactics or ruses. As a result, his or her valiant attempt to interpret the raw data is of little use to the platoons and squads in contact with the enemy.

Each company's NCOs would stand a better chance of determining what a crafty foe was up to. If the particulars of enemy maneuver and mind-set were additionally part of their formal training, they could gather their own opposition insights. What they saw on patrol would become a type of "human intelligence" at a time when spies have been virtually eliminated. Eastern armies are able to operate from the bottom up because they use lead squads for "recon pull." The more squads they allow to operate semi-independently, the more human intelligence they collect.

Miscreant Apprehension

The countless thousands of battalion-sized sweeps in Vietnam occasionally uncovered a weapons cache or hastily vacated camp. Whenever they stumbled upon a hidden infiltration route, they generated a firefight. But, overall, they netted too little of the enemy's supplies and reinforcements to forestall final defeat. The cordons were equally ineffective. They sometimes trapped a rear party, but the parent unit generally lived to fight another day. Perhaps the best example is what happened at the Hue City Citadel. During the nights of 21, 22, and 23 February 1968, no less than a "division minus" of North Vietnamese regulars successfully exfiltrated the allied cordon, taking their wounded and weapons with them.[14]

Western military leaders have difficulty grasping how this was accomplished. To escape the sweeps, the enemy simply hid below ground or in trees. With enough of a diversion from their rear party, they could also escape an ever-tightening cordon that way. Such things are, after all, part of their *moshuh nanren* heritage (the *ninja's* Chinese predecessor).[15] To escape the cordon around the Citadel, the enemy sent individual squads out at half-hour intervals. After swimming the Perfume River in the shadow of a bridge, they squirmed through the sewer ditches of southern Hue until reaching a ridgeline that other units had kept open. Concurrently, the wily foe sent casualty-laden porters out to the east. First, they moved through a hidden tunnel in the wall, then across a partially submerged bamboo bridge, and finally through several miles of recently constructed (and still controlled) trench.[16] (Both evolutions will be discussed in more detail later.) Central to the whole success of this operation was the enemy's willingness to decentralize control and widely disperse his underarmed personnel.

A lesson of Vietnam that is still true today is how hard the guerrilla is to catch in his own back yard. In essence, he must be drawn out of his normal area of operations and into a trap. Or he must be tracked down in much the same way a policeman looks for a criminal. The British had great success tracking terrorists in Malaya. The resulting dispersion of effort was their key to success.

Civil Affairs Programs

Often, headquarters-organized civil affairs programs make little impact on each separate community. They attempt instead to improve some aspect of a whole region's centralized infrastructure (like its electricity grid). When the center of that grid is predictably sabotaged, no one benefits from the original effort. Or an attempt is made to move all supporters into a fortified zone, thereby leaving their original property unprotected. A somewhat varied, and less grandiose, effort from which every community could immediately benefit would have more effect. But then, that would take decentralization of control and simultaneous representation in many places

All Three Would Be Better Served by More Dispersal of Effort

Whether intelligence gathering, miscreant apprehension, or civil affairs, more could be accomplished at the local level by tiny detachments. Their contribution to local security would also help with the more idealistic goals of counterinsurgency: (1) hearts and minds; (2) fair elections; and (3) freedom from fear.

In a 4GW conflict, the most strategically important ground is the village or neighborhood. It cannot be won by motorized patrol or smart bomb. It must be discreetly outposted. In most, there will be concurrent activity in all four aspects of 4GW—martial, political, economic, and psychological. The key to dominating that activity is again local security. For example, if that neighborhood is being terrorized by a *Hezbollah*-like-element, its citizens will be less likely to oppose that element's electoral candidate. And if that neighborhood becomes too restive, an allied assault may damage its economic infrastructure. The best way to provide some semblance of local security is a U.S.-anchored CAP platoon. The implication is clear. To stand any chance of winning a 4GW conflict, America will need squads with enough skill to operate alone.

With advanced tactical techniques (to include urban escape methods), the American squad within each CAP platoon could safely contribute to all four aspects of 4GW. Its corpsman/medic could provide medical assistance. Members with construction experience could rebuild infrastructure. With a little instruction in urban mantracking and law enforcement, some of the GIs could help their indigenous police counterparts to identify and arrest local miscreants.

The villages of Vietnam and neighborhoods of Baghdad share the same scourge. Each contains a tiny group of brutal extremists (cell) that wants all residents to obey their agenda. To win either war, each of the thousands of village/neighborhood cells must be countered by a tiny Western contingent. With a little unconventional warfare training, U.S. troops could fill that role. The community focus has been an integral part of the Islamists' so-far-undefeated formula. Of late, the Chinese army has been fielding far more people who are specifically trained for this type of mission.

Countering China's Less Obvious Threat

An astonishing 20% of the PRC's ground forces are now martial-arts-qualified special operators.[17] The PLA currently maintains an active force of 2.25 million but only 1.6 million are ground forces.[18] With a PLA reserve of 1.2-1.5 million and 13 million males reaching mandatory-service age every year, the ground force could quickly grow.[19] If the 320,000 existing special operators are qualified in *ninja*-like obscuration, squad assault, and light-infantry instruction, then the West has a real problem. (The 100,000 special operators in the Light Infantry Training Guidance Bureau of China's closest ally appear to be well qualified in all three.[20])

Any new Cold War with China must be largely handled at the local level by equally well trained U.S. special operators and infantrymen. They will never exist in sufficient numbers until the U.S. military acknowledges the limitations of its current training methodology. Within the retired community lies sufficient expertise in such matters, but organizational pride has thus far precluded its utilization.

While U.S. special operators have been tasked with the training of indigenous forces, most have too little light-infantry experience to accomplish such a mission. For a very good reason, they have no knowledge of advanced assault and escape technique. In high-intensity warfare, America's special operators are used only to locate opposition targets for subsequent attack by supporting arms or heavy infantry.[21] In other words, they have been largely relegated to a reconnaissance role.

Much Depends on the Meaning of "Distributive Operations"

The concept of "Distributive Operations" (those in which squads operate alone) has been recognized for years as the next step in the U.S. Marine Corps' tactical growth. They are not only the best way to counter insurgents, but also to take minimal frontline casualties in conventional war. Most strongpoint-matrix defenses and multiple-penetration assaults are based on what individual squads can accomplish alone. The advent of shoulder-fired thermobaric weapons makes routine dispersion of the U.S. rifle company mandatory.

Because the American military has traditionally opted for firepower over surprise, Quantico and Benning tend to view "Distributive Operations" as flooding a battlefield with tiny groups of forward observers. Because those groups also know something about reconnaissance and conventional infantry maneuvers, they are expected to survive. Such an expectation might be a realistic at Fort Irwin or 29 Palms, but it is not in Lebanon or on the Korean Peninsula. Israel's decision to pull out of southern Lebanon seven years ago was based on the decimation of one of its naval special-operations teams. All the riflemen of China's ally receive training in both conventional and unconventional warfare. In addition, each of its companies has two or three "Light Infantry Training Guidance Bureau," *ninja*-qualified commandos attached. There, they function as full-time tracking, assault, and training cadre.

Thus, for the U.S. infantry to pursue "Distributive Operations," it must first give its riflemen more light-infantry skill. Those riflemen must be able to move around unobserved, hide in plain sight, and escape an encirclement without the help of supporting arms. Neither the Corps' reconnaissance elements, nor America's best special operators currently have enough of those kinds of skills. The Navy's brave Sea, Air, and Land (SEAL) personnel, who lost their lives in the Kunar region of Afghanistan a couple of years ago, did so because they were unable to move around unobserved. Then, they were unable to disguise their trail. Then, they were unable to hide inside, or break out of, an enemy cordon. Like reconnaissance teams, most special operations contingents are never expected to assault a prepared enemy position (one with protective barbed wire, mines, and interlocking machinegun fire). They therefore lack enough infiltration and assault technique (e.g., the German "stormtrooper" method of WWI) to escape an enemy encirclement.

To move forward on "Distributive Operations," the U.S. infantry will need a "bottom-up" training method—one in which squad members collectively develop their own tactical techniques through field experimentation. Until Benning and Quantico recognize this, their squads (no matter how heavily armed) won't be able to safely step outside their parent unit's protective umbrella. Through bottom-up training, squad members develop better initiative, tactical technique, and decision-making ability. The doctrinally driven, standardized approach to training will never produce squads that can operate alone. Nor will it permit the most useful definition of "Distributive Operations."

New Islamist Tactics Are Immune to Electronic Surveillance

During the summer of 2006, an Islamic fundamentalist movement successfully thwarted an invasion by the region's most powerful nation. The Israeli army is nearly as "high-tech" as its U.S. counterpart. Yet, throughout its 33-day war in southern Lebanon, Israeli troops "rarely saw the enemy until they were shot at."[22] *Hezbollah* made good use of remotely controlled cameras and firing devices.[23] But its real secret to success was as old as the battle for Iwo Jima—below-ground fortifications and communications.[24]

Israel's high-tech surveillance and weaponry were no match for *Hezbollah's* low-tech network of underground tunnels.[25]
— *Washington Post,* 11 September 2006

The enemy in Afghanistan has found another way to thwart advanced electronic surveillance. His soldiers enter the country individually or in pairs through Pakistani border crossings like Charman, Badini, and Torkham.[26] After blending with the normal flow of traffic for two or three days, some end up at one of the many subterranean waystations from the Soviet-Afghan War. Others muster in groups of 200-300 at training camps in the Afghan mountains. Each camp is near one of the many arms depots established at the end of the Taliban regime.[27] As soon as the fighters are trained, they disperse into dozens of vehicles for the trip to their objective.[28] For a particularly well-watched objective, they infiltrate on foot. As many as 400 fighters have been involved in attacks against police stations and army outposts.[29] One suspects platoon-sized elements working in concert. A small platoon could elude satellite-borne thermal imaging by simply entering a house with a mud roof. The Taliban fighters in Ghazni and Zabul provinces are known to operate in groups of 20-25 men.[30] Once the attack is completed, the members of each unit again widely disperse to prevent being targeted by Western supporting arms.[31]

Iraq Provides Another Insight into the Future

In Iraq, just as in Vietnam, the most impressive firepower the U.S. could muster has failed to quell insurrection. However "smart," shells and bombs still damage infrastructure, resupply the foe with explosive, alienate the population, and discredit the local law-enforcement community.

Thus, while countering Communist and Islamist expansion, U.S. leaders cannot discourage enemy explosions with those of their own. No amount of supporting arms—however good for morale or the U.S. economy—will ever stop IEDs and suicide bombers. Military historians report that, if anything, bombardment tends to induce the other two maladies. America and France had just pouring tons of huge shells and bombs into the hills above Beirut in 1983 when the Marine Barracks was truck-bombed. In the low-intensity wars of the 21st Century, the most-advanced U.S. planes, tanks, and artillery pieces will make no more difference than the "best military hardware of its day" did in Vietnam.

Neither will the latest advances in electronic intelligence gathering. By swimming in two's and three's through a population, the enemy has discovered how to negate their effect. What he has achieved through dispersion and decentralized control should give U.S. planners a hint on how to stop it.

While the scope of the expansion now approximates an unconventionally fought WWIII, it must be handled piecemeal as if it were an undeclared Cold War. Otherwise, the unimaginable could too easily happen. The heavy work must go to America's infantry squads. As in WWII, each must be ready to assault a prepared enemy position. Unlike in WWII, it may have do that single-handedly one moment and, in the next, assist local authorities with miscreant apprehension. In essence, the U.S. squad of the future must be both assault and police qualified. While decidedly inconvenient, this particular truth is no longer negotiable. If—like after Vietnam—it is again ignored, America will become an embattled island with little influence over the rest of the world. In an age where rogue nations possess nuclear-tipped intercontinental missiles, this is not a viable foreign policy.

Mantracking Not That Different from Police Work

Among the most useful of the light-infantry skills is mantracking—following a foe's footprints and other sign along the ground. While most U.S. infantrymen do not currently have this ability, it would definitely help them to more safely close with the enemy. Just by looking at the ground, they could tell when their adversary was near. Mantracking has many of the same attributes as a criminal investigation. As their goals are similar, so can be their methods. The next chapter will determine to what extent more knowledge in police procedure might help the contemporary American infantryman.

9 The Law Enforcement Dimension

- How can a police effort limit revolutionary expansionism?
- What does law enforcement have to do with 4GW?

FOR "LOCAL SECURITY," LAWS MUST BE OBEYED

(Source: FM 19-95B1/2 [1978], cover; DA Pam 550-175 [1989], p. xxxvii)

Countering the New Dynamics of Revolution

Armed Communist uprisings have had little trouble shifting into the political arena. Several did so in the 1980's throughout southern Africa, and others are doing so today in South Asia. "Political wings" of Maoist factions have already accomplished the following: (1) assumed control of Calcutta; (2) been the first ruling party of Bangladesh; (3) joined the ruling coalition in Sri Lanka; and (4) arranged a full partnership with the Nepalese government.

Islamist revolts can also easily transition into politics. Sunni fundamentalists have won elections in Sudan and Palestine, while

Shiite fundamentalists are well on their way to controlling the governments of Lebanon and Iraq. True democracy can only be generated from the bottom up. Without enough local security in the villages and neighborhoods of a restive nation, its prospective voters will be too susceptible to coercion.

Local security involves more than just repelling armed attack. It involves locating and disciplining law breakers. Even trustworthy local police could not handle the former. And local militias cannot be allowed to help with the latter. Thus, a tiny Western contingent could make all the difference. If that contingent were skilled enough to survive without ever having to resort to bombardment, its members could pass for foreign aid workers in the law enforcement sector. What better way could there be to play down their presence? They would no longer be perceived as occupiers

To fill this role, U.S. infantry squads must be as well trained in police procedure as they are in unconventional warfare. Then, by anchoring CAP platoons, they could make a strategic contribution to the effort. Without political stability, there can be no victory in a 4GW conflict. That has been the unpleasant lesson of Iraq.

> Fourth generation war is marked by non-national networked entities who provide too few targets for bombing to have any effect other than the effect of creating more recruits for their ranks. 4GW forces thrive on devastation and insecurity of the people; increasing the devastation and insecurity, as in with most military approaches, is counterproductive in that they do nothing more than create greenhouses for terror. What are needed . . . are small near-autonomous units of truly light infantry that can play the role of police force rather than occupiers in the greenhouses of terror. It requires a military paradigm shift away from centralized control and micromanagement.[1]

Would U.S. Military Procedure Work in an American City?

What if someone set off an IED in New York City? Would the New York City Police Department (NYPD) do the following: (1) immediately trample all over the detonation site; (2) make no attempt to look for the shovel and other implantation tools; (3) not collect bomb fragments or residue; (4) not search for where the lookout and trigger man respectively stood; and (5) not scour the area for foot- and finger-prints? Upon learning from an unknown bystander of "who in the neighborhood might be sympathetic to the bomber," would they further do the following: (1) kick in the door of the house believed to be that of the suspect; (2) brashly interrogate any males present though women and children are clearly terrified; and then (3) take those males into custody in a country where such trips are often permanent? If the NYPD operated that way, there would be an armed uprising in Brooklyn.

Add to that the sectarian divide between Sunni and Shiite that the U.S. has helped to widen in Iraq, and standard U.S. counterinsurgency procedure becomes a recipe for disaster. It's a recipe for disaster because it makes too little an attempt to obey civil law. As such, it alienates the population and further polarizes U.S. military personnel. It may comply with military law and even the Geneva Conventions, but it generally ignores the parameters of civil law. In a place at the brink of civil war, both sides will try to get the occupier to do their bidding. Shiites will falsely accuse Sunnis and the other way around. Thus, a tip from a lone bystander is not sufficient justification for a full scale, military raid on a local resident's house. That's the reason for search warrants in New York City. There, a legal expert has to be convinced that there is sufficient evidence to warrant the intrusion of privacy. That evidence usually comes from several corroborating sources—to include physical evidence from the scene of the crime.

And so the endless cycle repeats itself. Order-oriented U.S. service personnel receive a nebulous intelligence report that *al-Qaeda* is about to attack again. Fully motorized, they roll like sitting ducks out of their cozy base and into their assigned neighborhood. The inevitable happens. They quickly destroy or never look for the physical evidence that would have led them to who actually did it. With their strong-arm approach, they further alienate the local population. And then, they return to their bases more convinced than ever that any Iraqi who won't fully answer their questions is an insurgent sympathizer.

Bystanders won't always level with NYPD detectives either. That's because they are scared of retribution from the crime's perpetrator(s). But the detectives don't immediately come to the conclusion that everyone that remains silent is aiding and abetting a criminal. Where local citizens are hesitant to help, they simply dig further for physical evidence or other leads. That's the way professional policing is accomplished. The civilian is always given the benefit of the doubt. Until U.S. military units adopt some of the time-honored procedures of professional police work, they will continue to have trouble quelling insurgency.

U.S. Policemen Already Operate in a 4GW Setting

To succeed, U.S. law enforcement agencies must pay close attention to the sensibilities of local populations. They attempt to minimize the political, economic, and psychological fallout of every case. Many of their methods of investigation and apprehension would be of great help to the GIs who must anchor a CAP platoon. Tacticians they are not (e.g., Waco). By neither are they naive enough to think that valuable leads can be obtained by coercion.

To function effectively within a CAP platoon, the members of each U.S. squad would have to undergo something of a paradigm shift. Instead of "those who close with and destroy the enemy," they would have to see themselves as "protectors of the weak," and "public servants." No longer would all suspects be perceived as potential targets.

To survive alone as police augment, each group of fourteen GI's would have to master some of the lesser known light-infantry skills—e.g., sensory perception and urban escape. Too much armament and technology makes that much less likely to seem important. With the constantly rehearsed techniques of a *ninja,* no GI would ever be surprised again, much less captured.

Police Goals

As a matter of normal procedure, U.S. police personnel protect not only innocent bystanders, but also the criminals themselves. This law enforcement *mantra* just happens to coincide with one of the best synopses of battlefield morality ever written. Contrary to what U.S. troops are told in training, the name of the game is killing as few enemy soldiers as possible. That's because peace is the ultimate objective.

> The hypothesis of legitimate defense, which never concerns an innocent but always and only an unjust aggressor, must respect the principle that moralists call the principium inculpatae tutelae (the principle of nonculpable defense). In order to be legitimate, the "defense" must be carried out in a way that causes the least damage and, if possible, saves the life of the aggressor.[2]
>
> — Pope John Paul II

How Police Procedure Accomplishes Those Goals

Policemen are not allowed to preemptively fire at a suspect. Assumed be innocent, he cannot be harmed until he makes some life-threatening gesture toward the arresting officer or another person. In those rare instances where he is known to be a convicted murderer, he can be fired upon while running away.

The most successful policemen never maltreat detainees. They have learned that any information obtained through forceful interrogation is generally a fabrication. The idea that the suspect is innocent until proven guilty shapes their every action. To punish the evil-doer, they must first prove beyond a reasonable doubt that he is guilty. That takes far more investigative effort that most infantrymen are allowed.

Adding Criminal Investigation to the Role of Infantryman

The U.S. Army has a whole branch dedicated to criminal investigation. Its Criminal Investigations Division (USACIDC, or simply CID) is manned by active-duty Army personnel. It could easily train or augment Army infantrymen tasked with a CAP platoon mission.

Unfortunately, the Marine Corps has no such internal criminal investigative capability. Its serious offenses are solved by the Naval Investigative Service (NIS). As the NIS is manned by civilians, it could not successfully augment a CAP platoon.[3] Nor is any active-duty Marine military policeman (MP) qualified to teach CAP platoon members about criminal investigation. That means all Marine infantrymen will need additional training on this subject. They and their buddies will be unable to pacify a neighborhood without monitoring its illegitimate activities. As a side benefit, they should receive more support from the residents they have risked so much to protect.

10 A Thorough Investigation

- Why must GIs be able to differentiate between sects?
- How can jailing every suspect hurt a 4GW effort?

COLLECTING/CORRELATING MANY TINY DETAILS

(Source: FMFM 2-1 [1980], p. 13-1)

A Somewhat Different Perspective

While a Western military commander seeks friendly morale and enemy discomfort, a criminal investigator looks only for truth. He cares not if his investigation shows fault with his parent command. In a 4GW setting, the precise assessment of small matters holds more significance than it did in the past. Now the action is so disjointed and free wheeling that anything not working must be immediately discontinued. That cannot happen where commanders are hesitant to acknowledge any error that might demoralize their troops or impugn a superior. To win at 4GW, the troops must be able to do more than just follow orders and fire their weapons. While widely dispersed and under decentralized control, they must assume full responsibility for their own actions. In a media-scrutinized setting, they will no longer be able to attribute their excesses to following orders. Any deviation, however slight, from generally accepted moral behavior will become a strategic embarrassment for the country.

While many U.S. military leaders feel that their enlisted personnel only behave morally in war because of the control they wield, this was not the experience of one Vietnam-era company commander.[1] His troops regularly displayed more moral restraint with regard to probable enemy sympathizers than he or his battalion commander thought necessary. It was peer pressure that held the morally challenged among them in check. Thus, a more prevalent investigative attitude within the U.S. military would do no harm to its cohesion.

More on the 2GW Syndrome

To overwhelm the opposition, 2nd-Generation Warfare (2GW) depends largely on bombardment. Its proponents make only a cursory effort to distinguish combatants from other indigenous personnel. The Japanese had thousands of Korean forced laborers on Iwo Jima,[2] yet most U.S. casualty totals make no mention of their fate. That the record keepers had trouble differentiating a Korean hostage from a Japanese soldier probably means that the troops did too.

Life was so cheap in Asia in those days that the oversight may have had little impact on the outcome of the war. But in Islamic countries, every noncombatant fatality brings with it a blood feud that can last for generations. That is why the U.S. military's high-tech, albeit 2GW, approach to counterinsurgency has so far failed in Iraq and Afghanistan.

To make matters worse, the GIs of today have no more insight into the heritage of their multi-ethnic foes than their grandfathers did. Returnees from the wars in Iraq and Afghanistan refer to their fleeting nemesis only as the "haji" or "muj." Most have no idea of the subtle differences between Sunni and Shiite, much less Imami and Ismaili Shiite, or Mustalian and Nazari Ismaili.[3] They have never been told that to be a good Salafist, fundamentalist Sunni Wahhabis (like bin Laden) must cooperate with fundamentalist Shiites (like Iran's Khamenei, Lebanon's Nasrallah, or Iraq's al -Sadr).[4] How, then, can they sort through all the disinformation to determine who their most probable attacker will be? Not knowing which sects pioneered suicide bombing and improvised explosive devices (IEDs), they will have less chance of finding their fabricators. Some detective-technique knowledge would help to bridge that gap.

4GW Too Widely Dispersed for Traditional Combat

In a worldwide War on Terror, each IED explosion, suicide bombing, and assassination must be initially treated as a local crime. Like a neighborhood/village police detail, the resident CAP platoon should first look into each incident. Within the context of that CAP platoon's own intelligence gathering effort lies the best chance to determine the perpetrator and his motive. Its members would know if strangers had entered their area (or if residents had left).

First, the platoon closes off the scene of the incident to pedestrian and vehicular traffic. (This is done with yellow crime scene tape or its equivalent.) After interviewing onlookers and sweeping the enclosure for clues, it determines whether the incident was an attack on the Coalition or otherwise motivated. As a host nation becomes more volatile, there is more chance of organized crime and civil war. Any number of things can trigger a shooting or explosion. While every execution-style killing might look like an attack against a government sympathizer, many will be the result of drug deals, gang feuds, extortion, and passion. Both the Communists and Islamists have learned how to capitalize on chaos. Their new method of war is to create so many incidents that Coalition forces can't react to them all. As they try, they uncover strategic targets. Instead of dispatching an armored column to each occurrence, Coalition headquarters must allow local outposts to respond initially. When all incidents are first referred to the local CAP platoon, more of the Coalition's manpower will be available to protect dams, electricity generators, fuel depots, and the like. How much the CAP platoon knows about police work will largely determine whether or not it can successfully assume such a role. Of particular importance will be their knowledge of basic criminal investigative procedure. The whole idea is to solve as many problems as possible at the local level, so the nation as a whole doesn't descend into anarchy.

How the Rules of Evidence Apply to Detention

Without enough evidence to reasonably suspect someone of a crime, he should not be arrested (or shot for not stopping when told). Nor should his front door be kicked in, his family terrified, or his watchdog neutralized. There are several categories of evidence: (1) physical, (2) testimonial, (3) documentary, and (4) behavioral.[5] Within each are varying degrees of credibility. For example, an eyewitness account carries more weight than a hearsay recollection. Unless the suspect has been apprised of his Miranda rights (not to incriminate himself), his own comments are inadmissible in a U.S. court. That's because people will attest to almost anything under enough duress. They can also be tricked into saying things that look bad out of context. Thus, all military interrogations must be conducted under some semblance of civility, whether "lives are at stake" or not. If less effort had been dedicated to grilling Guantanamo detainees and more to infiltrating *al-Qaeda*-affiliated organizations, the War on Terror would be a lot closer to being won right now.

The Collection of Physical Evidence

Physical evidence ordinarily consists of body materials (e.g., blood), objects (e.g., bullets), and impressions (e.g., fingerprints). But it can be any tangible article that tends to prove or disprove a point in question. Its purpose can be to reconstruct a crime, identify participants, or confirm/discredit an alibi. Physical evidence can be of five different types: (1) transient; (2) pattern; (3) conditional; (4) transfer; and (5) trace.[6] The last two refer to the exchange that occurs when two objects come into contact. They are based on Locard's exchange principle.

1. Perpetrator will take away traces of victim and scene.
2. Victim will retain traces of perpetrator and may leave traces on him.
3. Perpetrator will leave behind traces at the scene.[7]

Later in the discussion (next chapter), an attempt will be made to establish every possible link among four variables: (1) crime scene; (2) victim; (3) suspect; and (4) physical evidence. Thus, almost any hint of what happened may eventually become pertinent. Trace evidence includes not only hairs, fibers, and residue, but also microscopic matter not visible to the naked eye.[8] A U.S. infantryman would obviously have evidence-gathering limitations, but by thinking small he could come up with enough.

How evidence is collected, marked, and stored is as important as its chain of custody. Each item should be photographed from long and short range before being collected.

There are two types of physical evidence: (1) class evidence, or that which cannot be forensically identified with a specific source to the exclusion of all others; and (2) individual evidence, or that which can. In the first category are things like fibers, soil, wood, and plant materials. In the latter are body fluids, hair, prints, and handwriting.[9]

Criminal investigative technology has now reached to the point where whole books are dedicated to it. Mostly widely studied is the use of DNA (deoxyribonucleic acid) evidence. An essential material in the chromosomes of a human-cell nucleus, it transmits a hereditary pattern. As its complete profile is also unique for each individual, DNA evidence is now widely sought. DNA analyses can now be run on blood, semen, saliva, urine, feces, perspiration, ear wax, nasal mucus, vomit, hair, and skin remnants. Just by offering a suspect a cigarette, one can collect enough saliva for DNA testing. With modern methods, something as innocent as a used stamp can possess a DNA signature.[10] The only trick is how to collect this type of evidence without contaminating it. One of the best references on the subject is *Practical Homicide Investigation,* 4th edition, by Vernon J. Geberth.

There are also ways to detect the past presence of body fluids (those that have already been washed off). Most involve a chemical reagent or special light. Some of the detection chemicals can be applied with a cotton swab. They include phenolphthalin (Kastel-Meyer), leucomalachite green (LMG), and orthotolidine. Others, like luminol and tetramethylbenzidine (TMB), can be sprayed. Still others require some other application method or an alternate light source (ALS). Within this last category are hemaglow, leucocrystal violet (LCV), and flourescein. Luminol is probably the easiest to use, but it can be affected by household cleaners. LMG and LCV do not allow for further DNA testing where blood has been discovered in small amounts. An ALS is simply a device that creates high intensity light in the visible spectrum. Its wave lengths can vary from ultraviolet to infrared.[11]

Among the objects with distinctive signatures are bullets. Once fired, they carry the unique detonation characteristics of the gun through which they passed. Shell casings will only reveal which type of gun was used. But they and almost all objects found at a crime scene can have fingerprints on them. (See Figure 10.1.)

As DNA can now be extracted from fingerprints, how they are collected becomes more important. Powders will not generally interfere with DNA collection, but sprays do.[12] Fingerprints can be

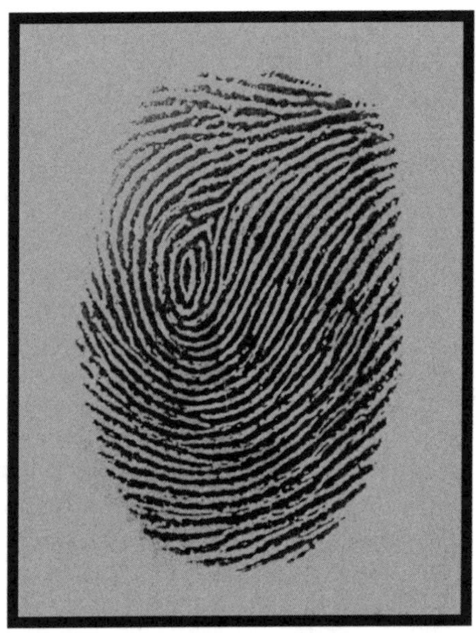

Figure 10.1: The Most Common Type of Hidden Evidence
(Source: Courtesy of Taylor & Francis, from *Practical Homicide Investigation*, by Vernon J. Geberth, © 2006 by Taylor & Francis Group, 2006, p. 611)

visible (from the transference of some contaminant), latent (from skin secretions), or plastic (embedded in a pliable surface). Pliable surfaces include putty, gum, wax, soap, tar, resin, clay, and stamp/envelop glue. Amazingly, latent fingerprints can now be extracted from the victim's bare skin for up to one and a half hours after those prints were made.[13]

Tire- and foot-prints also have characteristics that will often connect them to a particular vehicle or individual. In many cases (even in the city), they can be followed to the perpetrator's hiding place.[14]

With a special test, bullet holes will now provide the direction from which they were fired. They can therefore be used to pinpoint the shooter's location.[15] With a little DNA evidence from that location, his shooting days would be numbered.

Identification of Suspects

Suspects can best be identified through physical or testimonial evidence. Things like hypnosis, polygraph, and interrogation are a poor substitute. One of the most modern techniques is psycholinguistic analysis. This is the examination of spoken or written words for clues about their origin and motivation.[16] While well-known informants can help the investigator to guess who is responsible, jail-house "snitches" can't. They have too much to gain from altering the truth.

Crime Scene Procedures

In an occupier setting, the most common "crime scene" is that of a kidnapping, assassination, or IED detonation. First, the event must be reported and a determination made as to the possibility of intercepting perpetrators. Then, the crime scene is taped off to prevent unauthorized entry and physical-evidence contamination/theft. Any area that might reasonably contain associated footprints or tire tracks must be included. While the immediate area is the most important, other areas can also be vital. They include any point of entry, avenue of escape, suspect vehicle, suspect residence, or location of associated physical evidence. The principal area should be hastily sketched and photographed, and then initially kept empty.

Under no circumstance, should it be used as a casualty collection center or command post. If any threat still exists, weapons can be confiscated as long as precautions are taken not to damage latent fingerprints.

After medical assistance has been summoned for the victims, attention must be paid to any dying declarations they may want to make. Before they are moved, they should be photographed, and the approximate trajectory of whatever hit them determined. After all injured persons have been attended to, and if the crowd is still friendly, a step-by-step investigation can commence. If the crowd is not friendly, the investigation's key steps may have to be hastily attempted. The same holds true if weather or darkness threaten to obliterate the evidence.

Next, all assembled onlookers must be asked about what happened. They are separated from one another and questioned by someone who can quickly take notes. As some of the more distant onlookers may be associated with the crime, they should be detained first. Of interest are offender descriptions, license plate numbers, and direction of travel. From the latter, a perpetrator route or destination can be sometimes determined. Particular attention should be paid to the time sequence of events. Whether or not suspects can be later eliminated will depend largely on their alibis.

Concurrently, the crime scene should be systematically searched by someone who knows something about mantracking. Until it has been thoroughly sketched and photographed, all evidence must be left alone. And nothing else should be touched or added, like using the telephone or discarding a cigarette. A crime scene kit would include the following: (1) barrier tape; (2) evidence collection equipment (e.g., tape recorder, surgical gloves, flashlight, magnifying glass, tweezers, metal detector, measuring tape); (3) fingerprint kit (e.g., powders, brushes, ink pad, cards, reagents); (4) photography kit; (5) sketching and mapping kit; (6) casting kit (e.g., plaster, mixing bowl, casting forms); (7) evidence collection containers; and (8) ALS.[17] If no reagent or ALS is available, the widely available "black-light" bulb people use to detect pet stains may also serve the purpose.

In summary, proper crime scene procedure involves a five-part sequence: (1) take steps to arrest the perpetrator immediately, if possible; (2) protect the crime scene; (3) detain and identify witnesses and/or suspects for follow-up investigations; (4) take notes; and (5) assess the crime scene.[18] (See Figure 10.2.)

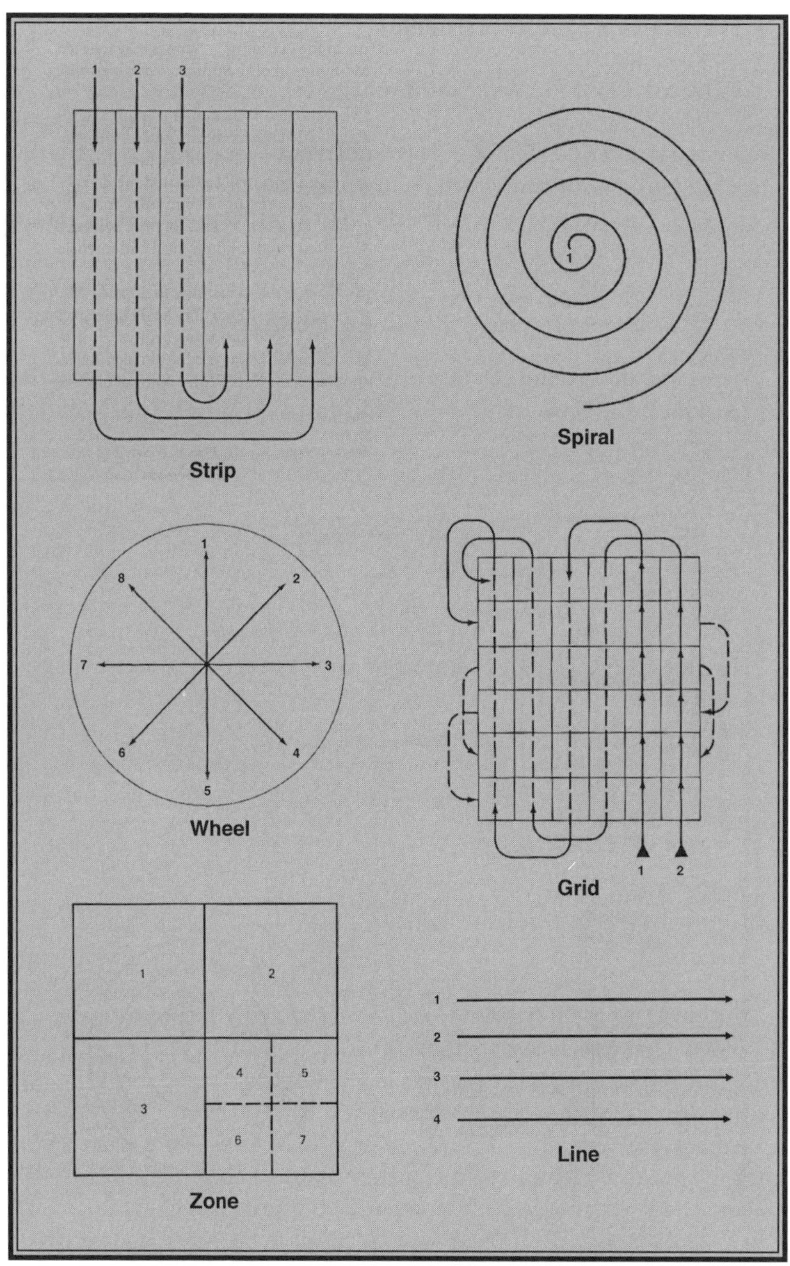

Figure 10.2: Crime Scene Search Patterns

(Source: Courtesy of Taylor & Francis, from *Practical Homicide Investigation,* by Vernon J. Geberth, © 2006 by Taylor & Francis Group, pp. 182-184)

Crime Scene Search Patterns

Often, the last known location of the victim or detonating device forms the center of a crime scene. Generally, there are five patterns. (Refer back to Figure 10.2.) For those that involve more than one searcher, all should follow the same well-marked path in and out of the taped-off area. It is usefully the same route followed by the first person on the scene.[19]

The strip method is specifically intended for large open areas. It involves several people searching back and forth along parallel lanes.

In a relatively small space, the spiral can be quite effective as long as its executor moves in gradually larger but still roughly parallel circles.

In the wheel method, searchers muster at the center and move outwards in different directions. It risks damaging evidence at the center and overlooking it at the periphery.

Best for a large area is the grid method. In it, searches move as in the strip method but cover every inch of ground twice. After searching from one direction, they shift to its perpendicular.

In the zone method, the area to be searched is divided up into squares or sectors. Then, an officer is assigned to each. This method is often used indoors. (See Figure 10.3.)

Heavily vegetated outdoor areas are often examined by scores of personnel on line. This type of search pattern is called the line method.

Extensions of the Crime Scene

Chronic miscreants have favorite places to hide anything that might link them to a crime, e.g., a handgun, detonating device, or shovel. In determining those places, one is limited only by his imagination, understanding of the local populace, and research into past events. Islamic IED "spotters" and "trigger men" probably exit an area along the same line the wires were laid. Any water well, garbage pit, or building site along that likely avenue of egress should be searched. On every detonation device will be latent fingerprints. Finding their rightful owner will do more good than "rounding up the usual suspects" on grandiose sweeps.

A crime scene can be any place that may contain evidence of

a crime. So, there exist "mobile" crime scenes that are sometimes continuing.[20] A good example is a kidnapping. To investigate it, one must go to wherever the kidnap victim may have paused during his abduction. It can stretch for many miles.

Trained mantrackers would be more likely to spot the obscure

Figure 10.3: Most Indoor Searches Require the Zone Method
(Source: FM 10-76Y1/2 [1977], cover)

clues. That's why every CAP platoon should have at least one formally trained mantracker. He could also prove invaluable during the pursuit and apprehension phase of each incident.

11 Pursuit and Arrest

- How does one pursue a criminal in enemy territory?
- Can he still be arrested without harm to the community?

KILLING EVOKES VENGEANCE

(Source: FM 100-20 [1981], p. 198)

There Is Nothing Wrong with Traditional Detective Work

In recent years, forensic science has moved to the forefront of criminal investigation. There are a number of reasons for this. Physical evidence holds the most weight in court. New methods are being developed every day to extract DNA and other trace elements from tinier and older sources. And, of course, many hours can be saved that might otherwise have been spent following up on leads. But the U.S. infantrymen in a CAP platoon setting will have more access to time than to fancy chemicals. He should therefore not be the least bit hesitant to give his best Sherlock Holmes impression.

Old-fashioned detective work was fairly straightforward, albeit time consuming. It involved establishing a comprehensive list of suspects and then ruling those suspects out, one at a time. Most useful in the elimination process was the ability to confirm or refute each alibi. Once the time and place of the crime had been firmly established, that only required a series of secondary investigations.

Thus, in retrospect, it is easy to see why common sense can be every bit as useful as forensics to solving a crime. This is a quality that most enlisted Americans still have in abundance. Of equal importance is learning to think like the opposition—something that many GIs attempt to do anyway. If each U.S. contingent is allowed to stay in its neighborhood/village long enough, much of what goes on there can be determined through public assistance, paid informants, and simple observation. That is not to say that occasionally gathering residue for DNA testing, or brushing a detonating device for fingerprints, might not help. These are things that almost anyone can do with very little initial instruction.

Reconstructing the Incident

After crime scene processing comes crime scene interpretation. It includes pattern analysis of things and behavior, further interrogation of people, tracking down leads, and getting help from forensic laboratories. After all the key witnesses and suspects have been advised of their rights and re-interviewed, they should be given the opportunity to sign a written statement. Tape recordings of those interviews will later be scrutinized for particular details and story consistency.

The goal now is to come up with a motive and temporal sequence of events. Incidents that have only to do with routine public discord are best left to the local police. U.S. CAP platoon members need only follow up on acts of insurgency.

Pattern Analysis

Any pattern in the physical evidence can reveal much more than one might expect. Where bullets have entered and exited an object must be carefully examined. If there are two or more holes in immovable objects (like walls, windows, screens, etc.), a line can be drawn between them and extended outward to determine the exact location of the shooter.

For any evidence that is inconsistent with the working hypothesis, some explanation must be found. In criminal activity and Eastern insurgency alike, the miscreant may purposely try to obscure his identify and even that he has committed an unseemly act. Before blowing something up in Vietnam, Viet Cong sappers would often throw down an 82mm mortar fin and ask for a few hastily aimed mortar rounds.[1] There is no telling how many other so-called coincidences were actually sabotage in that war.

Further Interviews and then Tracking Down Leads

What happened during an incident may not be entirely clear at first. There may not be any suspects at all yet. That's when the real fun begins. With the attitude that someone knows something, saw something, said something, or left something, the investigators canvas the neighborhood. Infantrymen who have developed the ability to spot things out of place, may discover hidden evidence or a perpetrator's ruse. Whatever people say of any substance becomes a "lead." Each lead must be followed until proven useful or false. Suspects are then repeatedly questioned about the crime to uncover any inconsistencies in their stories. To disguise the intent of the method, they can be asked to describe its various circumstances more thoroughly each time. In the process, they may reveal details that only the perpetrator would know. Anyone without an airtight alibi is obviously more likely to be the culprit.

In a kidnapping where the crime scene has already moved elsewhere, media exposure can help to locate the victim. As with wanted posters, phone tips now become the most important leads in the case. Upon receipt of one, the U.S. contingent at the initial kidnap site would simply refer the lead to a counterpart near the most recent sighting. That counterpart would then take the appropriate action. (See Figure 11.1.)

Modus Operandi

Criminals develop what is called a *modus operandi* or way of doing things. Many include habits that are so unusual as to rarely occur otherwise. If the truth be told, the majority of really serious crimes in Iraq are probably being committed by about 5% of the insurgent population. Thus, anything that can be done to track down specific perpetrators would be well worth the effort. The British counterinsurgency effort in Malaysia largely worked because of the tiny tracking teams dispatched after every incident. If a day-long curfew were imposed on a village or neighborhood in which an IED had been detonated, an experienced mantracker could probably determine whether the perpetrator was local. Then, with the help of fingerprints, that person could be arrested.

Making Use of Forensic Science

The U.S. members the CAP platoon need not be familiar with all of the latest ways of collecting evidence, just some of the tricks. A black light, for example, will show blood and urine stains that would otherwise be invisible. And "dusting" for fingerprints is no harder than it looks. The GIs must only be able to collect basic evidence without contaminating it.

The Surveillance or Stakeout

One of the most often-used police procedures is the surveillance or "stakeout." The only difference between it and a military reconnaissance mission is that the former usually involves watching a static location for a particular individual. When that individual emerges from a stakeout, he is often followed to his next destination.

Tailing a Suspect

There are a number of ways to unobstrusively follow a quarry. The most successful in an urban setting involves a number of indistinguishable people or vehicles. Whenever the quarry becomes the least bit suspicious, the lead pursuer passes him or turns a corner. Then, someone further back or on a parallel street takes over. Be warned, however, that some people have an uncanny ability to remember faces.[2] Others never forget a number like on a license plate. And still others have a well-developed "sixth sense" that warns them of impending danger.[3]

In the country, secretly following someone is about the same as "stalking" him. In the most common stalking technique, the pursuer always keeps an object between himself and the quarry.

The Apprehension

Policemen generally arrange an arrest so that the quarry has no way to resist. Instead of confronting him in the familiar confines of

Figure 11.1: POW Procedures Still Apply
(Source: FM 7-8 [1984], p. N-1)

his own home, they wait for him to go out for groceries. Then, posing as civilians on the street, they swarm in from all sides. U.S. military men might find such an approach too likely to produce fratricide. But most American policemen do not plan to use their weapons. That's because they are required by the laws of this country to use minimal force. In such an environment, prisoners are seldom mistreated. (See Figure 11.2.)

An Elusive Fugitive

Where a fugitive is difficult to catch, the apprehension procedures of a big-city detective can help. Most develop an extensive background profile on their subject, to include girl friends/wives, known associates, favorite haunts, and habits. If possible, they determine their quarry's cell phone number. This may later help them to get the suspect out into the open where he can be more safely arrested.[4]

In a big city like Baghdad, fugitives easily switch neighborhoods. Wanted posters and police flyers will often be needed to locate him. The posters are placed at all locations that people, who might want to exchange information for consideration in their cases or for profit, might see them. The flyers would be given to all CAP platoons and other police detachments.[5]

Once the fugitive's cell phone number is known, many things are possible. A woman can call him to arrange a meeting or to determine if he is at home. Or someone can tell him that the police are on their way and to get out while he can. That call must come from an undisclosed recipient, unregistered cell phone, or phone with the Caller ID (identification) avoidance option.[6]

If only the suspect's pager number can be determined, he can be called on an undercover phone equipped with Caller ID. When he calls back, he will unwittingly reveal his phone number. Most phone companies can also determine the location from which a call has been made.[7]

Arresting a Particularly Elusive or Dangerous Suspect

Arresting a wily quarry requires almost as much planning as a deliberate infantry attack. First, the subject's location must be thoroughly reconnoitered. The complete physical layout of that location must be determined. All front-door particulars are important: (1) durability of security screen or grate; (2) whether the screen door is locked; (3) composition of the front door; (3) number of locks on the front door; (4) which way the doors open; and (5) type of door knob. Then, a complete survey must be made of rear exits, fire escapes, rooftop, rear yard, security apparatus, alarms, dogs, etc. In most Muslim countries, the front courtyard is also a concern.[8] Finally, a way secretly to approach the location must be found. Policemen are not authorized to demolish an occupied structure and everyone in it, so they depend more on surprise.

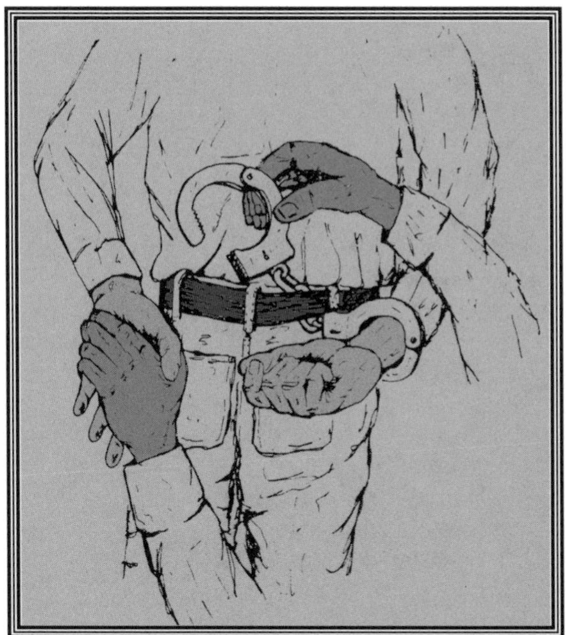

Figure 11.2: All Suspects Are Presumed Innocent
(Source: FM 19-95C1/2 [1978], p. 2-106)

If the fugitive has been particularly active in the insurgency, he may also have boobytraps, an escape tunnel, or a hidden room. With someone like this, no attempt should normally be made to enter his residence. There are ways of preparing a building for defense that can make such an expedition virtually suicidal for the best trained of urban assault troops. Those ways normally involve a combination of makeshift surveillance devices (e.g., mirror shards in series, tiny wall or floor holes, squeaky boards, etc.) and hidden explosives. It is thus important that someone like this be lured out into the open. For American policemen, there is a legal limit to how much trickery can be used. That is the subject of the next chapter.

12 The Sting

- What are the ways to lure an insurgent out into the open?
- Can what he does then provide useful information?

"PSEUDO-OPERATIONS"

(Source: FM 31-73 [1967], p. 201)

A Working Definition

In law enforcement lingo, the term "sting" applies to a situation that undercover police create to determine who may have been committing a certain type of offense in a particular locale. It is not the same as ensnaring a known criminal. By fooling all those who may have something to hide, the police attempt to establish who actually does. In effect, they are arriving at a more complete list of suspects. A perfect example is a fake "fence" for stolen merchandize. With it, officers posing as store workers can determine who, in a given neighborhood, would be most likely to have committed a burglary.

However, all those who hawk stolen goods are not burglars and cannot be treated as such. They only have stolen merchandise in their possession. To arrest any for burglary, the police will have to thoroughly investigate—and acquire much more evidence on—any sting-derived suspect.

The term "sting" can also be applied to an unlawful activity, as in the motion picture of that name. In the movie, high rollers from the late 1920's are relieved of their funds in a fake betting parlor for horse race enthusiasts. Staged radio announcements and time-delayed ticker-tape reports provide the "house" with better than average odds.

The 4GW military equivalent of a "sting" might look something like this. Communist NPA guerrillas have been operating—far from home—on the Zamboanga Peninsula of southwestern Mindanao. To secretly undermine Western oil interests, they may be masquerading as Muslim raiders. However, there is no direct evidence of this. Rumors are circulated that a Philippine army platoon is unhappy with all the collateral damage that Philippine artillery has caused around Liguasan Marsh. The platoon's desertion is staged, and it flees to the NPA's favorite refuge. With something the NPA wants, namely information about Philippine Army dispositions, the platoon does whatever it can to appear to switch allegiances. It runs some fake, supply-gathering raids on government outposts to demonstrate its intent to operate as a guerrilla faction. Its leader makes no attempt to physically link up with the NPA but confides frequently with local residents and welcomes new members. Through those relationships, he hopes to plant a seed in the mind of the NPA commander. That seed is the whereabouts of some poorly guarded British oil company workers. Waiting at their location is, of course, a Philippine Army ambush. If the NPA commander takes the bait, what his casualties say to their captors should be enough to confirm or deny the original suspicion. Their statements will establish, once and for all, if the displaced Communists have been passing themselves off as *Abu Sofia, Abu Sayyaf,* MILF, or MNLF. By uncovering such a highly deceptive strategy, one might prevent a powerful Communist sponsor from trying something similar, elsewhere in the world.

Police Entrapment

Of course, there is a legal limit to how much people can be

fooled into incriminating themselves. Anything over that limit is called "entrapment." It is comparable to "leading a witness" (putting words into their mouth). An example would be an undercover officer suggesting a crime and then asking his quarry if he wants to participate. For the fruits of a sting to be legitimate, the quarry must be the first person to suggest money for sex, guns for money, bombing a Coalition vehicle, or whatever the crime may be. There are rules, because it is the criminal justice system that must punish the offender.

Some police stings can just barely violate a subject's rights. In the process, they still ruin any chance of help from the courts. An example was recently reported from Australia. To secure confessions, undercover Victoria police officers recruited suspects into mock crime gangs. In the process, they may have circumvented a generally accepted legal principle—the right to silence. After luring the subjects into the fake gangs, the policemen asked them to reveal any past crimes that might bring "heat" (unwanted police attention) down on the gangs. While such confessions have been ruled legally admissible in Australia,[1] they would almost certainly be disallowed in Miranda-conscious America.

It is also improper to "trick" a retailer into breaking the law. In one U.S. state, law enforcement personnel may have crossed that line with regard to alcohol and cigarettes. They sent minors into stores with people who were obviously of age. They also dressed minors to appear older than they really were. Across that particular state, any retailer or employee who falls for such a ruse can be issued a license suspension or heavy fine.[2] To support a totally legitimate sting of this nature, 13- and 14-year-olds would have to dress normally, go into stores alone, and freely answer all questions concerning their age.

Legitimate Ensnaring of Established Fugitives

Not all trapping constitutes entrapment. There are any number of legally admissible traps for known criminals. Some are too lethal to be of much use in a 4GW environment. For example, nothing really productive could come from luring an *al-Qaeda* leader into a public building and then destroying it and all of its occupants with a cruise missile. While difficult for U.S. leaders to envision, most Communist and Islamist movements are run from the bottom up. That means cell leaders literally do not know who they work for. They know where they can go for support and that's about it. Almost all management is by exception. So, those movements can operate just fine without any high-level leadership at all. Killing bin Laden and al-Zawahiri on the same day would make little difference to the overall effectiveness of *al-Qaeda*. Their martyrdom would serve almost as much purpose as their presence. Of course, low-level Islamist and Communist commissars do control important action. They are the ones who routinely terrorize individual villages and neighborhoods. Every time one is arrested on some charge that will stick in his country's legal system, that country comes closer to peace.

Legitimate Law Enforcement Stings

There has been at least one textbook written on which types of stings are legally proper.[3] The most common examples of legitimate stings involve undercover police personnel pretending to be in the market for drugs or guns. Or they establish pawn shops that will accept any merchandize. Appearing to be in the market for services (rather than things) more easily qualifies as illegitimate entrapment.

Below is a list of recent, high-visibility stings. Though at least one looks overly contrived, no determination can be made as to their legitimacy without knowing more about them. It goes without saying that the fake hit man cannot suggest the murder, nor can the fake drug customer suggest the buy.

- An undercover detective, posing as a hit man, schemes with a husband out to kill his wife.
- A heroin dealer is busted by undercover officers, one of whom poses as a wheel chair-bound customer.
- A "drunken" decoy cop staggers in the New York subway to lure a mugger.
- Doctors involved in shady insurance scams are busted by cops after being caught on video.
- Police photograph a staged "murder-for-hire" to nab a woman who wants her husband killed.

Police stings for fraud involve services. A look at one by the Federal Trade Commission (FTC) confirms that those services must never be explicitly offered.

> Using undercover investigators and special computer tools, the FTC identified business opportunity advertisements that made earnings claims without including cautionary language required by the FTC's Franchise Rule. The investigators posed as prospective investors and listened to sales pitches from operators who hyped the business opportunity and touted the earnings potential. Then the investigators were given "references"—supposedly successful owners and operators of the business opportunity who could verify the earnings claims. In the course of their investigations, the FTC staff uncovered evidence that some of the "references" didn't own or operate a business. They were shills—actors paid by the operations to pose as successful and prosperous owners.[4]
>
> — FTC News Release, 20 June 2002

Military "Sting-Like" Episodes from History

While fighting several Communist factions in Rhodesia in the 1970's, the Selous Scouts instituted "pseudo-operations." By pretending to be guerrillas themselves, they could infiltrate an enemy-infested area and locate its other occupants. To enhance their credibility, the Scouts had a full portfolio of ruses: (1) pretending to raid Rhodesian farms; (2) entering guerrilla camps in blackface with white hostages in tow; (3) posing as members of a neighboring country's armed forces; and (4) faking hits on informers.[5]

Never short on initiative, U.S. Special Forces personnel have tried a few fairly innovative tricks in Afghanistan. One pretended—on the enemy's radio net—to be a transiting-unit commander in need of a guide.[6]

How a Few Stings Might Help in Iraq

Here's how an effective trap for known criminals in Iraq might be combined with a sting for their government accomplices. For a

Muslim militant faction, an isolated U.S. infantry squad is an irresistible target. To capture or kill its members, that faction would dispatch its most seasoned fighters—those who normally function as recruiters/trainers.

The urban defense is the strongest of the tactical mediums, so all U.S. squad members should be able to hide at the last moment and then gradually winnow out their attackers. They would need only a CAP platoon night formation that automatically draws any attackers to its center. By shifting all indigenous police and soldiers away from that center on initially passive two-man ambushes, the U.S. squad helps the quarry to approach and becomes the bait. Then, with a few hidden claymores and a secret escape bunker, it easily dodges the enemy thrust. Upon hearing a commotion at the headquarters building, all indigenous personnel then activate their ambushes. When the sun next rises, the enemy commander has 20-30 fewer recruiters/trainers and the CAP platoon has more local stature. One or two units may have already tried this scheme in the Iraqi theater. Its every detail is covered by Chapter 13 of *Militant Tricks*.[7]

But what of the indigenous police who are additionally Mahdi Army members? They would have, in all likelihood, led in the attackers. It is here that a concurrent sting might help the platoon to survive. Each tribal clique or subordinate group within its indigenous police squad could be surreptitiously told of a different vulnerability to the U.S. headquarters building. The attackers' entry method would then indicate which clique or group had assisted the enemy.

Military Variations

The American way of war is based on firepower, not surprise. As such, it involves very little deception at the small-unit level. Unaccustomed to all but the most basic diversions, U.S. enlisted personnel tend to consider all tricks helpful in war. They aren't. That's why so many paragraphs have been dedicated to the relative legality of various police stings. While legality and morality are not always the same, the former still provides some way to assess the effectiveness of a military sting. Now that 4GW is the norm, the killing of the enemy's frontline soldiers may no longer help to win the war. This is particularly true of Muslim cannon fodder.

As was shown in Chapter 9, all that killing is also a little short on being moral. This is an age in which the soldier must, in effect, love his enemy in order to win the war. GIs must treat Islamic militants as they would want to be treated. That means paying serious attention to how military stings are designed. For example, it would be a bad idea to endanger those who are just curious. It would be a bad idea to arrest those who would accept money to join a fake guerrilla movement. And, once a list of suspects had been established, it would be a bad idea to ignore evidence that might exonerate them. In a 4GW environment, truth and justice really do matter. That has been proven once again by a U.S. Special Forces Group in *al-Qaeda's* southwestern Philippine bastion. A hundred years ago on Jolo island, U.S. soldiers could do nothing more than chase 600-1,000 Moros (Muslim insurgents) up a volcano and kill them, in what is still locally remembered as a massacre.[8] Time and events have since proven how much good that did.

> Today, a crucial but little-known battle in the expanding war on terror is under way on Jolo Island. Designed to "wage peace," as Linder [U.S. contingent commander] says, it's an innovative, decidedly nonviolent approach by which U.S. military personnel—working with aid agencies, private groups and Philippine armed forces—are trying to curtail terrorist recruitment by building roads and providing other services in impoverished rural communities. The effort, known to experts as "the Philippines model," draws on a "victory" on the Philippine island of Basilan, where U.S. forces in 2002 ended the dominance of Abu Sayyaf without firing so much as a single shot. "It's not about how many people we shoot in the face," Linder said. "It's about how many people we get off the battlefield."[9]
>
> — *Smithsonian,* December 2006

Results can be less than satisfactory when U.S. troops enter another nation with good intentions, but then try to combine their limited powers of deception with a heavy hand. With that traditional but thoroughly outmoded formula, they can easily fan latent animosities between local factions. Those animosities may later appear to diminish, but will still smolder and could eventually lead to a civil conflagration. At least that's what came of the British tinkering—in the name of peace—with what had been a traditionally amicable relationship between Muslims and Hindus in India. And that's why every U.S. CAP platoon member must be thoroughly versed in international law and any local variations. He must know what evidence is admissible in that nation's courts. While serving with indigenous police of unknown persuasion, he cannot afford to be a party to any injustice. That being said, the particulars of a military sting can be further explored.

The military sting must be designed for the specific acquisition of things or information from a particular population segment. In many developing countries, one of the enemy's principal objectives is oil. Sometimes that objective is secretly pursued by Communist elements with the sole purpose of discouraging Western oil company competition. Other times, it is openly pursued by Islamist elements with the overall purpose of damaging infrastructure and undermining the credibility of the existing government. With regard to the former, poorly guarded Western oil workers might attract pseudo-Islamists and thus function as a sting. In the case of the latter, a poorly guarded pumping station might draw regular Islamists and serve as an ordinary ambush.

In the Russians' second (more successful) assault on the capital of Chechnya in 2000, they lured its Muslim defenders into hidden minefields by leaving an exit route open.[10] While that ruse qualifies more as a trap for known criminals than a sting, it still has some of the information-gathering qualities of a sting. With it, the Russians ascertained how to destroy other dissident factions without revealing their ruse.

Inherent Perils

In any sting or other type of undercover operation, the enemy is often too numerous and close for comfort. A response to every possible reversal must therefore be planned in advance. To maintain any degree of stealth and deception, those responses would necessarily derive from unconventional warfare.

13 The Only Defense Is ___ Unconventional

- Why have GIs had so much trouble beating guerrillas?
- What will it take to blunt Chinese and Islamist expansion?

(Source: FM 90-8 [1986], p. C-21)

Few Links between Police Work and Conventional War

Local security does not automatically ensue from the "successful" application of conventional warfare. As the Western variant becomes "higher tech," it departs even further from maneuver. Fire superiority is still its primary objective, and heavy ordnance is hard on roads, fuel pipes, communication lines, electricity grids, sanitation facilities, and governance apparatus. Wherever local infrastructure is damaged, criminals and terrorists are not far behind. As after any natural disaster, they come to exploit the frustration that shortages of basic services generate. That's why U.S. police departments don't employ heavy ordnance while assaulting a criminal hideout. Most of their highly visible failures over the years have come from accidental fires.

U.S. SWAT (Special-Weapons Assault Team) operations may look like their military counterpart, but they aren't. The difference is largely in the type of grenades used. SWAT teams use concussion grenades to preserve the lives of hostages and criminals alike. As evidenced by the Hadithah incident in Iraq, U.S. infantry squads don't.[1] Those who believe their country to be morally superior in all things will not want to hear what comes next. Over the years, their Communist adversaries have routinely used concussion grenades on assault.[2] Even the WWII-era Japanese had grenades with thin, nonserrated casings for reduced fragmentation.[3] To achieve some measure of lethality, the WWII Germans had to afix a special serrated sleeve to their thin-skinned potato mashers.[4] As late as 1989, Soviet troops were still throwing concussion grenades in Afghanistan (just as their grandfathers had against Hitler's Nazis).[5] Of course, those foes weren't trying to save defenders with their concussion grenades; they were trying to keep their own assault troops from having to rush fully ready defenders. Still, it is a good example of how effective minimal force can be.

So, if a "police action" is to be part of the U.S. military's answer to Islamist and Communist expansion, it must not be like that in Korea. Nor can it be of the traditional "top-down" variety. By April 2007 (according to six of America's most highly respected periodicals), the *Hezbollah*-like Mahdi Army had already infiltrated most of the police departments in central and southern Iraq.[6] Any law enforcement assistance effort must therefore be highly decentralized. Without something more than barbed-wire, bunkers, and on-call airstrikes, tiny U.S. contingents will have trouble surviving. They must look elsewhere for some measure of safety—namely, from the annals of "unconventional" warfare. During their everyday routine, they cannot be too easily accessible. Then, when unavoidably surrounded, they must be able to disappear temporarily like guerrillas. That will not be easy, because even America's best special operators lack that degree of light-infantry skill.

A Working Definition for "Unconventional Warfare"

The term "unconventional warfare" (UW) is almost never used

by American GIs, because it's not part of their military tradition. McGraw Hill's *Science and Technology Dictionary* defines UW as that which includes guerrilla war, escape/evasion, and subversion. It is conducted in enemy territory by indigenous personnel supported/directed by an external source.[7] That sounds a lot like 4GW by proxy. It's how Iran and Pakistan have traditionally vied for Afghanistan. It's how Iran has now all but annexed Iraq. And it is how China is currently influencing most of South Asia. The U.S. military's definition of UW is similar but suggests the term can be applied to almost any activity that undermines the foe.

> A broad spectrum of military and paramilitary operations, normally of long duration, predominantly conducted by indigenous or surrogate forces who are organized, trained, equipped, supported, and directed in varying degrees by an external source. It includes guerrilla warfare and other direct offensive, low visibility, covert, or clandestine operations, as well as the indirect activities of subversion, sabotage, intelligence activities, and evasion and escape.[8]
>
> — U.S. Dept. of Defense, 2003

The "UW" that U.S. Special Forces personnel study is an Americanized and bureaucratized rendition of the Asian original. Their dual mission of "Foreign Internal Defense" tends to dilute the equation. Thus, they spend more time on counterguerrilla than guerrilla operations, on raids than sabotage, and on long-range reconnoitering than short-range infiltration. Still, they are the best that America has to offer in this regard, and their progress over the last few years has been in the right direction.

Wikipedia Encyclopedia specifies how UW interfaces with 4GW's political arena. It says UW's "long-term goals are coercive or subversive to a political body."[9] The Chinese treatise on "unrestricted warfare" comes immediately to mind.[10] So does America's obsession with democratizing the world. If she is to succeed, she must first develop a UW defense to the Chinese initiative.

Learning to Think Like a Chinese

China badly wants Taiwan. While the PRC may be preparing to take it back by force, many students of Eastern deception believe that preparation to be a feint. Now, with a Yangtze River dam, China would never risk an all-out war with the West. Its bid to acquire Taiwan will be more devious and multifaceted. First, it will secure the sea lanes for its African and Iranian oil by promoting Islamist or pro-Chinese hegemony throughout the Malay Peninsula. Without better training in small-unit tactics than the U.S. can provide, that region will have no more chance of surviving than Vietnam did. In control of the Malacca Straits, the Chinese will be in a perfect position to blackmail the U.S. on more than just Taiwan. To effectively shortstop the Maoist method, one needs world-class small-unit maneuver techniques. Despite clever semantics to the contrary, America has no true light infantry. Unlike those in Communist armies, her junior infantrymen receive no unconventional warfare training. Without hearts-and-minds-ruining bombardment, they cannot fend for themselves when outnumbered. Might the PRC be planning to exploit this weakness worldwide?

If the Chinese were to invade Taiwan, U.S. trained Taiwanese troops would have little chance. To win, they would need the same "soft," below-ground strongpoint defense with which North Vietnamese militiamen blunted the Chinese invasion of 1979. Those tactics are not of Western origin.[11]

The Chinese Version of a Sino-Islamic Coalition

While the rogue Islamist states have traded oil for U.N. protection and military assistance, their arrangement with China does not follow the Western definition of a coalition. In fact, no arrangement with Communist China will ever follow the Western model. Its ruling party has relied on too much deception, and not enough good will. In all probability, Islamist leaders have been hoodwinked almost as badly as their Western counterparts. The first chapter showed how PRC agents could have infiltrated *al-Qaeda*. It further demonstrated how the Muslim Brotherhood (current government of Sudan), *Sepah, Hezbollah,* and *Hamas* have all been manipulated by the PRC. That this reality is so different from the average Westerner's perception is no coincidence. China has excelled at deception since the days of Sun Tzu. Still, the infiltration of Islamist organizations might have only been to impart or test advanced tactical techniques. It does not necessarily imply active aggression.

Sun Tzu also liked to fan enmity between common foes. For

an atheistic nation, that might mean stirring up trouble between the world's two biggest religions. Such a strategy would involve arranged confrontations between Muslim extremist factions and Western fundamentalist leaders. Most suspicious of recent U.S. events was the D.C. sniper incident as Congress decided whether or not to invade Iraq. While Chalabi's concurrent lobbying was probably Iranian inspired, the handler's degree of mind control over the young shooter was still troubling. One cannot help but imagine a "Manchurian Candidate" type of arrangement in which the wrong organization was implicated.

In the world of Eastern intrigue, the actual instigator routinely masks any link to the perpetrator. Eastern nations camouflage their strategic initiatives through strings of proxies. That way when *Hamas* does something, the average American never suspects a fledgling superpower had something to do with it. He or she has never been told that Iran has often functioned as China's instrument, *Hezbollah* as Iran's instrument, and *Hamas* as *Hezbollah's* instrument. Ideological differences are involved, and everyone knows that people of differing faiths can't cooperate. Who (if anyone) was ultimately behind 9/11 is no longer at issue. What is at issue is the unabated growth of a Chinese Co-Prosperity Sphere. Nations with atheistic or totalitarian ideologies have no business exporting democracy or demanding free trade. Though ostensibly peaceful, their so-called "foreign assistance" can prove lethal. The idea of a Sino-*al-Qaeda* connection is not new. Several books have been written on the subject, and any number of articles by well-respected journalists. Yet, to the average American, the idea seems so radical as to border on insanity. Whether it is true is not nearly as important as how the U.S. military prepares for the future. Those who must reestablish world peace will require UW training, not smarter bombs. Mao is still the recognized expert on insurgency. His method has so far proven immune to firepower/technology and does not need direct PRC backing to succeed.

What Has Been Missing from U.S. Decision Making

U.S. leaders have tried many things to reverse the downward spiral in Iraq and Afghanistan. That none have worked could indicate a false assumption. For a number of reasons, politicians won't easily entertain misgivings about their military. Yet, it is an established fact that "top-down" bureaucracies tend to be least efficient at their bottom echelons, and "bottom-up" bureaucracies tend to excel there. That is why the U.S. military has yet to outmaneuver guerrillas or East Asian soldiers at short range. To minimize the loss of American lives, it fights defensively with too little regard for collateral damage. Instead of abjectly denying this obvious reality, the U.S. military establishment should plan a winning strategy around it.

Might "unconventional warfare" be nothing more than that which avoids the bureaucratic inertia of a highly structured military? Without overly centralized control, its tactics appear asymmetric. Without large-unit action, its small units are better able to take care of themselves. And without a steady diet of standardized training, its individuals are more unpredictable, survivable, and potentially useful.

Tacticians agree that the urban defense is the strongest maneuver medium. Intelligence experts see most future combat occurring in heavily populated areas. Why not base future U.S. strategy on fighting defensively from a myriad of tiny, neighborhood/village outposts? This would no longer be "too risky" if U.S. soldiers and Marines received what their Far Eastern counterparts have gotten for 60 years—concurrent training in UW. In war, final victory must take precedence over personal sacrifice, otherwise the latter has no meaning. Out of a misguided attempt to keep U.S. riflemen safe, U.S. leaders have denied them the chance to reach their full warrior potential. That potential extends not only to surviving on their own, but also to making strategic contributions on their own.

How All of This Might Be Possible

Within this book's next part will be the specific problems (and solutions) of the members of a lone U.S. squad that happens to get in the way of the Chinese dragon or Islamist mob. When surrounded by 100 times their number in a heavily populated area, they must know how to save themselves. As was evident in Mogadishu in 1993, no amount of headquarters advice, quick-reaction force, or standoff bombardment will be enough to get the job done. To save themselves, while still managing to accomplish their mission, those 14 young Americans will need their own portfolio of UW techniques. That is the content of what is to follow.

Part Three

Prerequisite Unconventional Warfare Skills

"What difference does it make to the dead, the orphans and the homeless, whether the mad destruction is wrought under the name of totalitarianism or the holy name of liberty or democracy?"
— Mahatma Gandhi

(Source: Mahatma Gandhi, "Non-Violence in Peace and War," n.p., n.d.)

14 Finding an Enemy Weakness

- Why do America's foes make so few tactical mistakes?
- What aspects of the situation do they still ignore?

EVERY FOE'S WEAKNESS IS IN HIS PATTERN

(Source: FMFM 2-1 [1980]. p. 5-1)

Which Parts of UW Should Be Assimilated

The usual definition of UW embraces three categories of activity: (1) guerrilla operations; (2) escape and evasion; and (3) subversion. Only the first two will be discussed here, because the third pertains to undermining the existing regime. As such, it is beyond the purview of the U.S. infantry unit. Subversion can occur in all three of the nonmartial 4GW arenas. Combat troopers must only remember that their actions have repercussions: (1) in politics through adverse media coverage; (2) in economics through infrastructure damage; and (3) in psychology through too little respect for religious custom.

Getting beyond the "Hype"

For every Western soldier's shortcoming, the Eastern soldier is often attributed a strength. When on a roll like at Singapore in 1941, the latter's reputation can quickly exceed his ability. His actual strengths, relatively speaking, derive from more chance to operate alone than Western counterparts. Due to insufficient wherewithal, a heritage of bottom-up problem solving, and abundance of people, his nation has a greater appreciation for individual effort than do most Western countries. For the same reasons, his superiors place more emphasis on surprise than firepower. This makes them more dependent on small-unit maneuvers. As a result, the Eastern soldier gets more practice at three things: (1) exercising initiative, (2) making his own tactical decisions, and (3) helping to develop his own tactical techniques. Still, he is only a man. As such, he is just as prone to mistakes in judgment as the Western soldier. Often misled about his traditional adversary's resolve, he becomes doubly vulnerable.

Ostensibly to save lives, U.S. commanders fight slowly, methodically, and defensively. All the emphasis on "force protection" in Iraq is a perfect example. To avoid U.S. sweeps and cordon operations, the enemy has only to become adept at hiding below ground, sniping, and boobytraps. He also gets good at camouflaging his strongpoints from direct observation. These are the things he correctly assumes that Western commanders deem inconsequential.

Easterners More Capable at Unexpected Scale

The Eastern opponent achieves most of his success from fighting at a scale that is smaller than what most Western commanders deem strategically significant. For example, with unlimited access to more equipment, the Western commander worries little about lone saboteurs. As long as he can go where he wants and shoot as much as he wants, he considers himself to be winning. All the Eastern soldier or guerrilla has to do is dodge all of the firepower and wait. He does so by widely dispersing, and then hiding in spider holes, well walls, trees, civilian garb, and any other place GIs don't have the time to look.

Once enough attention is paid to this smaller scale, more than just Saddam Hussein will be found. While widely dispersed, Eastern fighters are well beyond the protective umbrella of any parent unit. Unless imbued with some fanatical code of honor, they should be easier to capture. That assumes, of course, that Western forces are widely enough dispersed and loosely enough controlled themselves. Their tempo of operations must also be slow enough to allow individual units time to carefully look around. For every enemy soldier captured, there will be one less extended family with a multigenerational *jihadist* grudge.

Enemy Predictability

Because of the problems the U.S. military has had with counterinsurgency, Eastern fighters are widely thought to be unpredictable in combat. The newest official term for this situation is "asymmetric warfare." The word "asymmetric" implies no symmetry to what the enemy does. While loosely controlled and widely dispersed guerrilla units might display more tactical variety than ordinarily expected, they are still predictable. Eastern armies intentionally develop maneuvers that are the opposite of what Western forces do under similar circumstances. They have additionally institutionalized the "false face and art of delay." That means their small-unit leaders almost always use a feint and then wait for their Western adversary to make the incorrect first move. To beat them, the Westerner has only to study past battles. He then can correlate every feint with possible maneuvers. After spotting that feint (often a Western formation), he simply looks to his flank or rear for the real attack.

The Enemy in Afghanistan

To limit reprisals during the Soviet-Afghan War, a varied assortment of *mujahideen* factions often participated in the same operation. They rehearsed separately (or not at all) at their home base, rendezvoused after dark, and then enjoyed limited communication during the actual attack. As most had been told to shoot at something (to confuse defenders as to which outpost was actually under assault), this lack of coordination normally made little difference. However, any interruption to the plan could have easily led to disaster. Unable to support each other, the various factions would have been destroyed piecemeal by a more astute enemy.

U.S. and Russian forces fight in much the same way, so the shortcomings of the *mujahideen* are probably still true of the Taliban. As the *mujahideen* became less afraid of their largely predictable and increasingly besieged adversary, they developed two bad habits: (1) neglecting to provide local security while deep in their own territory; and (2) using the same ambush sites over and over.[1]

The Soviets' expeditionary force depended almost entirely on artillery and air support and seldom went after their opposition on the ground (particularly after an ambush). As a result, that opposition became used to a particular way of fighting. A more responsive occupier would have capitalized on that pattern.

While the Afghans instinctively sought to damage or capture Soviet supplies, they couldn't see why it should be done secretly (to limit the response and protect the method). As a result, they had trouble embracing tactical innovation. The Pakistani ISI's leader who was responsible for their training and tactical advice made the following observation.

> In fact, what was wrong with my method was that it lacked noise and excitement. It was not their [the *mujahideen's]* way to fight, with no firing, no chance of inflicting casualties, no opportunity for personal glory and no booty. Their method was to bombard the posts with heavy weapons by night at long range, move closer to fire mortars, get 30-40 men to surround them, and at short range open up with machineguns, RPGs and RLs (rocket launchers). If the garrison withdrew, the posts were captured and the mujahideen secured their loot in the form of rations, arms and ammunition, all of which could be used or sold. Then, only then, was the charge laid on the fuel pipeline. If the garrison stuck it out, the pipeline remained untouched.
>
> It often took a serious setback, with quite severe casualties, to force a *[mujahideen]* Commander to review his methods. Like most soldiers the Mujahid hated digging. He was decidedly unhappy in a static defensive role; it was alien to his temperament; it restricted his freedom to move, and he could seldom be convinced of the need to construct overhead cover. Similarly, his fieldcraft was often poor as he was disinclined to crawl, even when close to an enemy position. The hard stony ground, or the possibility of mines, may have had something to do with it, but I had the impres-

sion that it was a bit beneath his dignity. Walk, or crouch perhaps, but crawling was seldom acceptable.[2]

— Brigadier Yousaf, Afghan Service Bureau Chief

An Example of the Type of Thing to Look for in Afghanistan

As evidenced by the strongpoint defense in Figure 14.1, *al-Qaeda* and its Taliban allies are far more sophisticated defensively than Western commanders would like. The rectangular compounds are arrayed in concentric circles around the headquarters buildings. Each can direct a steady stream of machinegun bullets across its neighbor's front on either side. To assault any of those compounds, Western troops would have to

Figure 14.1: *Al-Qaeda's* Strongpoint Defense in Waziristans
(Source: Courtesy of Associated Press, photo captioned "Al-Qaeda Cornered," from "U.S. Assists Pakistan in Battle," by Riaz Khan, 20 March 2004, © 2004)

endure interlocking machinegun fire from both flanks. While the whole array looks pretty impressive, a closer look reveals some weaknesses as well as one or two additional strengths. (See Figure 14.2.)

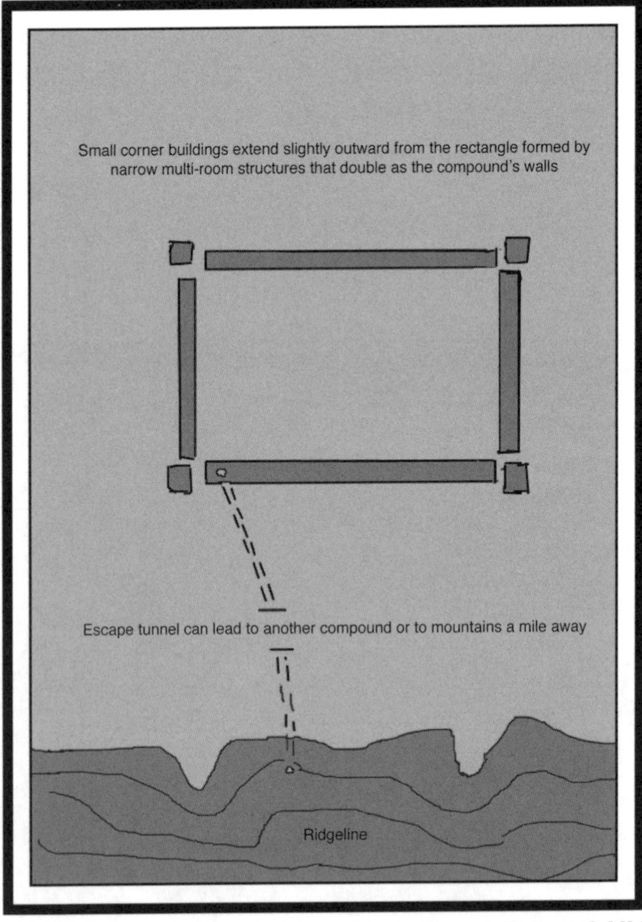

Figure 14.2: ***Fort Affords Visibility & Fire at Base of All Walls***
(Source: From photo captioned "Mullah Omar Slept Here," in "The Strange Case of Haji Bashar Noorzai," by Bill Powell, *Time Magazine*, 19 February 2007)

A rare news photograph shows small corner buildings extending slightly outward from the rest of the rectangular compound. That rest is formed by narrow multi-room structures that double as walls. Sentries in those corner buildings thus have a clear view of what happens along the base of those walls. Even at night, the whole structure's mud stucco surface would create a false horizon against which any commando activity would be clearly silhouetted. On a more positive note, the narrow spaces between corner buildings and the rest of the compound would provide no fewer than eight points of entry to the fortress.

The flatter portions of southern Afghanistan are supposed to be covered with similar arrays of walled compounds. Very probably, they have been constructed in much the same way. They will be easier to seize by surprise than by traditional fire and maneuver.

The Enemy in Iraq

The principal instigator of Iraq's instability (PRC-backed Iran) has been employing a largely misunderstood and thus highly successful strategy. That strategy depends, in large part, on America's continuing obsession with Sunni *al-Qaeda*. While U.S. units have been feverishly training Iraq's police force and army to take over the counterguerrilla effort, the former has been heavily infiltrated by Shiite militiamen. Most of the police departments that could not be infiltrated have been forced to abandon their law-enforcement function. Well aware that the Shiite-dominated Iraqi regime cannot disarm/dismantle those militias without losing its power base, the instigator has only to wait. Once the U.S. Congress fully realizes that the conflict has deteriorated into a civil war, it will bring home the troops. Then, as the strength of the radical element grows within Iraq's internal security establishment, so too will it grow within Iraq's government. A neighborhood police detachment can have the same effect on how people vote as an overbearing ward boss. This is particularly true in a Muslim country where what people believe to be true often comes to them over a public address system before daily prayers.

The Iranian Revolutionary Guard has been operating with relative impunity throughout central and southern Iraq since the start of the war. Its current presence seems not particularly to bother Iraq's pro-Iranian regime, and its initial presence may have actually been requested by the West (as in Afghanistan) to help oust the previous regime. Thus, there is every probability that Iran's plans for the real heartland of Shiism are right on track.

But within the instigator's strength also lies his weakness. Iran has demonstrated so little respect for the West's ability to see through and stop its method, that it will continue to do most of the same kinds of things. Among the most prevalent have been physical assaults on uncooperative police stations.

An Example of What to Look for in Iraq

The assaults on police compounds have invariably involved an inside man and one or more suicide vehicles (to penetrate the perimeter wall). As such, they didn't require much tactical sophistication. It should not be all that hard for a technological superpower to so rig each station with remotely controlled surveillance and firepower to make it a trap for unwanted visitors. After all, Middle Eastern architecture is perfectly suited for such a scheme. The walls are thick enough to obscure cameras and claymores and also to limit blast and fragmentation. That the roofs are flat adds to the number of kill zones. In addition, the spaces between the buildings are so narrow, twisted, and numerous that the enemy couldn't easily retreat.

Therein lies the secret to a successful defense of Iraq. The Muslim militant won't expect America to fight on that small a scale. Nor will he alter his methods to reverse any setbacks at that level. His very identity revolves around a willingness to closely engage infidels. He can't refuse to seek them out without sacrificing that identity.

A Communist Foe

Most of the world's Communists now live in Asia. Because Americans lack a heritage of Sun-Tzu-like ruses, they are thought by Communists to be overly gullible. In effect, Asian Communists suffer from the same thing as most Westerners—arrogance. And this arrogance is their greatest weakness as well. They have become so awed by their frontline tactical superiority that they don't expect

Americans in their rear areas. That makes their assets of strategic significance easy to attack on the ground by skilled, long-range infiltrators.

An Example of What to Look for in Southeast Asia

An armed rebellion still smolders in Tibet. As recently as 2000, a Chinese bomber aircraft was seen refueling at Lhasa airport and a military truck convoy heading west. That convoy consisted of nothing more than a string of rickety, and thoroughly unguarded, 2 1/2 ton trucks. Within each cab were two PLA support personnel who appeared distrustful of either their moral mandate or of their ability to survive.[3] Largely without religion, Chinese soldiers are highly superstitious. As was discerned by a former U.S. Marine turned freelance combatant during the Vietnam War, such superstitions can make the things they guard much easier to attack after dark. Convinced of forest demons, lone sentries become quickly confused and intimidated by disembodied whispers projected toward them.[4] That makes the strategic assets they transport and guard more vulnerable to surreptitious ground attack. As masters of camouflage and dispersion, those rear-area soldiers are much less likely to act irrationally after an attack by aircraft or long-range artillery/missiles.

Only Missing Are Americans Who Can Get That Close

Asians are highly adept at defensive formations and maneuvers. Most are so heavily dug in that supporting arms generally can't hurt them, and then they systematically move rearward. To make matters worse, they regularly employ dummy positions, obstacles, and watch-standers. That's why Americans seldom saw their opposition at Iwo Jima, Seoul, and Hue City. And that's why they often took fire from all sides.

Thus, the Eastern enemy's weakness does not lie in the design of his tactics but rather in their execution. The only way to spot such a weakness is to get close enough to differentiate between what is real and what is not. Without more short-range reconnaissance skill, this will be as hard for contemporary U.S. soldiers and Marines as it was in WWII, Korea, and Vietnam. Eastern infantry units regularly provide their riflemen with *ninja*-like sensory-perception techniques. As a result, those riflemen are not easy to approach undetected. U.S. infiltrators will need commensurate skills just to keep from getting detected while inbound. Once they reach a point just outside the enemy's formation, those same skills should enable them to discern enough detail to find a weakness.

Imparting such "lower echelon" abilities will require training on a scale much smaller than what U.S. service personnel currently receive. To even determine what they are, instructors will have to repeatedly subdivide all areas considered to be "basics" (e.g., shooting, moving, and communicating). They must also add and then subdivide all areas considered to be common knowledge (e.g., microterrain appreciation, harnessing the senses, night familiarity, discreet force at close range, combat deception, and tactical-decision making). How U.S. soldiers and Marines acquire these "micro-skills" would also be different from the accepted norm—no more classroom memorization, and almost all field experimentation. (See Figure 14.3.)

Something Different

Anything too close to the American experience probably does not qualify as true UW. That's why Figure 14.4 only shows training that can strictly be proven to have been given to East Asian guerrillas. By so limiting the entries, one can preclude any logical—but still bogus—fillers that would almost certainly derive from Western guesswork. Later chapters will contain similar summaries on other topics.

The term "sapper reconnaissance" is used by both references to describe what the North Vietnamese Army (NVA) taught the Viet Cong (VC). One of those references contained a captured curriculum. As Asians have a different definition of "sapper" than most Westerners, a major insight into what might actually constitute UW reconnoitering and intelligence gathering could result. It is known that both the VC and the NVA regularly sent people to look at the inside of future attack objectives.[5] To an Asian, the term "sapper" only applies to someone who can enter an enemy's position unobserved. Asian sappers can do so easily through barbed wire.[6] (Unlike the person in Figure 14.3.) Thus, one can quickly see that UW ground intelligence gathering is more of an art form than any Western (technological) equivalent. Prior knowledge of every enemy mine/machinegun's location gives the attacker a much better chance of success. How enemy lines are again penetrated during the subsequent attack will be saved for the next chapter.

Embedded within each entry in Figure 14.4 is at least one technique. Techniques can only be derived and maintained through continual experimentation and practice.

NVA Sapper Training

While the below description is of internal NVA training, that which reached the VC was undoubtedly similar. Crossing swampy ground and dry leaves will correlate well with the next chapter's UW chart on how to get close enough to actually penetrate an enemy position. The excerpt below confirms the Asian sapper's ability to transit protective barbed wire.

Figure 14.3: *Eastern Sappers Crawl through Barbed Wire*
(Source: FM 21-75 [1967], p. 32)

The training was elaborate. We learned how to crouch while walking, how to crawl, how to move silently through mud and water, how to walk through dry leaves. We practiced different ways of stooping while we walked. In teams of seven men, we practiced moving in rhythm to avoid being spotted under searchlights, synchronizing our motions, stepping with toes first, then gradually lowering heels to the ground, very slowly, step by step.

Wading through mud, we were taught to walk by lowering our toes first, then the rest of the foot. Picking our feet up, we would move them around gently [to break any suction], then slowly pull up the heels to avoid making noises. If you just pulled them up, without first moving them around gently, you'd make sounds. The same thing would happen if you didn't put your toes down first. We used the same methods for walking through water. On dry leaves, we'd sling our weapons over our

Short-range scouting of enemy's rural position

<u>Sapper skills (before & after entering foe's position)</u> [&]

- Advance knowledge of how enemy bases are laid out and what installations they contain
- Ability to sneak through obstacles
- Observation methods
- Reconnaissance methods

<u>Psychological strategies (yojutsu and genjutsu)</u> [#]

- Spiritual refinement (seishin teki kyoyo)
    - Achieving a relaxed mental state
- Mind control (saiminjitsu)
    - Scouting attitude (sekkojutsu)
    - Enhancing one's external awareness
        - Concentrating on sensory perceptions
        - Paying attention to detail
        - Reading the thoughts of others
        - Perceiving danger
        - Making decisions
        - Visualizing the task to be accomplished

Figure 14.4: UW Guerrilla Course for Reconnoitering

Listening stops $

Sensory enhancement #

Seeing at night (ankokutoshijutsu)
- Fully adapting one's eyes to the darkness
- Keeping one eye closed near (and not looking at) any light
- Scanning an object without looking directly at it
- Watching for unexplained shadows (ankokutoshi no jutsu)

Enhanced peripheral vision through defocusing exercises

Hearing
- Listening for stealthy footsteps at 30 yards
- Cupping hands behind ears while tilting head with open mouth

Smelling
- Sniffing while closing mouth and concentrating on upper nose

Tasting
- Sampling the air with one's tongue

Touching
- Sensing a person nearby without actually touching him

Collecting intelligence #

Observing the foe from his perimeter (monomi-no-jitsu)
Memorizing defensive details

Short-range scouting of enemy's urban position

Collecting intelligence #

Scanning a room through the crack of a gradually opening door

Source Code:

Ninja methods for guerrilla use against Japan's Samuri (1460-1650) [7]
& N. Vietnamese methods for Viet Cong use against GIs (1965-1973) [8]
$ N. Korean Light Infantry Trng. Guidance Bur. methods (1992-2007) [9]

Figure 14.4 (Cont): UW Guerrilla Course for Reconnoitering

backs and move in a bent-over position using hands as well as feet. We were taught to move the dried leaves away with our hands, then pull our feet up underneath our palms so that we wouldn't step on the leaves. We'd keep moving that way until we neared the objective. Time made no difference. In training, it might take two or three hours to crawl like this through five fences of barbed wire.

> ... [To reconnoiter a position from the inside,] we would first have to crawl through the barbed wire, but without cutting the wire or removing the mines—we couldn't leave any traces. We were supposed to tie the wire up with string and mark the mines on the route we were following.[10]
>
> — Nguyen Van Mo, 40th Mine Sapper Battalion

Rare Recollection of Actual VC Sapper Penetration

Very seldom in the annals of warfare are there detailed descriptions of what actually occurs during a sapper reconnaissance. Below is one from the Vietnam War. Within it lies a classic diversion of an enemy sentry. When the sentry lights his cigarette, he temporarily ruins his night vision. Unlike Westerners, Asians will almost always wait for an opening instead of trying to force their way through nonconducive circumstances.

> Once [in the Mekong Delta in 1965] I got into the middle of Cai Be [South Vietnamese Army] post where the district chief's office was. It was fifteen days prior to the attack and takeover of the post by our battalion. I was accompanied by two comrades armed with submachineguns to protect me in case my presence was discovered while I was nearing the post entrance. I was then wearing pants only and had in my belt a pair of pincers, a knife, and a grenade. At one hundred meters from the post I started crawling and quietly approached the post entrance with the two comrades following me. At twenty meters from the post, my comrades halted while I crawled on. At the post entrance there was a barbed-wire barricade on which hung two grenades. Behind the barricade stood a guard. I made my way between the barricade and the stakes holding up the barbed wire fence. I waited in the dark for the moment when the guard lit his cigarette. I passed two meters away from him and sneaked through the entrance. On that occasion I was unable to find out where the munitions depot was but I did discover the positions of two machineguns and the radio room. I got out at the back of the post by cutting my way through the barbed wire.[11]
>
> — Reconnaissance sapper, 261st VC Battalion

Of Particular Interest to the U.S. UW Enthusiast

Easterners continually practice all movement techniques so that they, in effect, become muscle memory. While trying to infiltrate an enemy position, one would eventually encounter unexpected terrain or obstacles. As he had never rehearsed for them before, he might have trouble overcoming them. As noted in Figure 14.4, the *ninja* has a solution for just such an occurrence. Called "visualization," it involves rehearsing—in one's mind—what one is about to do. By thinking through every detail and possible hang-up, he then more effectively accounts for them.

15 Obscure Approach

- Can a UW attack surprise the foe if its approach doesn't?
- How do Asian guerrillas get so close to their objectives?

GIS CAN BECOME PHANTOMS TOO

(Source: FM 19-95B/CM [1978], cover)

The Movement Continuum

America's traditionally Eastern foes don't defend in the same way it does. They use broad bands of squad- and platoon-sized strongpoints that are made to look like a linear defense through the liberal use of dummy obstacles and positions. To make matters worse, many of those strongpoints are below ground and so well camouflaged that GIs can walk over them without knowing it. Add to that puzzle some forward outposts with roving sentinels between, and the U.S. reconnaissance sapper has quite a task ahead. Even if he gets close to the leading row of strongpoints unseen, he may still incur problems from behind. If a security patrol or roving sentinel sees his footprints, those footprints with lead them right to him. Thus, the prospective sapper must thoroughly prepare for

Distant approach to an enemy position

Navigation [&]

Moving through enemy country [#]

- Predicting the weather (ten-mon)
- Knowing and using terrain features (chi-mon)
  - Staying off the horizon
  - Blending with one's background
  - Fully utilizing all available cover
    - Lost-track pivot for darting behind cover
    - Entering pivot for turning corners
- Land navigation
  - Celestial dead reckoning (determining direction from the stars)
  - Terrain association (following linear terrain features like streets)
- Crossing open areas
  - In full moonlight
    - Predicting the shadows of natural and man-made objects
    - Moving quickly from shadow to shadow
      - Semi-prone rushing stance
  - In subdued light
    - Moving slowly and steadily from spot to spot
    - Motion so slow as to be indistinguishable to the naked eye
    - Rolling-travel method (taihenjutsu)
- Turning step for continuously scanning for enemy
- Walking like the wind over long distances (taijutsusosoku shugyo)
  - Scouting in actual battle (jissensekko gijutsu)
- Crossing a road or trail at low spot, curve, or otherwise covered place
- Changing direction in tall grass to avoid its unnatural motion
- Moving about in the mist (muton yuho)
- Traversing an area in pitch darkness
  - Stealthy step or running on tiptoe
- Remaining perfectly still under sudden, artificial illumination
- Avoiding one's reflection in standing water while near the enemy

Close approach to an enemy position

Camouflage [&]

- Hiding in plain sight

Figure 15.1: UW Guerrilla Instruction for Approach March

Flare training [&]
Closing with the enemy's line of defense [&]
Several crawling methods
How stealthfully to negotiate dry leaves
How stealthfully to negotiate swamp

Source Code:

Ninja methods for guerrilla use against Japan's Samuri (1460-1650) [1]
& N. Vietnamese methods for Viet Cong use against GIs (1965-1973) [2]
$ Chinese ally's Light Infantry Trng. Guid. Bur. methods (1992-2007) [3]

Figure 15.1 (Cont): UW Guerrilla Instruction for Approach March

three things: (1) crossing the final 1,000 yards to the objective; (2) negotiating the 100 yards in front of the sentries; and (3) bypassing those sentries. Anything less would be asking for trouble.

Figure 15.1 shows how UW-trained forces have met the first two challenges. Most notable in their distant approach is the ability to avoid any natural or artificial horizon (see Figures 15.2 and 15.3), cause any reflection, or make any unnatural shadow. It

Figure 15.2: Mounds Provide a Horizon to Foes at Their Base
(Source: MCRP 3-02H [1999], fig. I-3)

Figure 15.3: Lighter Backgrounds Create "False Horizons"
(Source: MCRP 3-02H [1999], fig. I-5)

involves a knowledge of terrain-associated movement that far exceeds anything available through U.S. military schools. The last challenge—bypassing the sentry—will be briefly discussed in this chapter but not thoroughly assessed by UW experts until the next. That's because sapper penetration is tantamount to an infiltration attack.

To get some idea of what such a penetration might entail, an imaginary objective has been arranged. (See Figure 15.4.) It is rumored to contain a well-hidden bunker in which valuable intelligence is kept. (See Figure 15.5.) The only way to get at that intelligence is through a deliberate assault. But first, a sapper reconnaissance is in order. If the bunker doesn't exist, there is no reason for an assault. If it does exist, knowing how the defenses are laid out will save lives. (See Figure 15.6.) But, those who are to perform this U.S. sapper reconnaissance must first fully embrace the lessons of Figure 15.1.

Most of the Laws of Nature Are Incorporated into *Ninjutsu*

What the *ninjas* discovered is much like what wild animals do while hunted. When caught in a car's headlights, those animals freeze. Similarly, the *ninja* remains stationary beneath a parachute flare.

In broad daylight, a deer crosses a thickly wooded area slowly and an open area quickly. Similarly, the *ninja* moves quickly between shadows on a moonlit night.

A deer passes unseen through a farmer's field by following the low vegetation in its irrigation ditch. Similarly, the *ninja* crosses a road or trail at a low spot, between curves, or in deep shade.

The deer is never far from cover, and neither is the *ninja*. He is constantly aware of the nearest solid object and how best to reach it.

For a deer, all of the above-mentioned rules change during periods of reduced daylight. At dawn or dusk, he slowly crosses the open area. On a moonlit night, the *ninja* also has a way of moving so slowly that he is hard to detect.

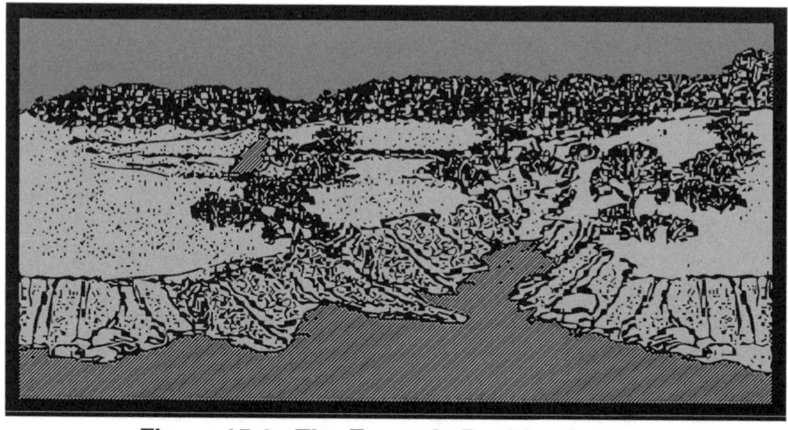

Figure 15.4: The Enemy's Position Looms
(Source: FM 7-8 [1984], p. 69)

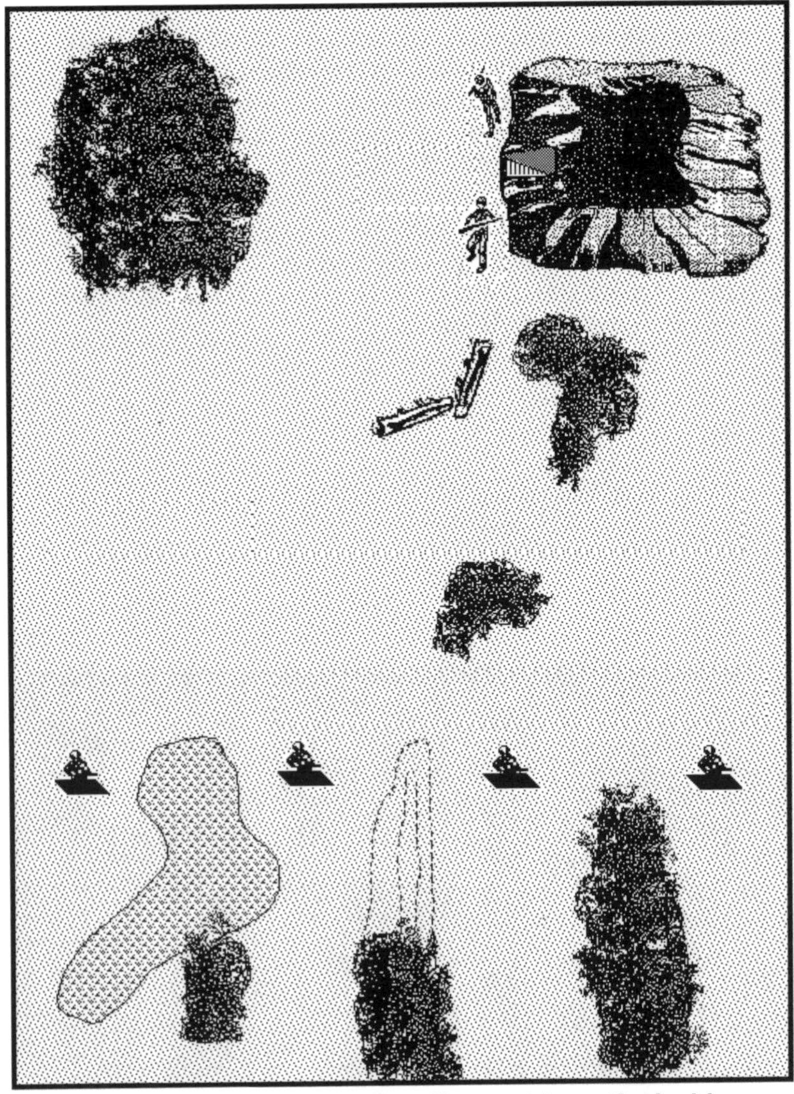

Figure 15.5: What's Really of Interest Is on the Inside
(Source: Courtesy of the Posterity Press, from *The Last Hundred Yards*, © 1997 by H.J. Poole, p. 242)

Sound and Odor Can Be Dead Giveaways

The hunter has great trouble approaching an animal from an upwind position. It can hear or smell him long before seeing him. That's why the *ninja* has intentionally enhanced his powers of hearing and smelling. In fact, when the wind blows just right, a master *ninja* can smell a Western stalker coming up behind him at 200 meters and hear him at 30.[4] Thus, the attention the VC paid to crossing dry leaves and swampy ground had a specific purpose. It was probably applied to other mediums as well.

Figure 15.6: There's Only One Safe Way to Find Out What It Is
(Source: FM 7-8 [1984], p. B-8)

The U.S. sapper should primarily remember to run his final (interior) reconnaissance of the enemy position from downwind. By so doing, he will more quickly identify the sentry locations in

1. DITCHES/DEPRESSIONS THAT LEAD INTO AN ENEMY CAMP, BUT INSIDE OF WHICH, THERE ARE NO DEFENDERS POSTED.

2. PLACES WHERE THE FIELDS OF FIRE HAVE NOT BEEN CLEARED.

4. WHERE WET AREAS EXTEND INSIDE THE ENEMY'S LINES.

3. APPROACHES TO POSITIONS MANNED BY HABITUAL SLEEPERS.

5. AREAS IN DEEP SHADOW.

Figure 15.7: Probable Gaps in Enemy Lines
(Source: Courtesy of the Posterity Press, from *The Last Hundred Yards*, © 1997 by H.J. Poole, p. 242)

his lane and any subsequent diversions. He will also reduce the chances of telegraphing his own presence through odor or sound. Then, the wind-driven vacillation of the vegetation will at least be along the same axis as his approach. And the rebounding shrubbery may partially mask his movements.

Most Sentries Have Weaknesses

Eastern sentries very probably make the same mistakes that U.S. sentries do. One of the most common is digging their fighting holes just behind the "military crest" of a hill instead of directly on top of it. As each sentry's downhill view is now partially blocked, a low crawler can sneak almost to his hole. The ideal position for a fighting hole gives its occupant an uninterrupted field of vision to his neighbor's hole on either side and downhill beyond grenade range. Any exception can easily be exploited by an experienced short-range infiltrator. As most sentries don't like to dig in damp or gullied locations, they invariably become "gaps" in the line. There are others. (See Figures 15.7 and 15.8.)

Figure 15.8: Sentries Have Limitations
(Source: FM 5-20 [1968], p. 31)

Luckily for America, most Eastern armies now also promote their most situationally astute and tactically skilled personnel beyond sentry duty. Like the U.S. military, they entrust that tedious mission to tired, homesick, recently recruited, and overly controlled teenagers. Those teenagers pose a risk to sappers only to the extent that they are recently positioned, near superiors, or otherwise free to fire their weapons.

The longer the average sentry has guarded the same post, the easier he is to bypass. He has already seen moving shadows in the night. After having reported them, he has been reprimanded by superiors who would have rather slept. Unless he is on full alert after being just moved to an area or warned of an impending attack, he does not have the authority to fire his rifle or throw a grenade. Depending on how far he is from his superior, that authority might take many minutes to acquire after having clearly seen an infiltrator.

From the overcommitment that low rank fosters, the Eastern defender has probably learned how to sleep while appearing not to. Like the average GI, he spends most of every day on patrol or working party and most of every night on watch. After a couple of hours of late-night duty, he may appear to be looking downrange, but his mind is undoubtedly somewhere else. An experienced infiltrator knows the difference. He watches for the head turning, shaking, and rubbing that characterizes a tired person trying to stay awake. If he sees none of these standard mannerisms, he assumes that the sentry is either dreaming of home or intensely focused on something to his front. The difference between the two lies in the hour and previous events. If the sentry has been on watch a while, it's 3:00 A.M., and nothing has changed to prompt a stare, the sapper can be fairly well assured that his quarry is dreaming. Under these kinds of conditions, he does not require a diversion to pass him. Just as a tired motorist can be unaware of leaving a highway, so too can a tired sentry be unaware of being passed by a short-range infiltrator.

Then There Are Any Number of Natural Sentry Diversions

Within a normal night, there will be many distracters to what a sentry sees, hears, and does. (See Figures 15.9 to 15.11.) Should

SENTRY HAS NO NIGHT VISION WHEN CLOUD COVERS MOON

HE CAN'T SEE INTO SHADOWS IN THE DIRECTION OF DISTANT FLARES OR IN ANY DIRECTION RIGHT AFTER THEY GO OUT

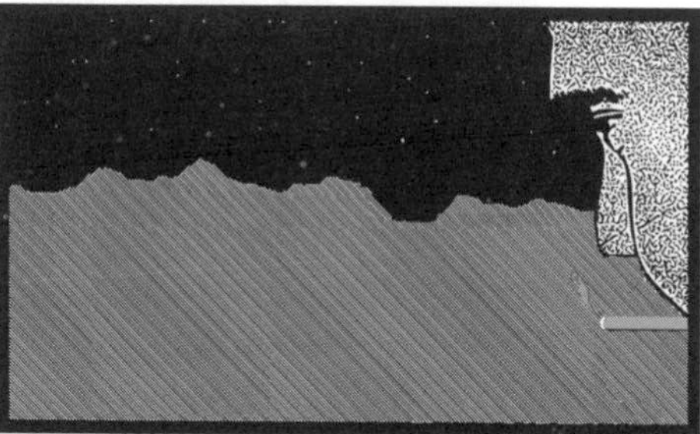

HE HAS NO NIGHT VISION RIGHT AFTER PUFF ON CIGARETTE

Figure 15.9: Distracters to a Sentry's Night Vision

(Source: FM 7-11B1/2 [1978], pp. 2-11-A-4.2 , 3-11-A-4.2; OPNAV P34-03 [1960], p. 40)

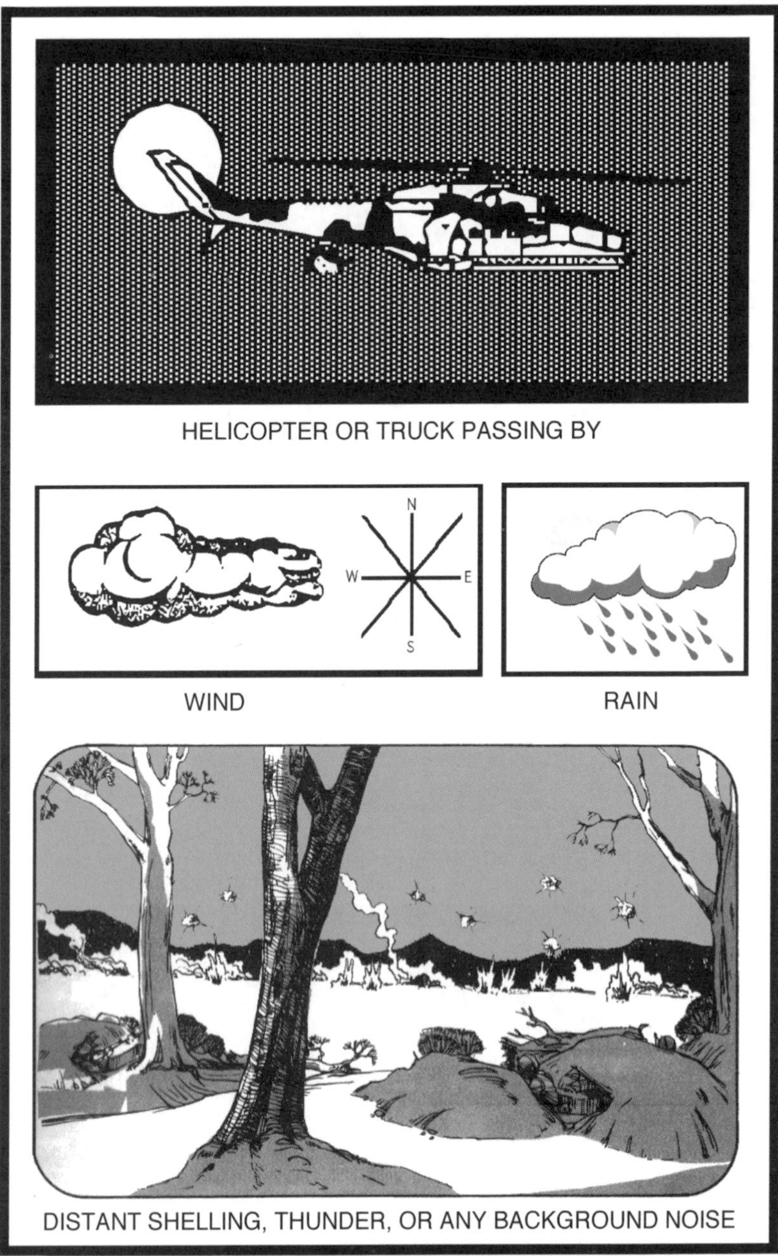

Figure 15.10: Distracters to a Sentry's Hearing
(Source: FM 7-8 [1984]. p. 4-25; MCO P1500.44B, p. 15-26; MCI 7311B, p. 115; Corel Gallery Clipart, Weather, #46A004)

WATCH CHANGE

SUPERIOR CHECKING LINES

ANY UNEXPECTED OR BOTHERSOME OCCURRENCE

Figure 15.11: Distracters to a Sentry's Attention

(Source: FM 90-5 [1982], p. 2-12; FM 100-5 [1994], p. 37; Corel Gallery Clipart, Bird #06D047, Insect #23B080)

that sentry does not fall asleep while sitting up, the short-range infiltrator can wait for one of these distractions before making his move.

A highly experienced pair of infiltrators could create their own distraction. As will be evident from the UW training chart in the next chapter, *ninjas* have made how to divert a lone sentry into an art form. Once one realizes that hypnosis is nothing more than overfocusing on one thing at the exclusion of everything else,[5] he begins to imagine the *ninja's* vast repertoire. The most obvious trick would be to create a diversion for one's partner. It would work best for a three-man American team. That way, two could get through enemy lines to accomplish the subsequent mission, while the third stayed behind to cover their withdrawal.

Should the U.S. Sapper Team Be Detected

Should the American sapper team become convinced that they have been spotted (e.g., overhear nervous sentry talk), all is not lost. There are any number of reasons why those sentries will either do nothing or take an inordinate amount of time reacting. (See Figure 15.12.) Unbelievable as it may seem, the sapper team can often just pull back during this totally predictable delay in the proceedings.[6] To then resume its mission, it would have only to move laterally into a different infiltration lane. Of course, there are exceptions to this rule. If the enemy unit has just moved into the area, it may be trigger-happy the first few nights. Luckily, people tend to shoot high at night. As throwing a grenade or detonating a claymore does not compromise a sentry's location, they cannot be totally ruled out. Whether they occur will depend on the sentry's instructions and degree of initiative.

An Imaginary Case

No American serviceman will ever agree to sneak into an enemy's fortified camp without first being shown the various ways to offset the obvious dangers. Minimally, the actions of the sapper must logically make sense to a survival-oriented Private First Class (PFC). Figures 15.13 to 15.18 take the reader through an ap-

NOT QUITE SURE OF WHAT HE JUST SAW OR HEARD

AWARE OF HOW EASY IT IS TO IMAGINE THINGS AT NIGHT

NOT ALLOWED TO GIVE AWAY HIS POSITION BY FIRING

CAN'T REACH HIS SUPERIOR BY RADIO OR LAND LINE

WOULD HAVE TO WAKE UP HIS PARTNER TO REPORT SIGHTING

DOESN'T WANT TO BOTHER HIS SUPERIOR AGAIN

GOT CHEWED OUT LAST TIME HE REPORTED HIS SUSPICIONS

WOULD RATHER NOT BELIEVE THE ENEMY IS COMING

IS MORE USED TO TAKING ORDERS THAN MAKING DECISIONS

OFTEN PUNISHED FOR SHOWING TOO MUCH INITIATIVE

HAS FALSE SENSE OF SECURITY WITH WHOLE UNIT NEARBY

NEVER TOLD HIS ENEMY IS GOOD AT SNEAKING THRU LINES

CONSTANTLY REMINDED THAT HIS UNIT IS BEST IN WORLD

NOT WELL TRAINED AT SHORT-RANGE INFILTRATION HIMSELF

NEVER TOLD THAT ALL SENTRIES HAVE WEAKNESSES

UNAWARE OF ALL THE DISTRACTERS TO VISION

UNAWARE OF ALL THE DISTRACTERS TO HEARING

UNAWARE OF ALL THE DISTRACTERS TO ATTENTION

SO OVERCONTROLLED THAT HE FEELS LITTLE RESPONSIBILITY

BECOMING EMASCULATED BY DEFENSIVE COMBAT

WOULD RATHER BE HOME

SIGHTING HAS ALREADY STARTED TO BLUR IN HIS MEMORY

Figure 15.12: Distracters to a Sentry's Ability to Act
(Source: Courtesy of the Posterity Press, from *The Last Hundred Yards*, p. 228, © 1997 by H.J. Poole)

proximate sequence of events. For the best chance of succeeding, both U.S. sappers should have "silencers" attached to their M-4 rifles.

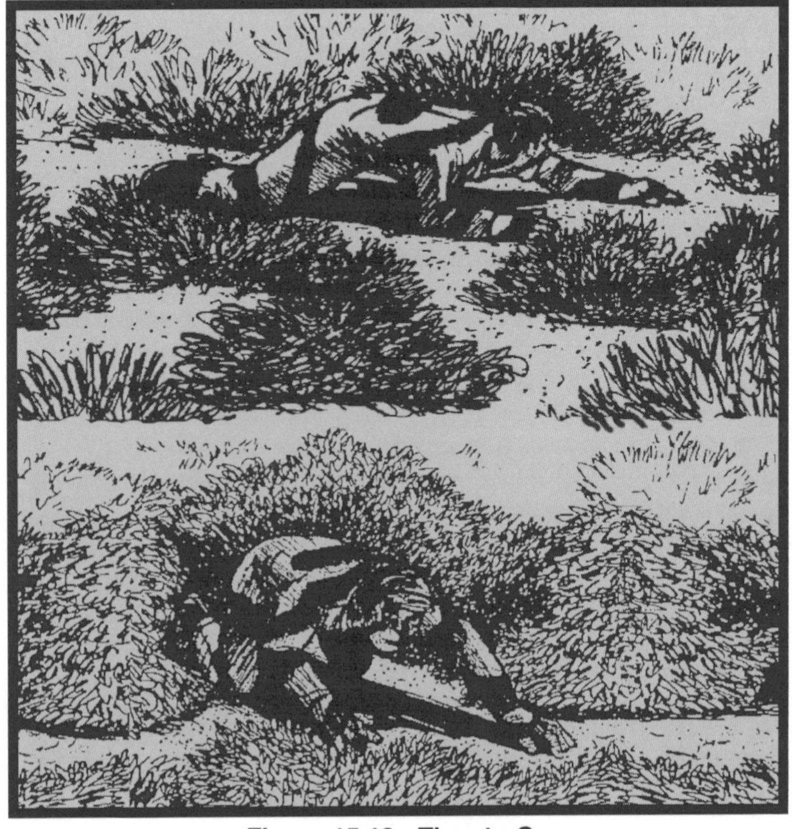

Figure 15.13: Time to Go
(Source: MCRP 3-02H [1999], fig. I-2)

Once the Sapper Reconnaissance Is Complete

So far on this enemy objective, only two lives have been risked. If it holds a strategically important enemy asset, the sapper pair can often destroy it before leaving. Then, no ground assault will be necessary. No matter how much firepower gets projected ahead of time, ground assaults cost lives. There is no amount of conventional ordnance that will seek out and destroy every well-camouflaged and heavily dug-in machinegun. To have any chance of neutral-

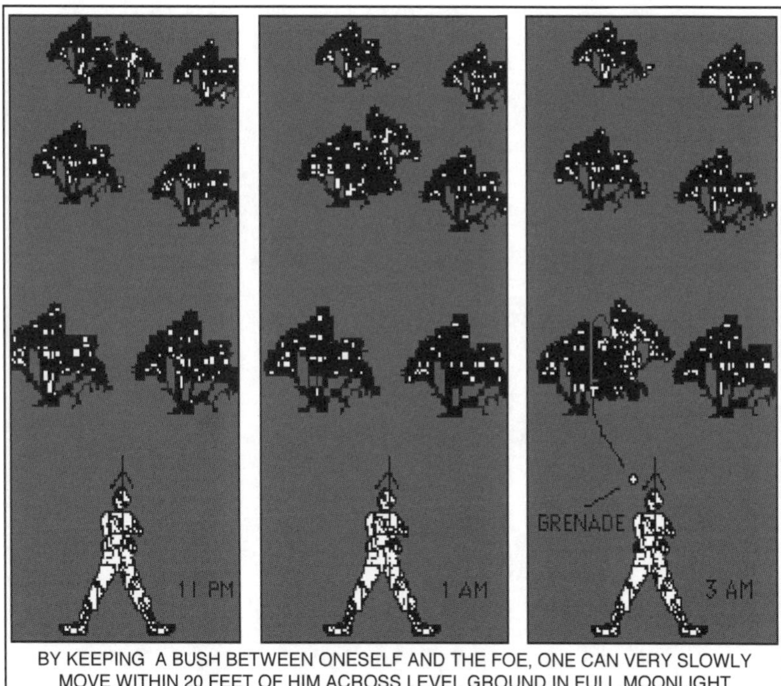

BY KEEPING A BUSH BETWEEN ONESELF AND THE FOE, ONE CAN VERY SLOWLY MOVE WITHIN 20 FEET OF HIM ACROSS LEVEL GROUND IN FULL MOONLIGHT

Figure 15.14: The East-Asian Stalking Approach
(Source: Courtesy of the Posterity Press, from *The Last Hundred Yards*, © 1997 by H.J. Poole, p. 230)

PRIOR TO THE PENETRATION ATTEMPT

BY STUDYING THE VEGETATION PATTERNS AT THE OBJECTIVE THRU BINOCULARS, TWO GI'S PICK LANE WITH A LIKELY GAP

THE TWO U.S. SAPPERS STRIP OFF ALL OF THEIR EQUIPMENT EXCEPT FOR BACK-SLUNG WATER, EXPLOSIVE, TIMER, & M-4

THEY CAMOUFLAGE THEMSELVES TO LOOK LIKE WHATEVER IS MOST COMMON IN THEIR LANE—BUSHES, GRASS, ROCKS

DURING THE APPROACH

AT DUSK, THE TWO GIS MOVE UP THEIR LANE WELL AWARE OF THE POSSIBILITY OF OUTPOSTS WITH ROVING SENTINELS

THEY HAVE CHOSEN A FULLY MOONLIT NIGHT SO THAT THE DEFENDERS' NIGHT VISION DEVICES WILL BE USELESS

IF THEY HAD PREVIOUSLY FOUND THE FOE TO HAVE THERMAL IMAGING, THEY WOULD HAVE WAITED FOR A RAINY NIGHT

UPON SPOTTING THE SENTRY IN THEIR LANE, THEY STALK HIM—KEEPING MOUNDS OR VEGETATION BETWEEN THEM

TO CROSS OPEN GROUND, THEY GO SO SLOWLY THAT THEIR MOVEMENTS WILL NOT BE DISCERNIBLE IN MOONLIGHT

THEY GET WITHIN 20-30 FEET (GRENADE RANGE) OF THE ENEMY SENTRY IN THEIR LANE BY 2:00 A.M

BYPASSING THE SENTRY

FROM 2:00 TO 3:30 A.M., THEY STUDY THE GROUND THEY MUST CROSS, VISUALIZE DOING SO, AND WAIT FOR A DIVERSION

WHEN THAT DIVERSION COMES, ONE TAKES A BEAD ON THE SENTRY'S HEAD WITH HIS WEAPON, AND THE OTHER MOVES

AFTER PASSING THE SENTRY, THE FIRST TAKES A BEAD ON THE BACK OF THE SENTRY'S HEAD AND THE SECOND MOVES

GETTING BACK OUT

AFTER THE TWO HAVE PERFORMED THEIR RECON OR SET THEIR TIMED CHARGE, THEY REVERSE THE PROCEDURE

Figure 15.15: Penetration Sequence for Objective without Wire

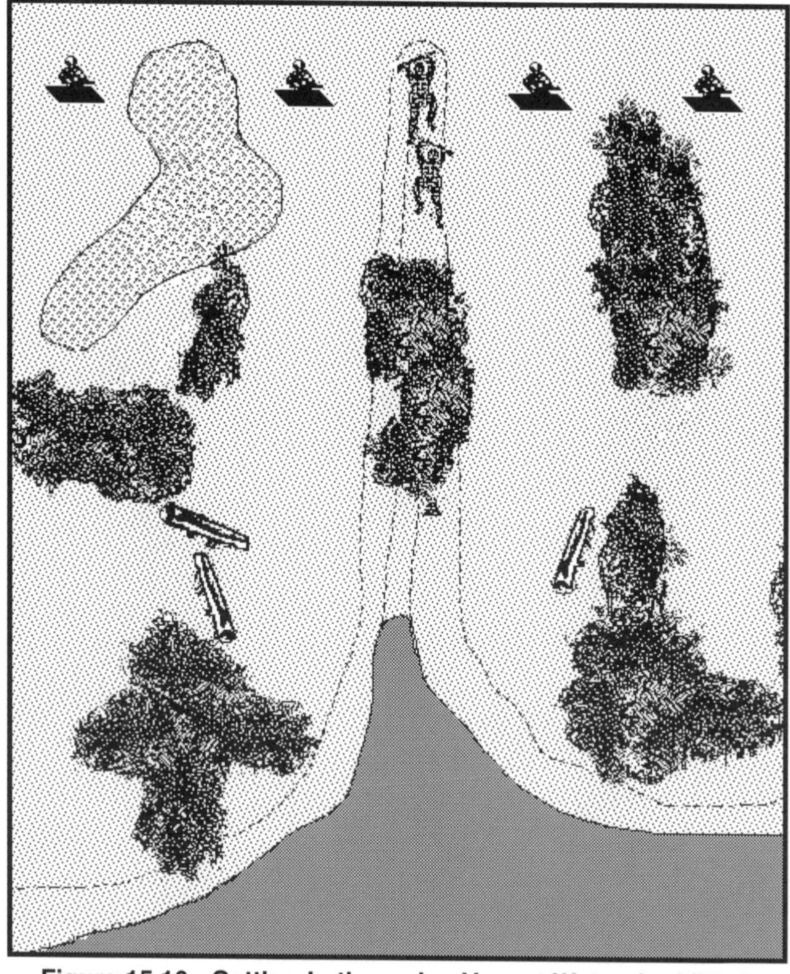

Figure 15.16: Getting In through a Vacant Watershed Ditch
(Source: Courtesy of the Posterity Press, from *The Last Hundred Yards,* © 1997 by H.J. Poole, p. 240)

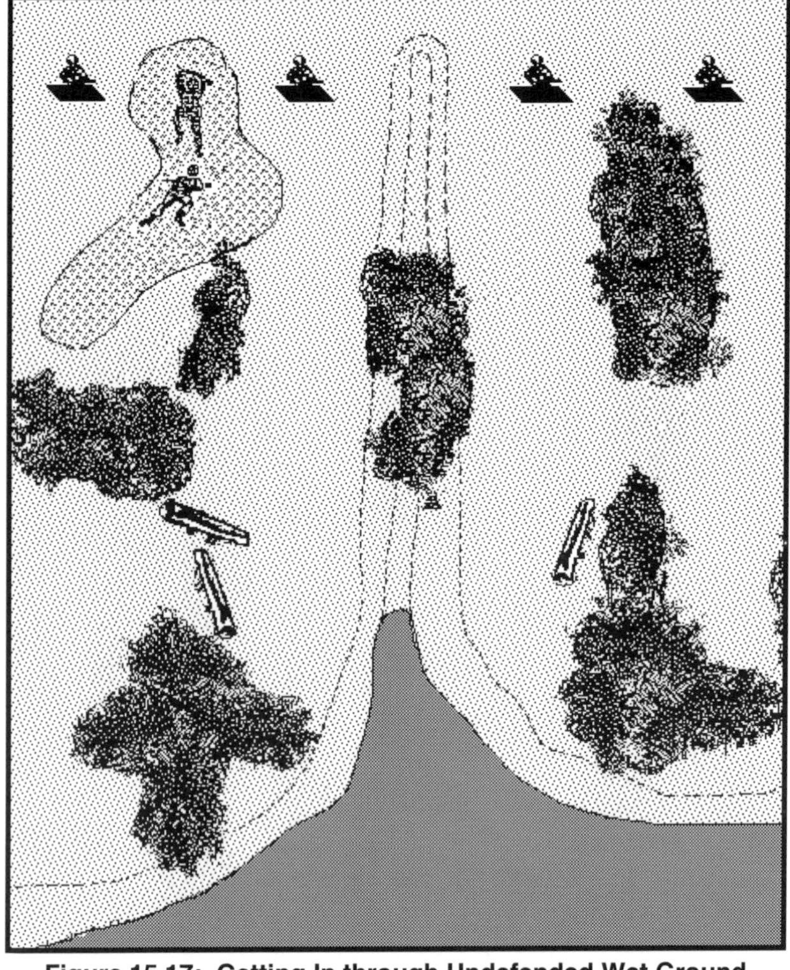

Figure 15.17: Getting In through Undefended Wet Ground
(Source: Courtesy of the Posterity Press, from *The Last Hundred Yards*, © 1997 by H.J. Poole, p. 240)

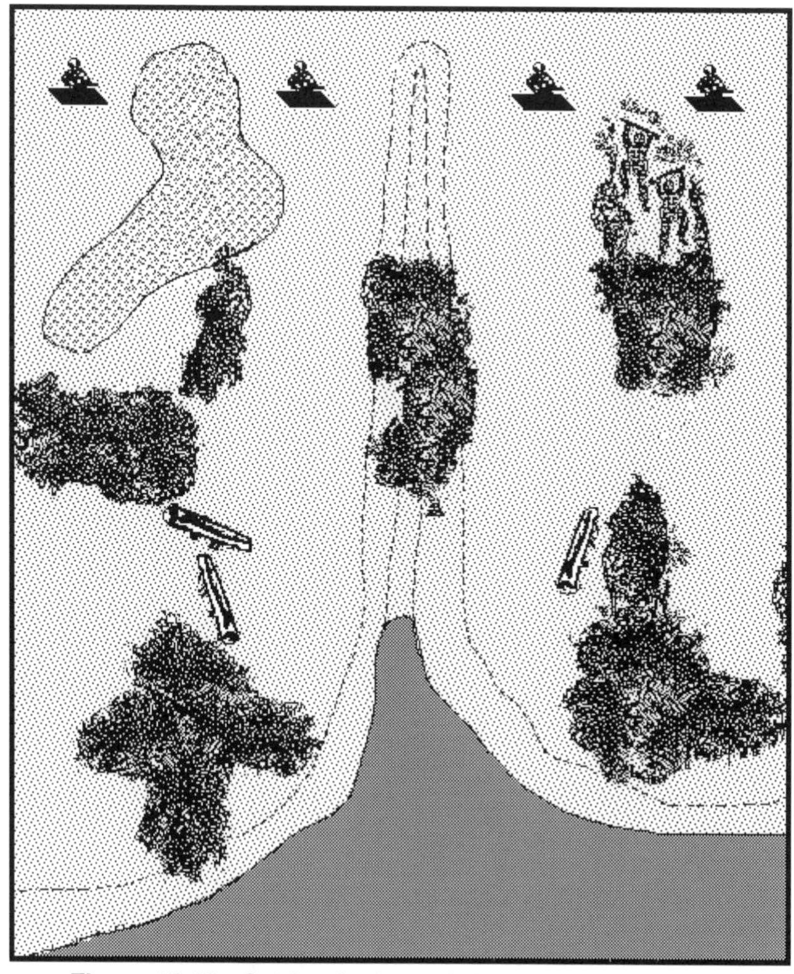

Figure 15.18: Getting In through Uncleared Vegetation
(Source: Courtesy of the Posterity Press, from *The Last Hundred Yards*, © 1997 by H.J. Poole, p. 240)

izing every machinegun, their locations must first be established. Most of the time, all can be found through sapper reconnaissance. The next chapter will discuss how further to minimize the risk of ground assault.

16 Disguising the Attack

- Why should a ground attack look like something else?
- What are the ways to disguise one?

MAKE QUARRY THINK IT'S "MINES" OR "MORTARS"

(Source: FM 7-8 [1984], p. F-1)

What Delineates "Sapper Recon" from Infiltration Attack

Just to reconnoiter a possible ground attack target, diminutive Asian sappers have for years crawled right through multiple rows of intact barbed wire.[1] Partially because Western soldiers are larger and less conditioned by their culture to be patient, they have no such military heritage. Therefore, against any wire-protected objective, U.S. troops should try no inside reconnoitering and instead run a "short-range-infiltration" attack in which the wire is quietly vaulted or separated. That "wire" must be a hastily strung single row, not the more daunting standard.

For such an attack, several tiny teams of soldiers or Marines would move up an equal number of roughly parallel lanes, each already determined to hold a promising gap. Each team's goal is first to negotiate any obstacles and then sneak between two enemy fighting holes. To accomplish the parent unit's mission, only one team has to get through. While there are few examples of such an attack in U.S. history, there are many in East Asian history. The relatively recent one below has luckily been documented in some detail. Please note the extent to which each sapper was trained and then allowed to operate without any headquarters' interference. All NVA/VC sappers were trained in light-infantry maneuvers, and all NVA/VC light infantrymen were trained in sapper techniques.[2] Until American soldiers enjoy the same level of training and trust, they will be unable to match the feat. That's the same as saying GIs will be unable to totally surprise a prepared enemy position. Of course, all of this takes a complete willingness to get down flat on the ground and commune with nature. (See Figure 16.1.) There are no economy-bolstering vehicles involved.

> [The] local NVA [special-operations detachment] probably served as guides for the [VC] sappers during pre-assault recons and their attack itself. . . . It was the sappers alone, however, who negotiated the wire obstacles and infiltrated the base. . . . With weapons slung tightly across their backs, grenades attached to their belts, and faces and bodies blackened, they slid snake-like through the brush, silently, patiently, an inch at a time, listening, watching, gently feeling the ground ahead of them. They neutralized trip-flares encountered along the way by tying down the strikers with strings or strips of bamboo they carried in their mouths. They snipped the detonation cords connected to claymores, and used wire cutters on the concertina, careful to cut only two-thirds of the way through each strand, then breaking each noiselessly with their hands, holding it firmly so the large coil wouldn't shake.[3]

This account mentions techniques for obstacle breaching, but none for sentry passing. While the latter surely existed, they must now be ascertained from how the three UW experts trained guerrillas. (See Figure 16.2.) Immediately apparent from the first page of the chart is the subterranean option—tunneling beneath

Figure 16.1: Much Depends on the Lowly Bush
(Source: Gallery Graphics, Mac/EPS, *Flowers, Trees, and Plants 2*, "Shrubs")

Between the line of departure and inside of barrier

Bluffing defenders #
Falling in behind a returning sentry or incoming patrol

Burrowing beneath enemy obstacles $
Crossing enemy obstacles &
Sapper methods
Negotiating minefields
Getting through wire
Transiting floodlit areas

Entering enemy's fortress (chiku jo gunryaku heiho) #
Using rain, snow, or fog to restrict the defender's vision and hearing
Choosing an overcast night
Leaping over low bushes (or obstacles)
Crawling over a low wall or fence

Silent assault

Short-range infiltration $ &
Stealthfully crossing surfaces (ninja-aruki) #
Sweeping step for clearing away obstacles in grass
Small step for shallow water and dry leaves (ko ashi)
Hands-and-knees crawl
Forearms-and-toes crawl
Serpent crawl
Dragon crawl

Figure 16.2: UW Guerrilla Course for Silent Rural Attack

Bypassing an enemy sentry #

Discovering the sentry's weaknesses (nyudaki no jitsu)
Deceiving the sentry's senses
 Avoiding eye contact with the sentry
 Knowing the limits of the sentry's peripheral vision
 Directing sentry's attention elsewhere (yojigakure no jitsu)
 Preconditioning sentry to the sounds and sights of infiltration
 Covering one's noise with wind's rustling of leaves
Masking footfalls with natural sounds or enemy conversations
 Staying downwind of sentry so as not to project any odor
 Blinding sentry with a flash or keeping bright light to one's rear
Psychological strategies (yojutsu and genjutsu)
 Mind control (saiminjitsu)
  Clouding a sentry's mind
   Hazing the sentry
   Distracting the sentry through hypnotic suggestion

Source Code:

Ninja methods for guerrilla use against Japan's Samuri (1460-1650) [4]
& N. Vietnamese methods for Viet Cong use against GIs (1965-1973) [5]
$ Chinese ally's Light Infantry Trng. Guid. Bur. methods (1992-2007) [6]

Figure 16.2 (Cont): UW Guerrilla Course for Silent Rural Attack

Figure 16.3: Most Forward Movement Must Be by Crawling
(Source: FM 21-75 [1967], p. 67)

the obstacles. Within the "entering the enemy's fortress" part are references to what might best be described as individual acrobatic moves. Some would work for diving over barbed wire or streams of machinegun tracers. As late as 2000, a Chinese military-magazine cover showed a PLA soldier flying parallel to, and about four feet off, the ground.[7] He wasn't wearing much gear.

U.S. troops might find this kind of physical activity more helpful to their survivability in combat than running around the block in tennis shoes. Why, then, has the latter become the norm? It must have something to do with how much gear their superiors (and the gear manufacturers) expect them to carry. For America to have any chance of improving its UW capabilities, the gear lobbyists and their unsuspecting active-duty minions will have to take a breather. Much less small-arms ammunition is necessary for 3GW and 4GW because its use badly compromises the element of surprise. Short-range U.S. infiltrators will need little more than a silenced M-4 with oversized magazine, an explosive charge with timer, and a little water. Anything more than that, to include excess clothing, will cause them to exude a pheronone (scent) signature.[8] If the wind is blowing in the wrong direction, that signature will alert any woods-wise or sensory-enhanced Easterner to the infiltrator's presence. (See Figures 16.3 and 16.4.)

Figure 16.4: Camouflage Netting May Help near Enemy Sentry
(Source: FMFM 1-3B [1981], p. 4-9; FM 5-103 [1985], p. 4-4)

Disguising an Infiltration Attack

Any form of ground incursion will obviously be more effective if the quarry can't identify it as such. On Guadalcanal,[9] and again in Vietnam,[10] two different Asian adversaries made sapper-placed explosives look like lucky artillery/mortar hits. Their sappers did so by detonating hand-placed explosives during incoming indirect-fire barrages on the U.S. positions. Though many years apart, both adversaries also made spider-hole-launched tank attacks look like stationary mine detonations. Their one-man outposts had only to follow a simple procedure: (1) attach a string to a surface-deployed but hidden landmine; (2) pull the mine beneath the tread of an approaching tank; and then (3) hide below ground until dark.[11]

Thus, any serious attempt by U.S. forces to run a UW (guerrilla-like) infiltration attack must necessarily entail a great deal of deception. If it doesn't, its particulars will soon become known to the enemy, and it will only work once. Most obvious of these deceptions is to fool the quarry into thinking he is under attack by indirect fire alone. That's the essence of the famous German Stormtrooper assault technique of WWI. But, any noise whatsoever tends to diminish the element of surprise, so U.S. forces must look Eastward for more stealthy alternatives. (See Figure 16.5.)

Figure 16.5: There Are Several Ways to Silently Cross Wire
(Source: Podgotovka Razvegchika: Sistema Spetsnaza GRU, © 1998 by A.E. Taras and F.D. Zanuz, p. 279)

A distant mortar or artillery barrage might divert the sentries' attention, but it would also wake up their superior. A better choice might be having someone snap a branch or two on the opposite side of the enemy's perimeter. (See Figure 16.6.) Unfortunately, that too would send an alert. One of the best diversions is a preplanned illumination concentration. If it were several miles behind the attack force, it would make no noise. It would partially illuminate the objective, and all but blind its defenders. Lastly, it would cause moving shadows from the various bushes, rocks, and trees that lined that side of the perimeter. Under those kinds of conditions, crouching attackers could virtually walk up on their quarries as long as they made no noise. Through it all, the sentries' superior would either sleep or remain unaware of any frontline trouble. Unable to get permission to fire, any sentries who finally detected the assault would be hesitant to do anything about it. However, urban terrain presents more of a challenge.

Figure 16.6: Even Russians Climb Trees
(Source: Podgotovka Razvegchika: Sistema Spetsnaza GRU, © 1998 by A.E. Taras and F.D. Zanuz, p. 153.)

More Acrobatics May Be Required in the City

Offensive urban combat is the most dangerous kind. No amount of unit overwatch can protect the individual soldier as he crosses each open area. As he moves between buildings or past a window while in one of those buildings, he can be shot from too many locations. Thus, each soldier is largely responsible for his own survival. To move in such a way as to dodge every bullet, that soldier must first thoroughly understand what constitutes cover in a three-dimensional battlespace. For example, alcoves may protect him from overhead fire, but they are killers if they contain a door. Then, any alcove occupant will throw a shadow beneath that door and be easily shot through it.

Once the soldier fully appreciates the differences in terrain, he must then develop appropriate movement skills. Otherwise, he will be unable to secretly enter buildings from the top, change stories without using stairs, and quickly descend into the sewer. Continually traveling up and down as well as sideways logically entails a whole new category of climbing technique. As anyone can attest who has had to climb a rope to a second story window while fully loaded, muscle power alone will not get the job done. (See Figure 16.7.)

The UW experts have more detailed advice for urban combat. (See Figure 16.8.) It is here that their affinity for treetops first

Figure 16.7: Urban Combat Requires Structure Climbing
(Source: Podgotovka Razvegchika: Sistema Spetsnaza GRU, © 1998 by A.E. Taras and F.D. Zanuz, p. 147.)

Between line of departure and inside of structure

Entering enemy's fortress (chiku jo gunryaku heiho) #

- Ramparts crossing
  - Pole or limbless-tree climbing without any equipment
  - Climbing tree with spiked hand and foot bands (shuka & ashika)
  - Leaping from tree to tree
  - Rope throwing (nawanage)
  - Pulling occupied treetop over wall with grappling hook (kaginawa)
  - Ascending a building's trellis or drain pipe
  - Jumping from rooftop to rooftop
  - Moving along a horizontal pole or "leaping ladder" (tobi bashigo)
  - Crawling or using a pulley (kasha) to cross an outstretched rope
- Ramparts scaling
  - Vertical-surface running (shoten no jutsu)
  - Running up an inclined plank
  - Rock climbing
  - Stone or brick wall climbing
    - While facing either towards or away from the wall
  - Rope climbing
  - "Loop," "spider," and "hanging-rope" ladders (bashigo)
- Entering an inaccessible structure (shinobi-iri)
  - Effortlessly moving through a window opening
  - Climbing stairs along the wall
  - Opening a door so as not to let in any light

Silent assault

Stealthfully crossing surfaces (ninja-aruki) #

- Walking across wooden floor on unrolled sash (obi)
- Sweeping step for planks and straw mat (nuki ashi)
- Side step for moving through narrow spaces or a threshold
- Cross step for a building's shadow or tight passageway (yoko aruki)
- Using cat's claws (neko te) to crawl along rafters

Bypassing an enemy sentry #

- Manipulating the sentry's thought processes
  - Interchanging truth with falsehood (hojutsu)
  - Altering the perception of truth and falsehood (kyojitsu tenkan ho)
  - Playing on the sentry's needs and fears
- Predicting sentry's next move by fixing one's gaze at base of his neck

Figure 16.8: UW Guerrilla Course for Silent Urban Attack

Actual passing strategies
- Not casting a shadow into the sentry's field of vision
- Cross-stepping behind sentry so as to watch him
- Staying below sentry's shoulders to escape his peripheral vision
- Melting around a corner
- Tapping sentry on shoulder and doing "lost-track" pivot
- Pinching sentry on ankle and rolling behind his resting place

Source Code:

Ninja methods for guerrilla use against Japan's Samuri (1460-1650) [5]
& N. Vietnamese methods for Viet Cong use against GIs (1965-1973) [6]
$ Chinese ally's Light Infantry Trng. Guid. Bur. methods (1992-2007) [7]

Figure 16.8 (Cont): UW Guerrilla Course for Silent Urban Attack

Figure 16.9: Passing an Asian Sentry Is More of a Chore
(Source: Courtesy of Orion Books, from *World Army Uniforms since 1939*, © 1975, 1980, 1981, 1983 by Blandford Press Ltd., Part II, plate 88)

appears. By also operating above and below ground in rural terrain, they have made that medium three-dimensional as well, and thereby captured many of the advantages of urban terrain. Even the Westernized Russian army has this tradition. (Refer back to Figure 16.7.)

How the three UW experts train guerrillas for urban combat might provide a few clues as to which new movement techniques might be necessary. (Refer back to Figure 16.8.) Within "ramparts scaling" and other segments of this chart are references to wall, tree, trellis, drain pipe, and stair climbing. There are other mentions of crossing between buildings on planks, ropes, and ladders. And, there are strategies for passing sentries. (See Figure 16.9.) All involve some form of acrobatic maneuver. One could reasonably conclude that to acquire much UW capability in the city, every U.S. unit would have daily to practice such things. Almost all East Asian armies already do so. Even the Russian Army does.

> The Red Army had extensive experience in cities in World War II. . . . The effect of these experiences is apparent in Soviet training today. For instance, the standard obstacle course that all Soviet soldiers negotiate at least weekly as part of their physical training is designed to build skills specifically suited to combat in cities. It includes vaulting low obstacles, climbing walls, walking balance beams, diving under low doors, and jumping through windows.[12]

The Chart Reveals a Whole New Level of Required Skill

That no one in America knows much about fighting like an urban guerrilla should be sufficient evidence that the U.S. military lacks the techniques to do so. Successfully to perform a UW infiltration attack in the city, such techniques would be necessary. Figure 16.8 provides a number of examples. Within the chart are ways to silently cross wooden floors and climb stairs. There is even a technique for opening a door without letting in any light. While such things may seem elementary and mundane to high-ranking U.S. military leaders, they would be of great interest to someone who was trying to secretly enter an enemy headquarters and then return home to tell about it.

Within the city, any attempt at an infiltration attack would invariably involve passing enemy sentries from the rear. Whichever teams got through the foe's outer defenses would very likely encounter interior watchstanders who blocked their way to the subsequent target. As painfully evident from Figure 16.9, getting past one of those watchstanders might take special and advanced training. Figure 16.8 provides a good starting point for the development of such training. While fixing one's gaze at the base of a sentry's neck may help to predict his next move, it might also alert him. Staring at the back of someone's head will often cause them to turn around.[13] One might be better served by watching the sentry's upper back while trying to stay out of his area of peripheral vision. According to the chart, the latter can best be achieved by staying below his shoulder level and not casting a shadow.

Touching a sentry on one side to move around his other should be left to *ninjutsu* experts. Still, the whole idea of so controlling a foe as to make him incapable of responding to an obvious intrusion is an intriguing one. It will be covered next.

17 Precluding a Counterstroke

- Can a breakdown in surprise during an attack be fixed?
- What's the best way to preclude counterattack?

THOSE NOT UNDER ASSAULT POSE LESS THREAT

(Source: FM 100-20 [1981], p. 54)

Surprising the Foe Though Already Detected

Most dismounted attacks are preceded by a some attempt, however inept, at a surreptitious approach. Then something goes wrong, the element of surprise is compromised, and the attack starts to cost lives. Once committed to an assault, most U.S. units are both unwilling and unable to abort that assault. So doing would constitute an exception to their heritage and thus violate their creed. The average unit keeps on coming at a now fully alerted enemy and—in the process—takes too many casualties. With two "guerrilla-like" changes to standard operating procedure, many of those casualties could be avoided. Americans are by nature a brave people, and most grow up in a fairly volatile environment. That gives U.S. privates the ability to resume an assault after being initially allowed to get down or even pull back.

A quick look at what the three UW experts would say about a no-longer-secret attack might provide an alternative to stopping. Figure 17.1 implies a willingness to still assault under certain circumstances. It further promises to run with abandon through the inside of the enemy's perimeter. The first would only be an option if a pair of prerequisites were met: (1) the attack—though noisy—had yet to warn defenders of a ground assault; (2) the element of surprise could be reestablished through one of more ruses. Randomly moving through an enemy camp would only be possible if the assault troops' fire had been so limited as to preclude fratricide.

Rebuilding the Element of Surprise

For every potential compromise to the element of surprise, the attacking unit must have an "on-call," preplanned diversion. For example, if a shot were to come from its daytime envelopment route, its base-of-fire machinegun could obscure the source of that shot by opening up immediately. Similarly, if an explosion were to happen in the same place, a supporting MK-19 grenade launcher could likewise obscure its whereabouts. In both cases, the idea is to so quickly mask the alarm that they enemy misinterprets its location. By not aiming at the actual objective, both automatic weapon operators additionally convince its defenders that another location is under attack.

It's almost impossible to run a night attack without triggering a trip flare. (See Figure 17.2.) After so doing, a *ninja* could make the sound of a wild animal and bound away. City-raised Americans might be better off letting defenders arrive at such a conclusion on their own. They should quietly take cover and be careful not to respond to any but the most well-directed reconnaissance by fire. After a 30-minute delay in the proceedings, enemy leaders will probably forget about the whole incident. To make sure they do, a fleet-footed GI could move to their perimeter's other side and snap a big branch.

Between the line of departure and inside of barrier

Enemy obstacle crossing &

Crossing trenches

Noisy assault

Raids &

Assault techniques &

Attacks from ambush &

Night firing &

Demolition work &

Attacks on bunkers &

Attacks on bridges &

Trench fighting &

Source Code:

Ninja methods for guerrilla use against Japan's Samuri (1460-1650) [1]

& N. Vietnamese methods for Viet Cong use against GIs (1965-1973) [2]

$ Chinese ally's Light Infantry Trng. Guid. Bur. methods (1992-2007) [3]

Figure 17.1: UW Guerrilla Instruction for Noisy Attack

Figure 17.2: The Inevitable Trip Flare
(Source: FM 7-8 [1984], p. 3-57)

In this way, the element of surprise could hopefully be reestablished after every setback. To succeed, a ground attack must only fool its quarry as to the direction from which the main assault comes. Should any of the preplanned ruses fail and too much of the element of surprise be lost, then the attacking unit must pull back. It can often successfully resume its offensive later that night, simply by coming in from a different direction. The only possible exception might be after partially transiting the enemy's barrier system (barbed wire). Then, continuing with the assault—though somewhat costly—might be less dangerous that trying to get back out.

The most serious of the setbacks to surprise is the shooting of small arms. For this reason, every participant should be armed with something that goes "boom" instead of "bang." On an active battlefield, there are so many booms during the average day, that positional defenders almost never think "ground assault" after hearing a nearby boom.[4]

The Simultaneous Firing of Rifles Connotes "Assault"

To fool the enemy as to which direction the assault is coming, there are two options. Do a lot of small-arms firing from one side, and then quietly attack from the other. Or, don't fire any unsilenced small arms at all. Below is how the NVA taught the VC to do it. It combines the absence of a recognizable signature by the assault element with a way to keep the defenders' heads down.

> Success in the [NVA/VC] attack is dependent on being able to breach the perimeter undetected. The assault is violent and invariably from more than one direction. It begins with a preparation, usually mortar and RPG fires. . . . Small arms are not employed except to cover the withdrawal in order to avoid disclosing the location of attacking forces. Once defending troops are forced into the bunkers, penetration of the perimeter is effected. Mortars cease firing, but the illusion of incoming fire is maintained through the use of RPGs, grenades, and satchel charges.[5]
>
> – *NVA-VC Small Unit Tactics & Techniques Study*
> U.S. Department of Defense

Specifics of the NVA/VC Assault

To surprise the defender of a carefully prepared position, most East Asian armies use what has come to be known as "stormtrooper" technique. By the spring of 1918, every German infantry squad knew how to apply it single-handedly. That squad would blow its bangalore during a precision artillery barrage and then assault with only bayonets and concussion grenades when the artillery shifted.[6] Fifty years later, the NVA followed 82mm mortar rounds with satchel charges, and 61mm mortar rounds with thin-skinned "potato mashers." If the whole nine-man NVA squad got through the barbed wire undetected, it stayed in column with an RPG man in the lead.[7] That RPG man could shoot whenever he wanted (and his companions drop fragmentation grenades into bunker apertures) without ruining the indirect-fire deception. If the squad was fired upon, its riflemen could shoot to the side and down without endangering each other or sister squads. Where it met light resistance coming through the wire, the first of its three-man "cells" (fire teams) deployed on line inside the breach.[8] When there was heavy resistance, the whole squad assaulted on line. Through it all, the light machinegunner carried his RPD by the handle, and all AK-47 men fired in the semi-automatic mode.[9] Everyone maintained several yards of interval, trotted, and shot from the waist or a "combat-glide" stance (rifle in the eye-muzzle-target position with buttstock off the shoulder).[10] Unlike the standard U.S. infantry assault, each composite technique in the NVA procedure had surprise rather than firepower as its ultimate goal.

The NVA night attack in the movie *Platoon* meshes well this research and may even reveal a few refinements to the method.[11] When one is developing UW attack techniques for an army that presently has none, it makes little difference whether the line between truth and fiction gets blurred a little. The whole idea is to envision something (from whatever source) that is promising enough to merit field testing. Thus, an in-depth, yet objective, look at the movie rendition would still be appropriate to upgrading U.S. military capabilities.

The setting for the film depiction is a string of three of four American fighting holes in the jungle. Their occupants have cleared only part of the vegetation to their front and have no protective barbed wire. The sun has long since set, and intermittent aerial flares are now create moving shadows in the woods. A tripflare goes off—either accidentally or on purpose. Already on high alert, the GIs detonate their claymores. If the enemy had already taken cover or turned those claymores face-down, their shrapnel might not have hurt anyone. Next, NVA RPG gunners destroy the only covered American fighting hole (bunker) in that sector. Notably absent at this time is any fire from an enemy machinegun. Without shooting their rifles, several tiny columns of NVA soldiers then assault this portion of the U.S. line all at once. As each consists of only a few men, it is probably a three-man fire team. Each has a rifleman in the lead who, when near an occupied U.S. hole, thrusts his bayonet or shoots downward. All columns quickly proceed across the string of holes and toward the middle of the U.S. position. Making no apparent attempt to stay on line or maintain their interval (relative spacing), all columns then converge on the center. There, one NVA soldier throws a satchel charge into the U.S. command bunker while others shoot totally surprised support personnel at pointblank range.

The initial loudspeaker propaganda and subsequent whistle blasts are theatrical embellishments. Both had been used in Korea, but by the Vietnam era were deemed wasteful of surprise. Further, the NVA probably didn't allow much horizontally directed small-arms fire from upright personnel at the center of a U.S. position. They preferred bayonets and concussion grenades to fratricide. During Operation Buffalo, they did permit some shooting by soldiers who had cut off and encircled small American contingents. But each of those soldiers was in the prone position and behind some kind of cover (like a rock). And each only took single, well-aimed shots when his quarry looked away. If any of those U.S. contingents had been on slightly higher ground, those bullets would have traveled upward and missed any NVA soldier on the other side of the circle. On that same operation, some of the encirclers climbed trees so as to be able to shoot downwards at the embattled Marines.[12] It would appear that NVA headquarters had discovered that by only shooting upwards and downwards, its assault elements could safely pass though the same battlespace from any direction.

To What Extent Is Coordination Really Necessary?

Implicitly evident in the film is the NVA's complete disregard for coordination between columns. It is true that most Communist countries have less respect for human life than their non-Communist counterparts. But they also attribute more worth to their infantrymen than non-Communist countries. When well-enough trained, each of their riflemen becomes a tremendous asset. Unable to keep up with the West in "high-tech" weaponry, they prepare each private to make a strategic difference. As such, they seldom unnecessarily risk frontline troops. So, the lack of coordination between NVA columns must have some explanation other than disregard for their safety.

Within that explanation may lie the elusive key to UW tactics. Perhaps the West has failed to understand UW because of one or more false assumptions. Its most blatant is that overwhelming firepower is the easiest way to win. If the assault columns cannot possibly shoot each other, what difference does it make whether they are properly aligned or well spaced? Without any horizontal firing by upright personnel, literally scores of those columns could randomly crisscross an enemy position without ever once harming each other.

That must be the principal difference between a UW and conventional-warfare attack. Within the latter, the emphasis on firepower creates an overriding need to closely coordinate all participant whereabouts and movement. Within the former, the emphasis on surprise permits more flexibility. To succeed at UW, one doesn't have to deal with all the restrictions on formation and maneuver that firepower demands. His assault elements will be perfectly safe though widely dispersed and loosely controlled. They must only obey a few ordnance expenditure rules.

Small arms are the weapon with the greatest kill radius, so they are the least used in UW tactics. They are either not fired at all, carefully aimed so as to hit only their target, or directed upwards or downwards. And fragmentation grenades are only dropped into holes or through apertures to preclude errant shrapnel. For all other applications, there is the concussion grenade and bayonet.

What about "Recon Pull"?

Prepared enemy positions (those fronted by barbed wire and interlocking bands of grazing machinegun fire) require deliberate attacks. To "hastily" attack one without preliminary reconnaissance and rehearsal is the recipe for disaster. Unable to reconnoiter an

Allied defense in depth, the German Stormtroopers of WWI developed the concept of "recon pull." Already well practiced in a foolproof way to secretly penetrate Allied lines, the Stormtroopers simply determined what was ahead as they made their way through each successive layer.

Thus, any U.S. UW attack against the unknown interior of an objective could usefully bring this idea into play. In other words, its participants need not know every detail of their subsequent target before passing through enemy lines.

The Proposed U.S. Technique for a Noisy UW Attack

Not all missions can be accomplished through silent infiltration. For example, if the target were surrounded by several rows of well-constructed and well-watched barbed wire, no U.S. soldier could get anywhere near it quietly. The concertina top is soft so a ladder won't work, and hang gliders are too heavy to haul around. If the subsequent mission involves intelligence gathering at a highly protected site, sappers couldn't accomplish it anyway. That's a job for one or more reinforced infantry squads. And those squads must mask at least one of their movements with noise (getting through the wire).

U.S. troops do not have an RPG equivalent. Whereas an RPG's backblast is minimal, that from a U.S. bunker or tank buster can prove lethal to anyone behind it. Thus, the most logical weapon for the lead man in any U.S. assault column is the old M-79 grenade launcher. It did not break or misfire as easily as its replacement (the M-203). Its squat dimensions and buckshot rounds were perfect for close-quarters fighting, and its high explosive rounds excellent for many types of standoff targets. A good M-79 man could put one of his projectiles through a bunker aperture. Each of his accompanying riflemen would carry several hand grenades—fragmentation for anything below ground and concussion for that above. Also armed with silenced M-4 rifles, they would only be authorized to shoot downward and to the side so as not to endanger each other or a sister squad. A low-velocity/soft-tipped M-4 round would have little chance of passing through an enemy soldier and hitting someone else, or of ricocheting. That's why Japanese infiltrators had wooden bullets on Guadalcanal—to facilitate close-range shooting by elements unable to coordinate.

At the end of each column would be someone carrying its internal "supporting arm"—a Shoulder-Launched Multipurpose Assault Weapon (SMAW). As his backblast area would always be clear going in, he could easily fire over the heads of his comrades. Those in flank columns could also fire to the outer side. In a noisy attack that involves an indirect-fire deception, the double thump of a SMAW round being fired and then impacting would simply enhance the illusion.

A Name for the American UW Technique

Such a maneuver would most logically be called the "flying-column assault." In the West, the term has historically been applied to a combined-arms task force—e.g., one with its own artillery and cavalry elements.[13] The British experimented with much smaller and completely dismounted flying columns late in WWI. But it is doubtful that any were squad sized.

This U.S. flying column must be composed of carefully outfitted assault troops. They should have both sufficient ordnance and the mobility to crawl along the ground if necessary. They must further be able to hear every muted sound. That means knee pads, elbow pads, no helmet, and all gear closely fitted to their body. To conserve on bulk and weight, NVA assault troops used a vest full of AK-47 magazines for a flak jacket. While attempting the equivalent of a noisy infiltration, American UW assault troops will need not only M-4 magazines, but also grenades, an entrenching tool, a personal radio, and water. Figure 17.3 shows how all those items might be carried by the individual without limiting his range of movement. (The water is in a bag on his back and available through a tube over his shoulder; the miniaturized radio is on a head mount with prepositioned mouthpiece.)

In the tactical technique that is depicted on succeeding pages, all the American squads come from the same side of the enemy's perimeter. There is no real reason why they couldn't come from several different sides at once. If the first three men in each column could project and detect a beam of light that was not visible to the naked eye, they could keep their column from tangling with any other. While the lead man watched to the front, the second and third in trace could watch to the left and right, respectively.

An Imaginary Walk-Through

The stage is now set for a "visualization" of a possible UW attack technique for American soldiers and Marines. (Visualization is a term that *ninjas* use for an imaginary run-through, when no rehearsal is possible.) Whether it appeals to every officer is not nearly as important as if it seems feasible to three-fourths of every group of 20 or more junior NCOs. They and their men are, after all, the ones who must risk everything to try it.

Figure 17.3: American UW Noisy-Assault Specialist
(Source: *Courtesy of Edward Molina, © 2003*)

In this imaginary test case, the enemy is believed to have valuable intelligence in a heavily protected bunker some 100 yards behind his lines. That intelligence cannot be retrieved any other way but the old-fashioned one.

Figures 17.4 through 17.15 take the reader through the full sequence of events up to, and including, the actual assault on the bunker. For that subsequent attack, a Westernized version of the NVA's prone encirclement technique will have to suffice.

Upon learning of the mission (Figure 17.4), the three attacking squads crawl as close to the enemy position as they can after dark. They do so up roughly parallel lanes in the objective's watershed pattern (Figure 17.5). After assessing the enemy's defenses from close range (Figure 17.6), each secretly emplaces its bangalore (Figure 17.7). (The mistake the Japanese made on Guadalcanal was trying to put too many people through each breach.[14]) Then, the senior squad leader calls for a preplanned artillery barrage on the other side of the objective (beyond danger close range.) He walks the rounds up to its opposite side and asks for a tight three-round volley. Upon hearing those rounds roaring in, all three squads detonate their bangalores (Figure 17.8). With any luck, the defenders will think all explosions are part of the same "fire-for-effect" mission by a distant observer. Immediately after the wire is rent, the columns come flying through. The lead man may have to "carefully" shoot a sentry or two, as do a few of the people behind him. Wherever possible, the rest drop fragmentation grenades into fighting holes, air vents, and bunker apertures. (See Figures 17.9 and 17.10.) Through this process, all columns pass easily over the enemy's initial line of resistance and head for the intelligence bunker.

Continuously working in the background (by prearrangement) is a single U.S. 60mm mortar. Its rounds are landing where the artillery did—just behind the enemy's position. Its purpose is to keep up the deception that the foe is only under bombardment. The sound of mortar rounds leaving the tube and impacting will mask that of M-79's being fired and their projectiles exploding. It will also override grenade noise.

With any luck, the American UW assault troopers can grab the intelligence and escape before the majority of defenders even realize they are under ground attack. That majority has so far received no auditory evidence of a ground assault. That's only because all force has been projected through bayonet, grenade, and silenced small arm.

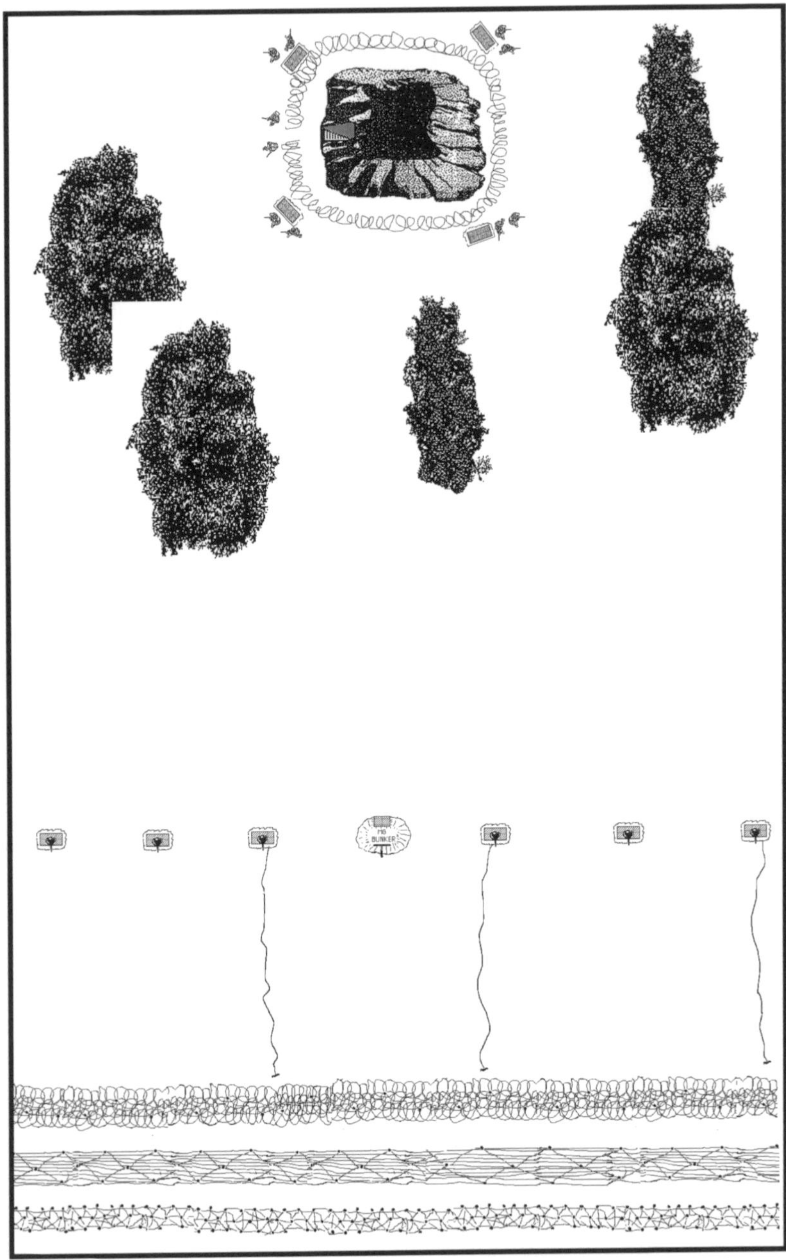

Figure 17.4: Mission Is to Retrieve Intelligence from Bunker
(Source: *The Last Hundred Yards*, Posterity Press, 1997, © 1994, 1995, 1996, 1998 by H.J. Poole, figs. 18.7, 19.3, 20.9)

Figure 17.5: Squads Crawl up Parallel Covered Lanes
(Source: FM 5-103 [1985], p. 4-4)

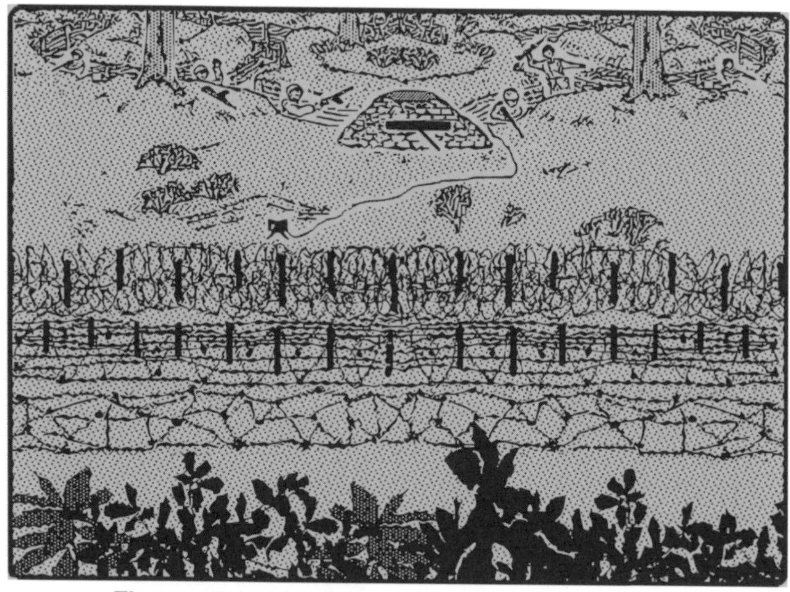

Figure 17.6: The Enemy's Lines from Up Close
(Source: FM 7-8 [1984], p. 3-28; MCO P1500.44B, p. 14-18)

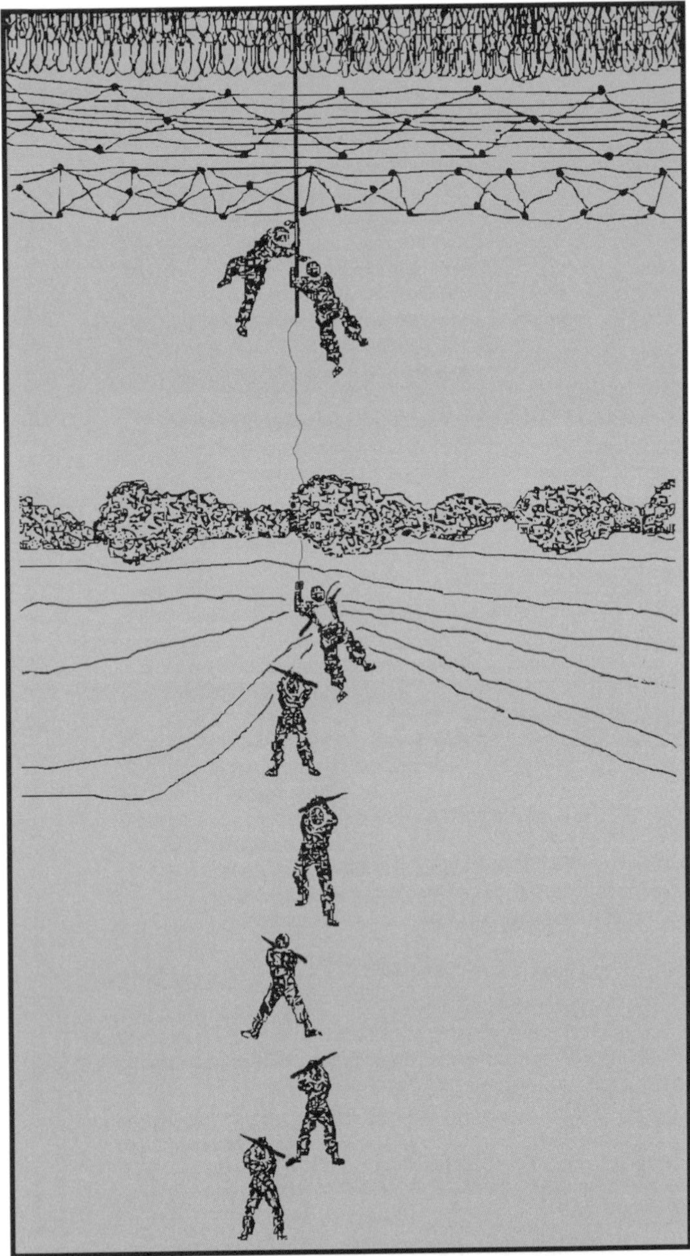

Figure 17.7: Each Squad Must Make Its Own Breach
(Source: *The Last Hundred Yards*, Posterity Press, 1997, © 1994, 1995, 1996, 1998 by H.J. Poole, fig. 18.5)

Figure 17.8: Bangalores Blown When Artillery Barrage Hits
(Source: *The Last Hundred Yards*, Posterity Press, 1997, © 1994, 1995, 1996, 1998 by H.J. Poole, figs. 18.7, 19.3, 20.9)

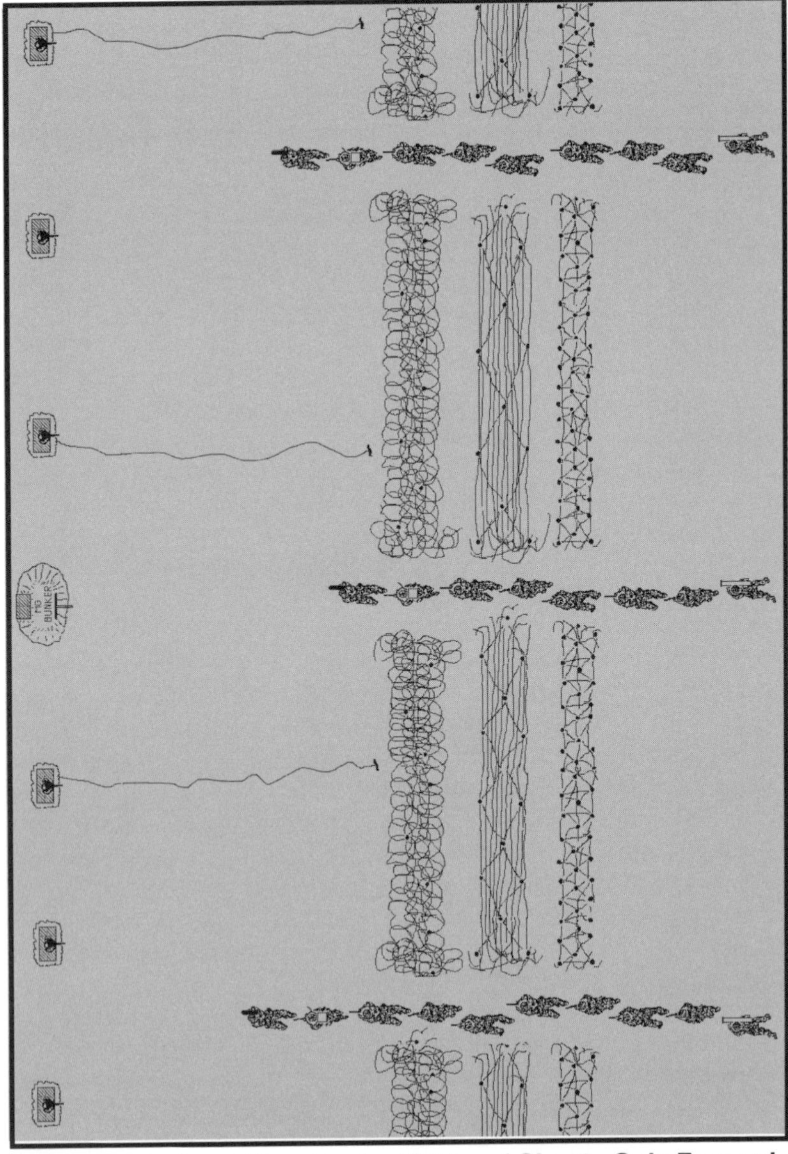

Figure 17.9: Lead Man Carries M-79 and Shoots Only Forward
(Source: *The Last Hundred Yards*, Posterity Press, 1997, © 1994, 1995, 1996, 1998 by H.J. Poole, fig. 18.7)

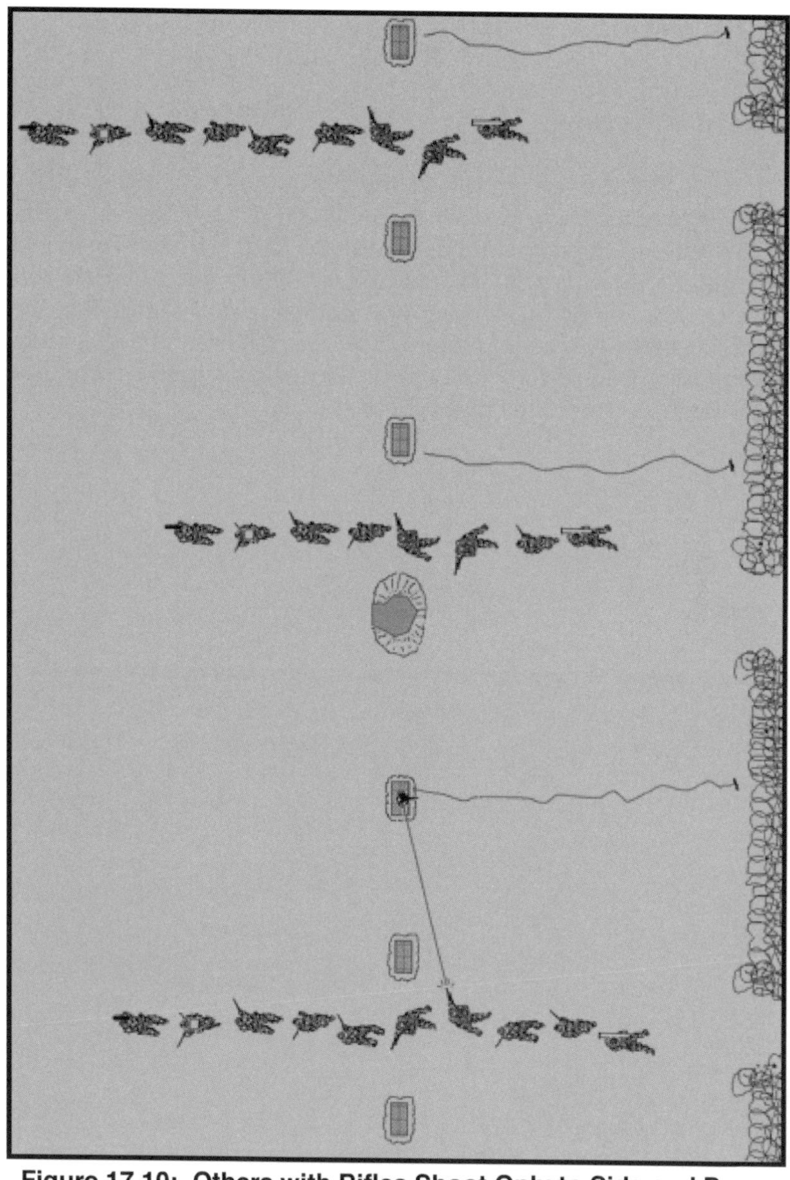

Figure 17.10: Others with Rifles Shoot Only to Side and Down
(Source: *The Last Hundred Yards*, Posterity Press, 1997, © 1994, 1995, 1996, 1998 by H.J. Poole, figs. 18.5, 18.7)

In the eyes of the UW experts, this evolution would thus qualify as a UW attack. Unlike its silent counterparts, it would require little additional training for U.S. troops. After a few well-supervised, live-fire walk-throughs, any American infantry unit could do it.

A Word of Warning

While Eastern lines may look linear, most are not. Instead, they are strings of tiny, squad-sized perimeters or trench segments that have been connected by dummy positions. This is to prevent aerial reconnaissance from pinpointing their locations. The gaps between are often fronted by the same row of barbed wire that protects the manned portions. To make matters worse, the front of each squad "strongpoint" can often be crisscrossed by grazing machinegun fire from those on either side and behind it.

Figure 17.11: Target of the Subsequent Attack
(Source: TM-E 30-480 [1944], p. 159)

All of this should make little difference to the U.S. UW assault contingent as long as the enemy remains unaware that a ground attack is underway. However, once he figures that out, what remains of their entry or escape could become much more difficult.

The Subsequent Mission

The whole reason for the penetration is the retrieval of intelligence from the enemy's command bunker. (See Figure 17.11.) Attacks like this are common in that part of the world where UW was born and has since become the preferred option. Well inside the heavily guarded Henderson Field perimeter on Guadalcanal, a three-man Japanese "patrol" attacked the First Marine Division command post in the late summer of 1942.[15]

So, for the three imaginary U.S. UW assault squads, the problem now becomes one of how successfully to operate after secretly entering the enemy's perimeter. Because of the indirect-fire noise that was required to secretly make the penetration, all defenders are now fully awake. With any luck, they still think that they are under attack by artillery and mortars alone. That puts them at the bottom of their holes and not looking around very much.

A "Limit of Advance" Permits Pre-Assigned Sectors of Fire

There still exists the problem of quickly taking down a subsequent, hardened target that has never been reconnoitered. Not only must it be secretly entered, but its contents must be retrieved intact—all without any friendly-fire losses. In a Westernized military, that calls for some control over movement and fire. Assigning the end of the bunker as the columns' limit of advance provides that opportunity.

In the dark, the flying squads proceed ahead through the inside of the enemy's perimeter until their intelligence bunker is spotted. Using existing vegetation as cover, they move up as close as they can without being detected by its sentries. Then, one squad goes just to the left of the objective, one just to the right, and the other hangs back in middle. (See Figure 17.12.) By technique, two shooters from each column know which parts of the bunker's defensive

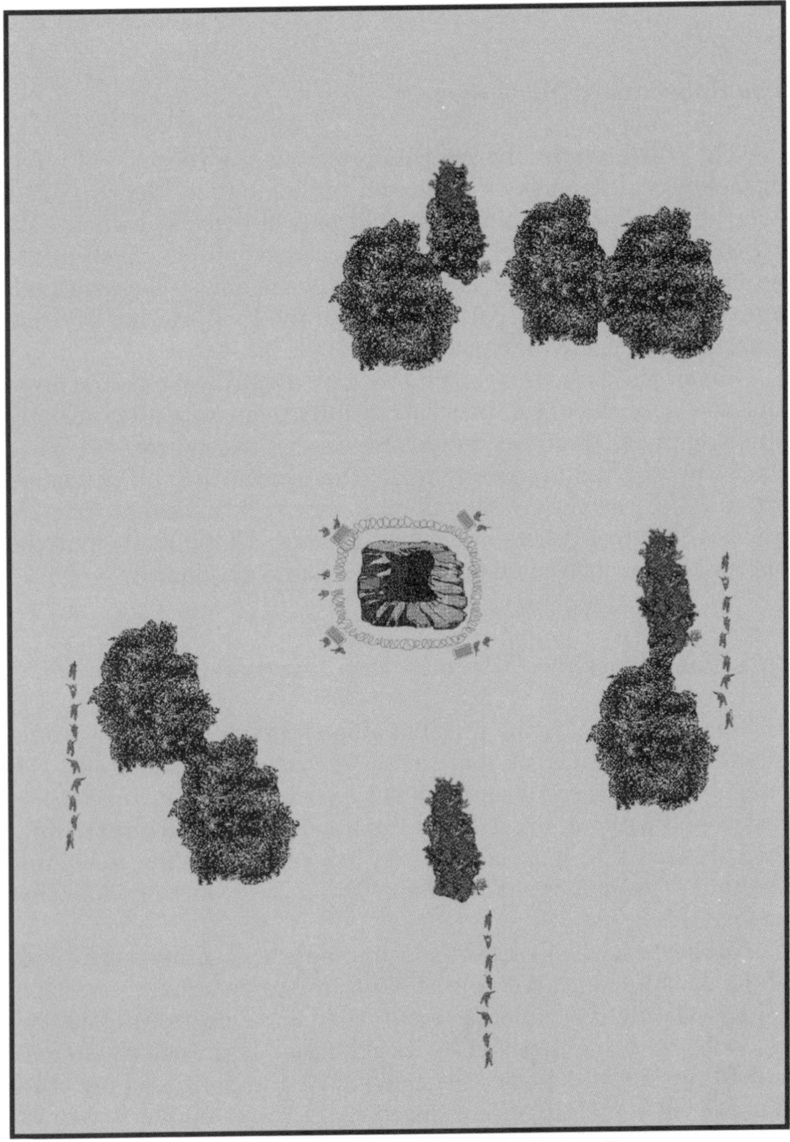

Figure 17.12: Flying Columns Stalk the Target
(Source: *The Last Hundred Yards*, Posterity Press, 1997, © 1994, 1995, 1996, 1998 by H.J. Poole, figs. 18.7, 19.3, 20.9)

ring to neutralize. Their respective columns also have pre-assigned sectors of fire that took effect at the limit of advance (end of the bunker). (In Figure 17.13, please note that these sectors preclude fratricide.)

Each shooter then crawls forward in his column's sector to a place where he can shoot all sentries in his assigned area of responsibility. He should now be automatically positioned so that any errant shot will either hit the elevated bunker or pass through an area so devoid of cover as to not possibly contain a GI.

As soon as he and his fellow shooters have whispered that they are ready over their personal radios, the senior squad leader (in the center column) gives the order to fire. Using the night vision sight on his silenced M-4, each shooter then takes out—in rapid succession—all the sentries in his pre-assigned area. (See Figure 17.14.) Any missed or astride a boundary must be dispatched by grenade toss. Only with screening and subsequent training will those shooters be ready for such an eventuality. To have any chance of entering a defensive hole, a thrown grenade must hit in front of that hole and then roll in.

Within each column, everyone else stays in single file. The file on the left can make sure that no one approaches the bunker from the left or front (direction of advance). The file on the right can prevent any interference from the right or front. There are good reasons for each squad to maintain its original, linear formation: (1) its members won't mask each other's fire in case of trouble; (2) the two who crawled off to neutralize the sentries know exactly where to find their comrades; (3) the column has only to reverse direction to quickly escape; and (4) everyone has a better idea of where the sister squads are. If the columns were to start shifting formation inside the enemy's perimeter at night, they might not be able to find their way back to the original breaches in the wire. Even over familiar ground, nighttime navigation can be difficult. By sticking to the same compass heading going in, all squads have a better chance of finding their subsequent target. By reversing that azimuth on the way out, all squads have a better chance of finding the prepared exit.

The simplicity of UW tactics is what permits their audacity. The flying column's movement is somewhat administrative and exposed, but the furtive behavior associated with a more "tactical advance" would invoke defender suspicion. During any aerial illumination, all column members most usefully get down on one knee.

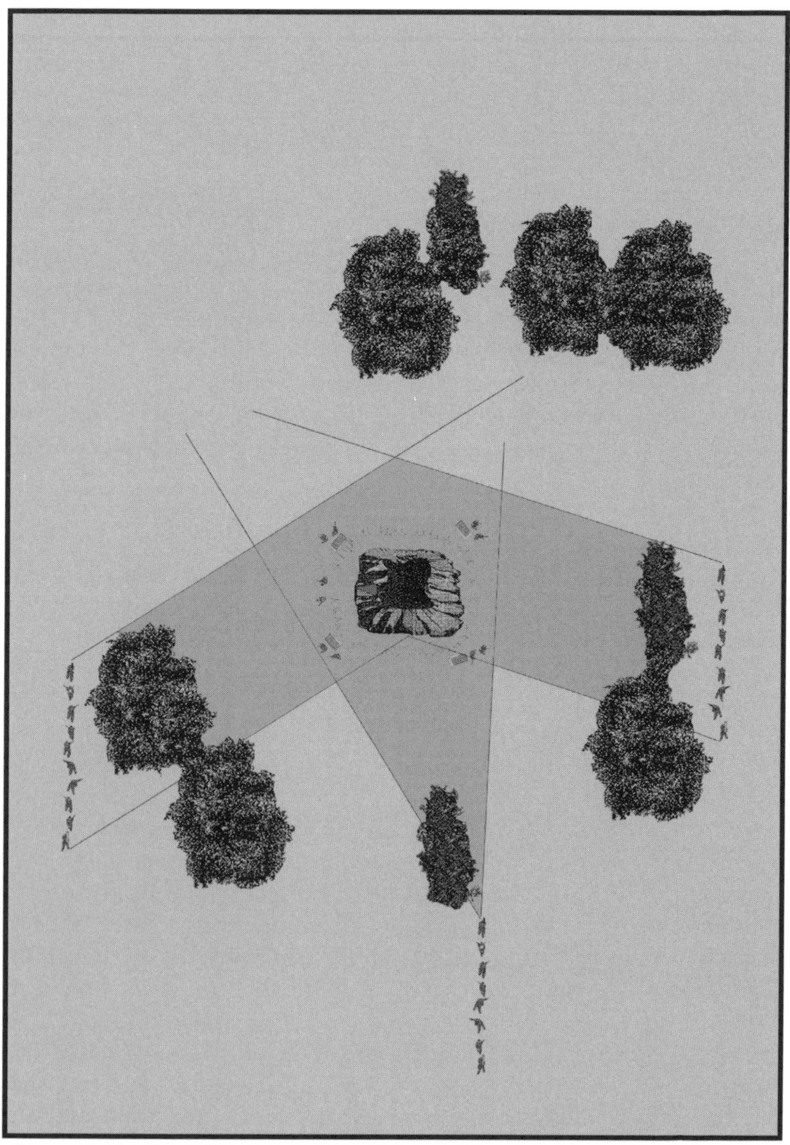

Figure 17.13: Shooters Know Fire Sectors at Limit of Advance
(Source: *The Last Hundred Yards,* Posterity Press, 1997, © 1994, 1995, 1996, 1998 by H.J. Poole, figs. 18.7, 19.3, 20.9)

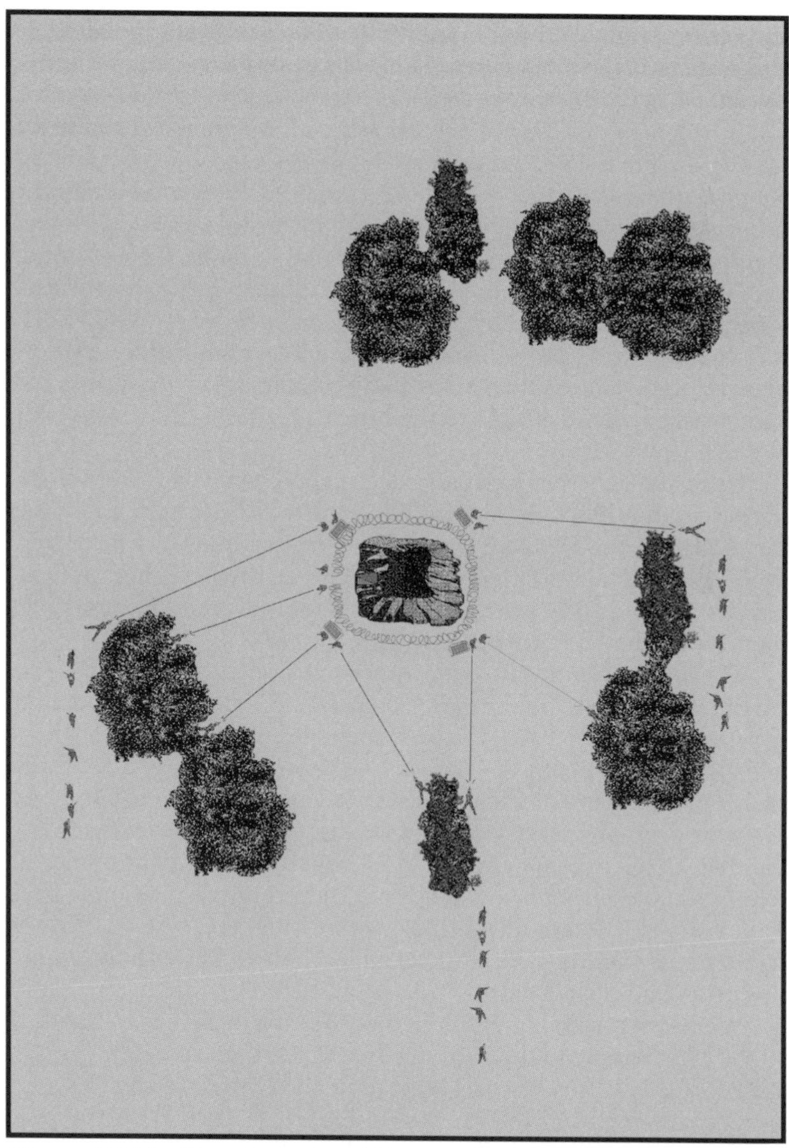

Figure 17.14: Shooters Crawl Up and Silently Dispatch Sentries

(Source: *The Last Hundred Yards*, Posterity Press, 1997, © 1994, 1995, 1996, 1998 by H.J. Poole, figs. 18.7, 19.3, 20.9)

An exceptional enemy commander will start firing his aerial flares within a couple of minutes of the initial American artillery barrage. If the columns have not yet closed with their subsequent objective, they have two choices—crawl the rest of the way or move only during lulls in the illumination. No longer able to use night vision scopes, the shooters will then have to fire during a lighted period.

In this age of advanced technology, all members of the flying squads should be able to communicate through face-mounted microphones. (Refer back to Figure 17.3.) If such sophisticated communication equipment is not available, they will only need a way to report their readiness to shoot and a return signal to do so. Those signals must be clearly detectable by all three columns but non-evocative of enemy suspicion. Ideally, they would make no noise at all. Early UW warriors used the calls of nonindigenous night birds. Today's Marines and soldiers might feel more comfortable with a sound so high as to be imperceptible to the human ear but still recognizable by some tiny gadget.

Once the sentries have all been dispatched, the leader of the center column has only to take two or three of his men and enter the bunker. (See Figure 17.15.) They project whatever force they need to secure the intelligence and return to their column. As killing, *per se,* does little to win an unconventional war, they may just capture the bunker's occupants.

Then, all columns reverse direction and head for the same barrier holes that they initially created. Should they encounter resistance from the back, the M-79 men are now in a good position to do something about it. For serious trouble, the Shoulder-Fired Multipurpose Assault Weapon (SMAW) men can turn around and fire over everyone else's heads (so doing will automatically empty their backblast areas). Through it all, whether upright or prone, all columns and their members maintain their relative positions. That way, everyone knows at all times where everyone else is. Within strange surroundings, formation rigidity helps with both technique execution and head counts.

Whatever resistance develops to the front will have to be handled by the SMAW man and his pistol. Just by turning sideways, he can automatically empty his backblast area and eliminate any fire from an adjacent sector of the line. (See Figure 17.16.) With the luck born out of skill, all three American flying columns escape unscathed before the enemy ever suspects their presence.

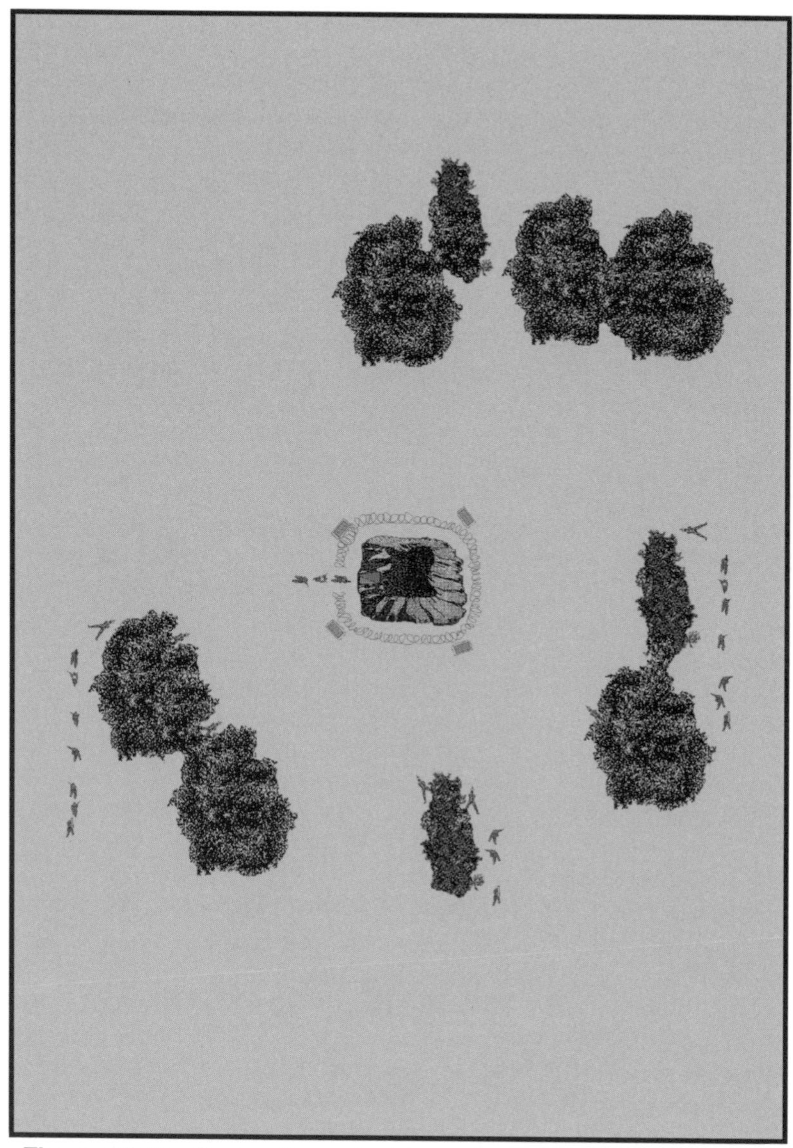

Figure 17.15: Center Team Retrieves Intelligence from Bunker
(Source: *The Last Hundred Yards*, Posterity Press, 1997, © 1994, 1995, 1996, 1998 by H.J. Poole, figs. 18.7, 19.3, 20.9)

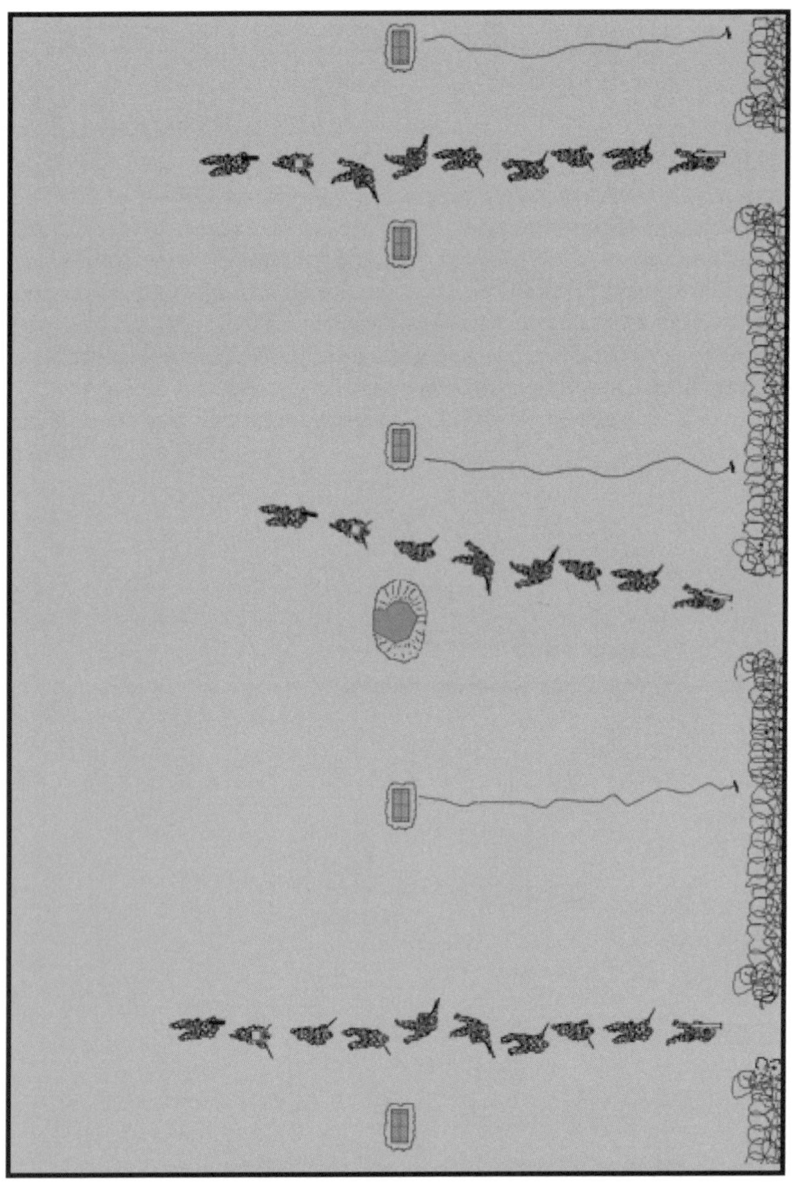

Figure 17.16: Columns Leave the Same Way They Came In

(Source: *The Last Hundred Yards*, Posterity Press, 1997, © 1994, 1995, 1996, 1998 by H.J. Poole, figs. 18.5, 18.7)

An Unpleasant Afterthought

The beauty of a UW technique is that it can be run more than once. By appearing to be something else, it only begrudgingly divulges its particulars to enemy investigators. Completely to obscure what has happened in this particular example, the bunker and all of its occupants would have to be blown up as if hit by a lucky artillery shell. (The number of lucky Japanese artillery hits on Guadalcanal far exceeded their statistical probability.[16]) And all of the gun-shot sentries would have to be further grenaded. As such things are grotesque and immoral, America's noisy UW assault troopers should not be expected to go there. In the UW arena of a modern (4GW) war, it is the side that best maintains the moral high ground that will normally win. How the flying columns get through the barbed wire would still stay secret, and that is the real strength of the procedure. Perhaps America's arms industry should start looking for a way to knock out a sentry at 50 feet without having to kill him.

If the Flying Columns Come from Different Directions

The above technique was specifically designed to appeal to a Western military's love of structured advance. That's the reason for the parallel columns and preassigned sectors of fire. Far-Eastern armies—the established experts on UW—would be more interested in bolstering the indirect-fire ruse and encircling the quarry. As such, their columns would probably enter the perimeter from different quadrants and then converge on the bunker. To take that bunker down, they would use only bayonet stabs and explosions. Before escaping, they would throw down a few 61mm mortar fins. Then, Figures 17.17 through 17.19 depict their last sequence of events.

By better protecting the element of surprise and technique particulars, the Eastern variation looks better on paper. But, as with all paper solutions, it has hidden flaws. Its grenades produce a lot of above-ground shrapnel that could easily hit friendlies and miss a hole-protected enemy. Its "converge on the sound of the explosions" coordination aspect makes no attempt to harness the new signaling and targeting technologies. The delay in bunker takedown that would probably result could cause enemy headquarters personnel

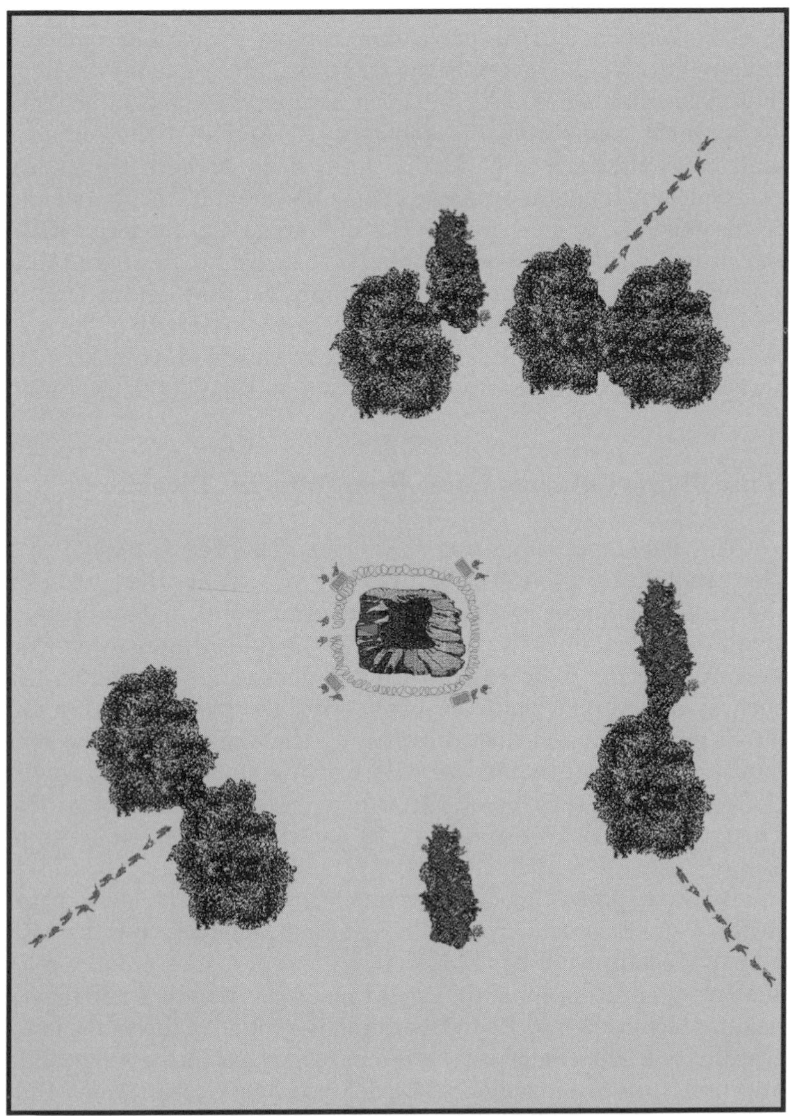

Figure 17.17: Columns Converge on Bunker from All Directions
(Source: *The Last Hundred Yards*, Posterity Press, 1997, © 1994, 1995, 1996, 1998 by H.J. Poole, figs. 18.7, 19.3, 20.9)

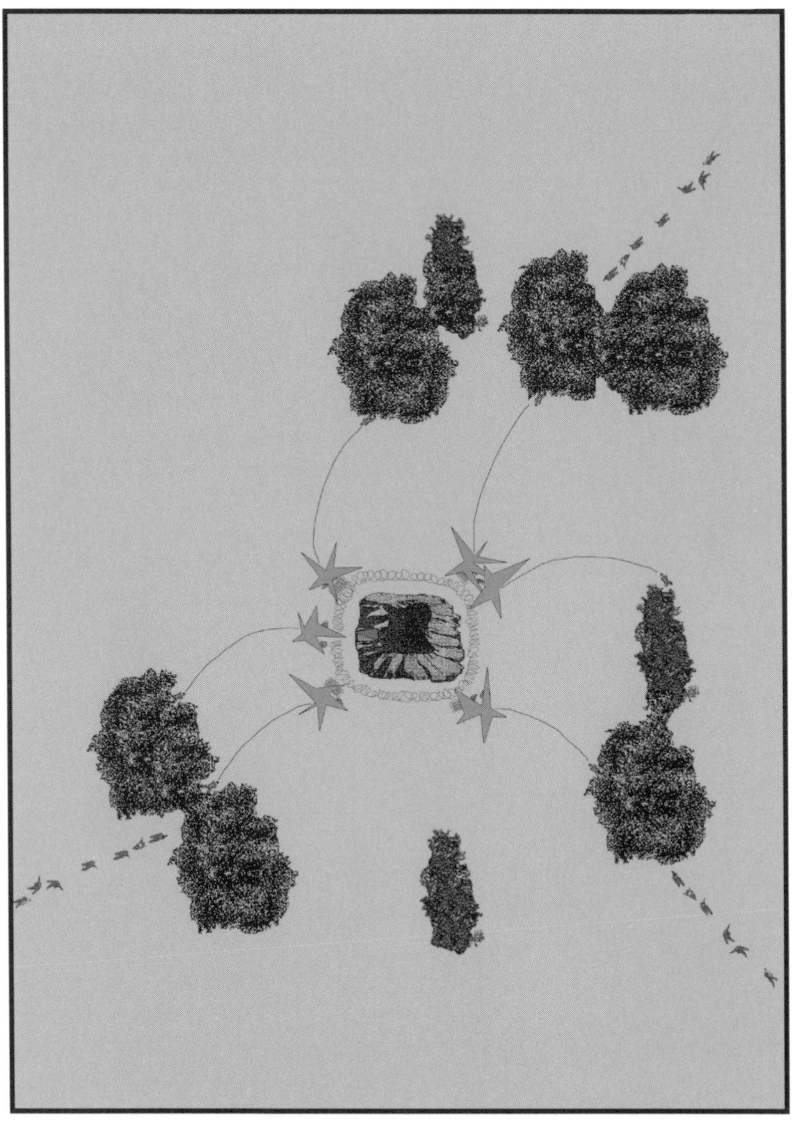

Figure 17.18: All Sentries Grenaded at Once

(Source: *The Last Hundred Yards*, Posterity Press, 1997, © 1994, 1995, 1996, 1998 by H.J. Poole, figs. 18.7, 19.3, 20.9)

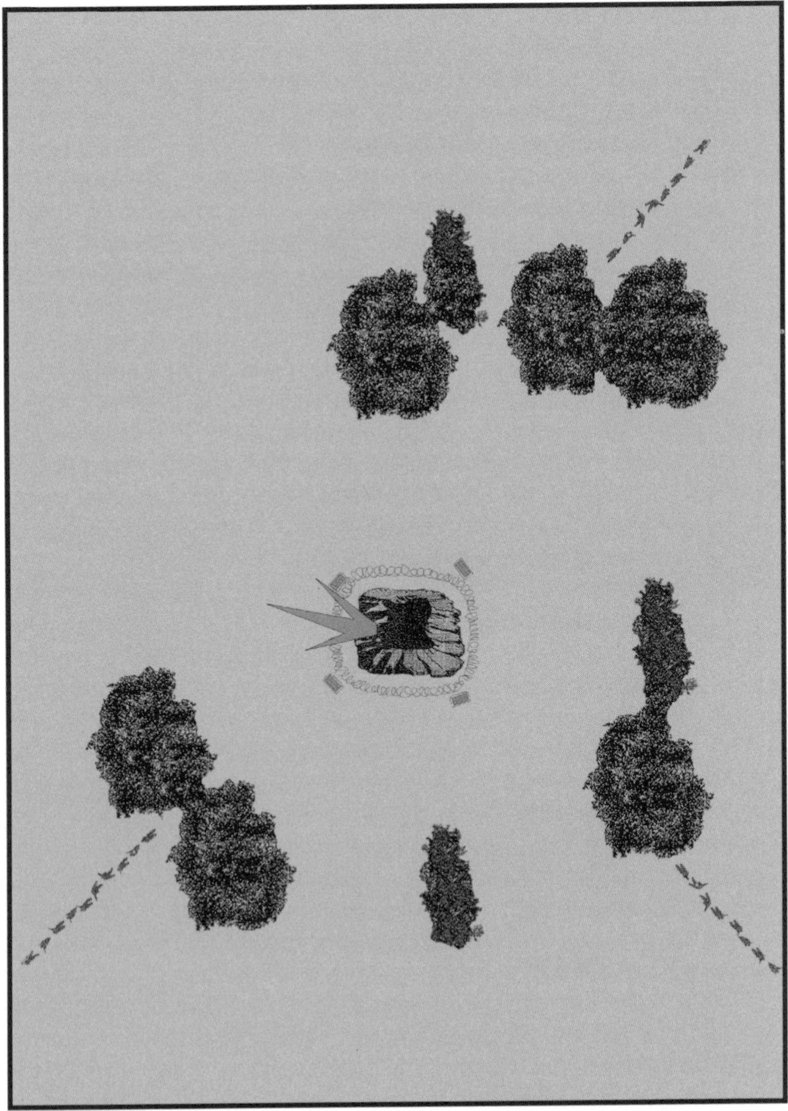

Figure 17.19: Bunker Blown to Resemble Lucky Artillery Hit
(Source: *The Last Hundred Yards*, Posterity Press, 1997, © 1994, 1995, 1996, 1998 by H.J. Poole, figs. 18.7, 19.3, 20.9)

to hide/destroy their intelligence. If Americans were to attempt this procedure, they would have to take with them any sentries or bunker occupants who survived the initial grenade blasts. No level of operational urgency would justify a violation of the Geneva Conventions. Those Conventions still apply inside an enemy perimeter. A few escape and evasion techniques from the next chapter might help America's flying columns to get back home with that additional burden.

18 Rural Escape and Evasion

- Is rural escape/evasion the same as outdoor survival?
- What makes it different?

(Source: FM 21-76 [1970], p. 43)

The Average GI's Perspective on Escape/Evasion

Most American infantrymen have never had to pull back, much less escape. Through manpower massing, overwhelming firepower, and measured advance, their superiors have generally saved them from any decision that inglorious. This has been going on for so long that any rearward movement whatsoever violates their organizational heritage. As a result, U.S. small-unit tactics manuals contain very little technique for breaking contact, and almost none for escaping or eluding one's pursuer. With a little more of that type of training, the SEAL team that got into trouble in the

Kunar Valley region of Afghanistan in 2005 might still be around.[1] Like it or not, tactical withdrawal becomes occasionally necessary when up against a more numerous and woods-wise foe. For then, it is either withdraw or be killed.

That's why escape and evasion (E&E) constitutes a full third of what is normally considered to be UW. While outdoor survival skills may help with its execution, they make no provision for the enemy and will not be discussed here. This chapter has only to do with how one's tiny U.S. detachment might successfully separate itself from a vastly larger and annihilation-bent enemy unit in rural terrain.

The History of E&E Training in America

American flyers have been trained in rural E&E since before WWII. U.S. Special Forces schools also include it in their curricula. One would think that something approaching the state of the art would have resulted from all that practice. But the underlying assumption in most U.S. E&E training is that all enemy armies fight like their American counterpart. Thus, when alone in enemy country, the U.S. flyer has only to watch for teeming beehives of defensive activity or noisy patrols. Of the world's major armies, only the French, British, and Westernized Russians still fight anything like U.S. forces do. Most militaries east of Istanbul have a completely different tactical tradition. They still sport all the vehicularization, supporting arms, and other "high-tech" trappings of a Westernized force, but they have those things mainly for show. All the gadgetry helps to discourage Western intervention. It, and the occasional Western formation, also help to make the standard offensive diversion more convincing. Old PLA manuals show the main attack by short-range infiltration from the rear,[2] while the Western quarry watches for a human wave from the front. Other Communist armies can defend while withdrawing, and escape while encircled. Yet, American troops are still told to expect a frontal confrontation with similar formations and maneuvers.

Even at the lowest echelons in the East-Asian Communist armies, units can quickly shift between mobile, guerrilla, and positional warfare.[3] In a protracted war, Mao identified the mobile mode as his primary and guerrilla mode as his secondary.[4] But the two are linked, and his armies could do both at once. He claimed that guerrilla warfare performed the role of strategic coordination in regular campaigns.[5] As guerrilla forces are widely dispersed, he probably meant that they provided most of the "real-time" human intelligence and then guided regular forces into position for surprise assaults. Thus, the modern-day Chinese Army is probably still UW capable despite all of its newfound wealth. Any thoughts that wherewithal could take the place of small-unit tactics were dashed on the plains of North Vietnam in 1979. There, poorly armed but well-situated North Vietnamese home guard units were able to blunt a fully supported Chinese invasion. They did so while regular counterparts were off subduing the Khmer Rouge in Cambodia.[6]

Thus, many countries in which U.S. forces might find themselves deployed are virtually crawling with very proficient enemy irregulars. And those irregulars don't live in huge base camps or noisily patrol. One of John McCain's contemporaries found that out the hard way during the Vietnam War. He was able to escape confinement in Hanoi alright, but then ran into trouble while approaching a U.S. base just south of the Demilitarized Zone (DMZ)—Gio Linh or Con Thien.[7] A lone enemy soldier simply popped up out of the ground and shot him as he ran back towards the north. There was no enemy encampment or patrol anywhere around. That lone North Vietnamese sentry was probably one of thousands of irregulars manning a wide band of tiny defensive outposts. Asian armies are not the least bit hesitant to widely disperse their personnel. Lone North Korean sentries were discovered in many of Seoul's buildings during the U.S. Marine assault on that city in September 1950.[8]

Unfortunately, the same tactical paradox applies to Iraq. Iranian *Sepah* and Lebanese *Hezbollah* are known to blanket a contested city with neighborhood detachments.[9] Each detachment then posts lone, civilian-dressed, and cell-phone-wielding lookouts on the street corners around its headquarters.[10] To effectively compete in Baghdad, U.S. forces would need their own "guerrilla-like" representation in every neighborhood. Without that representation, those forces can neither retrieve enough human intelligence nor have adequately qualified guides for raids. Most of the Islamist hideouts and activities therefore go unreported, and most of the raids are detected before they can do any damage.

Advanced rural E&E training would necessarily entail a thorough knowledge of mantracking and Eastern tactics. Below is a little-known defensive formation that might cause significant problems for an escaping U.S. detachment. It perfectly exemplifies what appears to be the central UW premise—that a military force can do a lot more maneuvering with smaller elements when unencumbered by firepower.

The Eastern Defensive Outpost Zone

Long before "technology," Eastern defenders had a sophisticated early warning system. Prior to WWI, just to the front of each Japanese stronghold was a string of one- or two-man outposts connected by roving sentinels. Those sentinels did more than just cover the ground between outposts. They were also able to apprise all outposts of what security patrols had come across. Thus created was a dynamic, protective screen that was in no way hampered by headquarters.

> When a patrol leaves the line of sentinels . . . , neighboring sentinels will be notified by moving sentinels or other means.[11]
>
> — Japanese night-fighting manual, 1913

In effect, the roving sentinels were themselves conducting tiny, loosely controlled patrols. They even had the authority to deviate from their appointed routes. On one occasion during the Nomonhan Incident of 1939, Japanese defensive scouts were able to shadow Russian infiltrators.[12]

Locating and Penetrating an Eastern Sentinel Screen

When a string of such outposts is suspected to one's front, it takes time to pinpoint the locations of any two in succession. Often, their only signature will be the slight movement and muted communication of a sentinel visit or watchstander relief.[13] Once their whereabouts has been established, there is still the little matter of moving between them without bumping into a roving sentinel.

> The patrol being hidden . . . , it should strive to discover the position of one sentinel; this being used as a base will

> assist in the discovery of the other posts and noncommissioned officer post. Having reconnoitered the intervening open ground, the enemy's method of security can be verified, and it can be judged whether or not it would be a good idea to enter the line of sentinels. To accomplish this, it is a good thing to follow directly after a passing moving sentinel or a visiting patrol.[14]
>
> — Japanese night-fighting manual, 1913

What All of This Might Mean to Rural E&E for Americans

Clearly, advanced E&E would have more to do with obscure movement than survival skills. Just being able to live off the land won't be enough. To escape, the small U.S. group or squad must know how to cover its tracks, lay a false trail, and discourage pursuit.[15] To keep from running into another enemy unit, it must obey certain rules.

One of those rules is not to follow "lines of drift." A line of drift is any bottleneck in the terrain that facilitates passage—like a streambed through thick jungle, or an elevated ridgeline through impenetrable swamp. Their friendly travel potential is so obvious to the enemy that they must be avoided. Escaping Americans must instead set off in a straight line (or connecting series of straight lines), and then somehow negotiate all obstacles in their way. At Camp Swampy (southern Lejeune's name during WWII), lone grid squares were intentionally flooded with student patrols in the late 1980's. While the plan was to generate contact between those patrols, it never came to fruition. All were following dead-reckoning azimuths and never saw each other.[16] That same lack of straight-line convergence would help an escaping U.S. contingent to avoid any additional enemy interest.

Other rules can be extracted from how the three UW experts train on E&E. (See Figure 18.1.) Most noticeable on their list is the need to blend in with surrounding terrain. To blend with nature, one must regularly commune with nature. Most U.S. infantrymen are now city raised. Regular squad-on-squad "free play" would help to fix the problem, but most waste what little field time they do get on canned exercises. And they receive no formal E&E training. (See Figure 18.2.)

Rural escape

Exfiltration [&]

Leaving without a trace [#]

Natural-element escape strategies (gotonpo)
- "Fire escape arts" (katonjutsu)
  - Firecrackers to simulate rifle fire
  - Masking one's movement with smoke
- "Wood escape arts" (mokutonjutsu)
  - Conforming to the crook of a tree
  - Climbing to a high place (tanuki gakure no-jitsu)
- "Earth escape arts" (dotonjutsu)
  - Stone concealment (sekiton jutsu)
  - Hiding in gap between two objects (uzura gakure no-jitsu)
  - Hiding under soft soil or the uprooted roots of a tree
- "Water escape arts" (suitonjutsu)
  - Breathing underwater through a hollow reed

Breaking contact [#]

Diversions
- Ventriloquism
- Scurrying or bounding away like a wild animal

Movements
- Rolling, leaping, or tumbling away (taihenjutsu)
  - Handspring methods
  - Rolling methods
    - Reverse-shoulder roll (chigari)
  - Leaping methods (hichojutsu)
    - Vaulting the foe
- Dodging to one side of and pivoting behind foe
  - Body drop methods
    - Forward breakfall (zempo ukemi)
    - Sideways-flowing rear-body drop (yokonagare)
    - Upright-flowing rear-body drop (tachinagare)

Leaving no recognizable trail [$]

Stepping on rocks and grass so as to leave no footprints
Breaking branches in direction other than escape route
Making false trail with footprints and discarded items

Escaping a trained tracker (tonpo) [#]

Leaving a recognizable trail and then retracing one's steps
Doubling back after the foe has bypassed one's concealed position
Abruptly terminating one's trail

Figure 18.1: UW Instruction on Rural Escape/Evasion

Rural evasion

Hiding (inton-jutsu) #

Camouflage skills
- Donning white clothing for snow or smoke
- Wearing black clothing at night
- Covering reflective skin with cloth or ashes

Other presence-obscuring skills (tonkei no jutsu)
- Constantly alert to the possibility of reflection (as in a mirror)
- Hiding in the shadows (jinton no jutsu)
- Trying not to reflect any rays of light
- Shallow breathing
- Hiding within plain sight (joei-on no jitsu)
  - Distorting one's silhouette (as with a cape)
  - Balling up like a stone
  - Posturing motionless in front of obvious cover

Waylaying a pursuer #

Moving around the opposite side of a tree as enemy scout passes it
Hiding behind a tree at the bend in a trail
Pretending to be a bush near the trail
Hiding within plain view (see techniques for hiding)
- Remaining perfectly still
- Not looking directly at the victim

Dropping on the enemy from above

Source Code:

Ninja methods for guerrilla use against Japan's Samuri (1460-1650) [18]
& N. Vietnamese methods for Viet Cong use against GIs (1965-1973) [19]
$ Chinese ally's Light Infantry Trng. Guid. Bur. methods (1992-2007) [20]

Figure 18.1 (Cont.): UW Instruction for Rural Escape/Evasion

Figure 18.2: U.S. Intantrymen Get No E&E Training
(Source: OPNAV P34-03 [revised 1960], p. 394)

According to the UW chart, one must be able to look like a rock, tree trunk, or bush at a moment's notice. Even Russians practice such things (See Figure 18.3.) It also talks about climbing trees. Since the Pacific island campaigns of WWII, Americans have not looked for their foes in trees. But they are still there. They have even climbed trees in Iraq.[17] Among the other recommendations is hiding beneath loose soil. It meshes perfectly with the tunneling predisposition noted in previous chapters. In summary, if the UW fighter can't pretend to be something in the two dimensional plane, he moves into the much-less-expected three-dimensional plane. Throughout, he applies his affinity for deception.

While all of this might be difficult for city-dwellers to accomplish, it would not be impossible if they had a good enough initial escape plan and subsequent route. Of course, they would also need to develop/practice various techniques for breaking contact, leaving without a trace, hiding, and waylaying a pursuer. Before each can be addressed, a good reason for avoiding a fight will have to be established.

Time to Go

All kinds of tactical opportunities await the unit that can widely disperse without being destroyed piecemeal. That is the underlying premise of the Marine Corps' recent push toward "distributive operations."

The problem is what to do when one of those tiny elements gets surrounded. There is considerable delay and risk associated with trying to clear an exit corridor with supporting arms. Even if the planes/artillery, observers, and radios are available, there is still no guarantee that the bombs/shells will kill enough of the enemy to make the escape possible. While seldom considered by U.S. arms manufacturers and government "technocrats," there is another way to save the beleaguered American element. Its members must be able to exfiltrate an encirclement and elude any subsequent pursuer. Other less-well-provisioned armies have used that approach for years. It risks no collateral damage, "friendly incoming," or loss of surprise. America's founding declaration attests to the fact that all cultures are equally endowed. Thus, anyone can pull off such an escape.

A Rural Escape Plan

In an encirclement, there would be two types of escape opportunities—those that coincidently presented themselves and those that were contrived. To arrive at a UW plan, one must imagine what a UW fighter would do.

Figure 18.3: Even Russians Learn How to Hide in Plain Sight
(Source: Podgotovka Razvegchika: Sistema Spetsnaza GRU, © 1998 by A.E. Taras and F.D. Zanuz, p. 373.)

While passing through enemy lines, the Asian infiltrator can quickly take advantage of any one of several naturally occurring diversions. Or he can wait for a lapse in the closest sentry's attention. Why couldn't an American exfiltrator operate the same way? Then, the techniques in Chapters 15 and 16 would apply. Of course, the Asian also has ways to create a diversion. Over the years, those ways have ranged from assault-simulating firecrackers to refugee-abundant breakouts. Thus, the first part of any rural escape plan must be the expected gap in enemy lines/alertness or some way to create one.

The Escape Route

Then, there is the need for a detailed escape route. Its viability will largely depend on how carefully it has been envisioned. It must facilitate both land navigation and obscure movement. The former is best provided by terrain association (following linear terrain features). But not one of those features can be a line of drift. The countryside is covered with tiny fingers and draws. Why couldn't the escape route be largely a composite of those? At a safe distance, one could also parallel the straight segments of a road or powerline.

While slow, the route promising the least amount of enemy interference is wet. It is comprised mostly of swamps, streamlets, and drainage ditches. Large stream beds would be lines of drift and too risky. Thus, only tiny watercourses would work for escape route "legs." There are many places to hide along tiny watercourses: (1) the occasional culvert; (2) the frequent vegetation; and (3) the ever-present opportunity to submerge. With the proper breathing apparatus, the most available option is not all that farfetched.

At the east end of Henderson Field on Guadalcanal, Lt. Joe Terzi asked for six volunteers for a "suicide mission" one hot night in September 1942. He and his six Marines were to man a listening post directly in the path a huge Japanese force that was bearing down on that part of the perimeter. With wisdom beyond his training, Lt. Terzi had correctly surmised that 3rd Battalion, 1st Regiment's best chance to stop that force required interrupting its momentum outside the wire. (If it had too easily reached Marine lines, its stormtrooper technique would have easily breached them.) When the Japanese showed up, all seven Americans started firing their Thompson submachineguns. Believing itself to have had prematurely stumbled upon the Marines' main line of resistance, the Japanese force became temporarily confused and very mad. It did its best to kill the tiny party of U.S. heroes. But, through the grace of God, those heroes did something that one had probably seen in an old cowboy movie. They all hid in the stream and did their breathing through hollow reeds.[21] Little did they know that this native American trick was also practiced by *ninjas* and their mainland predecessors.

Sometimes, a quick exit is more important than one precluding contact. Then, a treeline may be the way to go. In full moonlight, one can run along a treeline's shadow without being seen. Of course, one can also move between the shadows of separate trees as was described on Chapter 15's UW chart.

Every Escape Attempt Must Include Some Deception

To keep from being followed, the escaping element has two choices: (1) make no tracks; or (2) leave behind a false trail. For the first option, the UW chart recommends walking on rocks or tufts of grass. For the second, it suggests breaking branches in the direction opposite to that taken.

One of the oldest tricks is pretending to depart an area without actually leaving it. This might be particularly helpful during the hours of daylight. It is normally accomplished by making a false trail and then secretly doubling back to climb a tree. But, if the false trail were made by one man simulating many, then the rest of the group wouldn't have to go anywhere but up.

The chart also talks about hiding somewhere and then moving in the opposite direction after the enemy passes. There are more places for a single person to hide in the woods than one might think. They include, but are not limited to, the following: (1) in the upper portion of a hollow tree trunk; (2) under the roots of an upturned tree; (3) within a narrow crevasse or run-off ditch; (4) near the top of a leafy tree; (5) in an irrigation canal or deep streamlet; and (6) beneath an impassable tangle of vegetation. Figure 18.1 suggests other ways to "appear not to exist": (1) hiding in the gap between two objects; (2) balling up like a stone; and (3) standing motionless before obvious cover. Most Americans would not want to attempt the latter without first camouflaging themselves and then experimenting with poses.

In addition, one finds various man-made objects in rural terrain. Often, those objects have to do with irrigation, electrical power transmission, and highway construction. Few enemies will fully investigate the small culvert that happens every time a dirt road crosses a tiny draw. They are in no hurry to meet the fauna that might reside there.

Natural Ways of Discouraging Pursuit

As might be expected, Asia's UW fighters have a full portfolio of "non-mechanical" ways to permanently discourage pursuit. Among the more dramatic of these ways is to hide in the soft soil by the side of a trail and then to come up quietly behind one's pursuer. The famous "lost company" at Gallipoli may have moved on line across a parallel string of Turkish defenders who were lying just beneath the surface of the soil.[22] As those defenders rose up in unison through the thick smoke, each had only to shoot the closest British soldier in the back. A further Asian trick is to drop in on unwanted company from an overhead tree branch. Still another is to position oneself behind a big tree, and then move backwards along the base of that tree as the pursuer passes its front.

Of course, there are also many ways to just slow a pursuer. An experienced mantracker will look for sign up to 15 yards ahead. Regularly changing direction and not leaving much sign before and after each change of course will greatly slow his pursuit. Most effective is to almost reverse direction. He must waste many minutes looking for the next print to each side of the expected line of travel. An occasional false trail to the side would further delay his progress.

Minimizing one's human sign involves more than just footprints. There are also above-ground issues, like bent twigs, bruised leaves, and displaced dust. To avoid footprints, the quarry can step from rock to rock, root to root, or a combination thereof. When they run out, he can step on the harder ground at the base of each bush. If he tiptoes, he will leave no heel marks. Then, he has various composite techniques at his disposal. He might move past a tree, retrace his exact steps, and then jump to the blind side of that tree (a method used by some animals).[23] Or he might move 20-30 meters back along the stream he just came up and then carefully exit through a feeder creek or thick brush.

U.S. Techniques for Escape from Rural Encirclements

The rest of this chapter will be dedicated to visualizing the various ways in which an American contingent might successfully foil an enemy cordon. With enough practice and refinement, such "visualizations" could be turned into unit "techniques." As all are microterrain dependent, every U.S. infantry squad or special operations detachment will need a well-rehearsed portfolio of more than one before entering combat.

Two-dimensional art has its limitations. All subsequent illustrations will offer only an abbreviated version of the actual microterrain and vegetation that would exist in each case. Any actual segment of rural countryside would contain far more surface irregularities and plant clusters. Thus, the reader must complete each setting in his own imagination. The contour lines represent the depressions in each area's watershed pattern, and the bushes its thicker vegetation. An actual cordon would also be much larger and farther away from the trapped U.S. contingent. Figure 18.4 thus shows the predicament of an understrength U.S. squad or special-operation detachment. Its six men have found themselves completely surrounded by skilled opponents. In the past, this type of thing would have evoked great consternation within the American contingent and back at headquarters. In the future (should the U.S. military finally decide to evolve tactically), it will evoke only mild concern. The difference will be in the preparedness of the Americans involved—to escape an encirclement without outside help.

First on the list of UW expert recommendations for this sort of dilemma is exfiltration. (See Figure 18.5.) It generally requires darkness, but with tall grass or other ground covers, it might also be possible during the day. When ready to attempt such an escape, the tiny group of Americans breaks down into two-man teams. Each team heads for a different quadrant of the enemy cordon and begins looking for a viable gap. Before dawn, all penetrate that

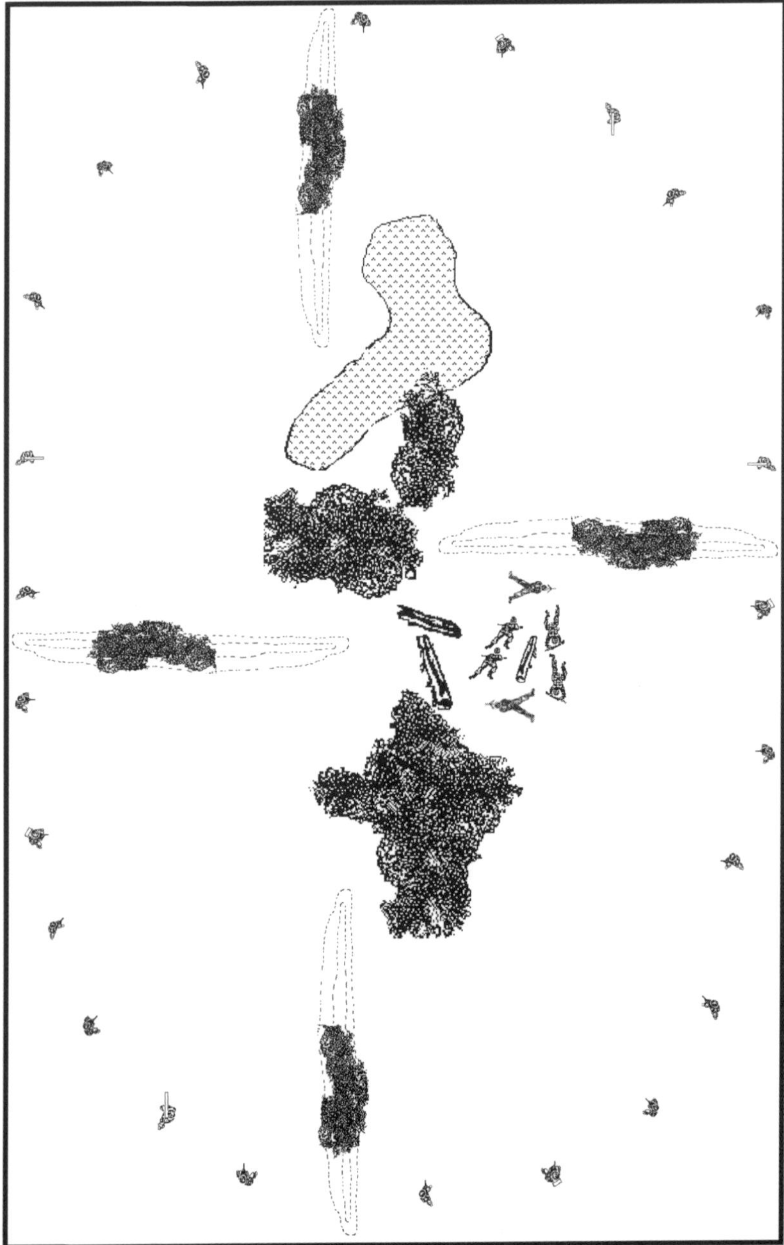

Figure 18.4: The Eventual Encirclement
(Source: FM 5-103 [1985], p. 5-10;TC 90-1 [1986], cover)

Figure 18.5: Exfiltration Is Not That Hard
(Source: FM 5-103 [1985], p. 5-10;TC 90-1 [1986], cover)

cordon through their respective sectors and make their way over to a predetermined rendezvous point. If the enemy has managed to encircle the Americans in a relatively uninhabited area, he must be assumed to know something about mantracking. Those Americans might be wise to carefully wend their way home before he finds his trap empty. The exfiltration technique is the same as for infiltration in Chapter 15.

The Lone-Party Diversion Ruse

U.S. small units have been too overcontrolled over the years to generate much trickery. As such, America's traditional foes don't expect much from that quarter. That makes them vulnerable to it.

There are places in wooded terrain where a single person can hide easily and several people can sometimes hide. The former include murky watercourses, rotting foliage, and hollow tree trunks. The latter include treetops, bramble bushes, and the root systems of overturned trees. Of course, the latter would only work if the enemy had been somehow drawn past the group hiding place. And the former would only work for the person doing the drawing, if he had slightly moved from the place of diversion to a foolproof hideout. Figures 18.6 and 18.7 are intended to depict such a sequence of events.

In Figure 18.6, a well-seasoned and confident U.S. volunteer starts sniping at several widely separated members of the enemy cordon from a point within easy crawling distance of a hollow tree trunk. As the members of that cordon converge on what they perceive to be the entire American team, they pay little attention to the tops of the trees they are passing. One contains the other five members of the U.S. unit. As soon as the volunteer believes his buddies safe, he crawls over to the dead tree trunk, enters through an opening at its bottom, and then climbs up into its fully enclosed middle.

In Figure 18.7, the U.S. volunteer snipes at the cordon from a place not too far from a murky or vegetation-choked stream. As the cordon tightens around the sniper, its members pay little attention to a tree that has toppled in a recent wind storm. In the soft earth beneath its exposed root ball are the other five members of the U.S.

Figure 18.6: Five Hide in Tree As One Diverts at Hollow Stump
(Source: FM 5-103 [1985], p. 5-10;TC 90-1 [1986], cover)

Figure 18.7: Five Hide under Roots As One Diverts at Stream
(Source: FM 5-103 [1985], pp. 4-19, 5-10;TC 90-1 [1986], cover)

unit. As soon as the volunteer knows his buddies to be outside the cordon, he crawls over to the stream, gets below the surface vegetation or murkiness and breaths through a hollow reed.

Be warned that neither ruse will work against an experienced tracker unless one has taken great pains to erase and disguise all tracks and other evidence of what has actually occurred. While Eastern armies have many more trackers than the U.S. military, those trackers may still not be attached to every unit.

A More Old-Fashioned Breakout

To be successful, all escape attempts need not be strictly silent or highly deceptive. As in the rural assault, it has only to deceive the enemy as to its exact location. Thus, any encircled American force must first hold out until dark. It can then do what it knows best—frontal assault. That assault will not be suicidal if it can meet a single, nontraditional condition—no shooting of unsilenced small arms. All the killing must be done by grenade or bayonet. The enemy will associate closely spaced explosions with a mortar attack. The techniques in Chapter 15 are followed until the two-man teams are within grenade range of the enemy holes in their lanes. Then, they grenade those holes and escape. (See Figure 18.8.)

A viable variation on that theme comes from this chapter's UW chart—firecrackers. Firecrackers can be ignited by fuse. While a long string of firecrackers went off at one side of the enemy's cordon, six Americans could conduct a silent assault at the other. That's because the firecrackers sound to the enemy like small-arms fire. This gives the opposition soldiers in the targeted sector the impression that the breakout is being attempted elsewhere. (See Figure 18.9.)

None of the escape techniques so far presented have involved any modifications to the existing terrain. Where time is available to slightly modify that terrain (as little as one full night), much more in the way of escape and diversion is possible.

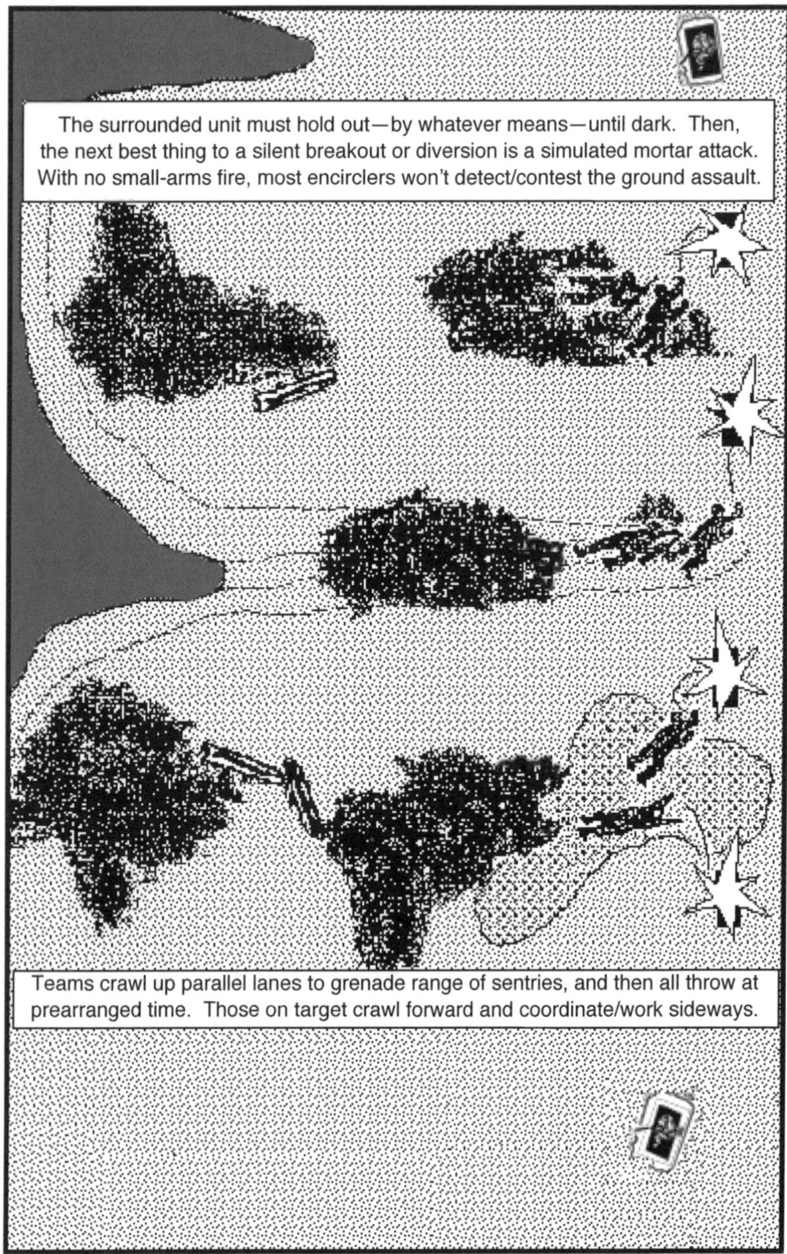

Figure 18.8: Best After-Dark Back-Up Is Fake Mortar Attack
(Source: FM 7-70 [1986], p. 420; FM 5-103 [1985], p. 4-6; MCI 03.66a [1986], p. 2-8; FM 23-30 [1988], p. 2-8; FM 7-1183 [1976], p. 2-VII-C-4.4)

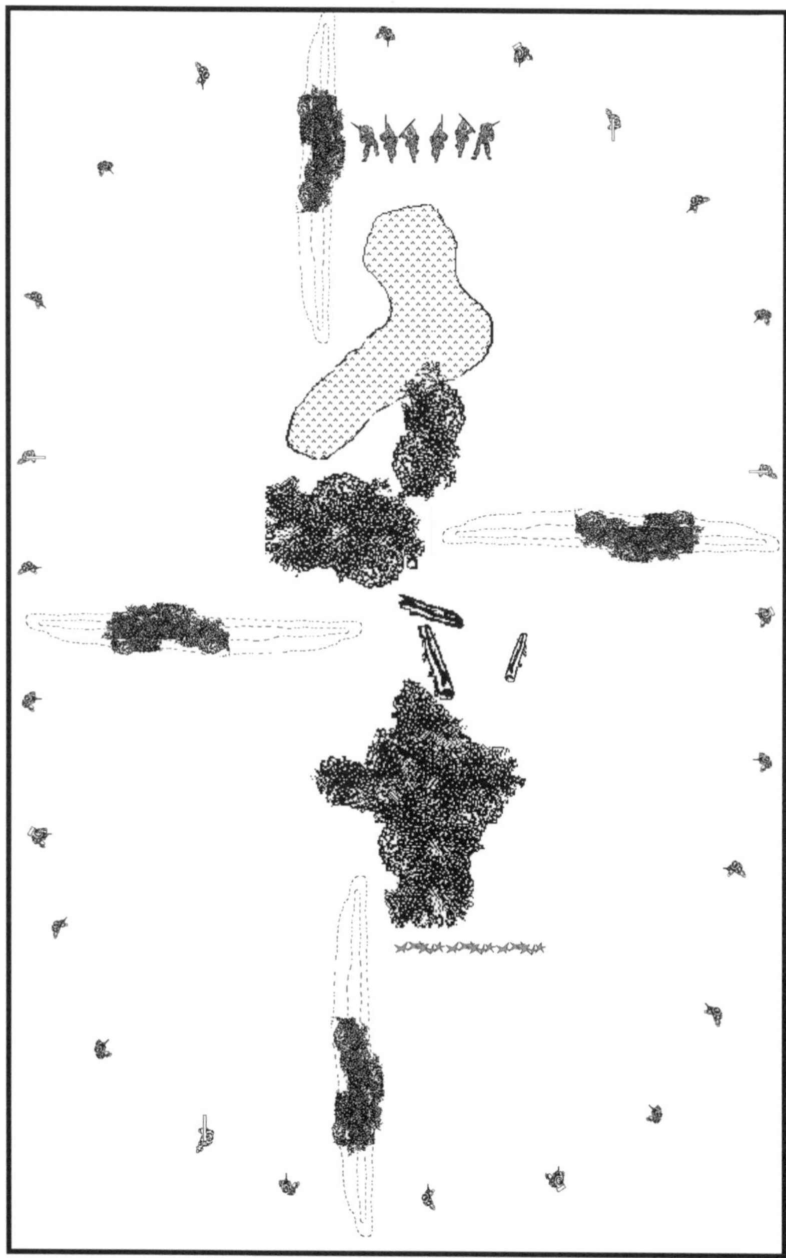

Figure 18.9: Non-Firing Rush Away from Fused Firecrackers
(Source: FM 5-103 [1985], p. 5-10;TC 90-1 [1986], cover)

19 Enhancing Rural Terrain

- Can rural terrain be altered to make escape more easy?
- What types of construction might be involved?

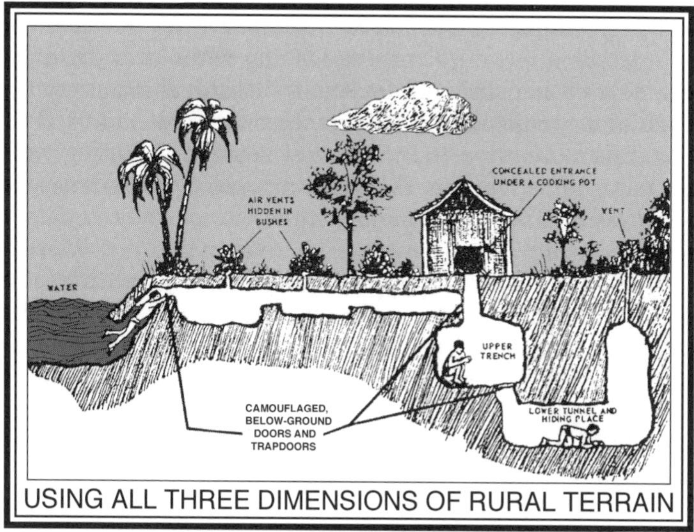

USING ALL THREE DIMENSIONS OF RURAL TERRAIN

(Source: FM 31-73 [1967], p. 246)

More UW Options in a Slightly Modified Landscape

Much more is possible in the way of reconnaissance and offensive maneuver when one is willing to wait below ground for an approaching foe or tunnel into his camp. And overhead foliage provides another medium through which an attacker can surprise his quarry or bypass that quarry's barrier system. Thus, one can make a good case for adding a little digging and tree modifications to his offensive game plan.

What a UW-oriented army can accomplish on defense with enough subterranean preparation has been described in great detail in *Phantom Soldier* and *The Tiger's Way*. The extent to which the Japanese depended defensively on the upper portions of the jungle canopy during WWII has yet to be fully determined. It now seems clear that many of their palm-tree-top positions on Guadalcanal were initially for early warning of ground advance and later for adjustment of supporting arms. Because those position occupants without working radios used rifle shots for alternate signals,[1] most official histories remember them only as snipers. The very few Marines hurt that way suggests otherwise.[2]

"Escape and evasion" (E&E) is not an issue that is completely distinct from offense and defense. After attacking, one could effectively preclude a counterstroke by leaving without any hint of his route or destination. In Vietnam, enemy assault elements routinely departed along trails different from the ones they had used to approach. But more often than not, they seemed to simply vanish.[3] Even a tactically advanced, rearward-moving Asian defense would not work every time. To compensate for its periodic breakdown, participants would need somewhere to hide in a hurry. More than one U.S. unit has had the unpleasant experience of fighting hard for a hill and then finding it, and the open ground behind it, virtually unoccupied.[4] Might elusive Asian attackers and beleaguered Asian defenders have both been taking refuge below ground—virtually beneath the feet of their Western pursuers? There is considerable evidence to that effect. Perhaps that's another way in which UW warriors avoid opposition firepower.

Thus, most of this chapter will be dedicated to showing how a tiny U.S. detachment can enhance its rural location to more easily elude the Chinese or Islamist dragon. America's infantry leaders should then be able to use this E&E capability to justify more daring small-unit offensive and defensive maneuvers. Only then, will they have any real UW capability of their own.

Below-Ground Escape Bunkers in Conventional War

By March 1945, the Japanese had made subterranean warfare into an art form. On Iwo Jima, they conducted almost all of their tactical withdrawals and counterattack marches below ground. All three main lines of defense were linked by tunnel, as were their composite strongpoints.[5] By the time the U.S. Marine assault force came ashore, only the area just north of Suribachi (the narrowest part of the porkchop-shaped island) remained unconnected to this network. The full extent of Japanese burrowing beneath Iwo Jima's northern hummocks was little known in the West until 1995. It was only then that a Nippon TV special revealed an array of connecting compartments with no fewer than four separate levels.[6] (See Figure 19.1.) In a cross-section of the island, the special further disclosed a master north-south tunnel linking all three main defense lines at or beneath the lowest level of their respective chambers.[7] (See Figure 19.2.) Thus, one could reasonably conclude that the main tunnel could only be reached by secret trapdoor in the floor of an opening above it. That's why the full extent of the tunnel system was unknown to Western historians for so long. When it came time to abandon a strongpoint or defensive line, a Japanese rear-party had only to collapse a minor part of the burrow to hide any hint of where the main force had gone.

Even on Luzon, the Nipponese showcased their newly discovered option for below-ground escape. (See Figure 19.3.) What a U.S. War Department sketch shows them to have excavated beneath each hilltop strongpoint may look like a bomb shelter,[8] but it wouldn't have withstood a very big bomb. Closer inspection reveals what may have been its actual purpose. With no tunnel leading directly to the central room, the structure had at least the potential of an underground hide facility. Beleaguered defenders could have easily collapsed or otherwise disguised all entrances to that room at the bends in those tunnels. Then, they would need only provisions and air ducts to live to fight another day. The surface opening to an air duct is, after all, not that hard to camouflage with a pile of ill-fitting rocks. As soon as the surface occupiers had headed for their next objective, those who had secretly withdrawn downward could have easily dug their way out.

By 1953, an Asian mainland country occupied by the Japanese for some 40 years had developed a similar subterranean methodology. That country's Soviet mentors recorded the particulars of what is believed to be one of the mountain strongpoints just above the 38th parallel.[8] (See Figure 19.4.) The tunnels between concentric trenchlines have to run just below the surface of the ground and are probably covered trenches themselves. But, their extensions then enter the mountain. Along them are any number of side rooms with no access to the surface. Those rooms are too far from the front lines to be used as refuge during a pre-assault bombardment. They, too, could have been inhabited for quite some time by those

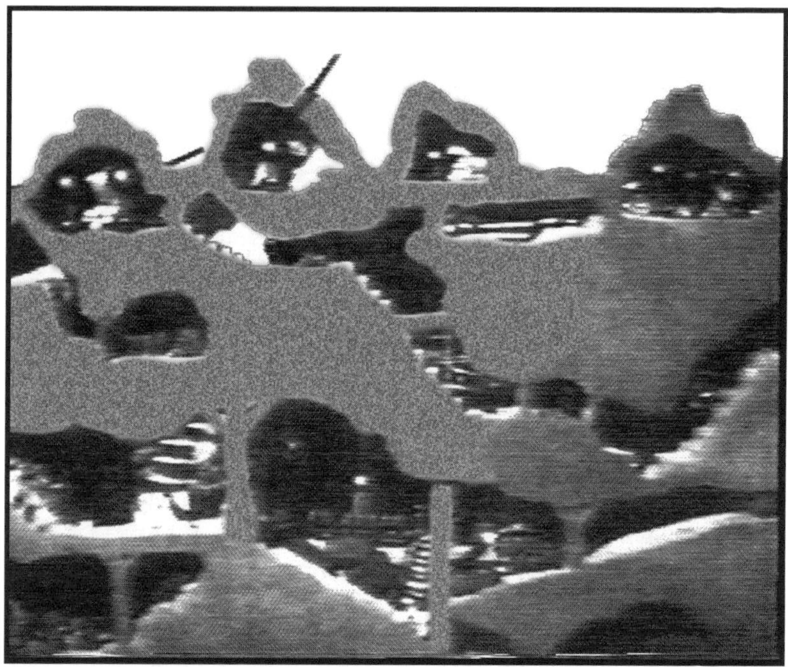

Figure 19.1: Hiding Places beneath the Hummocks on Iwo Jima
("What Cameramen Saw through Their Lenses," *A Tribute to WWII Combat Cameramen of Japan* series, © 1995 by Nippon TV, videocassette)

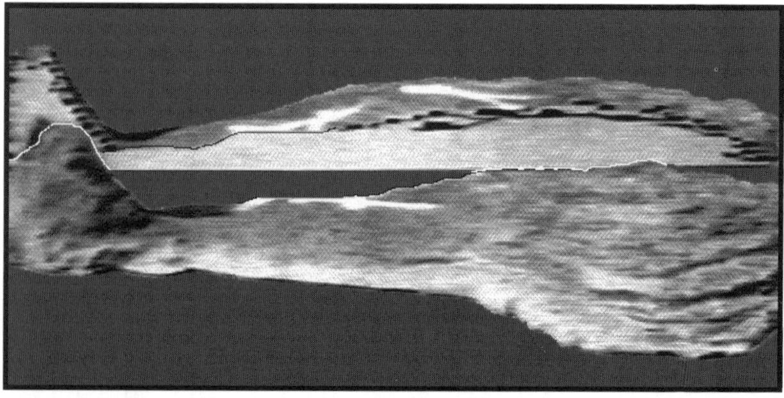

Figure 19.2: Main Tunnel between Bottom Tier of Huge Rooms
(Source: "What Cameramen Saw through Their Lenses," *A Tribute to WWII Combat Cameramen of Japan* series, © 1995 by Nippon TV, videocassette)

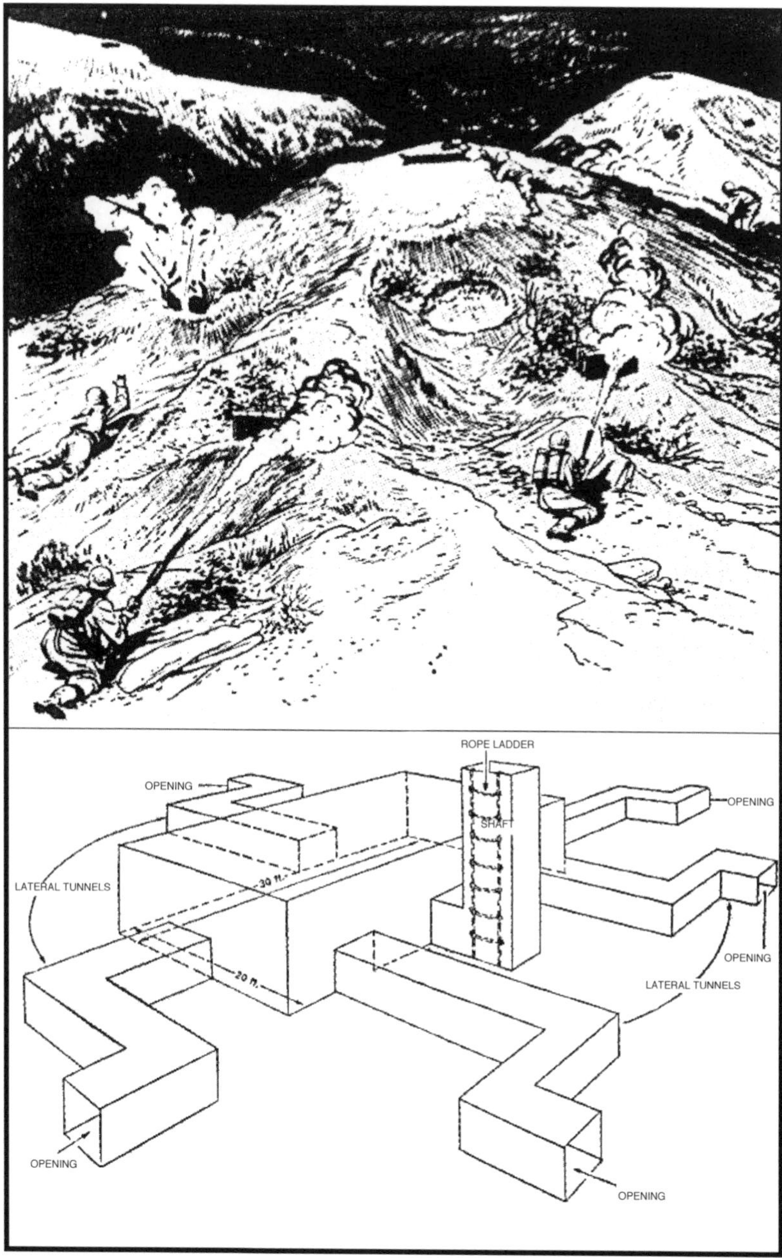

Figure 19.3: More Than Just a Bomb Shelter on Luzon in 1945
(Source: Courtesy of Osprey Publishing from U.S. War Dept. sketch, in *Japanese Army of WWII*, by Philip Warner, © 1972 by Osprey Publishing Ltd.)

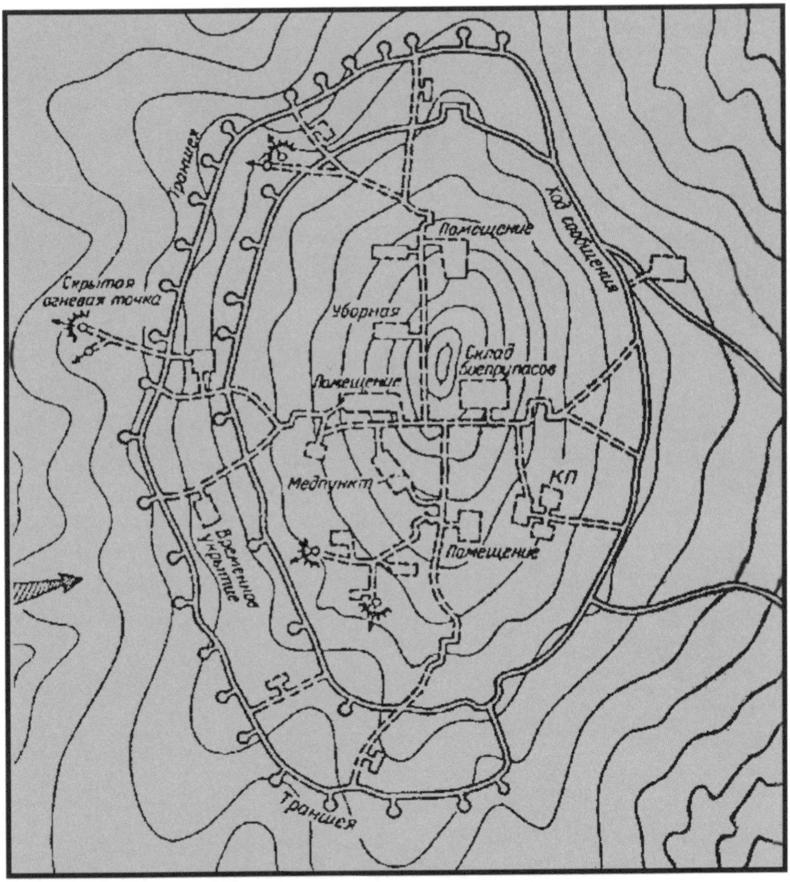

Figure 19.4: Korean Hill Covered with Escape Chambers
(Source: *Voina v Korea: 1950-1953*, by A.A. Kuryacheba, © 2002 by Polygon Publishers, p. 582)

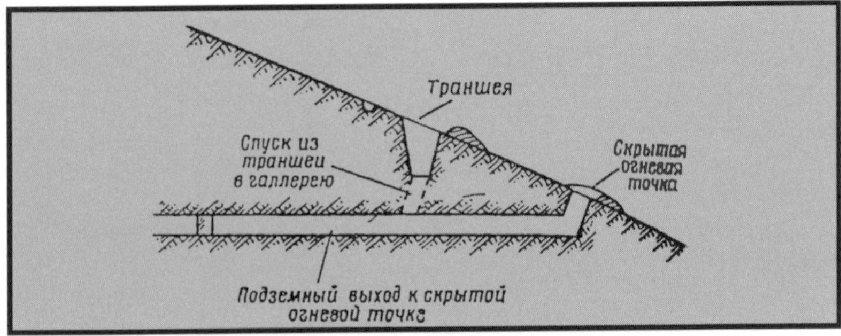

Figure 19.5: Secret Exit by Trapdoor to Sealed Tunnel
(Source: *Voina v Korea: 1950-1953*, by A.A. Kuryacheba, © 2002 by Polygon Publishers, p. 613)

evicted from the hill's surface fortifications. In that country's war museum are several photographs of troops manning just such a hill. There, a full-scale mock-up of a hill's underground living area also exists. With log-shored walls and ceilings, that area appears quite habitable. Just off the main tunnel are the following: (1) kitchen; (2) sleeping quarters; (3) bathroom; (4) separate storage rooms for food, water, and ammunition; (5) observation post with tiny view-port; (6) artillery or anti-aircraft chamber with cave-like opening; and (7) landline phone booth with surface access.[9] In Figure 19.5, the Russian artist shows how beleaguered frontline troops could have escaped another way. Trench-bottom trapdoors led to separate horizontal tunnels. In them, former defenders could have hidden for days or moved beyond the new surface dwellers' lines.

Enough has been said about the Vietnam War in previous works to prove that a third Asian army has learned to escape below ground. The entire coastal plain of Vietnam was dotted with subterranean facilities: (1) guerrilla cell headquarters; (2) infiltration route waystations; and (3) supply depots.[10] Those facilities were not normally linked by tunnel, but there were exceptions like Cu Chi. This chapter's title page drawing shows how much the art of subterranean warfare had advanced by 1970. The VC's favorite entrance to such a hide was below a well's waterline, and his favorite exit was beneath the surface of a regularly full irrigation ditch or stream.

Telling Displays at the PRC's New War Museum

In a tiny, barely accessible alcove of Beijing's massive new military museum lies a glass-enclosed scale model showing the extent to which the PLA understands subterranean warfare.[11] That this knowledge has not been fully applied in the past is no guarantee that it is currently idle.

Wonderfully recreated in the tiny mock-up is the main street of a Chinese village. This is no ordinary street. It has been thoroughly prepared by local guerrillas to counter the intrusion of Japanese occupiers. While most of this preparation has occurred below ground, some has to do with reaching and crossing rooftops. Such an image may evoke painful memories for Iraq veterans. Many remember rooftop activity during ambushes. But few have suspected a subterranean approach or exit. If that war lasts much longer, excavation may play a greater role, just as it has in Palestine.

First noticed by American soldiers in Korea, the "closing-V" ambush (or *Haichi Shiki*) has been part of Chinese military culture for centuries.[12] The tiny diorama in the Beijing's museum may depict a rare, three-dimensional version of that formation. Or it may simply show an early prototype of the U-shaped urban ambush that has been seen on countless battlefields since the late 1930's, including recent efforts to expel the Russians from Chechnya.[13]

As with many things Chinese, the detail of this tiny war scene tells the story. The Japanese lead element has already entered the village unopposed and is in the process of poisoning its well. The main body is still on the bridge at the edge of town and starting to take fire from a rooftop machinegun. The file that connects them is also under attack from not only the rooftops, but also from ground-level firing ports. One of those ports is beneath the heavy stone table of a grist mill. As such, it is unassailable.

The most interesting part of the display is in the cut-away view of what is occurring below ground. There is a maze of tunnels and rooms that span three separate levels. None of these openings are connected to the village well, however. The underground system has its own well with no ground-level signature. Ladders to the surface lie beneath the stone floor of a pagoda and full watering trough in a barn. A hay stack provides the air vent. All women and children are now housed below ground in temporary living quarters, and any guerrillas wounded in the fighting will be taken to a subterranean treatment room.

Immediately, one's attention shifts to the rooftops. Fighters are fanning out along the tops of the connecting one-story structures on both sides of the street. Their obvious intent is to finish off the connecting file so as to discourage any further intrusion by the main column.

That the display pertains to something that happened almost 70 years ago should make no difference to the true UW enthusiast. Until modern technology learns to see below ground, subterranean warfare will be the norm for those wanting to evict more powerful occupiers. Elsewhere in the Beijing museum are photographs of more recent occurrences. One is of contemporary Chinese infantrymen sleeping in a cave they have just dug. Another is of Chinese officers inspecting a man-sized tunnel in some Middle Eastern country. Still another is of a Chinese fireteam in the assault. The last would have little significance if the members of that fireteam were not wearing U.N. helmets.[14]

What All of This Has to Do with Future U.S. Missions

To successfully check Chinese and Islamist expansion, the U.S. infantryman will have one of two roles in coming years. He and his squad will either have to live and operate by themselves in enemy territory. Or he alone will have to train proxy guerrilla forces. Either way, he must know how to function like a guerrilla himself. His best tactical model will be the Viet Cong. Their NVA instructors have a winning record against two separate manifestations of Chinese aggression. While they were off defanging a Chinese guerrilla proxy in Cambodia, their home guard trainees single-handedly thwarted a fully supported Chinese invasion.[15]

The only real difference between how an Asian army prepares for battle below ground and how a guerrilla does so is in the scale. To best determine the latter, one must see how the UW experts taught guerrillas to enhance terrain. (See Figure 19.6.) The main themes of the chart are digging and hiding. The peripheral threads are swimming, attacking from below, and discouraging pursuit. The rest of this chapter will explore these subjects. How an isolated U.S. squad might escape capture will also be visualized. Among that squad's methods will be one or two with simulated boobytraps. Actual boobytraps are not recommended as they kill indiscriminately.

Guerrillas Depend More on Tiny Hides

The VC made good use of individual excavations in Vietnam. (See Figures 19.7 and 19.8.) Most had been farmers. Their closeness to nature gave them great insight into the most effective use of available camouflage.

There is nothing a young U.S. city dweller can't do—with enough research and experimentation—that a VC could. To build a subterranean hideout, the American's main challenge will be how to conceal its entrance. Of course, he must also figure out how to reinforce its walls and ceilings. As each ceiling's rigidity depends on what grows above, GIs should know which trees produce spreading root systems. (Refer back to Figure 19.6.) If few trees are available despite a rainy climate, each man may have to construct a temporary exit like that in Figure 19.8. Saddam Hussein escaped capture for many months by easy access to something similar.

Why U.S. Squads Must Have Guerrilla-Like Skills

Many feel that the U.S. Marine Combined Action Platoon (CAP) initiative from the Vietnam era is the answer to the Maoist and Islamist insurgencies of the present and future. As such, an imaginary U.S. squad has been assigned to work with a few indigenous

Rural attack

Attacks from tunnels under barriers &

Rural escape

Tunneling &

Leaving without a trace #

Natural-element escape strategies (gotonpo)
- "Metal escape arts" (kintonjutsu)
  - Disorienting pursuers with a metal blinding mirror
- "Wood escape arts" (mokutonjutsu)
  - Using low vegetation for concealment (moku ton jutsu)
- "Earth escape arts" (dotonjutsu)
  - Digging a hiding place
- "Water escape arts" (suitonjutsu)
  - Stealth swimming and flotation pots (suijutsu)

Use of mines and boobytraps &

Breaking contact #

Diversions
- Leaving behind booby traps to warn of pursuit

Rural evasion

Hiding (inton-jutsu) #

Waylaying a pursuer #

Assaulting the enemy from below

Source Code:

Ninja methods for guerrilla use against Japan's Samuri (1460-1650) [16]
& N. Vietnamese methods for Viet Cong use against GIs (1965-1973) [17]
$ Chinese ally's Light Infantry Trng. Guid. Bur. methods (1992-2007) [18]

Figure 19.6: UW Instruction on How to Enhance Rural Terrain

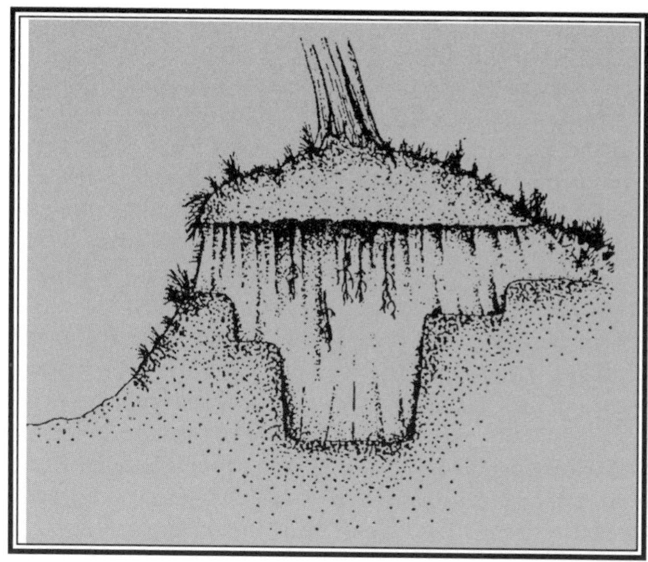

Figure 19.7: Certain Species of Trees Have Spreading Roots

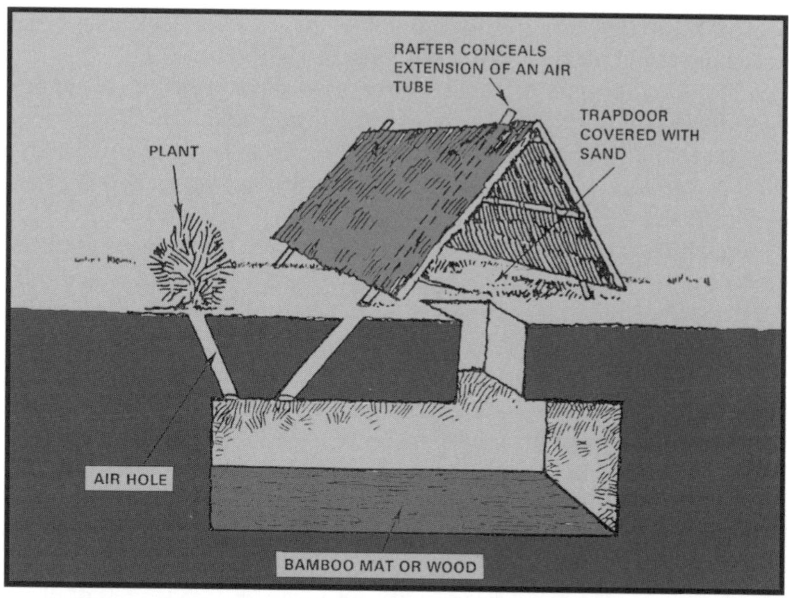

Figure 19.8: One-Man Escape Chamber from Scratch

(Source: FM 90-8 [1980], p. A-3)

police and soldiers to secure an area of southern Mindanao from *Abu Sayyaf* and NPA incursion. That area is roughly four miles square. At its center is a morass of partially flooded ground fed by several streambeds. (See Map 19.1.) The young Americans have been warned repeatedly by local villagers that their indigenous sister squads now contain enemy fighters. After spotting a Filipino cohort among hundreds of attacking NPA guerrillas one night, the Americans strike out on their own for a nearby swamp. Well briefed on the inherent dangers of a CAP mission, they have been secretly preparing that swamp to serve as a refuge.

Over the months, they have located several naturally occurring one-man hides throughout the relatively flat and open areas around the swamp. They include vegetation-covered pools, thick-topped trees, large bramble patches, hollow tree trunks, and road culverts. All have been appropriately modified to provide a place in which to avoid enemy searchers. Hollow reeds have been positioned/planted at the pools. Perches have been built in the trees. (Refer back to Figure 16.6.) Zigzag tunnels have been clipped in the sticker bushes. A step has been placed in the upper portion of a pair of hollow tree trunks. And all culvert centers have been stuffed with debris to prevent any telltale silhouette.

Additionally, any number of spider holes have been dug in all areas devoid of other hides. (See Figure 19.9.)

The U.S. squad members have also done a study of where friendly travel might be obscured but not impeded—thick stands of tiny trees, defiladed lanes, and the like. As a result of this study, they have located, and in some cases improved upon, the various conduits throughout the area. (See Figure 19.10 and Map 19.2.) Those which occurred naturally are partially covered game trails, a narrow gully that the map maker missed, and a long firebreak ditch. All provide concealment, and the last two would provide good cover in an otherwise exposed location during a firefight. Additionally, the GIs have marked off several "speed trails" across ground that lacks enough interest to allow pinpoint navigation. As long as those trails are used only for emergencies, they will not invite ambush. All entrances to bushy portions have been carefully obscured. In the Orient, such things are accomplished by tying bushes together long enough for them to grow together naturally.

Now the GIs are thinking like Native Americans and their Asian ancestors. They want a base camp in the swamp, so they will need secret conduits to and from that swamp's center. The watercourses

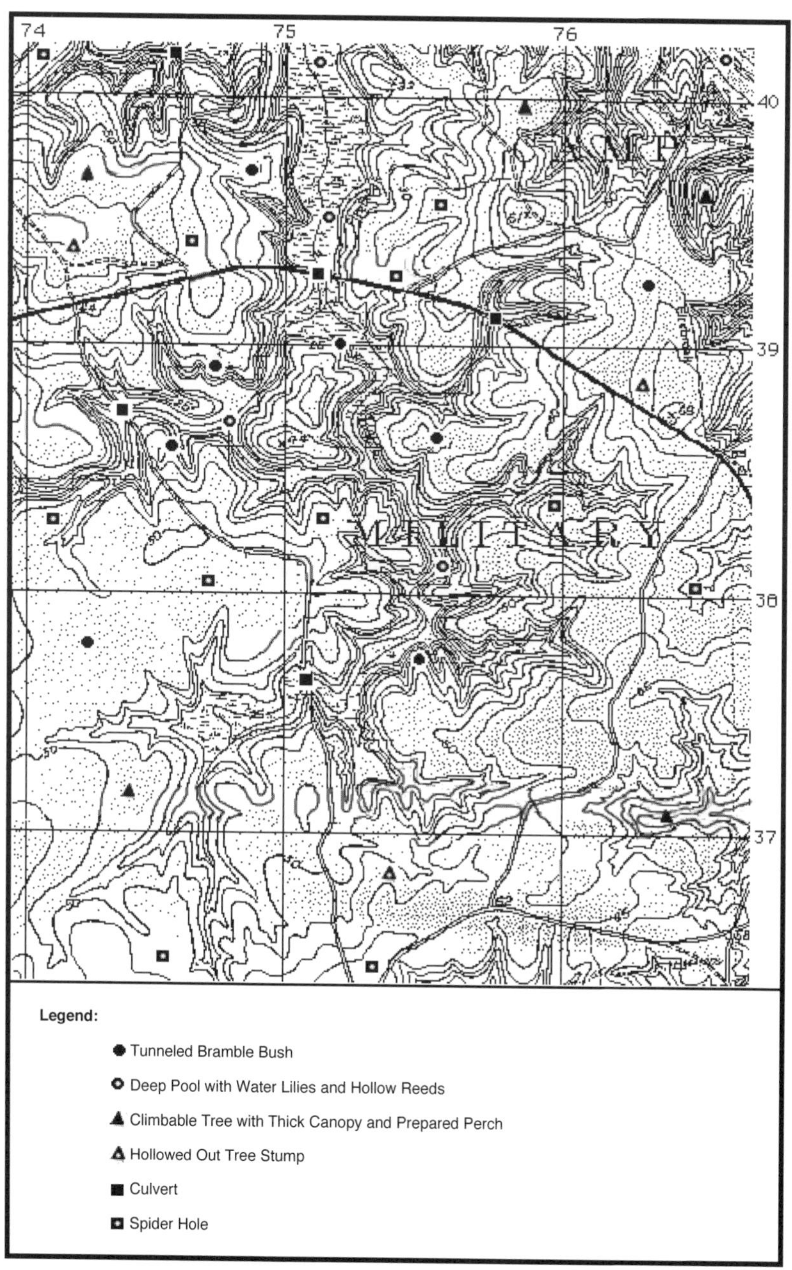

Map 19.1: U.S. Guerrilla-Prepared Rural Hides
(Source: U.S. Dept. of Interior, "Jacksonville South Quadrangle," 1:24,000)

Figure 19.9: Spider Hole Preparation
(Source: FM 7-8 [1984], p. D-15)

Figure 19.10: Taking Advantage of Every Fold in the Ground
(Source: FM 7-8 [1984], p. B-1)

already provide a few, but they want more. First, they locate a three-foot-high ledge that follows the contour of a finger to the east. The ground just below that ledge will make a defiladed crawl-way. Then, they remember an easy-to-follow route to the north that stays in deep shadow during any phase of the moon. To the southwest, they locate an area of heavily forested hard ground that, with a few carefully placed river rocks, should provide a footprint-resistant trail as far as the road. To follow most of that trail, one has only to move from one surface root to the next. Finally, the Americans create a decoy trail that should take any pursuers well past their refuge. Intentionally aligned with an existing road, it lies on an east-west azimuth. The idea is to lead pursuers onto the trail from one end or the other, and then so mysteriously exit its culmination that those pursuers continue to parallel the road. At the eastern terminus is a huge old tree with low, widely spreading limbs. GIs approaching it from the west can swing up onto one branch, move along it to a fork in the tree's trunk, enter another branch, and then exit it a full 60 yards from where they began. Close at hand will be ground that slopes gently into their swampy home. Some 80 yards from the western terminus of this "dead end trail" is a tiny brook that also leads into their refuge. GIs being chased to the west could go all the way to this trail terminus and then—over an exposed root system—backtrack to the brook without leaving a trace.

In essence, all members of this situationally dictated guerrilla unit have come to know every inch of the ground they will defend. Now, they must establish a headquarters.

The American Squad's Base Area

The "base area" is a Communist concept. It is an area in which a tiny guerrilla detachment can find temporary refuge. For a piece of real estate to qualify as a base area, it must be so difficult for an enemy to enter that he will normally not. A good-sized swamp makes a perfect base area. Somewhere in the deepest and darkest part of the swamp in Map 19.2, the GIs must find some place to harbor. It should have natural screening, a good supply of clean water, a secret underground escape facility, and an enemy diversion plan. Any close enemy approach to its precise location must be somehow averted. The VC used to regularly accomplish this feat with mines and snip-

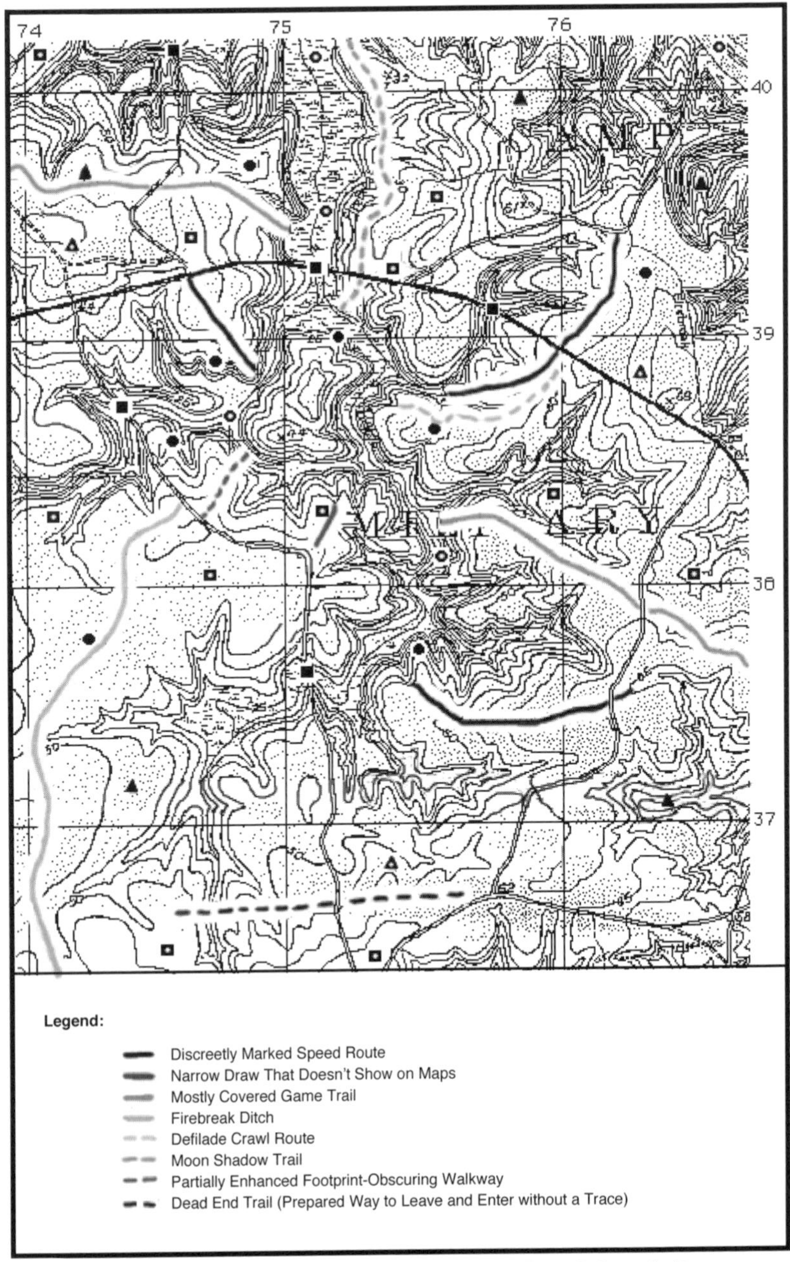

Map 19.2: U.S.-Guerrilla-Prepared Rural Conduits

(Source: U.S. Dept. of Interior, "Jacksonville South Quadrangle," 1:24,000)

ers. Every time an American sweep kept coming across mine-laced dikes, a Viet Cong sniper to its rear or flank would cause it to turn or delay (for a medevac) until dark. Either way the underground installation in the sweep's initial path would be safe.[19]

On a smaller scale in the woods, such things are best accomplished from defensive outposts with "observation lanes" prepared between them. These are narrow strips of ground in which the vegetation has been removed or shifted to one side. To create the impression that the whole area is uninhabited, those outposts must also be carefully manned. There can be little or no movement signature while entering, leaving, or occupying them. And each should have its own covered escape route.

If an island in the middle of the swamp (like at grid coordinates 751357 on Map 19.2) is to be the harbor site, then an underground escape facility must be prepared within its confines. That facility has to be much bigger than the one-man hides already constructed. If it is to be below ground, the easiest place to dig would be beneath the roots of an upturned tree. The trick then would be to somehow preclude any sign of human passage nearby. Asian guerrillas are fond of water entrances for precisely that reason. Thus, an upturned tree near the streambed would make a perfect spot. Any Americans wanting to escape that way could simply move from either direction up the rocky streambed to its entrance. They then have only to keep from muddying up the stream or moistening its bank. Much more could obviously be said about how to design such an escape facility. But those types of details are best left to the common sense and imagination of the junior enlisted personnel at the scene. Finally to win the so-called War on Terror, U.S. squads must be allowed to improvise.

Once the subterranean facility has been prepared, those GIs will be eager to take the fight to their tormentors. For a target, they will have their choice of NPA, *Abu Sayyaf,* MILF, or MNLF.

Doing Something to the Area's New Masters

Progressively to hurt a more powerful foe, one must find a vulnerability and then attack it in such a way that he never feels obligated to correct the deficiency. In Iraq for example, America's technological pride has been so damaged by the IED, that it has failed to take the most obvious countermeasure—dismounting the vehicles, outposting every neighborhood, and living off the local economy.

Well aware of the lessons of history, the hunted Americans decide to interdict the enemy resupply columns that move through their area. They are quite sure that those columns do not swagger down the middles of trails and roads, but rather sneak along the parallel treelines. When they do move cross-country, they are restricted by the amount of vegetation and contour interval. Where either is difficult, they follow streambeds or ridgelines for speed.

To interdict such a column, the tiny American force will first have to send out a fireteam-sized patrol to locate the exact trace of its passage. That patrol should go to places where the enemy might be seen from a distance or leave footprints. A treetop perch along an open stretch of ground would do for the former, and any soft ground along a line of drift would work for the latter (constitute a "track trap").

Later to ambush that column, a good site must be found. It should have its own interior cover (like a dead log). It needs natural obstacles to the front, and both sides (like a puddle, swampy ground, or tangle of old barbed wire). And, there is nothing quite like a covered exit route should the quarry start shooting. That route needs only to be deep enough for crawling. The foe may never realize he's been ambushed if the patrol sticks to claymores and grenades.

At some point, the GIs will want to start sabotaging the enemy's camp as well. Two men will first need a safe place from which to observe his frontline positions. Then, during some natural diversion, they will slip through a gap and create what looks like a chance occurrence. If that occurrence is to be a lucky mortar round, they will need a couple of 81-mm mortar fins, as well as their explosives and a timer. If they can slip back out the way they came before the explosion, they can repeat the feat over and over. Each time, they will take a different route home and carefully obscure their footprints.

Foiling the Eventual Pursuit

Sooner or later, one of these ambush or infiltration forays will incur a very large and determined pursuing force. If the Americans are able to elude that force long enough to enter their carefully prepared domain, they can escape its cordon by creating a diversion at one of their spider holes. (See Figure 19.11.) Of course, technology provides other ways to defeat a cordon.

The Technology Variant

Most infantry units will avoid any area they know to be mined. That creates an opportunity for a few GIs who must somehow survive a concentrated search by many times their number. Most of the U.S. cordons in Vietnam were second-hand-intelligence based and too porous to catch much. Similarly, an Eastern foe who had not yet seen or tracked his quarry would not be surprised by an empty cordon. Within this universal reality lies additional opportunity.

Figure 19.12 depicts six Americans hidden in a slight depression amidst relatively level and lightly vegetated terrain. Around themselves, they have built a simulated minefield. While the mines may appear to be tripwire or surface-prong detonated, they are actually set off by electrical charge or remote control from the depression. Thus, the Americans can selectively blow up portions of the cordon as it tightens around them. Each time they do so, the enemy will believe that one of his own personnel has caused the explosion. With any luck after the second or third blast, he will find some reason to bypass the area. To further enhance the ruse, a few of the internationally recognized signs for "minefield" could be posted.

Of course, one would hope that such a drastic and complicated ruse would never become necessary. If there were some way for the Americans to foil close pursuit, they might never have to endure such a thing. Technology can also help in that regard.

Technological Ways of Discouraging Pursuit

Unbeknownst to most veterans of the Vietnam War, many of the boobytraps they encountered were intended to discourage further searches in the same direction. In effect, the enemy had ringed each detachment headquarters, infiltration-route waysta-

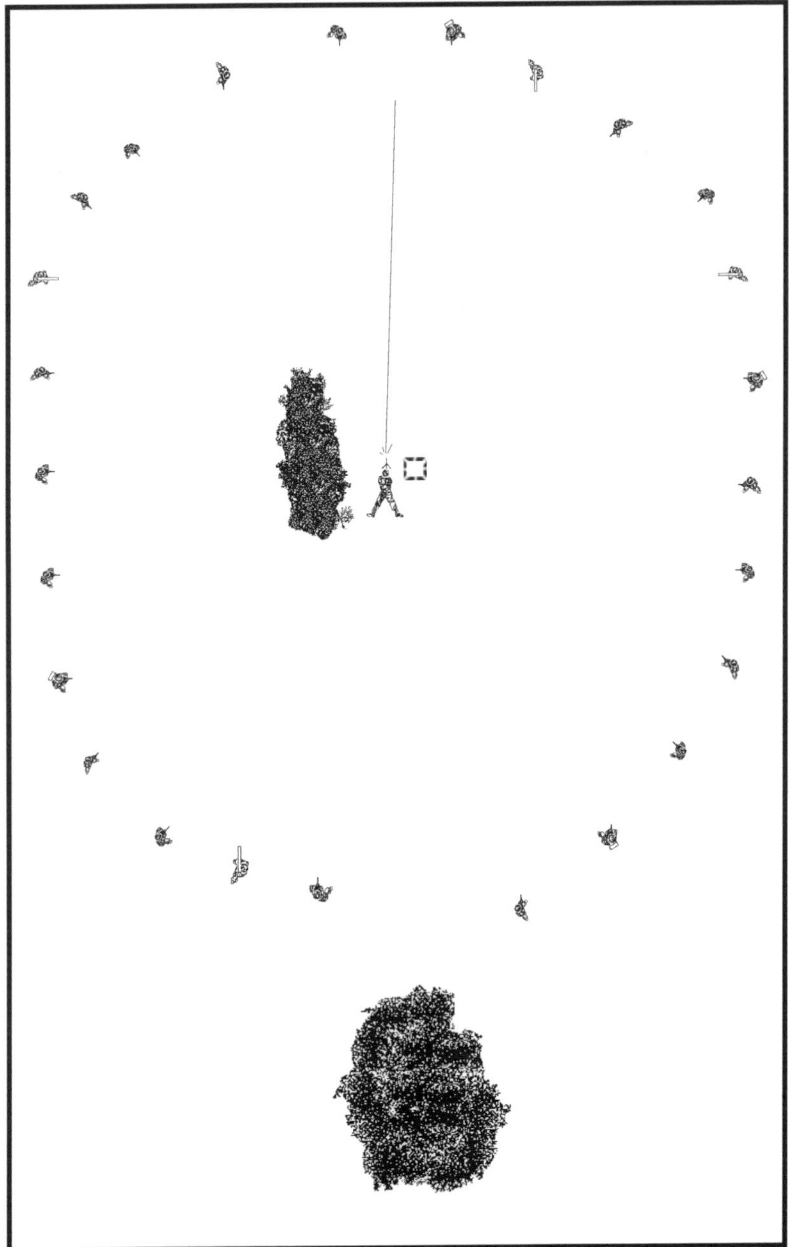

Figure 19.11: Five Hide in Bramble As One Diverts at Hole
(Source: FM 5-103 [1985], p. 5-10;TC 90-1 [1986], cover)

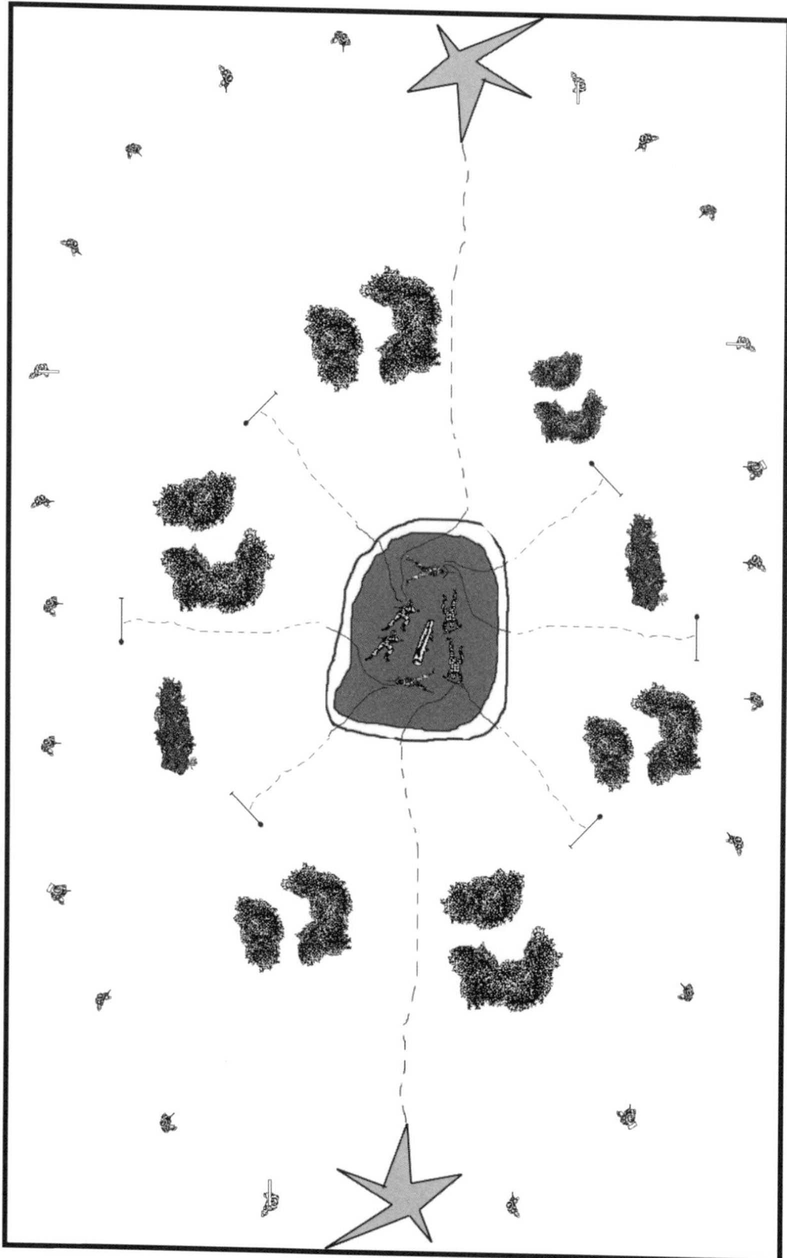

Figure 19.12: All Six at Hidden Depression in Fake Minefield
(Source: FM 5-103 [1985], p. 5-10;TC 90-1 [1986], cover)

tion, and supply depot with boobytraps. He knew that it was standard procedure for the American unit that encountered a minefield to retrace its steps and find some way around it. His ruse worked well, because U.S. forces found only a tiny fraction of what there was to find in the way of strategic assets. But boobytraps kill indiscriminately. That's why U.S. doctrine requires every soldier and Marine to get his battalion commander's permission before emplacing one. Even then, its precise location must be accurately mapped and passed up the chain.

Still, the idea of impeding a pursuer with something that at least simulates a minefield is compelling. An obstacle course of hidden tripwire-detonated "flash-bang" devices would qualify. Having committed to memory the exact location of all devices, its builder and his colleagues could easily avoid them as they ran through the pattern. (See Figure 19.13.) Even pursuers right on their heels would quickly lose interest in the chase after tripping the first "flash-bang." If at all interested in finishing the war alive, they would have no choice but to assume that the muted explosion had come from a misfiring boobytrap. Even after discovering the ruse, they would proceed more slowly.

The More Ready-to-Man Defensive Strongpoints the Better

All across Vietnam's coastal plain were vacant fortified villages, treeline-following trenchlines, and other bunker systems. The enemy may or may not have been originally forced to vacate them, but they still existed in great abundance. This gave the hard-pressed guerrilla squad plenty of places from which to hold out until dark. Then, it had two choices. It could barricade itself within the inevitable escape chamber and wait for the occupier to grow tired of looking. Or it could send one or two of its members at a time through the myriad of irrigation ditches that crisscrossed the countryside. As proved by Lt. Terzi and his valiant six on Guadalcanal, contemporary Americans can do as much and more. But they will never get the chance until their commanders stop hoarding control and fighting defensively under the pretext of limiting casualties. The best way to limit casualties while still winning a war is to help junior infantrymen to achieve their full battlefield potential. This is as possible in the city as it is in the woods.

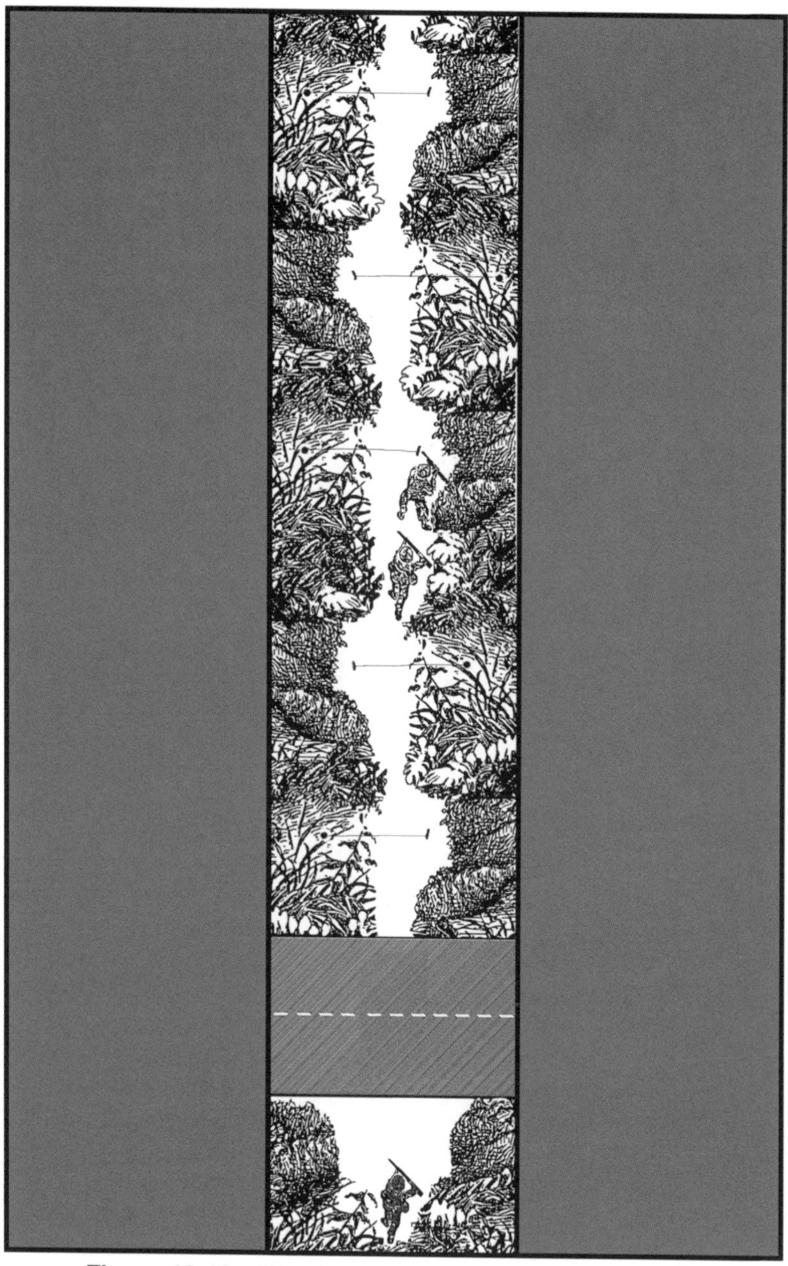

Figure 19.13: "Flash-Bang" Maze to Break Contact

(Source: FM 5-103 [1985], pp. 4-4, 4-6)

20 Urban Escape and Evasion

- Is it easier to escape an encirclement in the city?
- How might E&E trained infantrymen fare better in Iraq?

BUILDING AND GUTTER SHADOW CRAWLING

(Source: MCI 03.66a [1986], p. 210)

A Lost Opportunity?

In the fall of 2006, the U.S. government finally realized how important the security of each of Iraq's residential areas was to its survival as a whole. By late May 2007, 146 out of 457 of Baghdad's neighborhoods had been outposted by a combined force (company-sized or larger) of American and Iraqi troops. At the height of the U.S. "Surge" in July, only about half of Baghdad was being pacified in this way.[1] To provide a physical presence in all neighborhoods, the Coalition would have had to further disperse its assets—give each neighborhood a platoon instead of a company. But Coalition commanders must have considered such a wide dispersal of personnel unsafe. They were afraid that many of the platoons would be destroyed piecemeal. In other words, neither the GIs nor their Iraqi counterparts knew how to escape an encirclement. Should the war still be going when this work is released, the U.S. military might want to share some of its urban E&E techniques with the troops in that theater. By so doing, it could complete the outposting and win the war.

One can only assume that too many of America's top military leaders are unaware of what badly outnumbered and outgunned people can accomplish on defense in the city. A few lessons from history might help them to see why urban E&E training might help their people to win an urban guerrilla conflict.

It's Much Easier to Hide in the City Than in the Country

Built-up areas have always been good places for rebels to operate. That's partially because of their proximity to popular support. But it's also because of the terrain itself. From a tactical standpoint, urban terrain is unique; it favors even the untrained defender. Different rebel groups have tried different things over the years, but there are common threads throughout. For example, Warsaw ghetto rebels could move backwards through the crawl-spaces that occurred in normal building construction. The Irish rebels of 1920 had strings of safe houses for use during a retreat. This chapter will deal with how a U.S. squad might secretly exit a built-up area that they and two Iraqi squads had just ceded to a vastly larger Madhi Army contingent. Those who don't believe escape to be possible without first leveling an escape corridor with supporting arms can take heart from what happened in Poland many years ago.

The Defense of the Warsaw Ghetto

The Warsaw Ghetto fighters got their baptism of fire in January 1943. Poorly armed, they only had 143 revolvers, one machine pistol, and seven rounds of ammunition per weapon. There were 650 of them, divided into groups of 30.[2] Their secret to success was an intricate escape and evasion network. It could also be used to approach the enemy unseen.

> The Ghetto fighters constructed an intricate network of underground cellars and tunnels. Concealed retreats and passages for shifting and distributing the defense forces were also devised.[3]
>
> All inhabitants of the Ghetto prepared for what they realized would be their final fight. Hundreds of camouflaged bunker shelters were dug under the houses (including 618 air raid shelters), most connected through the sewage system and linked up with the central water supply and electricity.[4]

When the fighting finally broke out, Jewish freedom fighters poured a hail of bullets, grenades, and bombs down on the German infantry. Against the tanks, they tossed a barrage of gasoline-filled bottles. The battle raged from 19 April to 16 May 1943. Then, realizing the Ghetto could not be captured by any standard clearing operation, the Germans started to dam up and flood the sewers. Their commander destroyed the entire residential area by setting every block on fire.[5] Unbeknownst to the Germans, one of the two insurgent organizations had a tunnel from the central stronghold at Muranowski Square to the Michalin Forest outside the Ghetto.[6]

Hundreds of Jewish fighters nevertheless survived in the sewers and rubble. There was sporadic shooting throughout the summer of 1943, then things turned quiet.[7] In August 1944, the underground Polish army attempted to liberate Warsaw from German occupation. The remaining Jews took part, and the fighting soon turned brutal. At one point, an encircled Jewish enclave managed to secretly join another through the sewers.[8] This time, the Germans had to burn down 85% of the city to restore some semblance of order.[9]

A More Recent Example by a UW-Trained Adversary

At the end of January 1968, some 5,000 NVA and VC soldiers entered and attempted to hold Hue City during the Vietnam War.[10] As that force included the NVA's 4th, 5th, and 6th Regiments, it was every bit of a reinforced division.[11] After weeks of fighting, what was left of that division withdrew into the Citadel and then supposedly

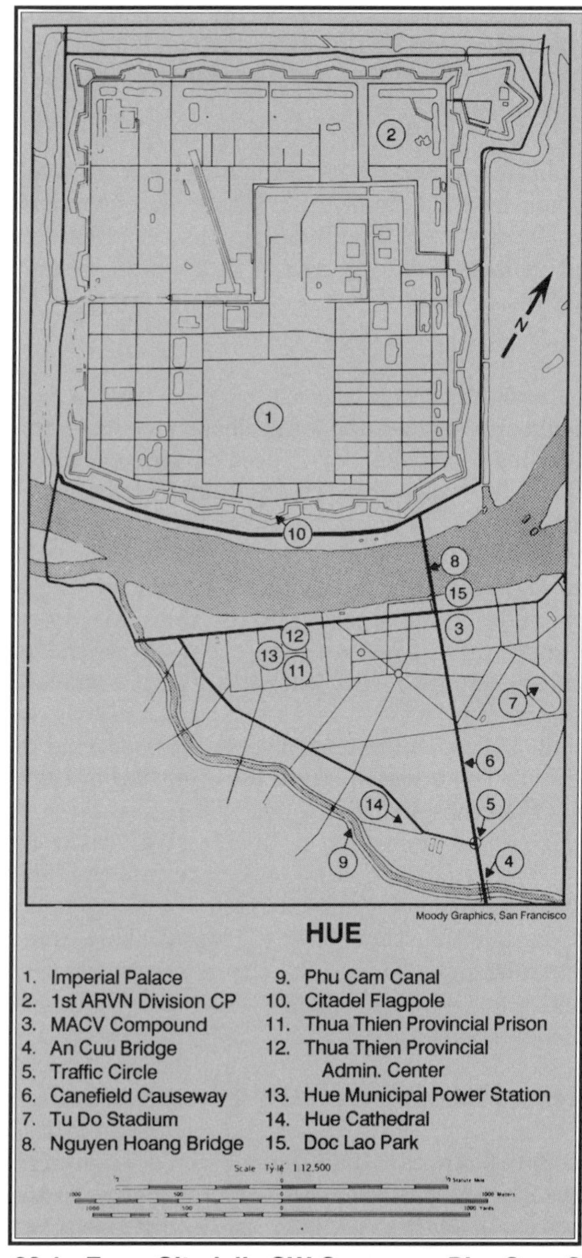

Map 20.1: From Citadel's SW Corner up Phu Cam Canal

(Source: Courtesy of Pacifica Military History, from *Fire in the Streets: The Battle for Hue, Tet 1968*, © 1991 by Eric Hammel)

into the Imperial Palace at its southeastern end.[12] (See Map 20.1.) Yet, when members of South Vietnam's elite Black Panther Company stormed that Palace on 24 February, they found it empty.[13] By that time, the Communist force had suffered 1,000 killed and as many wounded.[14] What happened to the nonambulatory casualties will be addressed in the next chapter. The issue at hand is what happened to those not tasked with carrying the wounded (as many as 2,000 soldiers). Something of a precedent had been set here. Though seemingly surrounded and out of options, an NVA "division minus" had somehow gotten away.

The Allies were not oblivious to the possibility of a breakout, but most of their units had been deployed to the west and north of the Citadel. These were the directions from which many of the NVA had come and the shortest route to the mountains. But that particular foe seldom withdrew along routes used for approach or otherwise predictable. Thus, one must look to the south and east of the fort for how the NVA "division minus" managed its escape. The empty Palace on 24 February should have come as no surprise. Citadel vintage forts often had built-in underground passageways between royal compound and moat.[15] While the Imperial Palace and Huu Gate were captured on the 24th, the extreme southern corner of the Citadel did not fall until early on the 25th.[16] Thus, the beleaguered foe had until then to complete his escape.

Central to Oriental military philosophy is the ability to disperse while under duress. Just because most of the foe entered the Citadel in battalion strength does not mean that he departed that way. NVA squads were accustomed to operating under decentralized control and, unlike their Western counterparts, could function as semi-independent maneuver elements in enemy-controlled areas. Over a long enough period of time, many NVA soldiers could have exfiltrated the Allied cordon. If one squad departed the Citadel's Nha Do Gate every 20 minutes, a fully manned regiment could have crossed the river in three nights.

As early as 16 February, the enemy commander had asked for permission to withdraw his troops from the Citadel.[17] Late on the night of the 21st, the U.S. Marine positions to his east were pummeled with rockets and mortars—very possibly to cover the sound of the first squads to leave to the south.[18] There were other diversions on the 22nd and 23rd.[19] The last involved a half-hearted ground assault at the northwestern end of the Citadel.[19] NVA forces maintained full control of the area between the eastern side of the Citadel and the Perfume River until the 23rd.[20] Thus, most of the mass exodus must have occurred between the 21st and the 23rd. At the Citadel's southwest corner, tiny groups of swimmers had the shadow of a bridge and the entrance to the Phu Cam Canal. (Refer back to Map 20.1.) Once in the Phu Cam, they had only to follow neighborhood drainage ditches to reach a fully protected exit corridor. A mere 500 meters away lay a ridgeline that extended to the south another 2000 meters. (See Map 20.2.) As late as 26 February, 2nd Battalion, 5th Marines still had to fight hard for portions of that ridgeline.[21]

How might these lessons of history be applied to the War on Terror? If U.S. squads were able to do the same kinds of things, that war might be a lot easier to win. Thus, the ethnically diverse and abundantly gifted American public must ask itself a highly revealing question. Are they and their relatives culturally inferior to East-Asian infantrymen, or just prevented from reaching their full battlefield potential?

Why Would Americans Run Away in the City?

A properly designed urban defense is nearly impervious to assault. But U.S. soldiers and Marines cannot win a guerrilla war from behind barbed wire and sandbags. They must instead interact with the local citizenry. The police station from which the lone U.S. squad would work might not withstand back-to-back truck bombs, intense fire from all sides, and follow-up demolitions. When capture or execution are the other alternatives, escape doesn't sound all that bad. Eastern armies have long accepted tactical withdrawal as an essential part of maneuver. A secret withdrawal is a lot easier to do a few men at a time.

Natural Urban Escape Routes

The city offers a myriad of hidden passageways. Working from the bottom up, what follows is only a partial list of those large enough to contain a man. First, there are the various subterranean conduits: (1) subways; (2) train tunnels; (3) storm drains; (4) aquaducts; (5) sewers; (6) catacombs; (7) old wells; and (8) abandoned mineshafts.

Map 20.2: Up Phu Cam's Runoff Ditch Feeders to the Ridge

(Source: *U.S. Marines in Vietnam: Fighting the North Vietnamese in 1967*, Hist. & Museums Div., HQMC, p. 212)

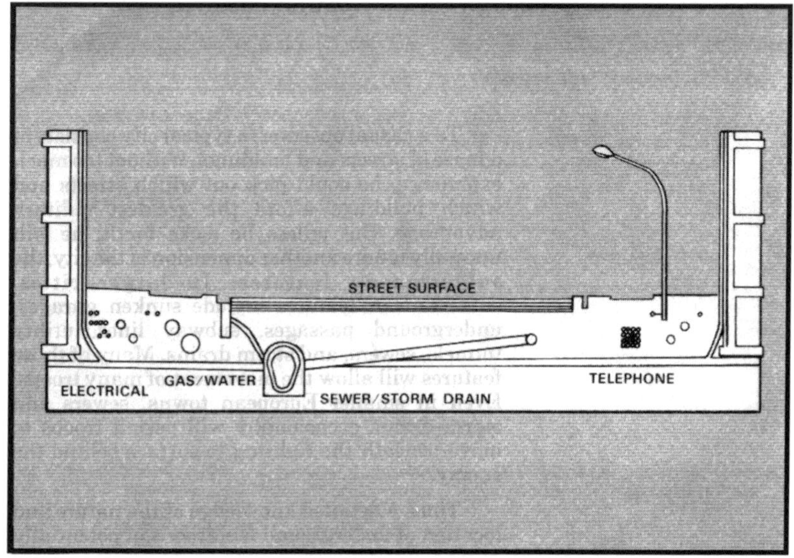

Figure 20.1: Storm Drains and Sewers
(Source: FM 90-10-1 [1982], p. J-2)

Figure 20.2: Crawl-Spaces beneath Houses
(Source: FM 90-10-1 [1982], p. B-37)

Figure 20.3: Breezeways between Buildings
(Source: FM 90-10-1 [1982], p. J-4)

(See Figure 20.1.) Then, there are the obscure passages at surface level: (1) covered drainage ditches; (2) crawl-spaces beneath houses; (3) breezeways between buildings; (4) roadside gutters; and (5) the narrow spaces behind bushes or trash. (See Figures 20.2 and 20.3.) Next, there are the naturally occurring avenues within buildings: (1) basements; (2) ventilation ducts; (3) eaves; (4) "dumbwaiter" or "dirty-laundry" shafts; (5) attics; and (6) rooftops. (See Figures 20.4 through 20.7.) Finally, there are various elevated paths: (1) tree branches; (2) guy wires; (3) telephone lines; (4) clothes lines; and (5) street-spanning signs.

By combining these conduits, one can come up with a fairly foolproof way to escape unhappy surroundings after dark. John Mosby once escaped almost certain capture by Union forces at his wife's house by simply exiting an upper floor window to take refuge on a nearby tree limb.

What Advice Would the UW Experts Have?

Figure 20.8 deals first with how an individual might break contact with one opposition group and then elude any others. Heavily

Figure 20.4: Basements
(Source: FM 90-10-1 [1982], p. E-11)

Figure 20.5: Ventilation Ducts
(Source: FM 90-10-1 [1982], p. B-12)

Figure 20.6: Eaves
(Source: FM 90-10-1 [1982], p. B-39)

implied is the advantage gained by exiting an encirclement one or two people at time instead of all at once (exfiltration versus frontal assault).

The difficulties that one man might have under such dire circumstances must first be discussed. If his capture seemed imminent, he might be willing to throw temporarily blinding powder into someone's face. After kicking a can while hiding, he might like to know how to sound like a cat. Upon being trapped in a building, he might want to use one of the following *ninja*-like tricks: (1) hide behind a door; (2) leave a door or window open without exiting the room; and (3) avoid casting any shadow or reflection. To then secretly leave that building, he could move hand over hand up the back of a metal staircase, ascend the overhang of a roof, or drop rice to warn

Figure 20.7: Roofs and Attics
(Source: FM 90-10-1 [1982], p. F-9)

of pursuit. After eluding the initial threat, he could hide in a place too small to normally hold a human being or impersonate an enemy soldier.

Only a few of these vintage techniques might apply to a whole group. That's why highly dispersed exfiltration is such an attractive option. However, several people could dress up like enemy soldiers, make their way along hidden passageways, or use a perilous overhang to acquire connecting roofs. The chart also makes mention of a diversionary fire or other explosion. Any group UW technique must take its inspiration from these few things.

Urban escape

Leaving without a trace #

Natural-element escape strategies (gotonpo)

"Fire escape arts" (katonjutsu)

Diversionary fire and other fire/explosive methods (kajutsu)

"Metal escape arts" (kintonjutsu)

Climbing the underside of a metal stair

"Wood escape arts" (mokutonjutsu)

"Earth escape arts" (dotonjutsu)

"Water escape arts" (suitonjutsu)

Breaking contact

Diversions

Blinding powders (metsubushi)

Releasing a drugged or pet animal when first noticed

Leaving behind rice to warn of pursuit

Imitating the sound of a cat or other small mammal

Movements

Ducking through or hiding behind a door

Ascending the overhang of a roof

Escaping a trained tracker (tonpo) #

Making a false exit (e.g., opening an outside door without leaving)

Urban evasion

Impersonating the enemy $

Hiding (inton-jutsu) #

Camouflage skills

Using various disguises (hensojutsu)

Impersonation (gisojutsu)

Other presence-obscuring skills (tonkei no jutsu)

Continually monitoring one's own shadow

Hiding in a place too small to normally hold a human being

Source Code:

Ninja methods for guerrilla use against Japan's Samuri (1460-1650) [22]
& N. Vietnamese methods for Viet Cong use against GIs (1965-1973) [23]
$ Chinese ally's Light Infantry Trng. Guid. Bur. methods (1992-2007) [24]

Figure 20.8: UW Instruction for Urban Escape/Evasion

Every Neighborhood Offers a Varied Escape Route

Once members of the U.S. squad had come to know every square inch of their assigned area, they could easily choose the best routes of unobserved egress. Any portions not in defilade (like most road crossings) could be more easily negotiated at night using some of the techniques in Chapter 15 (e.g., shadow crawling).

Figure 20.9 shows potential escape routes in all four cardinal directions from the squad's headquarters (marked by crosshatching) in an imaginary neighborhood. The route to the north starts at a home's foundation, moves across adjacent rooftops, follows a series of breezeways, dives through a covered drainage ditch, and finishes up in a deep gutter. It would secretly take its user(s) almost a quarter of a mile from their initial starting point. The one heading east follows a breezeway and then a series of deep gutters. The one to the south uses the narrow opening behind bushes/trash, moves through the subfloor crawl-spaces of several houses, and finishes up in a covered drainage ditch. Its westerly equivalent takes a covered drainage ditch across the road and then skips from rooftop to rooftop across an entire block.

Getting Out of the Headquarters Unobserved

Each building's architecture will dictate how many ways there are to depart it unseen. Figure 20.10 depicts the building in which the lone U.S. squad and their local counterparts have tried to provide neighborhood policing and security. It is a two-story structure with a steeply sloping roof. In other words, it has both eaves and attic. Formerly, the residence of a wealthy family, it also has a laundry chute. That chute is roughly two-feet square. It originates in an upstairs corner bedroom and terminates in a partially finished basement.

The GIs initially move to a saferoom on the second floor of their building. From there, they have two ways to escape the structure. The primary is through a closet into the eave space, up a framing hole into the attic, through a ventilation duct onto the roof, down tree limbs to the ground, and then through bushes to the next house. The alternate involves lowering themselves down a laundry chute (on a looped rope that can subsequently be retrieved) and exiting the basement through a window. (See Figure 20.11 for a diversion.)

Figure 20.9: Naturally Existing Escape Routes at U.S. Outpost

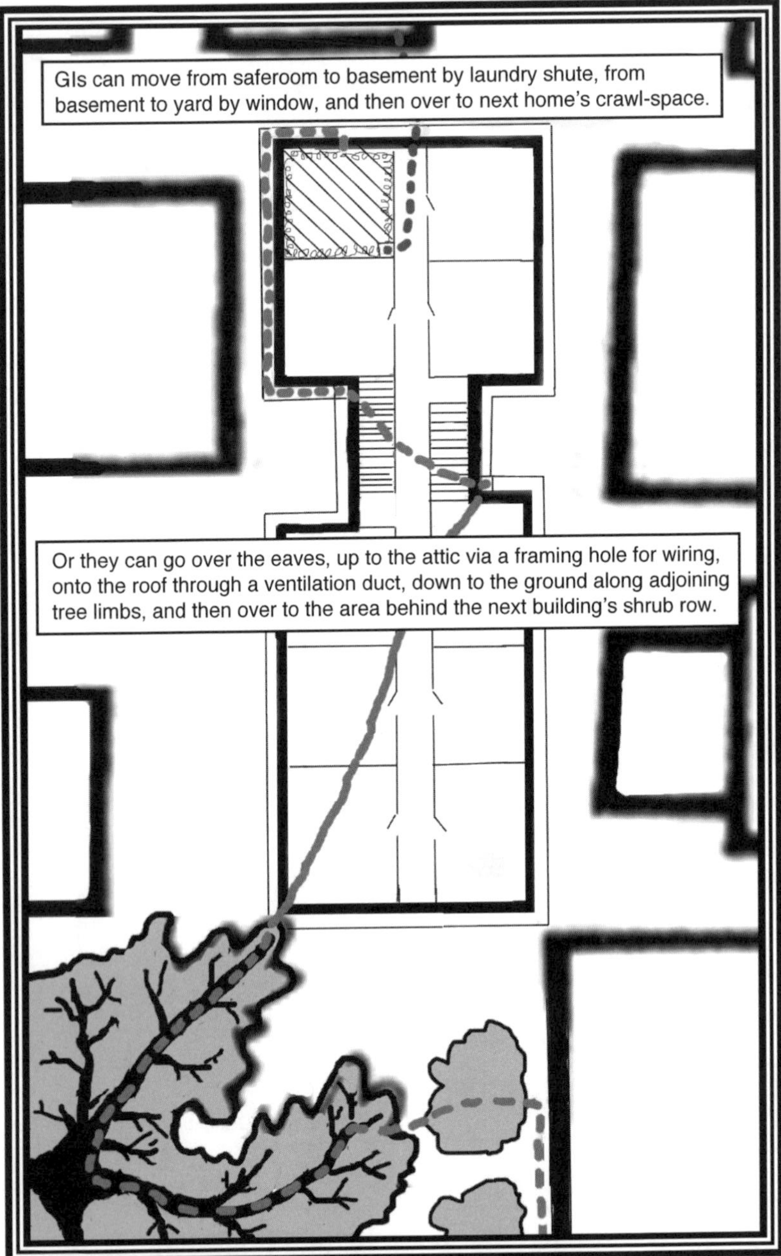

Figure 20.10: Secretly Leaving the Outpost Building

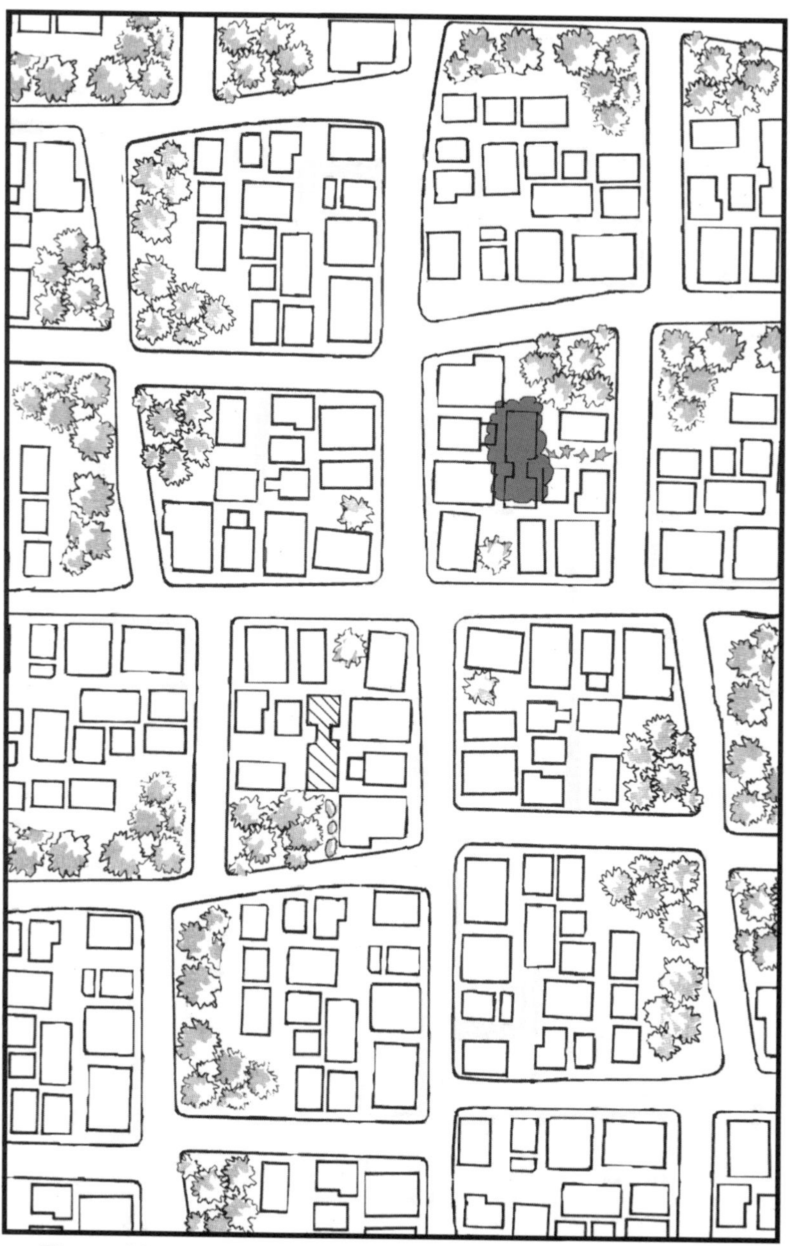

Figure 20.11: Remotely Set Fire-and-Firecracker Diversion

The Diversionary Fire

In Iraq or Afghanistan, normally Islamist factions from other places are involved in any full-fledged attack on a neighborhood police station. This creates the possibility of a diversion to facilitate escape. Should gun shots and billowing smoke be coming from a similar structure on an adjacent block, many of the attackers might start to doubt their guide's proficiency. Their indecisiveness would give the Americans a better chance to escape. (Refer back to Figure 20.11.) Of course, the odds for escape can also be increased by modifying the terrain.

21 Enhancing Urban Terrain

- What parts of the urban landscape are easily modified?
- How might those modifications allow more daring tactics?

SECRETLY EXPANDING A CITY'S TUNNEL NETWORK

(Source: FM 90-10-1 [1982], p. E-4)

All UW Options Possible When Urban Terrain Is Altered

Cities and towns are so diverse and multi-dimensional in composition that—with a little preparation—they provide a perfect place to apply every UW technique so far presented. If America's junior enlisted personnel were given enough time and leeway to "fix up" a neighborhood, they could accomplish far more reconnaissance and offensive maneuver than is normally possible. Just by extending and connecting existing sewers, those wanting to sneak up on the foe could secretly enter his barrier system. While cities have overhead foliage in which to hide, their biggest potential for elevated movement is along the rooftops of adjacent buildings. To span their intermittent openings, all that is required is some prestaged or portable gear. Built-up terrain also provides move overhead ways to bypass enemy obstacles. Existing telephone and guy wires can often be supplanted by silenced grappling hook and nylon rope. Once that rope is pulled taught, the average U.S. soldier or Marine would need only a carabiner clip and setting moon to make an uneventful passage. Those who find such a discussion farfetched should take a look at the 15 August 2007 edition of *China Daily*. It shows a modern PLA crossbow that could easily shoot a small grappling hook and attached nylon line 100 yards or more.[1]

What a UW-oriented army can accomplish on defense in the city though subterranean preparation has been thoroughly described in *Phantom Soldier* and *The Tiger's Way*. The extent to which the Japanese used below-ground conduits during the defense of Manila was never recorded. The sophisticated way in which they defended a Luzon hilltop in Figure 19.3 suggests underground rooms in Manila in which to elude the tightening Allied cordon. When the Allies finally assaulted what they believed to be the Japanese defenders' last-stand position (the Intramuros' Fort Santiago), they found only 2,000 refugees.[2] As will soon be abundantly clear, the North Vietnamese also incorporated excavation into their defense of Hue City. (See Map 21.1.)

An urban E&E capability could help the U.S. military to generate more urban offense and defense. After all, nothing larger than a squad can generate much surprise in most locales. Thus, just being able to operate in smaller increments would be of great help to both types of missions. When one of those increments gets surrounded by many times its number, its best chance of survival is to hide or pull back. That process can be greatly facilitated by excavating or otherwise improving a predetermined path. That type of construction is much more easily accomplished in the city than in the country. It requires less sophisticated camouflage and must only supplant existing passageways and alcoves. In urban terrain, there are also any number of spaces in which a small unit might take up temporary residence after a few cosmetic adjustments. Even relatively modern U.S. cities have the equivalent of catacombs (e.g., the old town beneath current street level in Seattle).[3]

The rest of this chapter will show how a tiny U.S. infantry squad might modify the area around its urban outpost to more easily evade

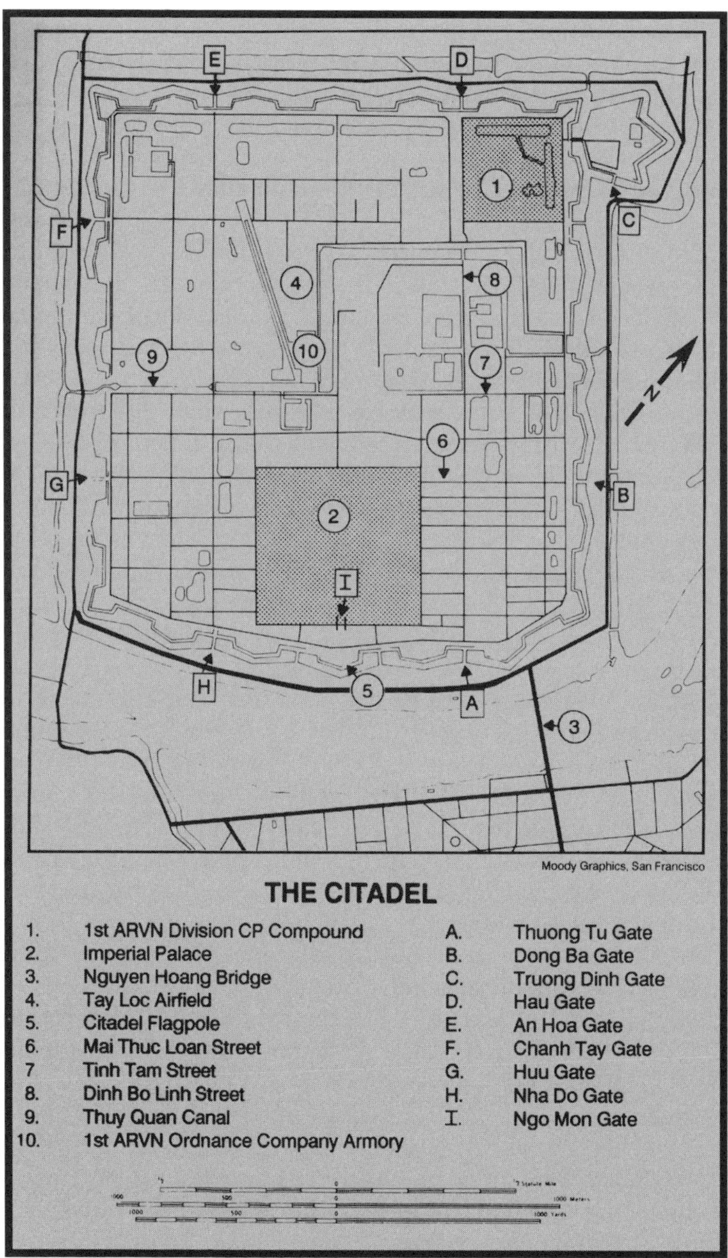

Map 21.1: The Citadel's Wall and Many Gates

(Source: Courtesy of Pacifica Military History, from *Fire in the Streets: The Battle for Hue, Tet 1968*, © 1991 by Eric Hammel)

the Chinese or Islamist dragon. With such squads, U.S. commanders should be able to mount a more daring initiative in Iraq. Without them, the handwriting is already on the wall.

Whatever Happened to the NVA's Hue City Casualties?

The NVA's watery, "southern" exit from Hue City's ancient Citadel was adequately covered in the last chapter. But how did that enemy "division minus" manage to evacuate its hundreds of serious casualties? They couldn't have swum the Perfume River. Another egress route must have come into play.

After the battle, there was an eastern corridor discovered that was better suited for casualty removal. With much of it covered and below ground, it was probably used throughout the 24-day battle for both reinforcement/resupply and evacuation. There are two possibilities for its first leg from the Imperial Palace: (1) an eastward-running passageway beneath the streets that was part of the Citadel's original design; or (2) a connecting series of tunnels that modern occupiers had dug through that portion of the Citadel's walls.

The NVA fought so hard for a street called Mai Thuc Loan that it became known to history as "Phase Line Green." It ran from the Imperial Palace to the Dong Ba Gate.[4] Beneath it may have been an ancient escape route from the Imperial Palace to the Perfume River. Or to its side may have been a covered drainage ditch that had been quickly deepened by its new defenders. After the Marines crossed over Mai Thuc Loan to attack other streets to the southeast, they did not closely watch it.[5]

The Citadel's southern walls were laced with Japanese tunnels from WWII that had subsequently been extended by the NVA.[6] Very probably, a secret passageway ran the length of the wall between Nha Do and Thuong Tu Gates, and another between Thuong Tu and Dong Ba Gates. That would explain why the Dong Ba Tower had been so easy for the NVA to reoccupy after each air strike.[7] This tower was just above the gate and also full of tunnels.[8] The other gates probably had hidden passageways above them as well. Then, any enemy evacuation column could have moved the full distance without ever having to emerge. On the 23rd of February, 1st Battalion, 5th Marines found fresh tunneling in the southeast Citadel wall.[9] (Refer back to Map 21.1.)

Whether a secret tunnel ran the full length of the southeast wall doesn't really matter, because its base remained in enemy hands throughout the night of 22 February.[10] Its top was not captured until after dawn on the 24th.[11] If the night of the 23rd was dark, a large enemy force could have moved unseen around the eastern corner of the Citadel by simply following the river bank. As previously documented, the VC still controlled the eastern approaches to the fort throughout this period.

Either way, from 21 to 26 February, the region east of the Perfume River remained free of Allied interference. The two South Vietnamese battalions initially operating in that area had been evicted by a large enemy force during the first few days of February.[12] That enemy force probably had, as its mission, to build and protect the evacuation route. The two South Vietnamese Ranger battalions later assigned to clearing that zone did not arrive in Hue City until 22 February,[13] and had not captured the built-up area between the northeast wall and the river until 25 February.[14] In other words, any Citadel defenders who could reach the road outside the Dong Ba Gate before the 25th were probably home free. The local VC establishment could have helped them to reach the covered trench. With VC porters and guides, even large evacuation columns would have had a relatively easy time of it. Any need for boats could have been easily eliminated with two Asian tricks: (1) a portable bridge with human stanchions over marsh or shallow water; (2) a bamboo bridge just beneath the surface of deeper water (i.e., the main part of the Perfume River).

About 4 March, 2nd Battalion, 5th Marines made the telling discovery just east of Hue City. While history recorded what they found as a reinforcement route, it would also have made a good egress route.

> Leaving the southern sector to the 1st Brigade, 101st Airborne on the 29th, the two Marine battalions [2/5 and 1/5] entered their new area of operations to cut off any NVA forces trying to make their way from Hue to the coast. Although encountering few enemy forces, the two battalions uncovered "fresh trench work along the route of advance, 3,000 meters long with 600 fighting holes." Captain Michael Downs, the Company F Commander, remembered a trench complex that "traveled in excess of five miles" with overhead cover every 15 meters. As Downs remarked, "that

> had to be a way to get significant reinforcements into the city." The search for significant North Vietnamese forces proved fruitless.[15]
>
> — *U.S. Marines in Vietnam: The Defining Year, 1968*
> History and Museums Division, HQMC

The Citadel defenders' rear guard may have gone east or south, or simply hidden in secret and well-provisioned underground rooms. After a week or two of laying low, hundreds of fighters could have easily blended in with the hordes of returning refugees. Besides 140,000 regular inhabitants, Hue had been host to tens of thousands of Tet pilgrims.

Matching This Feat on a Smaller Scale

To make more urban E&E possible through construction, one must remember two things: (1) the effectiveness of every hiding place and exit route will depend on how well its entrance is obscured; and (2) the enemy isn't stupid. In the Warsaw Ghetto, there is no proof that the Germans summoned mantrackers, but they did call for dogs. And they did a lot of shooting into suspicious walls, ceilings, and floors. Another of their tricks was to bust out all the windows of a building from the inside. If any window then appeared unbroken from the outside, it marked a secret chamber.[16] The valiant Ghetto defenders responded in kind—using every bit of their ingenuity to disguise their work.

Soon an underground city began to emerge beneath the Ghetto. Every person capable of building it did so. Not excavated from virgin soil, its larger spaces were created by walling-off "feeder" portions of the existing sewer system. Some were capable of housing dozens of people. With water, drainage, and wiring readily available, they had bunk rooms, kitchens, and lavatories. While their lights required a generator, the phones would work for short periods of time on batteries alone. Of course, there were a fair number of above-ground improvements as well—some 50,000 secret entrances to false rooms in subfloors, closets, eaves, and attics. The floor entrances varied from loose tiles and rug-covered trapdoors to toilets on hinges and removable hearths. The wall entrances consisted of everything from holes behind picture frames to false backs in cabinets and bookcases.[17] Of all the portals to a secret space, the moving toilet was probably the best thought out. The only tunnel not found by the Germans at Stalag Luft III after the legendary breakout of WWII's "Great Escape" was the one with a partially submerged entrance. The Allied fliers had brilliantly created a bathroom sump that did not properly drain (or leak beyond a certain point). Though its movable side began just above that point (the surface of the standing water), the Germans never suspected an optical illusion.

> "Tom" went from the dark corner of a hut corridor; "Harry" began under a stove. A tiled base was lifted to one side, revealing the top of a tunnel shaft. "Dick" started in a washroom beneath the drain cover. Hiding the tunnel entrance in a sump where dirty water collected was a master stroke. The Germans never did find "Dick."[18]
>
> — PBS's "Nova," 5 June 2007

While cellars could hold more supplies and their entrances be more easily concealed, attics provided better communication and escape routes. From those attics, Jewish fighters could sneak out onto the often-connected rooftops. Their tormentors were not anxious to follow, and many who did so took an unceremonious tumble to the pavement below.[19]

Of course, the tenements did not provide the only refuge. In stores and bakeries, Ghetto dwellers hid under counters, in unfired ovens, and beneath tubs. Some even tried to remove the stuffing from couches. False backs to packing crates provided discreet ways to enter secret rooms, and outside garbage piles made a perfect place to fabricate tiny niches.[20]

One way the gain access to a rooftop in the Warsaw Ghetto was to climb a rope ladder to a trapdoor in the attic ceiling. When wanting to move from one roof to another one story below it, the fighters positioned a mattress to soften their impact. Then, they stood on the edge of the first roof, jumped, landed on their feet, and fell forward onto the mattress.[21] Though never formally trained in UW, they had nevertheless become masters of a full sixth of its content. From their exploits, one might logically conclude that the best UW methods are born from experimentation at the small-unit level. Before checking to see what the UW experts might say about enhancing urban terrain (Figure 21.1), one could usefully amass a list of sheltered spaces and conduits.

A Summary of What Exists

Among the hiding places in the city are the following: (1) the same ones as in the country at parks, vacant lots, and yards; (2) those behind all walls, floors, and ceilings; (3) those in utility or ventilation shafts; and (4) those within or behind furniture and stored property.

Urban terrain provides several obscure passageways that, when combined, permit travel over considerable distances. The most common are as follows: (1) all those of a rural setting in parks, vacant lots, and yards; (2) public-service tunnels; (3) narrow spaces between buildings; (4) perfectly aligned spaces within touching structures; (5) aerial wires, braces, or signs; and (6) adjacent rooftops.

Obscuring Entrances and Connecting Conduits

The problem boils down to making secret entrances to all hides and conduits, and then linking the conduits of different types. Only in a row house situation would eave and attic spaces be easy to connect. So, the gap between buildings is most easily bridged at rooftop level with a long pipe or taut rope.

While movement between rooftops might be the most challenging, that below ground entails the most work. It takes a lot of digging to expand existing tunnels. (See Figure 21.2). Only at surface level could the job be done in a hurry. Wherever one's movement might be observed, refuse or rubble could be placed. Plus, there is always the opportunity for covered trenching under the guise of a public-works project. Armies that regularly practice such things incrementally do them more quickly than would normally be possible. Part of the tunneling on Iwo Jima was accomplished after the island was invaded.[22] At Hue City, the NVA needed less than 24 hours to prepare Phase Line Green well enough to withstand a four-day U.S. onslaught. It had supposedly been occupied by South Vietnamese forces just prior to the Marines' arrival.[23]

What the UW Experts Say

Enough of a framework now exists to try to imagine from Figure 21.1 what the UW experts might have known about enhancing

Urban attack

Entering enemy's fortress (chiku jo gunryaku heiho) #

Ramparts crossing

Through sewers, air shafts, other openings deemed inaccessible

Urban escape

Leaving without a trace #

Natural-element escape strategies (gotonpo)

Urban evasion

Hiding (inton-jutsu) #

Camouflage skills

Other presence-obscuring skills (tonkei no jutsu)

Source Code:

Ninja methods for guerrilla use against Japan's Samuri (1460-1650) [24]
& N. Vietnamese methods for Viet Cong use against GIs (1965-1973) [25]
$ Chinese ally's Light Infantry Trng. Guid. Bur. methods (1992-2007) [26]

Figure 21.1: UW Instruction on How to Enhance Urban Terrain

Figure 21.2: Storm Drain Feeder Branches Can Be Widened

(Source: MCRP 3-02H [1999], p. IX-1)

urban terrain. Only two themes appear, and both pertain primarily to routes: (1) moving through sewers, air shafts, or other openings deemed inaccessible; and (2) camouflage. Thus, one might try to cover an elevated passageway with ventilation latticework or create an entire room behind a tiny heating grate. Either way, the emphasis would be on optical illusion. The method might go something like this. First, lower the searcher's level of intensity through the clear view of an obvious opening. Then, create the impression that there is little chance of a passageway or hide behind the opening (make it too high, small, or legitimate). And finally, give the searcher some reason to ignore that possibility altogether (create an elsewhere-leading trail of false clues or active diversion). In Figure 21.3, the enemy sees an obvious entrance to an in-room bomb shelter and thus has less reason to suspect an alternative purpose for the opening. America's junior enlisted ranks are undeniably its most crafty. At the bottom of the heap, they have to be. With little urging, they would have no trouble applying the "false face and art of delay" that distinguishes East-Asian thought from American,[27] and thus forms the most likely model for UW deception.

Any unused space in a building's design can provide a secret living area. Most wiring and piping are in the walls, so that area can be easily modified to provide all the comforts of home without any telltale indicators. There is little mention of fake ceilings in the Warsaw Ghetto chronicles, only trapdoors leading to rooftops. But, in modern buildings, going up is often the only option. Their structural skeletons are too streamlined and walls too thin to provide traditionally vacant space (eaves, attic, etc.). Almost all unused space now exists above drop-down ceilings. Comprised of acoustic tiles and flimsy aluminum straps and hangers, their purpose is to hide ductwork and wiring. Just as the aluminum framework is suspended from the concrete floor above, so could a hiding platform. If its occupants were to ascend by rope ladder through a styrofoam tile's flimsy seat, the enemy would never suspect a thing. He would be more interested in the floors and walls. This ruse could be further enhanced by removing most of the room's furnishings, particularly those which might be used to reach its ceiling.

Finally, when thinking about how to permit more sophisticated UW techniques through some form of construction, one must acknowledge the ultimate deception. After installing a fake wall at the end of room of indeterminable depth, there would be no reason for those being hunted to leave at all. (See Figure 21.4.) Such an arrangement formed the plot of a recent movie. After gaining unauthorized access to a bank one night, thieves built a fake wall at one end of a large, shelf-lined document room. With nothing of any value missing the next morning, the bank's manager wrote off the whole incident as vandalism. A week later, all of his stocks and bonds disappeared in the middle of the day. The masking with shelves of the room's true depth must have made it hard for the bank workers to detect a change.

Now to Simulate the Winning of the Iraq War

It may now prove useful to show the worst that could happen if America were to more fully embrace the urban CAP platoon concept as part its last-ditch "Surge Policy" in Iraq. A single (though reinforced) U.S. squad has been sent to augment one squad each of Iraqi police and soldiers at the middle of a highly volatile part of greater Baghdad. Should those 16 young Americans get encircled by many times their number, they can expect no help from supporting arms or a rapid reaction force. They must therefore take responsibility for their own extraction.

With 15 men plus himself, the American squad leader first assigns eight two-man exfiltration lanes that radiate outward from his headquarters. He does so in such a way that the streets become lane boundaries. (See Figure 21.5.) Then he establishes a patrol regimen with his Iraqi counterparts in which each two-man team spends most of its time in a sector containing its exfiltration route. Unbeknownst to any Iraqi patrol members, the GIs will be initially looking for potential hides, covered routes, and friendly families. Once they have come to know every inch of those few blocks (and mapped every detail), they will ask their squad leader for help in modifying various aspects. Local laborers may be appropriate for some, but others will take the entire squad after dark (out of sight and mind of the general population). The whole idea is to so carefully prepare the neighborhood that this lone U.S. squad can easily escape it.

Determining the Two-Man Sector's Potential

The two-man teams initially look for things like rooftop niches

Figure 21.3: Removable Back to Obvious Shelter
(Source: FM 7-8 [1984], p. P-6.)

that are only accessible through gymnastic effort from the ground. They are also interested in heavily foliated trees that are just barely climbable. Within yards, alleyways, and vacant lots, they search for places where a bum might live beyond the sight of everyone else. They record the exact locations of all truck-portable trash containers. They also pay close attention to which windows and doors of uninhabited rooms are either unlocked or easy to force. (See Figure 21.6.)

Now they are in a position to recommend to their squad leader which areas within their respective sectors might make the best egress route for the squad as a whole. Some construction and shifting of refuse heaps may be necessary. (See Figure 21.7.)

This American squad has been thoroughly briefed on how important "hearts and minds" are to the winning of a guerrilla war. They know the CAP platoon approach involves more danger, but

Figure 21.4: The Beginnings of a Fake Wall
(Source: FM 7-8 [1984], p. P-7)

their level of light-infantry skill has been proportionately augmented through additional training. They are fully prepared to use minimal force to defend themselves and the community. Because they have had to live off the local economy, they are familiar with everyone in the neighborhood. As such, they have friends. Some of their friends have offered to hide the whole squad in case of trouble. Thus, they can add "safe houses" to their growing list of terrain associated assets. Strings of safe houses can prove very helpful during any escape attempt. (See Figure 21.8.)

To escape capture or worse, the U.S. squad may not have to go very far. With the proper modifications, its own headquarters building could provide a useful alternative. Two stories tall and with a flat roof, it has no distinctive features except for a narrow ledge at the top of each floor. By deflecting sunlight and rain from the windows below, that ledge helps to keep the building cool in summer

Figure 21.5: Exfiltraton Lanes from CAP Platoon Outpost

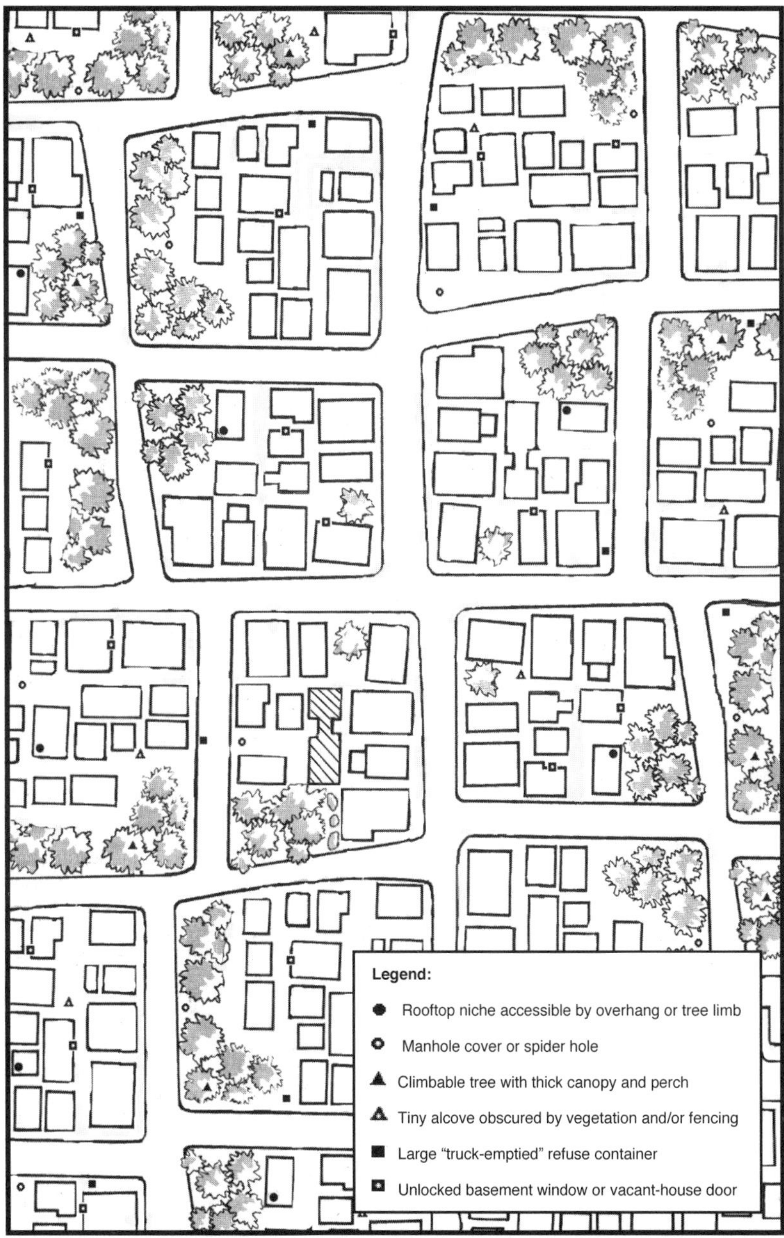

Figure 21.6: U.S. Guerrilla-Option Urban Hides

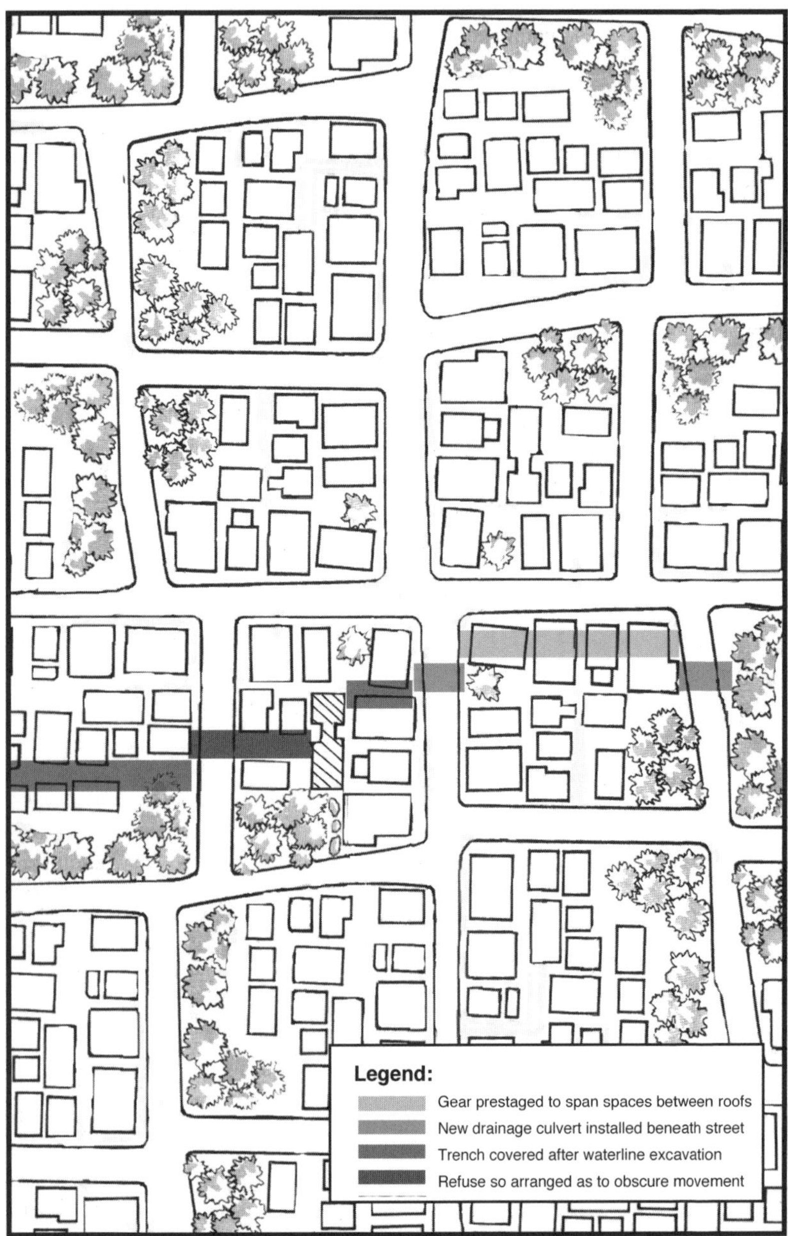

Figure 21.7: U.S. Guerrilla-Option Urban Conduits

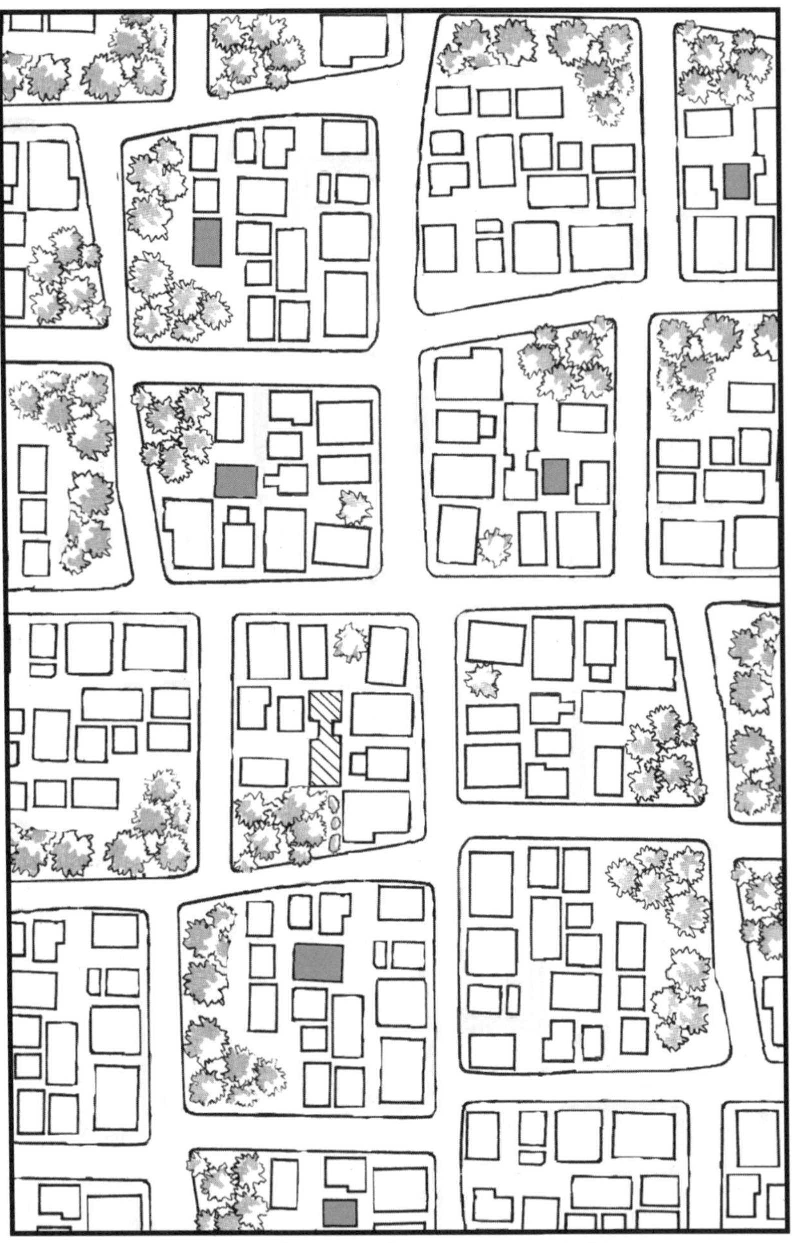

Figure 21.8: Strings of American Safe Houses

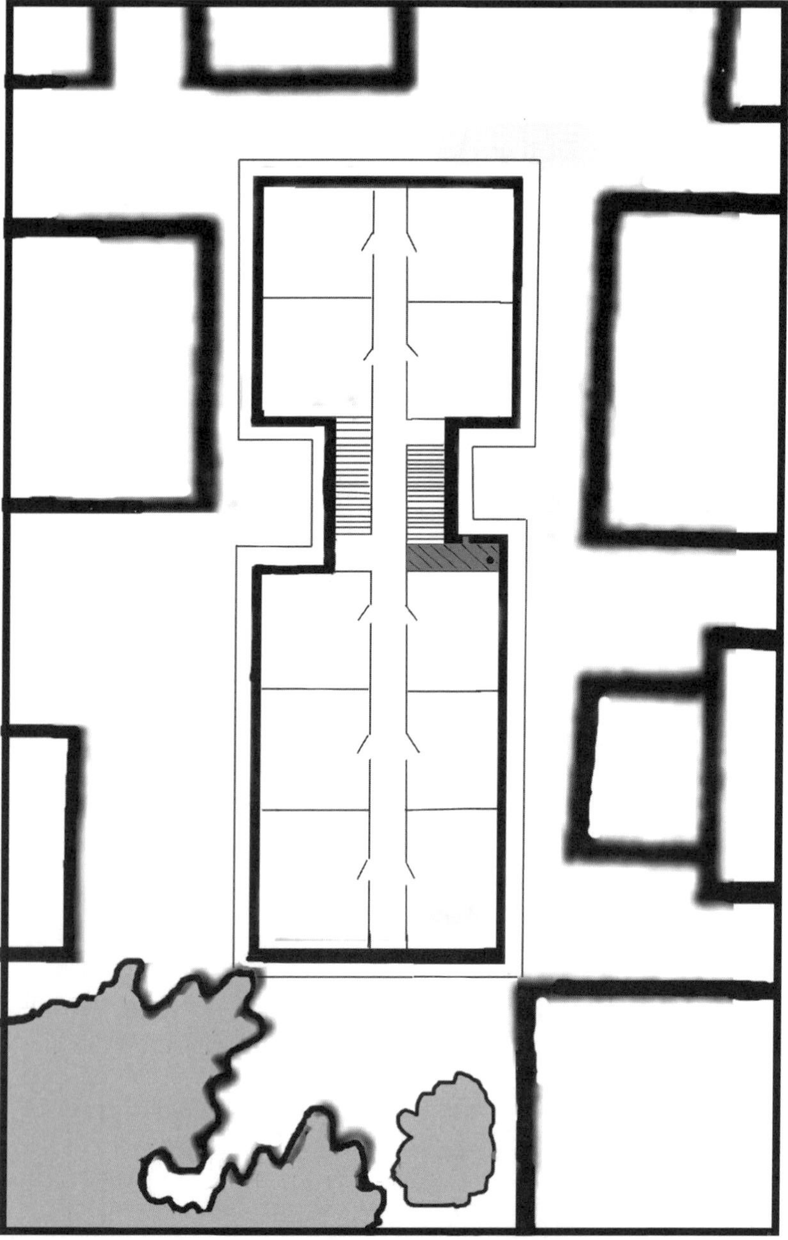

Figure 21.9: With Secret Safe Room, GIs Need Not Depart

and dry in winter. While the structure has a frame and floors of reinforced concrete, its exterior walls are brick. Its interior rooms are defined by thin wood-and-wallboard dividers. But the way the doors to those rooms and stairwell have been positioned has created an opportunity. One second story room is a perfect candidate for a little obscure shortening. (See Figure 21.9.) A fake wall at one end would produce an eight-foot-deep and twenty-four-foot-wide chamber in which 16 men could easily hide for a week. Its primary access would be through a ventilation grate in the drop-down yet adequately tall ceiling of a first-floor bathroom. Its alternate exit would be through a hole in the exterior wall over which the final layer of bricks has been left intact. Just beyond that hole is the narrow ledge that runs the circumference of the building.

A difficult structural scenario has been intentionally chosen to simulate Baghdad architecture and show how almost any limitation can be overcome. A chamber just above a bathroom would be easy to plumb. A second ventilation grille in the stairwell would be too high for inspection and provide enough air flow to keep the chamber's occupants from overheating.

After overrunning a Coalition headquarters, an Islamist element would have no reason to leave more than a few dozen caretakers in its vicinity. After hiding for a week, the U.S. squad could either recapture its building and resume normal activity or secretly move to another hide or safehouse to conduct guerrilla-like operations at night.

Business As Usual

To be most effective in an urban setting, the CAP platoon should provide local security through law enforcement. Even in a volatile neighborhood, that means "walking a beat" instead of patrolling, meeting residents instead of eyeing them suspiciously, and investigating incidents instead of reacting to them. Some of the members of this particular American squad have been formally trained in investigative procedure and mantracking. They can quickly cordon off the scene of a IED explosion, identify the footprints of its perpetrator, and follow them back to the place of detonation. There they can lift latent fingerprints or take a DNA sample. Finally, they know how to extract DNA samples for comparison from suspects without their knowledge. Most importantly, they have demonstrated enough commitment to the safety of this particular neighborhood to earn its residents' trust. Once the friendly "tips" start flowing in, the terrorists will be on their way out. Without enough support from the people (whether coerced or otherwise), guerrillas cannot operate. Rounding up and jailing untold numbers of the "usual suspects" hasn't worked so far for the Coalition. Its commanders would have better luck arresting only those for whom there was sufficient evidence for a trial.

Among the U.S. squad's other options are a police sting in a pseudo-guerrilla format that does not constitute entrapment. Just as John Dillinger had to be arrested outside the Biograph Theater in Chicago, so too must Iraqi terrorists be lured away from their dens. Their early warning apparatus is too sophisticated to permit any other approach. But, in addition to being police-qualified, this U.S. squad is also UW qualified. It has both a defensive and offensive UW strategy.

The Defensive Work-Up

To try to prevent their headquarters from being overrun, the U.S. squad develops a UW-oriented defense plan. Instead of bunkering, barbed wire, and final protective fires, that plan is predicated on disrupting the momentum of any attack force.

First required will be a terrain assessment from the enemy's perspective. Where would his advance party probably appear? How would his main attack force approach the Coalition building? Just prior to an attack in Ramadi in 2005, U.S. Marine lookouts detected the following: (1) people standing where they normally wouldn't; (2) cars suddenly doing U-turns; (3) people jumping out of vehicles with binoculars; and (4) people not showing up for work. Then, someone with a black flag appeared on a distant building, and a busload of about 50 middle-aged males drove by the target.[28] Before another attack in Iraq, members of the assault force crossed each street two men at a time after official looking checkpoints were set up to isolate the neighborhood. The U.S. CAP platoon contingent must be ready for either.

From the E&E assessment, the GIs already know which rooftops or heavily obscured ground areas might provide the best avenues of approach for the enemy. Where best to watch those avenues won't be hard for them to determine. If there is not enough manpower to physically outpost those places, then they will be visited by patrol every night. They might include ground-level views of long open areas against light-colored backdrops, or simply track traps. Wherever a human presence is not possible, a remote monitoring device will be used.

Should the outpost be right next to the route, those in it could disrupt the enemy's momentum without ever divulging their presence. All it takes is a command-detonated claymore that leads the quarry to believe he has hit a tripwire. Or the two men manning the outpost could move to another prearranged ambush position. With their in-depth knowledge of the neighborhood, they would have no trouble sneaking away after triggering their claymores. That knowledge and their E&E preparations would also give them the option of delaying the enemy for several hours with their small arms. In essence, they would then be functioning as a two-man defensive strongpoint that moves rearward under extreme pressure.

The Offensive Scheme

No American Marine or soldier will be ever be truly contented until he gets routinely to attack his opposition. The defensive way in which U.S. forces have been operating over the last half century grates against his very being. Thus, when the imaginary American squad finds evidence of an enemy headquarters, car-bomb factory, or torture chamber in its Baghdad theater of operations, it starts to plan its own assault.

The GIs must first locate a spot from which to more closely observe the suspected site of enemy activity. This most logically is the job of the two men in whose E&E sector the site belongs. They should be able to approach it unobserved and, if necessary, fashion an escape hide nearby. For an assault by the squad as a whole, that new observation post can function as an attack position. To more easily approach it, the squad could do any number of things to disguise its greater sound-and-movement signature. Among them might be the following: (1) the prestaging of weapons; (2) coming at the target from upwind to minimize the barking of dogs; or (3) adding the side entrances and ground floors of safehouses to their route.

Within E&E's smaller scale of combat lies an immense, and largely untapped arena of tactical maneuver. America's adversaries have used it for years. Not until its own infantry leaders learn to trust UW-and-police-trained NCOs will their country's fortunes of war improve. First must come the training. (See Figure 21.10.) As no one in America knows much about the squad applications of UW, that part of the training must necessarily be experimental in format.

Figure 21.10: Today's GIs Need Training in UW
(Source: FM 22-100 [1983], p. 230)

Afterword

What U.S. Forces Lack While Fighting Eastern Foes

The U.S. military may be good at many things, but it hasn't had any true "light infantrymen" since the days of Carlson's Raiders and Merrill's Marauders. Only cash-strapped or East-Asian nations still recognize the potential of dismounted "ground pounders." On many types of missions, two properly trained infiltrators can do what an armored brigade cannot. And they can do it with a lot less casualties and collateral damage.

Unfortunately, the U.S. "top-down" approach to training and operations is too highly structured to produce enough small-unit expertise. The Eastern "bottom up" approach works much better in that regard. The army of China's closest ally uses *ninja*-qualified special operators as training cadre. A few of its 100,000 "Light Infantry Training Guidance Bureau" commandos are attached to each line company. This gives that company's commander instant access to expert point men, short-range infiltrators, assault specialists, and E&E practitioners. The attached commandos subsequently impart enough UW skill to the rest of the company to create self-sufficient squads, fire teams, and riflemen. Should the situation dictate, each element will then be able to survive 10 times its number of Western counterparts.

As East-Asian Communist soldiers can easily shift between mobile (maneuver) and guerrilla warfare, GIs have too often faced what they perceive to be the latter.

Why U.S. Leaders Have Been Unable to Overcome the Shortfall

Within the Pentagon, the decision has apparently been made to opt for technological advance over tactical innovation. While Eastern "light infantrymen" seldom fire their small arms in the assault to promote surprise, U.S. troops shoot theirs as much as possible to "keep enemy heads down." Though the U.S. Marine Corps embraced the precepts of "maneuver warfare" in 1986, it has yet to apply them to small units. Several U.S. Army divisions also call themselves light infantry, but their vehicular and bombardment methodology belies that claim. While most Asian infantrymen receive training in both conventional and unconventional warfare, U.S. troops get only the former. This puts them at a decided disadvantage in any one-on-one encounter.

How an Eastern Foe Operates

What is normally called "asymmetric warfare" isn't without pattern. It is decentralized warfare in which small units are allowed to follow tactical guidelines instead of forced to obey doctrinal edicts. Within those guidelines are well-tested football-play-like "techniques" that are nearly the opposite of what a Western counterpart might do under similar circumstances. Those techniques easily catch overly controlled GIs by surprise.

In the Western world, special-operator- and light-infantry-type missions are normally separate and distinct. The operators locate the enemy and then ask the infantry to move in for the kill. Unfortunately, even Rhodesian light infantry rode around in armored personnel carriers and thus had trouble generating enough surprise to conduct a fruitful assault. The Russians tried using special operators both to find and assault their foe in Afghanistan, but that didn't work either. The Russian mind-set is largely Western, and its operators had too little assault technique.

Here's the part that gets really confusing (and controversial). What the U.S. military has been calling "conventional warfare" has been considered by most Eastern armies to be the less effective of two legitimate options since 1917. Because it is driven from the top down, it forces squads into illogical scenarios—like rushing machineguns and dying in place. Most Eastern armies now use a conventional "tactic" as their feint and an unconventional (or asymmetric) "tactic" as their primary maneuver/formation. They have, in essence, learned how to conduct maneuver warfare at the squad level. Because this type of warfare involves so little collateral damage, it perfectly complements 4GW.

Self-sufficient squads also make more productive large-unit operations possible. All Eastern armies use lone squads as lead elements in large attacks, and lone squads as building blocks of strongpoint matrix defenses.

The Urgent Need for Change within the U.S. Military

To execute what U.S. planners have recently been calling "distributive" or "infiltration" operations, advanced squad techniques will be required. Those techniques cannot be designed at some headquarters' think tank. They have to be developed through "bottom-up" experimentation at each line company. Then, instead of being bored by training and predictable in combat, the members of those companies will approach their potential through the dynamics of tactical competition.

The United States Marine Corps—with its Red Chinese Carlson Raider insight—stands a better chance of developing world class techniques, but the U.S. Army may get there first. If it were additionally to train its Special Forces personnel in advanced assault, guerrilla, and E&E techniques, it could use them as line company training cadre.

To generate the most momentum, an expeditionary force must operate from the bottom-up anyway—through "recon pull." That will not happen until senior U.S. commanders realize the lone squad's potential (like Gen. Ludendorff did near the end of WWI). To win a proxy-applied 4GW conflict, America will need squads that can disappear when necessary. At all other times, their members must function as foreign aid workers in the law enforcement sector instead of occupiers. Seldom, if ever, will they then need to endanger public support by resorting to heavy ordnance.

Most of America's institutions are decidedly "top-down." Top-down organizations tend to be least proficient at what they do at their lowest echelons. That's because initiative and decision making at those lowest echelons is often considered by those above to be disruptive. As a result, U.S. units get outsmarted by guerrillas and suffer unnecessary casualties at short range in more conventional scenarios. While official tallies of enemy casualties appear to refute this claim, most include large numbers of support personnel and civilians killed by rear-area bombing from high altitude.

To improve at short range during peacetime, each U.S. infantry company must be allowed to research the tactical techniques of other nations and experimentally derive its own. To continue to improve at short range in war, it must additionally gather its own intelligence and constantly modify its technique portfolio. In essence, each must run its own institution of higher learning (one that objectively considers all the options).

> A nation that draws too broad a difference between its scholars and its warriors will have its thinking being done by cowards and its fighting by fools.
> — Thucydides

To Conduct UW at the Squad Level

As was clearly demonstrated by Part Three, what differs between conventional and UW technique is subtle. Just as subtle is how America's squad training must change to properly develop either. Though so-far ignored by the Pentagon, these subtle difference are what will ultimately determine whether America can win another war.

How U.S. Riflemen and Small Units Must Be Trained

Both U.S. infantry branches could easily fix their short-range-combat deficiencies by simply endorsing the training method that Posterity Enterprises has fully developed and tested over the last 10 years.[1]

Most productive is the type of training that naturally occurs at the company level when headquarters is not trying too hard to justify its existence. Each company's NCOs must be allowed to collectively identify and fix their own deficiencies.[2] To improve any technique, they have only to statistically verify that its sequel generates more surprise or fewer casualties. Once assured of compliance with this quality control measure, the officers have only to learn from what they observe. They will soon realize their men's capabilities under various circumstances. To enhance initiative, decision making, and technique at the squad level and below, the commander has effectively removed himself and his officers of the day-to-day mechanics of squad training. Formerly viewed as the "main teacher," he moves into the more productive role of "main learner." He has only to insure that his senior training representative is good at facilitating the collective wisdom of lower ranks. (See Figure A.1.) Before being partially blamed for the Corps' morale problems after the Vietnam War, the Marine Gunnery Sergeant was the "principal . . . assistant to the company commander in supervising the training of the company."[3]

American GIs cannot be expected to beat guerrillas until they are trained like guerrillas. All East-Asian Communist armies provide their soldiers with unconventional warfare techniques. These

Figure A.1: Infantry Company Training Facilitator
(Source: FM 12-75Z3/4 [1979], cover)

techniques can be loosely described as "sneaking," "hiding," and "escaping." That's why East Asian soldiers can take on 10 times their number without a supporting-arms crutch.

Within the infantry school setting, the wrong type of quality control can virtually preclude any progress. Generally, a board is convened to review proposed changes to the standardized course of instruction. As anything of substance raises questions as to its doctrinal legitimacy, few are adopted. Board members spend most of their time insuring that all courses reflect only standard terminology. As ridiculous as this may sound to a civilian educator, it is what routinely occurs in the "educational" manifestation of a top-down military bureaucracy.

When board members agree on anything tactical, they have generally ignored substantive detail and arrived at a least common denominator (too simplistic a procedure). The Marine Corps' first maneuver warfare manuals were never staffed for that reason. To create a world-class tactical curriculum, what was once considered to be doctrine must now be embraced as guidelines. Then, student critiques must be allowed to determine instructor longevity. All instructors wishing to stay must subsequently acknowledge that their students are collectively smarter than they are. Instead of parroting paragraph headings, they will begin to look for missing or better steps in their topic's procedure. As long as each is allowed to add learning objectives to a well designed and sacrosanct list, he will remain happy and productive. He must, of course, be left in place for several years. By having to track the success of any tactical modification through friendly-casualty totals or surprise determinants (speed, stealth, and deception), he will provide his own quality control.

Modern War Requires a Different Type of Leadership

For leaders, top-down societies end up with "big-picture" thinkers who make little attempt to monitor detail. America's enemies have discovered this. They attack with cuts so small as to each appear harmless to a big-picture thinker. That type of threat is best thwarted at the small-unit level.

There is an alternative to the "charismatic" approach to leadership that has become so prevalent in the U.S. Armed Forces. Inspirational Americans exist in every generation, but the average junior officer would inspire more confidence by not pretending to know it all. What he has learned through Benning, Quantico, or his few years of service is only a small part of a very complicated picture.

While the Western officer tries to mold enlisted subordinates into what he only partially understands himself, his Eastern counterpart studies their capabilities and then tries to place them into appropriate situations. To stabilize the deteriorating situation in South Asia and elsewhere, all commissioned Americans must warm up to this alternate approach.

Helping the Rest of the World

South Asia is much like Africa. For slightly different reasons, both are highly susceptible to Chinese and Islamist expansionism. Within Africa, Iranian *Sepah* and Lebanese *Hezbollah* have been exporting revolution from Sudan—a country run by the Muslim Brotherhood and backed by China. *Al-Qaeda* has been exporting the same thing from Somalia. While their mutual goal appears to be *sharia,* oil and the Democratic Republic of the Congo's uranium are obviously in play. The U.S. command in Djibouti has had the right approach—waging peace instead of war—but not enough assets. To check the Communist and Islamist takeover of Africa, the West will need nothing short of a modern "Marshall Plan." The aid would have to be delivered directly to villages or families instead of through government channels. It would consist of things like village wells or cisterns, family solar-energy collectors, and individual inoculations. With this "bottom-up" approach, America could generate enough "believers in democracy" to eventually save their countries. Without it, millions will die (from drought, disease, and bombs) or go over to the expansionists. Life is so cheap in Africa, and armed fighters so easy to come by, that guerrilla movements must be gradually dried up in that part of the world. This can only be accomplished incrementally by diminishing the reason for their discontent or their base of support.

South Asia poses a different problem. *Al-Qaeda* is well rooted in Pakistan and Afghanistan, the Southern Philippines and Indonesia, and Malaysia. Islamists are on the move in southern Thailand, northwest India, and Afghanistan. But a far greater threat to the region is posed by the Communists. There are already pro-Chinese governments in Laos, Cambodia, Burma, and Pakistan. Under

Communist attack are those of India, Nepal, Bangladesh, and the Philippines. In South Asia, bypassing government channels to provide humanitarian aid will not be enough to reverse the trend. Here, the U.S. must finally field tactically proficient squads. How else can they show local forces the way to beat Maoist guerrillas? A painfully objective look back at history will emphasize the point. Either the South Korean and South Vietnamese soldiers were culturally inferior to their northern counterparts, or the U.S. military lacked the ability to give them sufficient training.

China has being using the same 4GW ploy all over the world. While Chinese oil, shipping, and construction companies gain influence over each nation's infrastructure (sometimes under the guise of foreign aid), their guerrilla proxies discourage Western competition. As all this occurs against a backdrop of Islamic rebellion, Western leaders never suspect the ruse. Unfortunately, Sun Tzu's backyard produces guerrillas who are so tactically proficient as to defy all conventional means of containment.

Though understrength, U.S. forces have yet to counter the Taliban upsurge in Afghanistan. As in Vietnam, they lack the tactical sophistication to surprise a "woods-wise" foe on the ground. Unless all aerial and artillery bombardment is halted, U.S. and NATO forces will lose what little popular support they have left. Key villages must be outposted for six months or more by U.S. squads with enough UW training to operate alone.

In other words, the glass is half full but quickly draining, and America still lacks any way to fill it further. This is what the veterans of Vietnam have been trying to tell the present leadership. They are proud of their record against the best light infantry in the world today. They don't want America to "turn that uncomfortable page" without first demanding that its firepower-and-technology-dependent military acquire more small-unit proficiency. Unbelievable as it may seem, America has yet to develop squads that can sneak up on a fully prepared larger unit, secretly attack it, and then safely escape. In the semantics of history, its military has failed to evolve tactically. Having sworn an oath to protect America from all threats foreign and domestic, Vietnam veterans are far from content with this long-standing and apparently intentional oversight. They want for their sons and nephews what they never got themselves—a concurrent block of dynamic (nonstandardized) training in modern (unconventional) warfare. Without it, they fear that the world situation will continue to deteriorate.

Notes

SOURCE NOTES

Illustrations:

Maps on pages 5, 9, 10, 31, 45, 67, 75, 80, 81, 83, 93, 94, 117, 121, 131, and 134 reprinted after written assurance from GENERAL LIBRARIES OF THE UNIVERSITY OF TEXAS AT AUSTIN that they are in the public domain.

Map on page 32 reprinted after written assurance from *TIME MAGAZINE* that this map from the NIC Changlang District One (India) website is not their property and probably in the public domain.

Map on page 33 reprinted after asking permission of the SCHOOL OF ORIENTAL AND AFRICAN STUDIES, Univ. of London. Copyright © n.d. by Klaus Schroeder. All rights reserved.

Map on page 34 reprinted with permission of *FRONTLINE* and WGBH, Boston. Copyright © 1996 by PBS and WGBH/Frontline. All rights reserved.

Map on page 56 reprinted after asking permission of ASIA TRAVEL, Singapore. The map appears at its website as map designator "asiatravel.com/ujungmap.html." Copyright © n.d. by Asia Travel. All rights reserved.

Map on page 95 reprinted after asking permission of *THE ECONOMIST*. Copyright @ 2006 by The Economist Group. All rights reserved.

Map on pages 138 and 139 reprinted with permission of Markus Hauser and PAMIRS.ORG. Copyright © n.d. by Markus Hauser. All rights reserved.

Map on page 135 reprinted with permission of PAKISTAN & THE KARAKORAM HIGHWAY, LONELY PLANET, and KHYBER GATEWAY. This map has Khyber Gateway designator "chitraldistrict.gif" and Lonely Planet designator "TG_PAK6_Chitral_District.pdf."

Pictures on pages 168 and 171 reproduced with permission of CRC Press, Taylor & Francis Group, Bocan Raton, FL, from *PRACTICAL HOMICIDE INVESTIGATION,* by Vernon J. Geberth. These pictures appear in pages 611 and 182-184 of the CRC Press publication, respectively.

Picture on page 203 reproduced after written assurance from ASSOCIATED PRESS that it is from a Pakistani handout of unclear origin.

Pictures on pages 242, 243, 244, and 289 reproduced with permission of Dr. Anatol Taras, Minsk, Belarus, from *PODGOTOVKA RAZVEGCHIKA: SISTEMA SPETSNAZA GRU,* by A.E. Taras and F.D. Zaruz. The illustrations are from pages 279, 373, 147, and 153 of the Russian publication, respectively.

Picture on page 246 reproduced after written assurance from Orion Books, London, that the copyright holders for *WORLD ARMY UNIFORMS SINCE 1939,* text by Andrew Mollo and Digby Smith, color plates by Malcolm McGregor and Michael Chappell, can no longer be contacted. It is from Part II (plate 88) of the Orion publication.

Pictures on page 306 reproduced after being unable to contact Nippon, TV, Tokyo, from "What Cameramen Saw through Their Lenses," *A TRIBUTE TO WWII COMBAT CAMERAMEN OF JAPAN* series.

Picture on page 307 reproduced after telephonic assurance from Osprey Publishing Ltd., London, that this is a U.S. War Dept. (public domain) sketch in *JAPANESE ARMY OF WORLD WAR II,* Men-at-Arms Series, text by Philip Warner, color plates by Michael Youens, page 25.

Pictures on page 308 reproduced after asking the permission of Polygon Publishers, St. Petersburg, Russia, from *VOINA V KOREE: 1950-1953,* by A.A. Kuryacheba, Voenno-Estorecheskaya Biblioteka. The two illustrations are from pages 582 and 613 of the Polygon publication.

Maps on page 330 and 347 reprinted with permission of Pacifica Military History, Pacifica, CA, from *FIRE IN THE STREETS: THE BATTLE FOR HUE, TET 1968,* by Eric Hammel. The illustrations are from pages xvi and xvii of the Pacifica Military Historypublication (artwork by Moody Graphics of San Francisco), respectively.

Text:

Reprinted with permission of RMS Reprint Management Services, Lancaster, PA, for ASSOCIATED PRESS, from the following article(s): (1) "Terrorists Train for Seaborne Attacks," by Jim Gomez, 18 March 2005.

Reprinted with permission of East-West Services, Springfield, VA, publishers of *GEOSTRATEGY-DIRECT,* from the following article(s): (1) "China's 'Comprehensive Warfare' Strategy Wears Down [an] Enemy Using Non-Military Means," 2 August 2006; (2) "Iran's Improved Fajr-5 Rockets Can Be Fired Remotely," 31 May 2006.

Reprinted after asking permission of U.S. Naval Institute, publishers of *U.S. NAVAL INSTITUTE PROCEEDINGS,* from the following article(s): (1) "Cutting China's 'String of Pearls'," by Maj. Lawrence Spinetta (USAF), October 2006.

Reprinted after being unable to contact *PEOPLE'S DAILY*, Beijing, from the following article(s): (1) "China Recruits Young Volunteers to Work in Laos," 29 March 2002; (2) "It Is Easy to Gulp Down But Difficult to Digest," 6 November 2003.

Reprinted after being unable to contact *ASIA TIMES ONLINE*, Hong Kong, China, from the following article(s): (1) "The Roving Eye," by Pepe Escobar, 4 October 2001; (2) "China to Europe Via a New Burma Road," by David Fullbrook, 23 September 2004.

Reprinted after asking permission of *HINDUSTAN TIMES*, New Delhi, India, from the following article(s): (1) "Banned Bangladeshi Group Training Indian Extremists," 1 September 2004.

Reprinted after asking permission of C. Hurst & Co., Ltd., London, UK, from *INSIDE AL-QAEDA: GLOBAL NETWORK OF TERROR,* by Rohan Gunaratna.

Reprinted after asking permission of *INTERNATIONAL HERALD TRIBUNE,* Neuilly Cedex, France, from the following article(s): (1) "Military Aid to Indonesia—Editorials and Commentary," Opinion Pieces by Will Jourdin Penestanan Kelod and John M. Miller, 9 January 2006.

Reprinted after asking permission of Jamestown Foundation, Washington, D.C., publishers of *TERRORISM FOCUS,* from the following article(s): (1) "Indonesians Infiltrate Southern Thailand's Insurgency," by Zachary Abuza, vol. III, issue 27, 11 July 2006.

Reprinted after asking permission of *TIME,* from the following article(s): (1) "Taking the Hard Road," by Simon Elegant, Asia Edition, 23 September 2002.

Reprinted with permission of Tibor Krausz and *THE CHRISTIAN SCIENCE MONITOR,* from the following article(s): (1) "Cambodia's Healing History Lessons," 11 December 2006.

Reprinted with permission of Dharma Adhikari and *THE CHRISTIAN SCIENCE MONITOR,* from the following article(s): (1) "Joy and Caution in Nepal's Peace Deal," 5 December 2006.

Reprinted with permission of Anuj Chopra and *THE CHRISTIAN SCIENCE MONITOR,* from the following article(s): (1) "Maoist Rebels Spread across Rural India," 22 August 2006.

Reprinted with permission of *THE CHRISTIAN SCIENCE MONITOR,* from the following article(s): (1) "How Al Qaeda Seeks to Buy Chinese Arms," by Scott Baldauf, 23 August 2002; (2) "Al Qaeda Massing for New Fight," by Scott Baldauf, 9 August 2002; and (3) "Riots in Bangladesh May Benefit Islamists," by David Montero, 30 October 2006.

Reprinted with permission of *INTERNATIONAL CRISIS GROUP,* Brussels, Belgium, from the following article(s): (1) "Indonesian Backgrounder: Jihad in Central Sulawesi," Asia Report No. 74, 3 February 2004.

Reprinted with permission of BRITISH BROADCASTING CORPORATION (BBC) NEWS ON LINE, London, from the following article(s): (1) "Profile: Hun Sen," 15 July 2004; (2) Cambodia Country Study, updated January 2006; (3) "Cambodia's 'Out of Control' Evictions," by Guy De Launey, 29 September 2006; (4) "Khmer Rouge Judges Begin Work," 4 July 2006; (5) "Cambodia Clamps Down on Dissent," by Guy De Launey, 7 January 2006; (6) "China Gives Cambodia $600m in Aid," 8 April 2006; (7) "Cambodian PM Denounces UN Envoy," 29 March 2006; and (8) Laos Country Profile, updated 1 January 2006.

Reprinted with permission of PARS International, New York, for *THE NEW YORK TIMES*, from the following article(s): (1) "China Competes with West in Aid to Its Neighbors," by Josef Polleross, 18 September 2006.

Reprinted with permission of *THE WASHINGTON TIMES*, from the following article(s): (1) "China-Made Artillery Seized in Afghanistan," by Bill Gertz, 12 April 2002; (2) "China-Trained Taliban," by Bill Gertz and Rowan Scarborough, 21 June 2002.

Reprinted after asking permission of *DEBKAFILE* and *DEBKA-NET-WEEKLY*, Israel, from the following article(s): (1) "China Moves Forces into Afghanistan," 6 October 2001; (2) "Chinese-Made Ammo in al Qaeda Caves Confirms," 17 December 2001; and (3) "Osama's Secret Citadel," 28 September 2001.

Reprinted after being unable to contact *NEWSMAX*, South Africa, from the following article(s): (1) "U.S. Bombs Chinese Network in Afghanistan, PRC Sold Taliban Advanced Air Defense System," by Charles R. Smith, 20 October 2001.

Reprinted with permission of Central Asia-Caucus Institute, Nitze School of Advanced Internat. Studies, Johns Hopkins Univ., Washington, D.C., publishers of *CHINA AND EURASIA QUARTERLY,* from the following article(s): (1) "Fact and Fiction: A Chinese Documentary on Eastern Turkestan Terrorism," by Yitzhah Shichor, vol. 4, no. 2, 2006.

Reprinted after asking permission of Scott Meredith Literary Agency, New York, NY, from *INSIDE THE VC AND THE NVA: THE REAL STORY OF NORTH VIETNAM'S ARMED FORCES,* by Michael Lee Lanning and Dan Cragg.

Reprinted after being unable to contact *ASIAN ECONOMIC NEWS*, Beijing, from the following article(s): (1) "China Pledges $12.4 Million in Aid to Cambodia," 12 December, 2005; (2) "China Ready to Offer Aid to Build 3rd Bridge across Mekong River," 20 November 2006.

Reprinted with permission of Random House, Inc., New York, from *CROSSING THE THRESHOLD OF PEACE,* by His Holiness John Paul II.

Reprinted with permission of Eliza Griswold and *THE SMITHSONIAN,* Washington, D.C., from the following article(s): (1) "Waging Peace in the Philippines," December 2006.

Reprinted with permission of Copyright Clearance Center, for AGENCE FRANCE-PRESSE, Paris, from the following article(s): (1) "Al Qaeda Has Drones," 13 September 2005.

Reprinted after being unable to contact Mohammad Yousaf and Leo Cooper Publishers, South Yorkshire, UK, from *BEAR TRAP: AFGHANISTAN'S UNTOLD STORY*.

Reprinted with permission of CENTER FOR DEFENSE INFORMATION, Washington, D.C., from the following article(s): (1) "East Turkestan Islamic Movement (ETIM)," by Seva Gunitskiy, 9 December 2002.

Reprinted with permission of Texas A&M Univ. Press, College Station, TX, from *SAPPERS IN THE WIRE: THE LIFE AND DEATH OF FIREBASE MARY ANN,* by Keith William Nolan.

Reprinted with permission of Random House, Inc., New York, from *INSIDE THE SOVIET AIRLAND BATTLE TACTICS,* by William P. Baxter.

Reprinted with permission of Random House, Inc., New York, from *PORTRAIT OF THE ENEMY,* by David Chanoff and Doan Van Toai.

Reprinted with permission of *THE GUARDIAN,* London, from the following article(s): (1) "Inside India's Hidden War," by Randeep Ramesh, 9 May 2006.

Reprinted with permission of *THE TRIBUNE,* Chicago, from the following article(s): (1) "Only Democracy Can Break Pakistan Terror Link," by Benazir Bhutto, Global Viewpoint, 16 August 2006.

ENDNOTES

Preface

1. ABC's Nightly News, 30 April 2007; Anne Gearan, AP, "Rice Cites Progress in War against Terror despite Iraq Violence," *Jacksonville Daily News* (NC), 2 May 2007, p. 5A.
2. John L. Esposito, *Unholy War: Terrorism in the Name of Islam* (London: Oxford Univ. Press, 2002), p. 7.
3. Memorandum for the record by H.J. Poole.
4. *Wikipedia Encyclopedia,* s.v. "Religion in China"; *CIA—The World Factbook* s.v. "China"; "Religion in China," *Voice of America (VOA),* 20 September 2006.
5. "Freedom and Justice," PBS's *China from the Inside,* part IV, NC Public TV, 17 January 2007.
6. Memorandum for the record by H.J. Poole.
7. "U.S. Government Drops Vietnam from List of Worst Religious Freedom Violators," from AP, *Jacksonville Daily News* (NC), 14 November 2006, p. 12A; "Freedom and Justice," PBS's *China from the Inside.*
8. Ibid.; Anthony LoBaido, "China behind Christian Persecution in S.E. Asia," *World Net Daily,* 22 March 2000; Constantine Menges, *China: The Gathering Threat* (Nashville, TN: Nelson Current, 2005), p. 2; John Pomfret, "China Expands Crackdown on Religions Not Recognized by the State," Washington Post, 5 September 2000, in *China: The Gathering Threat,* by Menges, p. 148.
9. Bill Gertz, *The China Threat* (Washington, D.C.: Regnery Publishing, 2002), pp. 11, 41; American couple (who had just traveled by train from Russia to Chongqing), in conversation with the author in June 2000.
10. "Freedom and Justice," PBS's *China from the Inside.*
11. Ibid.
12. Constantine Menges, *China: The Gathering Threat* (Nashville, TN: Nelson Current, 2005), p. 323.
13. AFP-published estimate in *Twentieth Century Atlas—Death Tolls;* Jean-Louis Margolin estimate in *The China Threat,* by Gertz, p. xxi; *Wikipedia Encyclopedia,* s.v. "Cultural Revolution."
14. Richard L. Walker, "The Human Cost of Communism in China," study for U.S. Congress, 1971, in *The China Threat,* by Gertz, p. xxi.
15. R.J. Rummel, *Death by Government* (N.p., n.d.), pp. 100-101, in *China: The Gathering Threat,* by Menges, p. 54.
16. Seventy-year-old Chinese man (in Shanghai airport), in conversation with author in June 2000.
17. Ibid.; Menges, *China: The Gathering Threat,* p. 55.

18. *Encyclopedia Britannica,* s.v. "Cultural Revolution," "Zhou Enlai," and "Deng Xiaoping"; *Wikipedia Encyclopedia,* s.v. "Nixon."
19. Menges, *China: The Gathering Threat,* p. 2.
20. "Power and the People," PBS's *China from the Inside,* Part I, NC Public TV, 10 January 2007.
21. Gertz, *The China Threat,* p. 12.
22. International Crisis Group, as quoted by Danna Harman, "How China's Quiet Support Shields a Regime Called 'Genocidal'," *Christian Science Monitor,* 26 June 2007, pp. 1, 11-13.
23. "The Spiritual War," Ephesians, chapt. 6, *The Jerusalem Bible* (Garden City, NY: Doubleday, 1966.

Introduction

1. H. John Poole, *Phantom Soldier: The Enemy's Answer to U.S. Firepower* (Emerald Isle, NC: Posterity Press, 2001), p. 248.
2. H. John Poole, *Terrorist Trail: Backtracking the Foreign Fighter* (Emerald Isle, NC: Posterity Press, 2006), pp. 17-38, 197-208, 223-246.
3. *Unrestricted Warfare,* by Qiao Liang and Wang Xiangsui (Beijing: PLA Literature and Arts Publishing House, February 1999), FBIS trans.
4. Ibid., table of contents.
5. "One-Point, Two-Sides Attack on Defensive Position," *Handbook on the Chinese Communist Army,* DA Pam 30-51, (Washington, D.C.: Hdqts. Dept. of the Army, 1960), p. 24; Poole, *Phantom Soldier,* fig. 7-1, p. 103.
6. Memorandum for the record by H.J. Poole.
7. *Unrestricted Warfare,* by Qiao Liang and Wang Xiangsui, pp. 54, 144, 145.
8. "U.S. Surveillance Plane Lands in China after Collision with Fighter," CNN Headline News, 1 April 2001; Gordon Lubold, "U.S. Seeks More Info on China's Military, *Christian Science Monitor,* 29 May 2007, p. 2.
9. "Spy plane" article series from *Washington Post*: (1) "China Says It Will Return Disassembled U.S. Plane," 25 May 2001; (2) "Surveillance Plane to Be Returned to U.S. in Pieces," 30 May 2001; (3) "U.S., China Agree on Plan to Return Spy Plane: U.S. Team Arrives in China to Begin Dismantling Jet," 7 June 2001; (4) "Disassembled Navy Plane Scheduled to Leave China Today," 3 July 2001; (5) "China Bills U.S. Over Collision: $1 Million in Surveillance Plane Dispute Termed 'Exaggerated' ," 7 July 2001; and (6) "U.S. to Pay China $34,567 for Costs of Downed Plane," 10 August 2001.
10. "China's 'Comprehensive Warfare' Strategy Wears Down Enemy Using Non-Military Means," *Geostrategy Direct,* 2 August 2006.

11. "China Forging Strategic Ties to Radical Islam," China Confidential, 21 July 2006.
12. Joseph Kahn, "Where's Mao? Chinese Revise History Books," *New York Times*, 1 September 2006.
13. *Wikipedia Encyclopedia,* s.v. "Moro Rebellion" and "Philippine-American War."
14. Todd Bullock, "Asia Most Likely To Shape U.S. Defense Policy, Scholars Say," U.S. Dept. of State's Bureau of Internat. Info. Programs, 25 September 2005.
15. Diane Sawyer (on assignment in North Korea), "Good Morning America," 16 October 2006.
16. Jasper Becker, *The Chinese* (N.p.: John Murray Publishers Ltd., 2000), p. 274.
17. Grant Evans and Kelvin Rowley, *Red Brotherhood at War* (London: Verso, 1984), p. 151; Menges, *China: The Gathering Threat,* p. 49.
18. Anthony Short, "Communism, Race and Politics in Malaysia," *Asian Survey,* vol. 10, no. 12, December 1970, pp. 1081-1089; Becker, *The Chinese,* p. 274; *Wikipedia Encyclopedia,* "History of Malaysia" and "Communist Party of Malaya."
19. *Mao's Generals Remember Korea,* trans. and ed. Xiaobing Li, Allan R. Millet, and bin Yu (Lawrence, KS: Univ. Press of Kansas, 2001), p. 154; George Robert Elford, *Devil's Guard* (New York: Dell, 1971), p. 200; *The Battle of Dien Bien Phu,* Visions of War Series, vol. 10 (New Star Video, 1988), 50 min., videocassette #4010.

Chapter 1: *The Sino-Islamic Connection*

1. "Fourth Generation War," FMFM 1-A (Draft Copy), by William S. Lind (Washington, D.C., 2005).
2. Poole, *Terrorist Trail,* pp. 238-240; "Seoul Train," PBS's *Independent Lens,* NC Public TV, 13 June 2006.
3. Kenneth Katzman, *Warriors of Islam: Iran's Revolutionary Guard* (Boulder, CO: Westview Press, 1993), pp. 82-84.
4. Poole, *Terrorist Trail,* p. 9; Watts Roba Gibia Nyirigwa, "Why 2011 Referendum Is the Only Hope for South Sudanese: Part One," *Khartoum Monitor,* 31 May 2006, p. 5; *Wikipedia Encyclopedia,* s.v. "National Congress (Sudan)"; "Sudan Unity Requires Secular State," *Khartoum Monitor,* 1 June 2006, p. 4; U.N. Mission in Sudan (unmis.org), s.v. "Political Parties."
5. PRC Ministry of Foreign Affairs (www.fmprc.gov.cn), s.v. "Chinese Embassies."
6. ABC's Nightly News, 28 July 2006.
7. "China . . . Pledged Monday," World Briefs Wire Reports (AP), *Jacksonville Daily News* (NC), 19 September 2006, p. 7.

8. "Hezbollah Leader Vows Not to Give Up Weapons," from AP, *Jacksonville Daily News* (NC), 23 September 2006, p. 4A; Ed Timperlake, "Clues How Chinese Missile Ended Up in Hezbollah's Arsenal," as posted on 26 July 2006 at access@g2-forward.org.
9. *Wikipedia Encyclopedia,* s.v. "United Nations Mission in Sudan"; *Sudan Country Study,* DA PAM 550-27, pp. 257, 258.
10. Edward Cody and Molly Moore, "Analysts Attribute Hezbollah's Resilience to Zeal, Secrecy and Iranian Funding," *Washington Post,* 14 August 2006; *Embassy World* (www.embassyworld.com), s.v. "Embassy Listings for North Korea"; privately owned British website (uk.geocities.com/hkgalbert/kpdo.html), s.v. "North Korea."
11. "Iran's Improved Fajr-5 Rockets Can Be Fired Remotely," *Geostrategy-Direct,* 31 May 2006.
12. Nicholas Blanford, "Hizbullah Builds New Line of Defense," *Christian Science Monitor,* 26 February 2007, pp. 1,10, 11.
13. H. John Poole, *Militant Tricks: Battlefield Ruses of the Islamic Insurgent* (Emerald Isle, NC: Posterity Press, 2005), pp. 68, 69; "Ahmadinejad Has Been Pushing for His Own Candidate," World News in Brief, *Christian Science Monitor,* 15 November 2006, p. 7.
14. Osama's Secret Citadel," *DEBKA-Net-Weekly,* 28 September 2001, as posted at vbulletin.thesite.org.
15. *Wikipedia Encyclopedia,* s.v. "Wahhabi" and "Salafi."
16. Sharon Behn, "U.S. Targets Aid to All Militants," *Washington Times,* 11 July 2007.
17. David Brunnstrom, Reuters, "U.S. Says Iran May Be 'More Involved' in Afghan Fight," *Christian Science Monitor,* 19 April 2007, p. 4; Jason Straziuso, AP, "Afghan Bomber Deadlier," *Jacksonville Daily News* (NC), 3 June 2007, pp. 1A, 8A; Richard Clarke, on ABC's Morning News, 7 June 2007.
18. "Al-Qaeda's New Front," PBS's *Frontline,* NC Public TV, 25 January 2005; Rohan Gunaratna, *Inside al-Qaeda: Global Network of Terror* (Lahore: Vanguard, 2002), p. 31.
19. Rohan Gunaratna, *Inside al-Qaeda: Global Network of Terror* (Lahore: Vanguard, 2002), pp. 158, 159.
20. Aaron Mannes, *Profiles in Terror: Guide to Middle East Terror Organizations* (Lanham, MD: Rowman & Littlefield, 2004), p. 22; Samuel P. Huntington, *The Clash of Civilizations and the Remaking of World Order* (London: Simon & Schuster UK, 1997), p. 176.
21. *Wikipedia Encyclopedia,* s.v. "Non-Aligned Movement."
22. "U.S. Hopes China Will Help Moderate Havana Meeting," *China Confidential,* 11 September 2006.
23. Anthony Boadle, "Absent Castro Overshadows Non-Aligned Summit," Reuters, 14 September 2006.

24. Jim Avila, "Dream Team of U.S. Bashers Gathers in Cuba," *New York Times,* 11 September 2006; Scott MacLeod, "A Date with a Dangerous Mind," *Time,* 25 September 2006, pp. 34.
25. Daniel Schearf, "China-North Korea Relations Tested as Reports Say Kim Jong Il to Visit Beijing," *VOA,* 24 August 2006; "Chavez's Whistlestop World Tour," BBC News, 1 September 2006.
26. Alejandro Kirk and Dalia Acosta, "Non-Aligned Summit Opens amidst Suspense over Castro," Inter-Press-Service News Agency, 21 September 2006; Ardeshir Ommani, "The Non-Aligned Movement Has Been an Organization of, More or Less, Deprived Nations of the Planet," *Iran Heritage,* 18 September 2006.
27. ABC's Nightly News, 18 April 2006; "Iran Signs $20-Billion Gas Deal with China," UPI, 20 March 2004; Poole, *Terrorist Trail,* pp. 17-38, 182-188.
28. Maj. Lawrence Spinetta (USAF), "Cutting China's 'String of Pearls'," *U.S. Naval Institute Proceedings,* October 2006, pp. 40-42.
29. Mark Sappenfield and David Montero, "China Woos India and Pakistan with Nuclear Know-How," *Christian Science Monitor,* 21 November 2006, pp. 1, 10.
30. *Wikipedia Encyclopedia,* s.v. "Gwadar."
31. David Fullbrook, "China to Europe via a New Burma Road," *Asia Times,* 23 September 2004.
32. Ibid.
33. Ibid.; Perry Castaneda Map Collection, Library of the Univ. of Texas at Austin, map designator "china_rel01.pdf."
34. "Crossing the Line: China's Railway to Lhasa," Internat. Campaign for Tibet, 10 July 2006.
35. Bill Weir, interview in Tibet, ABC's *Good Morning America,* 9 November 2006.
36. Daniel Ten Kate, "Thai Coup May Ease Violence in the South," *Christian Science Monitor,* 26 September 2006, p. 6.
37. New Delhi businessman, in conversation with author on 30 May 2006.
38. Howard LaFranchi, "U.S. Presses to Enforce N. Korea Resolution," *Christian Science Monitor,* 16 October 2006, pp. 1, 10; ABC's Nightly News, 15 October 2006; ABC Affiliate WCTI's Noon News, 16 October 2006.
39. Diane Sawyer (on assignment in North Korea), "Good Morning America," 16 October 2006; ABC's Nightly News, 16 October 2006.
40. ABC's Morning News, 20 and 24 October 2006; "China: North Korea Has No Plans for a Second Nuclear Test," from AP, *Jacksonville Daily News* (NC), 25 October 2005, p. 3A.

41. FOX's Morning News, 20 October 2006; Raphael F. Perl, "Drug Trafficking and North Korea: Issues for U.S. Policy," Congressional Research Service, Library of Congress, *Report for Congress RL32167,* 27 November 2006.
42. Katherine Shrader, AP, "Sanctions on North Korea," *Jacksonville Daily News* (NC), 13 October 2005, p. 5A.
43. Menges, *China: The Gathering Threat,* p. 304; Bill Gertz, *The China Threat* and *Washington Times* articles, and Constantine Menges and M. Sgro, "Deadly Weapons," Hudson Inst., 2003, in Menges, *China: The Gathering Threat,* p. 421.
44. Howard LaFranchi, "Will Iran, Korea Really Back Off Nukes," *Christian Science Monitor,* 18 July 2007, pp. 1, 12; Donald Kirk, "New Phase as N. Korea Shuts Down Reactor," *Christian Science Monitor,* 16 July 2007, p. 4.
45. D.J. McGuire, *Dragon in the Dark: How and Why Communist China Helps Our Enemies in the War on Terror* (Bloomington, IN: Authorhouse, November 2003), pp. ix, 41; Japan's *Sankei Shimbun,* as cited by South Korea's Yonhap News Agency, in *Dragon in the Dark,* by McGuire, p. 64; Con Coughlin, "N. Korea Helping Iran with Nuclear Testing," *Telegraph* (Britain), 25 January 2007; Menges, *China: The Gathering Threat,* pp. 303.
46. ABC's Nightly News, 19 September 2007; Ilene R. Prusher, "Israel Sends a 'Message' on Nukes," *Christian Science Monitor,* 19 September 2007, p. 6; Uzi Mahnaimi, Sarah Baxter, and Mike Sheridan, "Israelis 'Blew Apart Syrian Nuclear Cache'," *Times on Line* (UK), 16 September 2007; Uzi Mahnaimi and Sarah Baxter, "Israelis Seized Nuclear Material in Syrian Raid," *Times on Line* (UK), 23 September 2007.
47. Katherine Shrader, "North Korean Client List Is Said to Take In Iran, Syria, 16 Others," from AP, as posted on 13 October 2006 at access@g2-forward.org; Gertz, *The China Threat,* p. 103; Menges, *China: The Gathering Threat,*pp. 126.
48. "Israel Intercepts Dual-Use Military Shipment from China to Gaza, *World Tribune,* 4 May 2006; "Explosive Powder Found on Chinese Ship," FOX News, 8 November 2006.
49. ABC's Nightly News, 28 July 2006; *Wikipedia Encyclopedia,* s.v. "United Nations Mission in Sudan"; *Sudan Country Study,* DA PAM 550-27, pp. 257, 258.
50. Joseph S. Bermudez, Jr., *North Korean Special Forces* (Annapolis: Naval Inst. Press, 1998), p. 147.
51. FOX's Morning News, 20 October 2006; Menges, *China: The Gathering Threat,* p. 386.
52. China Winning Resources and Loyalties of Africa," *The Financial Times* (UK), 28 February 2006.
53. "North Koreans Assisted Hezbollah with Tunnel Construction," Jamestown Foundation, *Terrorism Focus,* vol. III, issue 30, August 2006.

54. Poole, *Tactics of the Crescent Moon: Militant Muslim Combat Methods* (Emerald Isle, NC: Posterity Press, 2004), chapt. 8; Poole, *Militant Tricks,* chapt. 3; Scott Peterson and Nicholas Blandford, "A Gauge of Iran's Hand in Iraq," *Christian Science Monitor,* 5 July 2007, p. 6.
55. Chinese Military Attache to the U.N., in phone call to the author about 1996.
56. Lin Biao, "Carry out the Strategy and Tactics of People's War," Marxist Internet Archive, n.d.
57. Ibid.
58. Ibid.
59. "It Is Easy to Gulp Down but Difficult to Digest," *People's Daily* (China), 6 November 2003.
60. NPR's Morning News, 3 November 2006.
61. PRC Ministry of Foreign Affairs (www.fmprc.gov.cn), s.v. "Chinese Embassies"; "Strong Chinese-Hamas Intelligence Connection," *DEBKAfile* (Israel), 19 June 2006.
62. "China Sending PC Priests Abroad as 'Intelligence Operatives'," *East-Asia-Intel,* 26 July 2006.
63. "China Winning Resources and Loyalties of Africa."
64. David J. Lynch, "China Elevates Its Economic Profile in Africa," *USA Today,* 3 November 2006, p. 8B; Menges, China: *The Gathering Threat,* p. 399.
65. "40% Top Chinese Students Choose to Study Abroad," from Xinhua, *China Daily* (Beijing), 13 August 2007, p. 1.
66. ABC's Nightly News, 18 April 2006; "Tribal Militants Claimed Responsibility for Another Attack on an Energy Installation," World News in Brief, *Christian Science Monitor,* 8 June 2006, p. 7; MEND photograph, in "Curse of the Black Gold: Hope and Betrayal in the Niger Delta," *National Geographic,* February 2007, pp. 88-117.
67. "Islam in Africa Newsletter," vol. 1, no. 1, May 2006, by Moshe Terdman and Reuven Paz, Project for the Research of Islamist Movements (Israel).
68. ABC's Nightly News, 7 January 2007.
69. Charles R. Smith, "U.S. Bombs Chinese Network in Afghanistan, PRC Sold Taliban Advanced Air Defense System," Newsmax.com, 20 October 2001; Gertz, *The China Threat,* pp. 82, 94.
70. Christina Lamb, "Britain Says Pakistan Is Hiding Taliban Chief," *The Sunday Times* (UK), 8 October 2006; Poole, *Militant Tricks,* pp. 122-144.
71. Scott Peterson, "Hostile in Public, Iran Seeks Quiet Discourse with U.S.," *Christian Science Monitor,* 25 September 2003, p. 7.
72. Stephen Graham, AP, "Latest Assault Leaves 2 Brits, Afghan Interpreter Dead," *Jacksonville Daily News* (NC), 6 May 2004, p. 8A.

73. Kochay and Rahim, as quoted in *Afghan Guerrilla Warfare,* by Jalali and Grau, pp. 59-61 and p. 21, respectively; Poole, *Phantom Soldier,* p. 138.
74. "China's 'Comprehensive Warfare' Strategy Wears Down Enemy Using Non-Military Means."
75. Ibrahim, as quoted in *Afghan Guerrilla Warfare,* by Jalali and Grau, p. 289.
76. Bill Gertz and Rowan Scarborough, "China-Trained Taliban," Inside the Ring, *Washington Times,* 21 June 2002, unedited version from www.gertzfile.com; Matthew Pennington, AP, "Pakistan Unsure If Target Is al-Zawahri," *Jacksonville Daily News* (NC), 21 March 2004, p. 5A.
77. Mir, *The True Face of Jihadis*, p. 97.
78. *Unmasking Terror: A Global Review of Terrorist Activities,* vol. I, ed. Christopher Heffelfinger (Washington, D.C: Jamestown Foundation, 2005); Mannes, *Profiles in Terror,* p. 67.
79. John K. Cooley, *Unholy Wars: Afghanistan, America, and International Terrorism* (N.p., n.d.), in *Pakistan: Behind the Ideological Mask,* by Khaled Ahmed (Lahore: Vanguard, 2004), p. 225.
80. Amir Mir, *The True Face of Jihadis* (Lahore: Mashal Books, 2004), pp. 103, 104.
81. "Mujahideen Training and Operating in China ('Eastern Turkestan')," Islamist website video, as extracted by Middle East Media Research Inst. (MEMRI), 8 November 2006.
82. *Encylopedia Britannica,* s.v. "Muslim Rebellions (China)"; Chien-peng Chung, "China's 'War on Terror': September 11 and Uighur Separatism," *Foreign Affairs,* July/August 2002.
83. Mohan Malik, *Dragon on Terrorism: Assessing China's Tactical Gains and Strategic Losses Post-September 11* (Carlisle, PA: Strategic Studies Institute, U. S. Army War College, October 2002), p.5; Gunaratna, *Inside al-Qaeda,* p. 172; Mannes, *Profiles in Terror,* p. 61.
84. Ibid., p. 59.
85. Ibid., p. 26.
86. Ibid., p. 173.
87. Ibid., p. 174.
88. Gertz, *The China Threat,* pp. 76, 78, 80, 91, 92.
89. Ibid., p. 82.
90. Sara Miller Llana, "Nicaragua Plans a Big Dig to Rival Panama Canal," *Christian Science Monitor,* 15 November 2006, pp. 1, 12; ABC's Nightly News, 1 March 2007.
91. Probable CIA official (McClean address and too much knowledge), in phone call to author around the middle of October 2006.

92. Antonio Garrastazu and Jerry Haar, "International Terrorism: The Western Hemisphere Connection," Organization of American States, *America's Forum North-South Center Update,* 2001; Sara Miller Llana, "Nicaragua Plans a Big Dig to Rival Panama Canal," *Christian Science Monitor,* 1 December 2006, pp. 1, 5.
93. "Power and the People," PBS's *China from the Inside.*
94. *CIA–The World Factbook* s.v. "China."
95. Michael Elliott, "The Chinese Century," *Time,* 22 January 2007.
96. John Pomfret, "Chinese Military Backs Beijing's Latest Warning to Taiwan," *Washington Post,* 24 February 2000, in China: The Gathering Threat, by Menges, p. 145.
97. "Bush Criticizes Planned Taiwan Referendum," from AP, Newsmax.com, 9 December 2003.
98. "Taiwan Election/Referendum, March 20, 2004," *Asia Media News Daily,* n.d., UCLA Asia Inst.
99. ABC's Nightly News, 19 January 2007.
100. Chisaki Watanabe, AP, "U.S., Others Concerned after China's Anti-Satellite Launch," *Jacksonville Daily News* (NC), 20 January 2007, p. 6A.
101. Peter Navarro, "Watch Your Flanks America," Opinion Piece, *Christian Science Monitor,* 26 February 2007, p. 9; Elliott, "The Chinese Century," p. 42.

Chapter 2: *Burma Thailand, and Malaysia*

1. *Malaysia: A Country Study,* DA Pamphlet 550-45, Area Handbook Series (Washington, D.C.: Hdqts. Dept. of the Army, 1984), pp. 50-55.
2. "Malayan Races Liberation Army Man," *World Army Uniforms since 1939* (London: Blandford Press Ltd., 1980), part II, plate 104 and accompanying inscription.
3. *Malaysia: A Country Study,* pp. 50-59.
4. Ibid., pp. 56-58.
5. Menges, *China: The Gathering Threat,* p. 388; PRC Ministry of Foreign Affairs (www.fmprc.gov.cn), s.v. "Chinese Embassies"; *Wikipedia Encyclopedia,* s.v. "Mahathir Mohammed" and "Abdullah Ahmad Badawi"; Admiral Thomas Moorher (former JCS Chairman), as quoted in "Trade Dollars Might Finance Military Power," by Robert L. Macginnis, *Los Angeles Times,* 22 May 2000, in *China: The Gathering Threat,* by Menges, p. 395.
6. *CIA–The World Factbook* s.v. "Malaysia"; *Country Profiles,* BBC News, s.v. "Malaysia."

7. *Philippines: A Country Study,* DA Pamphlet 550-72, Area Handbook Series (Washington, D.C.: Hdqts. Dept. of the Army, 1983), pp. 50, 51; Carl Hammer, *Tide of Terror* (Boulder, CO: Paladin Press, 2003), pp. 518, 521.
8. Daniel Ten Kate, "Thai Military Reformer Takes the Helm," *Christian Science Monitor,* 2 October 2006, p. 7; Gunaratna, *Inside al-Qaeda,* p. 202; Simon Montlake, "Malaysia's Ex-Leader Stays in the Game," *Christian Science Monitor,* 10 November 2006, p. 6; Simon Montlake, "Tension Grows between Thai Security Forces and Muslim Locals," *Christian Science Monitor,* 12 July 2005, pp. 7, 10; Carl Hammer, *Tide of Terror* (Boulder, CO: Paladin Press, 2003), p. 507; "The Emir" and "Gauging Jemaah Islamiyah's Threat in Southeast Asia," by Sharif Shuja, in *Unmasking Terror,* vol. I, ed. Heffelfinger, pp. 402, 403, 421.
9. "A New Wave of Violence Erupted in Muslim-Dominated Southern Thailand," World News in Brief, *Christian Science Monitor*, 3 February 2006, p. 7; Kate, "Thai Coup May Ease Violence in the South," p. 6.
10. Simon Montlake, "As Thai Insurgency Spreads, Government Opens Door to Dialogue," *Christian Science Monitor,* 25 April 2005.
11. "Violence Erupts in Southern Thailand," World Briefs Wire Reports (AP), *Jacksonville Daily News* (NC), 17 July 2005.
12. "A New Wave of Violence Erupted in Muslim-Dominated Southern Thailand," p. 7.
13. "Three Policemen Were Killed and Rail Service in Southern Thailand Was Disrupted," World News in Brief, *Christian Science Monitor*, 3 August 2006, p. 7.
14. Simon Montlake, "Thai Rebel Tactic: Divide the Faiths," *Christian Science Monitor,* 20 July 2005.
15. Kate, "Thai Military Reformer Takes the Helm," p. 7.
16. Montlake, "As Thai Insurgency Spreads, Government Opens Door to Dialogue."
17. Ibid.
18. Ibid.
19. Montlake, "Thai Rebel Tactic: Divide the Faiths."
20. Montlake, "As Thai Insurgency Spreads, Government Opens Door to Dialogue."
21. Kate, "Thai Military Reformer Takes the Helm," p. 7.
22. Kate, "Thai Coup May Ease Violence in the South," p. 6.
23. Montlake, "As Thai Insurgency Spreads, Government Opens Door to Dialogue."
24. Grant Peck, "Thailand's Military Ousts Prime Minister While He's in New York," *Jacksonville Daily News* (NC), 20 September 2006, p. 5A.

25. "New Political Parties Banned in Thailand," World Briefs Wire Reports (AP), *Jacksonville Daily News* (NC), 22 September 2006, p. 4A.
26. "The New Prime Minister of Thailand Said . . . ," World News in Brief, *Christian Science Monitor*, 19 October 2006, p. 7; "The Conciliatory Approach Taken by Thailand's Military," World News in Brief, *Christian Science Monitor*, 14 February 2007, p. 7; ABC's Morning News, 21 February 2007.
27. Evans and Rowley, *Red Brotherhood at War*, chapt. 7.
28. "Violence and Repression in Myanmar," PBS's *Frontline World,* NC Public TV, 31 October 2006; "Crackdown on Burmese Muslims," *Human Rights Watch Briefing Paper,* July 2002.
29. *Wikipedia Encyclopedia,* s.v. "Myanmar," "Burmese Way to Socialism," "Politics in Myanmar," and "Human Rights in Myanmar."
30. "Burma Road Map," National Geographic Society, 2003.
31. Fullbrook, "China to Europe via a New Burma Road."
32. *Wikipedia Encyclopedia,* s.v. "Administrative Divisions of Myanmar."
33. "Eastern Shan State Army (ESSA), Mong Tai Army (MTA), Myanmar National Democratic Alliance Army (MNDAA), United Wa State Army (UWSA)," *FAS Intelligence Resource Program,* 5 December, 1999, from its website, www.fas.org. (This work will henceforth be cited as "Eastern Shan State Army.")
34. *Wikipedia Encyclopedia,* s.v. "Burmese Way to Socialism."
35. "Eastern Shan State Army."
36. Azzam, as quoted in *Unholy War,* by Esposito, p. 7.
37. "Crackdown on Burmese Muslims."
38. Gunaratna, *Inside al-Qaeda,* pp. 204, 232.
39. "Crackdown on Burmese Muslims."
40. "Banned Bangladeshi Group Training Indian Extremists," *Hindustan Times* (New Delhi), 1 September 2004.
41. "The Roots of Extremist in Bangladesh," by Wilson John, and "The New Face of Al-Qaeda in Pakistan," in *Unmasking Terror,* vol. I, ed. Heffelfinger, pp. 298-306.

Chapter 3: *Southern Phillipines and Indonesia*

1. *Philippines: A Country Study,* p. 3.
2. Ibid., p. 25.
3. Ibid., p. 45.
4. Ibid., p. 50.
5. Carl Hammer, *Tide of Terror: America, Islamic Extremism, and the War on Terror* (Boulder, CO: Paladin Press, 2003), pp. 505-514; Gunaratna, *Inside al-Qaeda,* pp. 174, 183, 184; *Philippines: A Country Study,* pp. 50, 51.

6. *Philippines: A Country Study,* p. 4.
7. Ibid., p. 49.
8. Simon Montlake, "Where U.S. Is Gaining against Terror," *Christian Science Monitor,* 15 February 2007, pp. 1, 4; Simon Montlake, "Political Killings Traced to Philippine Military," *Christian Science Monitor,* 23 February 2007, p. 7.
9. Azzam, as quoted in *Unholy War,* by Esposito, p. 7.
10. *Wikipedia Encyclopedia,* s.v. "Bangamoro."
11. Hammer, *Tide of Terror,* pp. 505-514; Gunaratna, *Inside al-Qaeda,* pp. 174, 175, 183, 184.
12. Gunaratna, *Inside al-Qaeda*, pp. 178-181; Mir, *The True Face of Jihadis,* pp. 183, 184; "Sipah-e-Sahaba," by Animesh Roul, in *Unmasking Terror,* vol. I, ed. Heffelfinger, p. 314; "Comprehensive Report on Suspected Terrorist Support Network—Case Operations Kamikazi and Quarter Moon" (N.p., n.d.), p. 1, from *Inside al-Qaeda,* by Gunaratna, p. 178.
13. Gunaratna, *Inside al-Qaeda*, pp. 183.
14. Ibid., pp. 184-186.
15. National Commission on Terrorist Attacks upon the United States, chapt. 5 of its report, footnotes 59-61; "The Emir," in *Unmasking Terror,* vol. I, ed. Heffelfinger, pp. 402, 403.
16. Gunaratna, *Inside al-Qaeda,* p. 196.
17. *Wikipedia Encyclopedia,* s.v. "Oplan Bojinka" and "Ramzei Yousef"; "Path to 9/11," ABC News, 10 September 2006.
18. *Wikipedia Encyclopedia,* s.v. "Responsibility for the September 11, 2001 Attacks" and "Riduan Isamuddin"; "Profile: Al-Qaeda 'Kingpin'," BBC News, 28 September 2006; Erika Kinetz, "U.S. Congress Warms to Cambodia," *Christian Science Monitor,* 14 March 2007, p. 4.
19. "Mission in a War Zone," *Maryknoll Magazine,* January/February 2004, p. 25.
20. Ibid., pp. 24-28.
21. "Communist Party of Philippines/New People's Army (CPP/NPA)," *Terrorist Group Profiles,* Naval Postgraduate School, April 2006; *Philippines: A Country Study,* pp. xvii, xxix.
22. *Philippines: A Country Study*, pp. xvii, xxviii.
23. "Thousands of People Were Seeking Refuge in School Buildings," World News in Brief, *Christian Science Monitor,* 18 April 2007, p. 7.
24. "Abbu Sayyaf," *Terrorist Group Profiles,* Naval Postgraduate School, April 2006; Jim Gomez, AP, "Terrorists Train for Seaborne Attacks," *Seattle Post-Intelligencer,* 18 March 2005.
25. Gomez, "Terrorists Train for Seaborne Attacks."
26. J. Guinto, "President: MILF Has until June 1 to Cut Terror Links," *Philippine Daily Inquirer,* 13 May 2003.

27. Zachary Abuza, "Tentacles of Terror: Al Qaeda's Southeast Asian Network," *Contemporary Southeast Asia,* vol. 24, no. 3, 2002; Simon Montlake, "In Philippines, a Renewed Bid to Drive Out Terror Factions," *Christian Science Monitor,* 14 December 2004, p. 4.
28. *Wikipedia Encyclopedia,* s.v. "Moro Islamic Liberation Front."
29. "Islamist Rebels Ambushed Marines Looking for a Kidnapped . . . Priest", World News in Brief, *Christian Science Monitor,* 12 July 2007, p. 7.
30. Josef Polleross, "China Competes with West in Aid to Its Neighbors," New York Times, 18 September 2006.
31. Ian Story, "China and the Philippines: Moving beyond the South China Sea Dispute," Jamestown Foundation, *China Brief,* vol. VI, issue 17, 16 August 2006.
32. Robert A. Manning, *The Asia Energy Factor* (New York: Polygrave, 2000), in *China: The Gathering Threat,* by Menges, p. 379; Gertz, *The China Threat,* p. 187.
33. David G. Winneck, "The South China Sea Dispute Background Briefing," manuscript, 11 February 1999, in *China: The Gathering Threat,* by Menges, pp. 294-297.
34. Maria rost Rublee, "Foreign Policy Responses to Aggressive Territorial Moves: The Case of the Spratley Islands," *Internat. Affairs Review,* Summer 1996, in *China: The Gatheriing Threat,* by Menges, p. 295.
35. Winneck, "The South China Sea Dispute Background Briefing."
36. Ibid.; Richard Fisher, *PLA Modernization Gains Momentum* (N.p.: Heritage Foundation, 1997), p. 2, in *China: The Gathering Threat,* by Menges, pp. 294-297.
37. Menges, *China: The Gatheriing Threat,* p. 295.
38. Bill Gertz, "China Makes Upgrades to Island Base," *Washington Times,* 11 February 1999, p. A12, in *China: The Gathering Threat,* by Menges, pp. 294-297.
39. Ibid.
40. Pauline Jelinek, AP, "New Military Chiefs Have Know-How, New Outlook," *Jacksonville Daily News* (NC), 7 January 2007, p. 6A; "One of the Terrorist Leaders Most Wanted by U.S. Authorities," World News in Brief, *Christian Science Monitor,* 18 January 2007, p. 7.
41. Jean Duval, "The First Period of the Indonesian Communist Party (PKI): 1914-1926," Marxist.com, 12 April 2000; *Wikipedia Encyclopedia,* s.v. "Revolutionary Government of the Republic of Indonesia."
42. Menges, *China: The Gathering Threat,* p. 388; *Wikipedia Encyclopedia,* s.v. "Abdurrahman Wahid," "Indonesia," and "Susilo Bambang."
43. Josh Kurlantzick, "China's Charm Offensive in Southeast Asia," *Current History,* September 2006, republished by Carnegie Endowment for Internat. Peace.

44. Peter Stiff, *The Silent War: South African Recce Operations, 1969-1994* (Alberton, South Africa: Galago Publishing, 1999), p. 18.
45. Kurlantzick, "China's Charm Offensive in Southeast Asia."
46. "Chinese Missile Aid for Indonesia," Internat. Inst. for Strategic Studies (London), vol. 6, issue 6, August 2005.
47. Will Jourdin Penestanan Kelod, Opinion Piece, "Military Aid to Indonesia—Editorials and Commentary," *Internat. Herald Tribune,* 9 January 2006.
48. John M. Miller, Opinion Piece, "Military Aid to Indonesia—Editorials and Commentary," *Internat. Herald Tribune,* 9 January 2006.
49. U.S. Marine Colonel (company commander with British battalion in Malaysia in 1962), in military school graduation address the author attended about 1986; *Malaysia: A Country Study,* pp. 56-58.
50. *Wikipedia Encyclopedia,* s.v. "Communist Party of Indonesia."
51. Zachary Abuza, "Indonesians Infiltrate Southern Thailand's Insurgency," Jamestown Foundation, *Terrorism Focus,* vol. III, issue 27, 11 July 2006.
52. "A Breakdown of Southern Thailand's Insurgent Groups," by Zachary Abuza, in *Unmasking Terror: A Global Review of Terrorist Activities,* vol. III, ed. Jonathan D. Hutzley (Washington, D.C.: Jamestown Foundation, 2007), p. 355.
53. Simon Elegant, "Taking the Hard Road," *Time,* Asia Edition, 23 September 2002.
54. "Al-Qaeda Infrastructure in Indonesia," from *Inside al-Qaeda,* by Gunaratna, p. 200.
55. "Jemaah Islamiya (JI)," *Terrorist Group Profiles,* Naval Postgraduate School, April 2006.
56. Gomez, "Terrorists Train for Seaborne Attacks."
57. "Jemaah Islamiya (JI)," *Terrorist Group Profiles.*
58. National Commission on Terrorist Attacks upon the United States, chapt. 5 of its report, footnotes 59-61; "The Emir," in *Unmasking Terror,* vol. I, ed. Heffelfinger, pp. 402, 403; Simon Montlake, "Indonesian Terror Group Hobbled," *Christian Science Monitor,* 30 August 2005, p. 6; Nasir Abbas (captured *JI* operative turned informant), on CBS's "Sixty Minutes," 6 May 2007.
59. Ibid.
60. "Jemaah Islamiya (JI)," *Terrorist Group Profiles.*
61. "The Emir," in *Unmasking Terror,* ed. Heffelfinger, pp. 402, 403.
62. "Jemaah Islamiya (JI)," *Terrorist Group Profiles.*
63. Gunaratna, *Inside al-Qaeda*, pp. 184-186.
64. Jason Frenkel, "New Terror Target Warning," *Herald Sun* (Australia), 16 March 2005.

65. "Jemaah Islamiya (JI)," *Terrorist Group Profiles*.
66. Will Jourdin Penestanan Kelod and John M. Miller, Opinion Pieces, "Military Aid to Indonesia—Editorials and Commentary," *Internat. Herald Tribune,* 9 January 2006.
67. Carol Huang, "Al Qaeda in 2006," Briefing, *Christian Science Monitor,* 1 February 2007, p. 12; Nasir Abbas (captured *JI* operative turned informant), on CBS's "Sixty Minutes," 6 May 2007.
68. *Wikipedia Encyclopedia,* s.v. "Abdurrahman Wahid," "Indonesia," and "Susilo Bambang."
69. "Indonesian Backgrounder: Jihad in Central Sulawesi," *Internat. Crisis Group (Brussels) Asia Report No. 74,* 3 February 2004, p. 11.
70. Fabio Scarpello, "Indonesia's Jihadist Revival," *Christian Science Monitor,* 5 February 2007, p. 7.
71. *Wikipedia Encyclopedia,* s.v. "Mujahedeen KOMPAK."
72. Scarpello, "Indonesia's Jihadist Revival," p. 7.
73. "Gauging Jemaah Islamiyah's Threat in Southeast Asia," by Sharif Shuja, in *Unmasking Terror,* vol. I, ed. Heffelfinger, p. 421.
74. Ibid., p. 422.
75. Abdullah Sungkar and Abu Bakar Ba'asyir, letter to regional *jihadi* leaders, from "The Emir," in *Unmasking Terror,* vol. I, ed. Heffelfinger, p. 405.
76. The Emir," in *Unmasking Terror,* vol. I, ed. Heffelfinger, p. 403.
77. Ibid., pp. 402, 403.
78. Ibid., p. 392; Carl Hammer, *Tide of Terror,* pp. 517-520.
79. Carl Hammer, *Tide of Terror,* pp. 517-520.
80. Ibid.
81. "Gauging Jemaah Islamiyah's Threat in Southeast Asia," by Sharif Shuja, in *Unmasking Terror,* vol. I, ed. Heffelfinger, pp. 422, 423.
82. Ibid.
83. "No Survivors, Wreckage Found in Ferry Sinking," *Asian Economic News,* 3 July 2000.
84. "One of the Terrorist Leaders Most Wanted by U.S. Authorities," p. 7.
85. Zakki Hakim, AP, "Indonesian Jet Still Missing," *Jacksonville Daily News* (NC), 3 January 2007, p. 5A.
86. "Wednesday Brought Yet Another Major Transportation Accident to Indonesia," World News in Brief, *Christian Science Monitor*, 8 March 2007, p. 7.
87. *Washington Post* of 9 October 2001 and *Economist* of 20 October 2001, in *Tide of Terror,* by Hammer, p. 518.

88. "Out of the Woodwork," by Zachary Abuza, in *Unmasking Terror,* vol. I, ed. Heffelfinger, p. 416.
89. "Gauging Jemaah Islamiyah's Threat in Southeast Asia," by Sharif Shuja, in *Unmasking Terror,* vol I, ed. Heffelfinger, p. 423.
90. Scarpello, "Indonesia's Jihadist Revival," p. 7.
91. "Sipah-e-Sahaba," by Animesh Roul, in *Unmasking Terror,* vol. I, ed. Heffelfinger, p. 317.
92. "The Emir," in *Unmasking Terror,* vol. I, ed. Heffelfinger, p. 402.
93. "The Trial of Abu Bakar Ba'asyir," by Zachary Abuza, in *Unmasking Terror,* vol. I, ed. Heffelfinger, p. 427.
94. "Islamist Militant Groups Infiltrating the Relief Efforts in Aceh," by Stephen Ulph, in *Unmasking Terror,* vol. I, ed. Heffelfinger, p. 415.
95. Tom McCawley, "Indonesia's Terrorist Hunt Bears Fruit," *Christian Science Monitor,* 15 June 2007, p. 6.
96. Fareed Zakaria, "True or False: We Are Losing the War against Radical Islam," *Newsweek,* 2 July 2007, p. 38.
97. Bill Gertz, "China Makes Upgrades to Island Base," *Washington Times,* 11 February 1999, p. A12, in *China: The Gathering Threat,* by Menges, pp. 294-297.
98. "Gauging Jemaah Islamiyah's Threat in Southeast Asia," by Sharif Shuja, in *Unmasking Terror,* vol. I, ed. Heffelfinger, p. 421; "Jemaah Islamiya (JI)," *Terrorist Group Profiles,* Naval Postgraduate School, April 2006.
99. *CIA—TheWorld Factbook,* s.v. "Malaysia."
100. *Philippines: A Country Study,* pp. 50, 51.
101. Carl Hammer, *Tide of Terror*, pp. 507.
102. *Philippines: A Country Study,* pp. 50, 51.
103. Ibid., p. 4.
104. "Gauging Jemaah Islamiyah's Threat in Southeast Asia," by Sharif Shuja, in *Unmasking Terror*. vol. I, ed. Heffelfinger, p. 421.
105. *Wikipedia Encyclopedia,* s.v. "Abu Bakar Bashir."
106. "Great Expectations for Indonesia," *People's Daily* (Beijing), 17 August 2007, p. 18.
107. Energy Information Administration Map, from "A Natural-Gas Gang," *Time,* 16 April 2007, p. 16.
108. Ibid.
109. Scott Peterson, "Shiites Rising—Part One," *Christian Science Monitor,* 6 June 2007, pp. 1, 13-16.
110. Indonesian Army General Bambang Darmono, in interview with Orlando de Guzman, in "After the Wave," PBS's *Frontline World*, 26 June 2007.

Chapter 4: *Cambodia and Laos*

1. Nayan Chanda, *Brother Enemy: The War after the War* (New York: Collier Books, 1986), pp. 17, 18; Evans and Rowley, *Red Brotherhood at War,* p. 123.
2. *CIA—The World Factbook* s.v. "Cambodia"; Suzy Kim, "Saying I Do Willingly This Time," Backstory, *Christian Science Monitor,* 16 January 2007, p. 20.
3. Chanda, *Brother Enemy,* chapt. 10.
4. *CIA—The World Factbook* s.v. "Cambodia."
5. Ibid.
6. Tibor Krausz, "Cambodia's Healing History Lessons," *Christian Science Monitor,* 11 December 2006, p. 20.
7. *CIA—The World Factbook* s.v. "Cambodia."
8. Ibid.
9. *Country Profiles,* BBC News, s.v. "Cambodia."
10. "Profile: Hun Sen," BBC News, 15 July 2004.
11. Ibid.
12. Poole, "Terrorist Trail," Chapt. 10.
13. *CIA—The World Factbook* s.v. "Zimbabwe."
14. "Zimbabwe: Shadows and Lies," PBS's *Frontline / World,* NC Public TV, 27 June 2006.
15. Guy De Launey, "Cambodia's 'Out of Control' Evictions," BBC News, 29 September 2006.
16. "Khmer Rouge Judges Begin Work," BBC News, 4 July 2006.
17. Krausz, "Cambodia's Healing History Lessons," p. 20.
18. Memorandum for the record by H.J. Poole.
19. Guy De Launey, "Cambodia Clamps Down on Dissent," BBC News, 7 January 2006.
20. *CIA—The World Factbook* s.v. "Cambodia."
21. Adam Piore, "Cash-Strapped Cambodia Eyes Black Gold," *Christian Science Monitor,* 30 August 2006, p. 7.
22. Ibid.
23. *CIA—The World Factbook* s.v. "Cambodia."
24. Ibid., s.v. "Cambodia," "Malaysia," "Indonesia," "Laos," and "Burma."
25. Polleross, "China Competes with West in Aid to Its Neighbors."
26. "China Gives Cambodia $600m in Aid," BBC News, 8 April 2006, picture caption.
27. Ibid., main story.
28. Smith, "U.S. Bombs Chinese Network in Afghanistan, PRC Sold Taliban Advanced Air Defense System"; Malik, *Dragon on Terrorism,* p. 12.

29. Polleross, "China Competes with West in Aid to Its Neighbors."
30. "China Pledges $12.4 Million in Aid to Cambodia," *Asian Economic News,* 12 December, 2005.
31. "Cambodian PM denounces UN Envoy," BBC News, 29 March 2006.
32. *CIA—The World Factbook* s.v. "Laos"; *Country Profiles,* BBC News, s.v. "Laos."
33. Ibid.
34. Ibid.
35. *Encyclopedia of the Nations,* s.v. "Lao People's Democratic Republic"; *CIA—The World Factbook* s.v. "Laos."
36. Fullbrook, "China to Europe via a New Burma Road."
37. Ben Blanchard, Reuters, "Hu to Seal Laos Push at Vietnam Expense," *The Standard* (China's Business Newspaper), 18 November 2006.
38. "China Ready to Offer Aid to Build 3rd Bridge across Mekong River," *Asian Economic News,* 20 November 2006.
39. Elliott, "The Chinese Century," p. 34.
40. Raphael Perl, "Drug Trafficking and North Korea: Issues for U.S. Policy," Congressional Research Service Report RL32167 (Washington, D.C.: Library of Congress, 27 November 2006).
41. Lt.Col. Patrick Myers and Patrick Poole, "Hezbollah, Illegal Immigration, and the Next 9/11," *Front Page Magazine,* 28 April 2006.
42. "Militants Kill Five Afghans Involved in Opium Project," World News Wire Reports (AP), *Jacksonville Daily News* (NC), 19 May 2005, p. 5A; "Six Afghans Die in Rebel Ambush," World News Wire Reports (AP), *Jacksonville Daily News* (NC), 20 May 2005, p. 4A; Neamatollah Nojumi, *The Rise of the Taliban in Afghanistan: Mass Mobilization, Civil War, and the Future of the Region* (New York: Palgrave, 2002), pp. 135, 136.
43. *CIA—The World Factbook* s.v. "Laos."
44. David Fullbrook, "Beijing Pulls Laos into Its Orbit," Asia Times Online, 25 October 2006.
45. *CIA—The World Factbook* s.v. "China."
46. "China Recruits Young Volunteers to Work in Laos," *People's Daily* (China), 29 March 2002.
47. *Country Profiles,* BBC News, s.v. "Laos."
48. LoBaido, "China behind Christian persecution in S.E. Asia."
49. Ibid.
50. *Country Profiles,* BBC News, s.v. "Laos."
51. Frederic J. Frommer, "Anti-Terror Laws Keeping Out Old Vietnam War Allies," *Jacksonville Daily News* (NC), 21 February 2007, p. 4A.

Chapter 5: *Nepal and Bangladesh*

1. Dharma Adhikari, "Joy and Caution in Nepal's Peace Deal," *Christian Science Monitor,* 5 December 2006, p. 9.
2. "A Deal That Will Bring Communist Rebels into the Government of Nepal," World News in Brief, *Christian Science Monitor,* 10 November 2006, p. 7.
3. Bikash Sangraula, "Nepal's Decade of War Draws to a Close," *Christian Science Monitor,* 9 November 2006, p. 6.
4. Adhikari, "Joy and Caution in Nepal's Peace Deal," p. 9.
5. Bikash Sangraula, "Nepalese Hit the Streets—Again—for a Change," *Christian Science Monitor,* 27 June 2006, pp. 6, 7.
6. Adhikari, "Joy and Caution in Nepal's Peace Deal," p. 9.
7. Bikash Sangraula, "Nepal's Children Forced to Fight," *Christian Science Monitor,* 28 July 2006, p. 7.
8. "There Will Be No Year-End Strike in Nepal," World News in Brief, *Christian Science Monitor,* 26 December 2006, p. 7.
9. Bikash Sangraula, "Popular Protests Ignite Nepal," *Christian Science Monitor,* 11 April 2006, p. 6; Sangraula, "Nepal's Decade of War Draws to a Close," p. 6.
10. "A Two-Week Ultimatum Was Issued by Communists," World News in Brief, *Christian Science Monitor,* 3 May 2007, p. 7.
11. "India's Naxalites: A Spectre Haunting India," *The Economist,* 17 August 2006.
12. *Wikipedia Encyclopedia,* s.v. "History of Bangladesh."
13. David Montero, "Riots in Bangladesh May Benefit Islamists," *Christian Science Monitor,* 30 October 2006, p. 6.
14. Ibid.
15. Ibid.
16. David Montero, "Quiet Bangladesh Woken by Bombs," *Christian Science Monitor,* 18 August 2006, p. 6.
17. Sangraula, "Popular Protests Ignite Nepal," p. 6.
18. "Political Gatherings Were Banned in Bangladesh," World News in Brief, *Christian Science Monitor,* 20 November 2006, p. 7.
19. Ibid.
20. Montero, "Riots in Bangladesh May Benefit Islamists," p. 6.
21. Ibid.
22. Sangraula, "Nepal's Children Forced to Fight," p. 7.
23. Montero, "Riots in Bangladesh May Benefit Islamists," p. 6.
24. Poole, *Militant Tricks,* p. 128.
25. Montero, "Riots in Bangladesh May Benefit Islamists," p. 6.
26. "Banned Bangladeshi Group Training Indian Extremists."

27. "The Roots of Extremist in Bangladesh," by Wilson John, and "Extremist Mobilization in Bangladesh," by Kanchan Lakshman, in *Unmasking Terror,* vol. I, ed. Heffelfinger, pp. 298-304.
28. "Cops Seize Books from Abu Sayeed's House," *Daily Star* (Dakha), 19 February 2005, and "Political Violence, 1096 Killed in 52 Months," *New Nation* (Dakha), 17 March 2005, in "Extremist Mobilization in Bangladesh, by Kanchan Lakshman, in *Unmasking Terror,* vol. I, ed. Heffelfinger, p. 302.
29. *Wikipedia Encyclopedia,* s.v. "National Awami Party."
30. Ibid., s.v. "East Pakistan Communist Party (Marxist-Leninist)."
31. Ibid., s.v. "Communist Party of Pakistan."
32. Ibid.
33. Ibid., s.v. "Communist Party of Bangladesh."
34. Ibid.
35. Ibid., s.v. "Communist Party of Pakistan."
36. *Wikipedia Encyclopedia,* s.v. "Bangladesh Awami League."
37. "Bangladesh," *Library of Congress Country Studies* (Washington, D.C., 1988).
38. *Wikipedia Encyclopedia*, s.v. "Communist Party of Bangladesh."
39. "All Five Remaining Elections Commissioners in Bangladesh Quit," World News in Brief, *Christian Science Monitor,* 1 February 2007, p. 7.
40. Spinetta, "Cutting China's 'String of Pearls'," pp. 40-42.
41. David Montero, "China, Pakistan Team Up on Energy," *Christian Science Monitor,* 13 April 2007, p. 6.
42. *Wikipedia Encyclopedia*, s.v. "Bangladesh Awami League."
43. Spinetta, "Cutting China's 'String of Pearls'," pp. 40-42.

Chapter 6: *India and Sri Lanka*

1. "2002: Hindus Die in Train Fire," BBC News, 27 February 2002; *Wikipedia Encyclopedia,* s.v. "2002 Gujarat Violence."
2. Animesh Roul, "Trail from Mumbai Blasts Leads to Multiple Terrorist Groups," Jamestown Foundation, *Terrorism Focus,* vol. III, issue 29, 25 July 2006; "Parliament Suicide Attack Stuns India" and "2001: Suicide Attack on Indian Parliament," BBC News, 13 December 2001; *Wikipedia Encyclopedia,* s.v. "2001 Indian Parliament Attack."
3. Roul, "Trail from Mumbai Blasts Leads to Multiple Terrorist Groups."
4. "India's Naxalites."
5. "Background Note: Sri Lanka," U.S. Dept. of State, October 2006; *Wikipedia Encyclopedia,* s.v. "1971 Uprising."
6. Poole, *Terrorist Trail,* pp. 151-173.
7. Mark Sappenfield, "Bombs Fail to Ignite As Indian Imams Urge Calm," *Christian Science Monitor,* 14 September 2006, pp. 1, 11.

8. Randeep Ramesh, "Inside India's Hidden War," *The Guardian* (UK), 9 May 2006; *Wikipedia Encyclopedia,* s.v. "Naxalbari" and "Naxalite."
9. "India's Naxalites: A Spectre Haunting India."
10. Ramesh, "Inside India's Hidden War."
11. "Indian Security Forces Stepped Up Counterinsurgency Operations," World News in Brief, *Christian Science Monitor,* 8 January 2007, p. 7.
12. "India's Naxalites: A Spectre Haunting India."
13. Ramesh, "Inside India's Hidden War."
14. Anuj Chopra, "Maoist Rebels Spread across Rural India," *Christian Science Monitor,* 22 August 2006, p. 6.
15. *Wikipedia Encyclopedia,* s.v. "Naxalite."
16. Ibid., s.v. "West Bengal" and "Kolkata."
17. Ibid., s.v. "West Bengal" and "Kolkata."
18. Ibid., s.v. "Sino-Indian War."
19. Ibid., s.v. "Xinjiang."
20. Ramesh, "Inside India's Hidden War."
21. McGuire, *Dragon in the Dark,* p. 202.
22. "Banned Bangladeshi Group Training Indian Extremists."
23. *CIA—The World Factbook* s.v. "Sri Lanka."
24. Ibid.
25. *Wikipedia Encyclopedia,* s.v. "Janatha Vimukthi Perumuna (JVP)."
26. *CIA—The World Factbook* s.v. "Sri Lanka."
27. *Wikipedia Encyclopedia,* s.v. "Janatha Vimukthi Perumuna (JVP)."
28. Ibid.
29. Ibid.
30. Ibid.
31. Ibid.
32. Ibid.; *CIA—The World Factbook* s.v. "Sri Lanka."
33. *Country Profiles,* BBC News, s.v. "Sri Lanka: Timeline."
34. *Wikipedia Encyclopedia,* s.v. "Tamil Nadu" and "Mughal Empire."
35. "No More Tears Sister," PBS's *Point of View*, NC Public TV, 27 June 2006.
36. *Country Profiles,* BBC News, s.v. "Sri Lanka: Timeline."
37. "Liberation Tigers of Tamil Eelam (LTTE)," *Country Reports on Terrorism, 2005* (Washington, D.C.: U.S. Dept. of State, April 2006); "No More Tears Sister."
38. *Country Profiles,* BBC News, s.v. "Sri Lanka: Timeline."
39. "Liberation Tigers of Tamil Eelam (LTTE)"; "No More Tears Sister."
40. Ibid; *Country Profiles,* BBC News, s.v. "Sri Lanka."
41. "Liberation Tigers of Tamil Eelam (LTTE)."
42. *Country Profiles,* BBC News, s.v. "Sri Lanka,"
43. *Country Profiles,* BBC News, s.v. "Sri Lanka: Timeline."
44. "No More Tears Sister."
45. "Liberation Tigers of Tamil Eelam (LTTE)."

46. *CIA—The World Factbook* s.v. "Sri Lanka."
47. "Liberation Tigers of Tamil Eelam (LTTE)."
48. Anuj Chopra, "Sri Lankan Talks a Welcome Step for Weary Observers," *Christian Science Monitor,* 30 October 2006, p. 4.
49. "A Truck Packed with Explosives and Driven by Tamil Separatist," World News in Brief, *Christian Science Monitor,* 17 October 2006.
50. *Country Profiles,* BBC News, s.v. "Sri Lanka: Timeline."
51. "Liberation Tigers of Tamil Eelam (LTTE)."
52. Ibid.
53. "No More Tears Sister."
54. *Country Profiles,* BBC News, s.v. "Sri Lanka."
55. *CIA—The World Factbook* s.v. "Sri Lanka."
56. "Sri Lanka Offers Oil Block to India in Return for Construction of Railway," *Sri Lanka Newspapers,* 30 January 2007.

Chapter 7: *Pakistan and Afghanistan*

1. David Montero, "Pakistan: Delicate Dance of a Key Ally," *Christian Science Monitor,* 26 September 2006, pp. 1, 11.
2. David Montero, "In Border Zone, Pakistan Backs Off from Taliban," *Christian Science Monitor,* 26 September 2006, pp. 1, 5.
3. Gunaratna, *Inside al-Qaeda,* p. 40.
4. Ali Jalali and Lester W. Grau, *Afghan Guerrilla Warfare: In the Words of the Mujahideen Fighters* (St. Paul, MN: MBI Publishing, 2001), first published as *The Other Side of the Mountain* (Quantico, VA: Marine Corps Combat Development Cmd., 1995), p. 409.
5. Interviews with Pakistani religious party recruits and Taliban prisoners during 1999, in "Afghanistan: Crisis of Impunity," by Robin Batty and David Hoffman, *Human Rights Watch,* vol. 13, no. 3(c), July 2001, p. 29.
6. Montero, "Pakistan: Delicate Dance of a Key Ally," p. 11.
7. Khaled Ahmed, *Pakistan: Behind the Ideological Mask* (Lahore: Vanguard, 2004), p. 223; Mir, *The True Face of Jihadis,* p. 21.
8. Montero, "Pakistan: Delicate Dance of a Key Ally," p. 11.
9. Zulfiqar Ahmad, "Intra-MMA Friction Swells over NSC," *Daily Mail* (Islamabad), 30 May 2005, pp. 1, 5; Mir, *The True Face of Jihadis,* p. 95; Ben Arnoldy and Owais Tohid, "Why Koran Is Such a Hot Button," *Christian Science Monitor,* 16 May 2005, pp. 6, 7.
10. Montero, "Pakistan: Delicate Dance of a Key Ally," p. 11.

11. "Return of the Taliban," PBS's *Frontline,* NC Public TV, 8 January 2007; David Montero, "Attacks Heat Up Afghan-Pakistani Border, *Christian Science Monitor,* 12 January 2007, p. 6; ABC's Nightly News, 25 February 2007; Munir Ahmad (AP), "Pakistan President Denies Claim bin Laden Hiding inside Nation," *Jacksonville Daily News* (NC), 1 March 2007, p. 5A; Howard LaFranchi, "Pakistan: U.S. Ally, U.S. Dilemma," *Christian Science Monitor,* 29 March 2007, pp. 1, 10.
12. Montero, "Pakistan: Delicate Dance of a Key Ally," p. 11.
13. Montero, "In Border Zone, Pakistan Backs Off from Taliban," p. 5.
14. "Return of the Taliban."
15. Ibid.; Gunaratna, "Inside Al Qaeda," p. 42.
16. "Return of the Taliban."
17. Mannes, *Profiles in Terror,* p. 67; Mir, *The True Face of Jihadis,* p. 105.
18. Mir, *The True Face of Jihadis,* pp. 183, 184; "Lashkar-e-Jhangvi: Sectarian Violence in Pakistan and Ties to International Terrorism," by Animesh Roul, in *Unmasking Terror,* vol. I, ed. Heffelfinger, pp. 97, 325-329.
19. Khaled Ahmed, *Pakistan: Behind the Ideological Mask* (Lahore: Vanguard, 2004), p. 223; Mir, *The True Face of Jihadis,* p. 21.
20. David Montero, "The Bribe to Exit Pakistan," *Christian Science Monitor,* 30 April 2006, p. 5; "Return of the Taliban."
21. NPR's Morning News, 16 July 2007.
22. David Montero, "In Talks with India, Pressure Is on Pakistan," *Christian Science Monitor,* 15 November 2006, p. 6; Randeep Ramesh, "PM Accuses Pakistan over Mumbai Bombs," The Guardian (U.K.), 14 July 2006; Lamb, "Britain Says Pakistan Is Hiding Taliban Chief"; David Montero, "More Evidence of Taliban Leader Hiding in Pakistan," *Christian Science Monitor,* 19 January 2007, pp. 1, 4, 5; "Karzai Accuses Pakistan of Backing Taliban Insurgents," News Digest Wire Reports (AP), *Jacksonville Daily News* (NC), 13 December 2006, p. 2A.
23. Benazir Bhutto, "The Price of Dictatorship," *The Guardian* (UK), 23 August 2006, reprinted from "Only Democracy Can Break Pakistan Terror Link," by Benazir Bhutto, The Tribune (Chicago), Global Viewpoint, 16 August 2006.
24. Montero, "China, Pakistan Team Up on Energy," p. 6.
25. "Musharraf Opposes Ex-PM's Return," by the Agencies, *China Daily* (Beijing), 13 August 2007, p. 5.
26. Malik, *Dragon on Terrorism,* p. 5.
27. Robert D. Kaplan, *Soldiers of God: With Islamic Warriors in Afghanistan and Pakistan,* revised ed. (New York: Vintage Books, 2001), p. 217; Gunaratna, *Inside al-Qaeda,* p. 40.
28. Malik, *Dragon on Terrorism,* table 1.

29. Bill Gertz, "China-Made Artillery Seized in Afghanistan," *Washington Times,* 12 April 2002.
30. Scott Baldauf, "How Al Qaeda Seeks to Buy Chinese Arms," *Christian Science Monitor,* 23 August 2002; Malik, *Dragon on Terrorism,* table 1.
31. Gertz and Scarborough, "China-Trained Taliban."
32. Smith, "U.S. Bombs Chinese Network in Afghanistan, PRC Sold Taliban Advanced Air Defense System"; Malik, *Dragon on Terrorism,* p. 12.
33. McGuire, *Dragon in the Dark,* p. 10; Malik, *Dragon on Terrorism,* p. 12.
34. "China Moves Forces into Afghanistan," *DEBKAfile,* 6 October 2001; Malik, *Dragon on Terrorism,* p. 5.
35. "China Moves Forces into Afghanistan."
36. "Chinese-Made Ammo in al Qaeda Caves Confirms," *DEBKAfile,* 17 December 2001.
37. McGuire, *Dragon in the Dark,* pp. 127-150, 208; *Wikipedia Encyclopedia,* s.v. "East Turkestan."
38. "East Turkestan Islamic Movement (ETIM)," by Seva Gunitskiy, Center for Defense Info., 9 December 2002.
39. Ibid.; *Wikipedia Encyclopedia,* s.v. "East Turkestan Islamic Movement (ETIM)"; *Washington Post,* 27 August 2002, in *Tide of Terror,* by Hammer, p. 485.
40. "East Turkestan Islamic Movement (ETIM)."
41. Michael A. Lev, "U.S. Holds 300 Chinese Extremists, Beijing Says," *Chicago Tribune,* 28 May 2002, p. 5.
42. Gertz and Scarborough, "China-Trained Taliban."
43. Scott Baldauf, "How Al Qaeda Seeks to Buy Chinese Arms," *Christian Science Monitor*, 23 August 2002.
44. "Chinese-Made Ammo in al Qaeda Caves Confirms."
45. Scott Baldauf, "Al Qaeda Massing for New Fight," *Christian Science Monitor,* 9 August 2002.
46. Gertz, "China-Made Artillery Seized in Afghanistan."
47. Malik, *Dragon on Terrorism,* p. 9, table 1.
48. "Al Qaeda Has Drones," Agence France-Presse, 13 September 2005.
49. Bill Gertz, "China Trained Taliban and al-Qaeda Fighters Says U.S. Intel.," as posted 22 June 2002 on www.rense.com.
50. Abdel Bari Atwan, *The Secret History of Al-Qa'ida* (London: Abacus, an imprint of Little, Brown Book Group, 2006), p. 122.
51. James Millward, "Violent Separatism in Xinjiang: A Critical Assessment," East-West Center Washington, *Policy Study 6,* n.d.; Malik, *Dragon on Terrorism,* p. 26.

52. Yitzhah Shichor, Central Asia-Caucasus Institute, Silk Road Studies Program, "Fact and Fiction: A Chinese Documentary on Eastern Turkestan Terrorism," *China and Eurasia Forum Quarterly,* vol. 4, no. 2, 2006, pp. 89-108.
53. Martha Olcott, "The Great Powers in Central Asia," Carnegie Endowment for Internat. Peace (Moscow Center), October 2006.
54. Mark Sexton (U.S. Special Forces multi-tour returnee from Afghanistan in September 2006), in series of telephone conversations with author between 26 September 2006 and 1 February 2007.
55. Kathleen E. McLaughlin, "Centuries-Old Partnership Binds China, Iran Together," *San Francisco Chronicle,* 18 September 2006; *Wikipedia Encyclopedia,* s.v. "Military of Pakistan."
56. "Chinese Company gets EU Afghan Road Contract," DAWN Group of Newspapers (Pakistan), 2 December 2003; "Karzai Attends Starting Ceremony of Road Project," Pakistani News Service, 28 August 2006; "Chinese Gunned Down in Afghanistan," CNN, 10 June 2004; "Chinese Company to Reconstruct Afghan Road," *People's Daily* (China), 28 August 2006.
57. "Chinese Gunned Down in Afghanistan"; Sexton phone calls.
58. Sexton phone calls.
59. Globalsecurity.org, s.v. "Bamian."
60. *Wikipedia Encyclopedia,* s.v. "Hazara"; H.E. Mu. Mohsen Amiuzadeh (Deputy Minister of External Affairs of Asia-Oceania of the Islamic Republic of Iran), Special Address to the Federation of Indian Chambers of Commerce and Industry (New Dehli, 22 July 2003).
61. *Wikipedia Encyclopedia,* s.v. "Uyghur."
62. ABC's Nightly News, 7 December 2006.
63. *Wikipedia Encyclopedia,* s.v. "Pakistan-Administered Kashmir."
64. Ibid., s.v. "Tibet."
65. Ibid., s.v. "Aksai Chin."
66. Ibid., s.v. "Jammu-Kashmir."
67. "Xinjiang," by Hayder Mili, in *Unmasking Terror,* vol. I, ed. Heffelfinger, p. 347.
68. Ibid., s.v. "Karakoram Highway."
69. "China Moves Forces into Afghanistan."
70. Baldauf, "Al Qaeda Massing for New Fight."
71. "Osama's Secret Citadel," *DEBKA-Net-Weekly,* 28 September 2001.
72. Fred Weir, "Big Powers Jockey for Oil in Central Asia," *Christian Science Monitor*, 28 March 2007, pp. 1, 12.
73. Pepe Escobar, "The Roving Eye," *Asia Times,* 4 October 2001.
74. "Osama's Secret Citadel."
75. Richard Clarke (former U.S. antiterrorism czar), on ABC's Morning News, 7 June 2007.
76. Jason Straziuso, AP, "Afghan Bomber Deadlier," *Jacksonville Daily News* (NC), 3 June 2007, pp. 1A, 8A.

77. Richard Clarke, on ABC's Morning News, 7 June 2007.
78. ABC's Nightly News, 6 June 2007.
79. "Military: Iran Teaching Iraqi Militia to Build Bombs," from AP, *Jacksonville Daily News* (NC), 12 April 2007, p. 5A; Peterson, "Shiites Rising—Part One," pp. 1, 13-16.
80. Poole, *Militant Tricks,* pp. 139-141.
81. Graham, "Latest Assault Leaves 2 Brits, Afghan Interpreter Dead," p. 8A.
82. Kochay and Rahim, as quoted in *Afghan Guerrilla Warfare,* by Jalali and Grau, pp. 59-61 and p. 21, respectively; Poole, *Phantom Soldier,* p. 138.
83. "Inside America's Empire," PBS's *America at a Crossroads,* NC Public TV, 11 September 2007.
84. "China's Global Reach," *Christian Science Monitor,* 30 January 2007, p. 13; Weir, "Big Powers Jockey for Oil in Central Asia," p. 1.

Chapter 8: *What Hasn't Worked in the Past*

1. Gregory Fremont-Barnes, *The Boer War: 1899-1902* (Oxford, England: Osprey, 2003), p. 64.
2. *Philippines: A Country Study,* p. 25.
3. Simon Montlake, "U.S. Troops in Philippines Defy Old Stereotype," *Christian Science Monitor,* 1 March 2007, p. 7.
4. *Philippines: A Country Study,* p. 45.
5. *Malaysia: A Country Study*, pp. 50-59.
6. Poole, *Terrorist Trail,* p. 152.
7. *The Battle of Dien Bien Phu,* Visions of War Series, vol 10 (New Star Video, 1988), 50 min., videocassette #4010.
8. Gen. Vo Nguyen Giap, *Dien Bien Phu,* 6th ed. supplemented (Hanoi: Gioi Publishers, 1999), p. 113.
9. P.C. Smith (Marine platoon sergeant during the Vietnam War), in conversation with the author in December 2006.
10. Reid-Daly, *Pamwe Chete,* p. ii.
11. ZANU HQ, Chimoio, "Report on the Massacre at Nyadzonya by the Rhodesian Forces on 9 August 1976," dated 19 August 1976 (captured by the SAS during Chimoio Raid on 23/11/1977), in *Pamwe Chete,* by Lt.Col. R.F. Reid-Daly, pp. 241-247.
12. Poole, *Terrorist Trail,* pp. 185-187.
13. Montlake, "U.S. Troops in Philippines Defy Old Stereotype," p. 7.
14. Poole, *Phantom Soldier,* chapt. 13.
15. Haha Lung, *Nights of Darkness: Secrets of the World's Deadliest Night Fighters* (Boulder, CO: Paladin Press, 1998), pp. 8, 9.
16. Poole, *Phantom Soldier,* chapt. 13.
17. Menges, *China—The Gathering Threat,* p. 328.

18. *Wikipedia Encyclopedia,* s.v. "People's Liberation Army"; *Chinese Defense Today* (www.sinodefence.com), s.v. "Home Ground Forces Order of Battle."
19. Ibid.; *CIA—The World Factbook,* s.v. "China."
20. Bermudez, *North Korean Special Forces,* p. 147.
21. Sexton phone calls.
22. Ahmed Rashid, "Losing the War on Terror: Why Militants Are Beating Technology Five Years After Sept. 11," *Washington Post,* 11 September 2006, p. A-17.
23. Nicholas Blanford, Daniel McGrory, and Stephen Farrell, "Tactics That Have Kept the Middle East's Most Powerful Army at Bay," *The Times* (UK), 10 August 2006; Cody and Moore, "Analysts Attribute Hezbollah's Resilience to Zeal, Secrecy and Iranian Funding."
24. Ibid.; Kevin Peraino, Babak Dehghanpisheh, and Christopher Dickey, "Eye for an Eye," *Newsweek,* 14 August 2006, p. 22; Ravi Nessman, AP, "Israelis Step Up Offensive," *Jacksonville Daily News* (NC), 10 August 2006, p. 2A.
25. Rashid, "Losing the War on Terror, p. A-17.
26. Suzanna Koster, "Taliban Fighters Talk Tactics While Safe in Pakistan," *Christian Science Monitor,* 9 November 2006, pp. 1, 10; Ron Moreau, Sami Yousafzai, and Michael Hirsh, "The Rise of Jihadistan," *Newsweek,* 2 October 2007, pp. 24-28.
27. Ibid.
28. "Taliban Forces Are Regrouping in Afghanistan," World Briefs Wire Reports (AP), *Jacksonville Daily News* (NC), 15 September 2006, p. 5A.
29. Rashid, "Losing the War on Terror, p. A-17.
30. Koster, "Taliban Fighters Talk Tactics While Safe in Pakistan," pp. 1, 10.
31. Ibid.

Chapter 9: *The Law Enforcement Factor*

1. J. Mark Hord, "Review of Terrorist Trail," as posted at www.d-n-i.net and g2-forward.org on 31 January 2007.
2. His Holiness John Paul II, *Crossing the Threshold of Hope* (New York: Alfred A. Knopf, 1995), pp. 205, 206.
3. Naval Investigative Service website (www.ncis.navy.mil), s.v. "Join NIS."

Chapter 10: *A Thorough Investigation*

1. Memorandum for the record by H. J. Poole.

2. Bill D. Ross, *Iwo Jima: Legacy of Valor* (New York: Vintage Books, 1986), p. 341.
3. *Random House Encyclopedia,* electronic ed., s.v. "Shi'a," "Imamis," and "Isma'ilis."
4. *Wikipedia Encyclopedia,* s.v. "Wahhabi" and "Salafi."
5. Vernon J. Geberth, *Practical Homicide Investigation: Tactics, Procedures, and Techniques,* fourth Edition (Boca Raton, FL: CRC Press, 2006), pp. 572, 573.
6. Ibid., pp. 179, 180.
7. Ibid.
8. Ibid., pp. 180, 974.
9. Ibid., pp. 572, 573.
10. Karen Breslau, "A Cold Case Warms Up," Periscope, *Newsweek,* 19 March 2007, p. 10.
11. Geberth, *Practical Homicide Investigation,* pp. 574-590, 948
12. Ibid., p. 609.
13. Ibid., p. 705.
14. Poole, *Terrorist Trail,* chapt. 14.
15. Geberth, *Practical Homicide Investigation,* p. 623.
16. Ibid., pp. 714-718.
17. Ibid., pp. 188-192.
18. Ibid., p. 45.
19. Ibid., pp. 182-184.
20. Connie Fletcher, *Every Contact Leaves a Trace* (New York: St. Martin's Press, 2006), pp. 59, 103.

Chapter 11: *Pursuit and Arrest*

1. Memorandum for the record by H.J. Poole.
2. Ibid.
3. James Corbett, *Jungle Lore* (London: Oxford Univ. Press, 1953), p. 172.
4. Geberth, Practical Homicide Investigation, p. 938.
5. Ibid., p. 939.
6. Ibid.
7. Ibid.
8. Ibid., p. 940.

Chapter 12: The Sting

1. Ian Munro, "Covert Police Methods Revealed," and "Lawyers Warn against Police Stings," *The Age* (Melbourne), 8 and 9 September 2004.
2. Dan Creedon, "Standardize Police Sting Operations," HB 3162, *Oil Can, The* (N.p.), first quarter 2002.
3. John F. Smith, James R. Sheridan, and Dennis F. Yurcisin, *How to Set Up and Run a Successful Law Enforcement Sting Operation* (Upper Saddle River, NJ: Prentice Hall, n.d.)
4. "State, Federal Law Enforcers Launch Sting on Business Opportunity, Work-at-Home Scams," Federal Trade Commission, Office of Public Affairs, 20 June 2002.
5. Leroy Thompson, *Dirty Wars: Elite Forces vs. the Guerrillas* (Devon, England: David & Charles, 1991).
6. Sexton phone calls.
7. Poole, *Militant Tricks,* pp. 233-256.
8. Eliza Griswold, "Waging Peace in the Philippines," *Smithsonian,* December 2006.
9. Ibid.
10. M.J. Orr, "Better or Not So Bad? An Evaluation of Russian Combat Effectiveness in the Second Chechen War," chapt. 7 of "The Second Chechen War," *P31,* ed. Mrs. A.C. Aldis (Sandhurst, UK: Conflict Studies Research Centre, June 2000), pp. 96, 97.

Chapter 13: *The Only Defense Is Unconventional*

1. "20/20," CBS News, 18 March 2007.
2. DA Pamphlet 30-51, *Handbook on the Chinese Communist Army* (Washington, D.C.: Hdqts. Dept. of the Army, 7 December 1960), p. 74.
3. TM-E 30-480, Handbook on Japanese Military Forces (Washington, D.C.: U.S. War Dept., 1944; reprint Baton Rouge, LA: LSU Press, 1991), pp. 210-212.
4. *Handbook on German Military Forces,* TM-E 30-451, (Washington, D.C.: U.S. War Dept., 1945; reprint Baton Rouge, LA: LSU Press, 1990), pp. 402, 403.
5. *The Bear Went over the Mountain: Soviet Combat Tactics in Afghanistan*, trans. and ed. by Lester W. Grau, Foreign Mil. Studies Office, U.S. Dept. of Defense, Lt. Leavenworth, KS (Washington, D.C.: Nat. Defense Univ. Press, 1996), p. 97.

6. Rod Nordland, "Walk through Fire," *Newsweek,* 9 April 2007, pp. 40, 41; Dexter Filkins, "In Iraq, Armed Police Carry Out Militias' Work," *International Herald Tribune,* 25 May 2006, p. 4; interview of Western journalist of Iraqi descent, PBS's *News Hour with Jim Lehrer,* 22 May 2006; Tom Lasseter, Knight Ridder, "Iraqi Forces May Need Years of Preparation," *Jacksonville Daily News* (NC), 28 August 2005, p. 5A; Steven Vincent, "Shiites Bring Rigid Piety to Iraq's South," *Christian Science Monitor,* 13 July 2005; Steven Vincent, "Switched Off in Basra," *New York Times,* 31 July 2005.
7. *McGraw-Hill Dictionary of Scientific and Technical Terms* (2003), s.v. "unconventional warfare."
8. *U.S. Department of Defense Dictionary of Military and Associated Words, 2003,* s.v. "unconventional warfare."
9. *Wikipedia Encyclopedia,* s.v. "unconventional warfare."
10. *Unrestricted Warfare,* by Qiao Liang and Wang Xiangsui.
11. Poole, *The Tiger's Way: A U.S. Private's Best Chance of Survival* (Emerald Isle, NC: Posterity Press, 2003), pp. 167-173.

Chapter 14: *Finding an Enemy Weakness*

1. Jalali and Grau, *Afghan Guerrilla Warfare,* p. 404.
2. Brigadier Mohammad Yousaf and Maj. Mark Adkin, *Bear Trap: Afghanistan's Untold Story* (South Yorkshire, UK: Leo Cooper, n.d.).
3. Memorandum for the record by H.J. Poole.
4. Charles Soard (experienced infantry scout and frequent visitor to Vietnam), in telephone conversation with author, 28 March 2001.
5. Michael Lee Lanning and Dan Cragg, *Inside the VC and the NVA: The Real Story of North Vietnam's Armed Forces* (New York: Ivy Books, 1992), p. 211.
6. Memorandum for the record by H.J. Poole.
7. Poole, *The Tiger's Way,* tables 2.2 and 24.1.
8. Michael O'Brien, *Conscripts and Regulars: With the Seventh Battalion in Vietnam* (St. Leonards, Australia: Allen & Unwin, 1995), p. 215; Lanning and Cragg, *Inside the VC and the NVA,* pp. 55, 56; James F. Dunnigan and Albert A. Nofi, *Dirty Little Secrets of the Vietnam War* (New York: Thomas Dunne Books, 1999), pp. 276-279.
9. Bermudez, *North Korean Special Forces,* pp. 233, 234, 247, 248; *Inside North Korea: Three Decades of Duplicity* (Seoul: Inst. of Internal and External Affairs, 1975), p. 74.

10. Nguyen Van Mo, 40th Mine Sapper Battalion, as quoted in *Portrait of the Enemy,* by David Chanoff and Doan Van Toai (New York: Random House, 1986), pp. 161, 162.
11. Reconnaissance sapper, 261st VC Battalion, as quoted in Lanning and Cragg, *Inside the VC and the NVA,* pp. 211, 212.

Chapter 15: *Obscure Approach*

1. Poole, *The Tiger's Way,* tables 2.2 and 24.1.
2. O'Brien, *Conscripts and Regulars,* p. 215; Lanning and Cragg, *Inside the VC and the NVA,* pp. 55, 56; Dunnigan and Nofi, *Dirty Little Secrets of the Vietnam War,* pp. 276-279.
3. Bermudez, *North Korean Special Forces,* pp. 233, 234, 247, 248; *Inside North Korea,* p. 74.
4. Masaaki Hatsumi, *The Essence of Ninjutsu* (Chicago: Contemporary Books, 1988), pp. 15, 53-61; Lung, *Nights of Darkness,* pp. 70-74.
5. "Hypnosis," chapt. in *The Complete Manual of Physical Fitness and Well-Being* (Pleasantville, NY: The Reader's Digest Assoc., 1984), p. 330.
6. Memorandum for the record by H.J. Poole.

Chapter 16: *Disguising the Attack*

1. Memorandum for the record by H.J. Poole
2. Dunnigan and Nofi, *Dirty Little Secrets of the Vietnam War,* p. 279.
3. Keith William Nolan, *Sappers in the Wire: The Life and Death of Firebase Mary Ann* (College Station, TX: Texas A&M Univ. Press, 1995), p. 123.
4. Poole, *The Tiger's Way,* tables 2.2 and 24.1.
5. O'Brien, *Conscripts and Regulars,* p. 215; Lanning and Cragg, *Inside the VC and the NVA,* pp. 55, 56; Dunnigan and Nofi, *Dirty Little Secrets of the Vietnam War,* pp. 276-279.
6. Bermudez, *North Korean Special Forces,* pp. 233, 234, 247, 248; *Inside North Korea,* p. 74.
7. Memorandum for the record by H.J. Poole.
8. Lung, *Knights of Darkness,* p. 73.
9. Poole, *One More Bridge to Cross,* chapt. 11.
10. Memorandum for the record by H.J. Poole.
11. *Handbook on Japanese Military Forces,* TM-E 30-480 (Washington, D.C.: U.S. War Dept., 1944; reprint Baton Rouge, LA: LSU Press, 1991), p. 117.

12. William P. Baxter, *Soviet Airland Battle Tactics* (Novato, CA: Presidio Press, 1986), p. 104.
13. Poole, *The Tiger's Way,* p. 66.

Chapter 17: *Precluding the Counterstroke*

1. Poole, *The Tiger's Way,* tables 2.2 and 24.1.
2. O'Brien, *Conscripts and Regulars,* p. 215; Lanning and Cragg, *Inside the VC and the NVA,* pp. 55, 56; Dunnigan and Nofi, *Dirty Little Secrets of the Vietnam War,* pp. 276-279.
3. Bermudez, *North Korean Special Forces,* pp. 233, 234, 247, 248; *Inside North Korea,* p. 74.
4. Memorandum for the record by H.J. Poole.
5. *NVA-VC Small Unit Tactics & Techniques Study, Part I,* U.S.A.R.V., ed. Thomas Pike (Washington, D.C.: Archival Publishing, 1997), p. VI-5.
6. Bruce I. Gudmundsson, *Stormtroop Tactics—Innovation in the German Army 1914-1918* (New York: Praeger, 1989), pp. 146-149.
7. Nguyen Khac Can and Pham Viet Thuc, *The War 1858 - 1975 in Vietnam* (Hanoi: Nha Xuat Ban Van Hoa Dan Toc, n.d.), figs. 544 and 510.
8. Ibid., fig. 557.
9. *NVA-VC Small Unit Tactics & Techniques Study, Part I,* U.S.A.R.V., ed. Thomas Pike, p. X-5.
10. Can and Thuc, *The War 1858-1975 in Vietnam,* figs. 556, 557, and 565.
11. "Platoon," written and directed by Oliver Stone, produced by Hemdale Film Corp., Metro Goldwyn Mayer Home Entertainment, 1986, 1 hour, 59 min., videocassette #M208119.
12. Keith William Nolan, *Operation Buffalo: USMC Fight for the DMZ* (Novato, CA: Presidio Press, 1983), p. 79; Poole, *Phantom Soldier,* pp. 135, 136.
13. *Wikipedia Encyclopedia,* s.v. "flying column."
14. Poole, *One More Bridge to Cross,* chapt. 11.
15. *Jungle Warfare,* FMFRP 12-9 (Quantico, VA: Marine Corps Combat Development Cmd., 1989), p. 41.
16. Poole, *One More Bridge to Cross,* chapt. 11.

Chapter 18: *Rural Escape and Evasion*

1. ABC's Nightly News, 28 June, 10 July 2005; ABC's Morning News, 29, 30 June 2005; Daniel Cooney, AP, "Military Reveals Details of Crash," *Jacksonville Daily News* (NC), 7 July 2005, p. 4A.

2. "One-Point, Two-Sides Attack on Defensive Position," *Handbook on the Chinese Communist Army,* DA Pam 30-51, (Washington, D.C.: Hdqts. Dept. of the Army, 1960), p. 24; Poole, *Phantom Soldier,* fig. 7-1, p. 103.
3. *Mao Tse-Tung: An Anthology of His Writings,* ed. Anne Fremantle (New York: Mentor, 1962), pp. 132, 133.
4. Ibid.
5. Ibid., p. 125.
6. Poole, *The Tiger's Way,* pp. 168-173.
7. "Return with Honor," PBS's *American Experience,* NC Public TV, April 2007.
8. S.Sgt. Lee Bergee and PFC Fred Davidson, as quoted in *The Korean War: Pusan to Chosin, an Oral History,* by Donald Knox (San Diego: Harcourt Janovich, 1985), pp. 289-291.
9. Poole, *Tactics of the Crescent Moon,* p. 23.
10. Memorandum for the record by H.J. Poole.
11. *Night Movements,* trans. and preface by C. Burnett (Port Townsend, WA: Loompanics Unlimited, n.d.), originally published as Japanese training manual (Tokyo: Imperial Japanese Army, 1913), p. 73. (This work will henceforth be cited as *Night Movements.)*
12. Edward J. Drea, "Nomonhan: Japanese-Soviet Tactical Combat, 1939," *Leavenworth Papers No. 2* (Ft. Leavenworth, KS: Combat Studies Inst., U.S. Army Cmd. & Gen. Staff College, 1981), p. 62.
13. *Night Movements,* p. 83.
14. Ibid., pp. 83, 84.
15. Poole, *The Tiger's Way,* chapt. 16.
16. Memorandum for the record by H.J. Poole.
17. Capt. John B. Nalls, "A Company Commander's Thoughts on Iraq," *Armor Magazine,* February 2004.
18. Poole, *The Tiger's Way,* tables 2.2 and 24.1.
19. O'Brien, *Conscripts and Regulars,* p. 215; Lanning and Cragg, *Inside the VC and the NVA,* pp. 55, 56; Dunnigan and Nofi, *Dirty Little Secrets of the Vietnam War,* pp. 276-279.
20. Bermudez, *North Korean Special Forces,* pp. 233, 234, 247, 248; *Inside North Korea,* p. 74.
21. William H. Bartsch, "Crucial Battle Ignored," *Marine Corps Gazette,* September 1997, pp. 82-84.
22. *All the King's Men,* by Nigel McCrery (New York: Simon & Schuster, 1999), previously titled *The Vanished Battalion* (N.p., n.d.); "All the Kings Men," *Exxon Masterpiece Theater*, BBC in conjunction with WGBH Boston, NC Public TV, 26 November 2000.
23. Allan A. Macfarlan, *Exploring the Outdoors with Indian Secrets* (Harrisburg, PA: Stackpole Books, 1971), p. 90.

Chapter 19: *Enhancing Rural Terrain*

1. Unidentified NCO's comment to Chesty Puller, in *Fighting on Guadalcanal,* FMFRP 12-110 (Washington, D.C.: U.S. War Office, 1942), pp. 35-37.
2. Col G.C. Thomas USMC, Maj.Gen. Vandegrift's Chief of Staff, in *Fighting on Guadalcanal,* FMFRP 12-110 (Washington, D.C.: U.S. War Office, 1942), p. 65.
3. Memorandum for the record by H.J. Poole.
4. Ibid.
5. Lt.Col. Whitman S. Bartley, *Iwo Jima: Amphibious Epic* (Washington, D.C.: Hist. Branch, HQMC, 1954), p. 15; Keith Wheeler and the editors of Time-Life Books, *The Road to Tokyo,* World War II Series (Alexandria, VA: Time-Life Books, 1979), p. 42.
6. "What Cameramen Saw through Their Lenses," 85:00 min., *A Tribute to WWII Combat Cameramen of Japan* Series (Tokyo: Nippon TV, 3 August 1995).
7. Ibid.
8. U.S. War Dept. sketch, in *Japanese Army of World War II,* by Philip Warner (London: Osprey Publishing, 1972), p. 25.
9. Anonymous traveler to Pyongyang, in conversation with the author on 23 August 2007.
10. Poole, *The Tiger's Way,* pp. 117-126.
11. Memorandum for the record by H.J. Poole.
12. Joseph C. Goulden, *Korea: The Untold Story of the War* (New York: Times Books, 1982), p. 295.
13. "Chechen Ambush of an Armored Column," illustration, *Infantry Magazine,* January-February 2004, p. 41.
14. Memorandum for the record by H.J. Poole.
15. Bermudez, *North Korean Special Forces,* pp. 233, 234, 247, 248; *Inside North Korea,* p. 74.
16. Poole, *The Tiger's Way,* pp. 167-172.
17. Ibid., tables 2.2 and 24.1.
18. O'Brien, *Conscripts and Regulars,* p. 215; Lanning and Cragg, *Inside the VC and the NVA,* pp. 55, 56; Dunnigan and Nofi, *Dirty Little Secrets of the Vietnam War,* pp. 276-279.
19. Poole, *The Tiger's Way,* pp. 116-124.

Chapter 20: *Urban Escape and Evasion*

1. Kim Gamel, "Militants Claim to Have Killed Soldiers," *Jacksonville Daily News* (NC), 5 June 2007, pp. 1A, 2A; NPR's Morning News, 5 July 2007.

2. Nora Levin, *The Holocaust* (New York: Thomas Y. Crowell Co., 1968), pp. 343-352.
3. Ibid.
4. *Wikipedia Encyclopedia,* s.v. "Warsaw Ghetto Uprising."
5. Levin, *The Holocaust,* pp. 343-352.
6. *Wikipedia Encyclopedia,* s.v. "Warsaw Ghetto Uprising."
7. Ibid.
8. Levin, *The Holocaust,* pp. 343-352.
9. *Wikipedia Encyclopedia,* s.v. "Warsaw Uprising."
10. *U.S. Marines in Vietnam: The Defining Year, 1968,* by Lt.Col. Jack Shulimson, Leonard A. Blaisol, Charles R. Smith, and Capt. David A. Dawson (Washington, D.C.: Hist. & Museums Div., HQMC, 1998), p. 29.
11. Ibid., pp. 164-167, 213; George W. Smith, *The Siege at Hue* (New York: Ballantine Publishing, 1999), p. 235.
12. Eric Hammel, *Fire in the Streets: The Battle for Hue, Tet 1968* (Pacifica, CA: Pacifica Military History, 1991), p. 308.
13. Nicholas Warr, *Phase Line Green: The Battle for Hue, 1968* (Annapolis, MD: Naval Inst. Press, 1997), p. 217.
14. *U.S. Marines in Vietnam: The Defining Year, 1968,* by Shulimson et al, p. 213.
15. Memorandum for the record by H.J. Poole.
16. *U.S. Marines in Vietnam: The Defining Year, 1968,* by Shulimson et al, p. 352.
17. Smith, *The Siege at Hue,* p. 203.
18. Hammel, *Fire in the Streets,* p. 340.
19. Ibid.; *U.S. Marines in Vietnam: The Defining Year, 1968,* by Shulimson et al, p. 210.
20. Poole, *Phantom Soldier,* p. 187.
21. *U.S. Marines in Vietnam: The Defining Year, 1968,* by Shulimson et al, pp. 212, 213.
22. Poole, *The Tiger's Way,* tables 2.2 and 24.1.
23. O'Brien, *Conscripts and Regulars,* p. 215; Lanning and Cragg, *Inside the VC and the NVA,* pp. 55, 56; Dunnigan and Nofi, *Dirty Little Secrets of the Vietnam War,* pp. 276-279.
24. Bermudez, *North Korean Special Forces,* pp. 233, 234, 247, 248; *Inside North Korea,* p. 74.

Chapter 21: *Enhancing Urban Terrain*

1. "Aiming High," photograph, *China Daily* (Beijing), 15 August 2007, p. 2.

2. Thomas M. Huber, "The Battle of Manila," in CSI Home Publications Research MHIST [database on line] (Ft. Leavenworth, KS: Combat Studies Inst., U.S. Army Cmd. & Gen. Staff College, n.d. [updated 30 September 2002; cited 1 January 2003]), available from the CSI website at www-cgsc.army.mil/csi/research/mout/mouthuber.asp, pp. 2, 3.
3. Memorandum for the record by H.J. Poole.
4. Warr, *Phase Line Green,* introduction.
5. Ibid., last chapter.
6. *U.S. Marines in Vietnam: The Defining Year, 1968,* by Shulimson et al, pp. 199, 201; Hammel, *Fire in the Streets,* p. 274.
7. Warr, *Phase Line Green,* pp. 141, 142; Hammel, *Fire in the Streets,* p. 281.
8. Ibid.
9. Hammel, *Fire in the Streets,* pp. 349, 350.
10. Ibid., pp. 347-348.
11. Ibid., p. 351.
12. Smith, *The Siege at Hue,* pp. 9, 169.
13. Hammel, *Fire in the Streets,* pp. 339, 340.
14. *U.S. Marines in Vietnam: The Defining Year, 1968,* by Shulimson et al, p. 210.
15. Ibid., p. 213.
16. Leon Uris, *Mila 18* (New York: Bantam, 1983), p. 363.
17. Ibid.
18. "Great Escape," PBS's *Nova,* NC Public TV, 5 June 2007.
19. Uris, *Mila 18,* p. 363.
20. Ibid.
21. Ibid., pp. 373, 374.
22. Bartley, *Iwo Jima,* p. 15; Wheeler et al, *The Road to Tokyo,* p. 42.
23. Warr, *Phase Line Green.*
24. Poole, *The Tiger's Way,* tables 2.2 and 24.1.
25. O'Brien, *Conscripts and Regulars,* p. 215; Lanning and Cragg, *Inside the VC and the NVA,* pp. 55, 56; Dunnigan and Nofi, *Dirty Little Secrets of the Vietnam War,* pp. 276-279.
26. Bermudez, *North Korean Special Forces,* pp. 233, 234, 247, 248; *Inside North Korea,* p. 74.
27. Poole, *Phantom Soldier,* chapt. 3.
28. Mark Mosher (U.S. serviceman in Iraq), in e-mail to author on 13 May 2005.

Afterword

1. Poole, *One More Bridge to Cross,* chapt. 13.
2. Poole, *The Tiger's Way,* appendix C.

3. *Marine Rifle Company/Platoon,* FMFM 6-4 (Washington, D.C.: HQMC, 17 February 1978), p. 5.

Glossary

ABC	American Broadcasting Company	U.S. TV network
AIM	Armed Islamic Movement	Sudanese alliance of militant groups
AK-47	Russian and Chinese weapon designator	Eastern-bloc assault rifle
ALS	Alternate Light Source	Projector of light in visible spectrum
ASG	*Abu Sayyaf Group*	Radical Muslim sect in Philippines, alias *Harakat al Islamiyya*
B-2	U.S. aircraft designator	American jet bomber
BBC	British Broadcasting Corporation	British radio and TV network
BNP	Bangladesh National Party	Part of Bangladesh's ruling coalition
BRN-C	Barisan Revolusi Nasional (the suffix "C" can signify a Communist or Chinese faction)	One of two rebel groups in southern Thailand
CAP	Combined Action Platoon	Consists of one squad each of U.S. infantry, indigenous police, and indigenous army
CEIEC	China National Electronics Import and Export Company	PLA's arm to build electronic defense networks for allies

CENTCOM	Central Command	U.S. headquarters for South Asia
CIA	Central Intelligence Agency	U.S. spy organization
CID	Criminal Investigations Division	Short for USACIDC
CNN	Cable News Network	U.S. TV network
COSCO	China Ocean Shipping Company	PLA's civilian fleet
CP	Communist Party of Sri Lanka	Old Marxist/Leninist party of Sri Lanka
CP-C	Communist Party of Sri Lanka-Chinese faction	Newer Maoist party of Sri Lanka
CPB	Communist Party of Bangladesh	Marxist/Leninist party in Bangladesh, formerly CPEP
CPB-NAP-BSU	Communist Party of Bangladesh-National Awami Party-BSU	CPB faction that vied with Pakistani army for Bangladeshi independence
CPC	Communist Party of China	Maoist Party of China
CPEP	Communist Party of East Pakistan	Marxist/Leninist East-Pakistani party
CPI-M	Communist Party of India-Marxist	Indian Marxist party that adopted Maoist strategy
CPM	Communist Party of Malaysia	Maoist party in Malaysia
CPP(Pak)	Communist Party of Pakistan	Marxist/Leninist party of Pakistan
CPP(Phil)	Communist Party of the Philippines	Essentially Maoist, Filipino party

CPP(Phil)-ML	Communist Party of the Philippines-Marxist/Leninist	Marxist/Leninist faction of CPP(Phil) that maintained Maoist strategy
D.C.	District of Columbia	Location of the U.S. capital
DIA	Defense Intelligence Agency	U.S. intelligence organization
DMZ	Demilitarized Zone	Buffer area between combatant countries
DNA	Deoxyribonucleic acid	Human-cell molecule that carries a unique genetic code
E&E	Escape and Evasion	Avoiding capture and then eluding pursuit
ETIM	East Turkestan Islamic Movement	Uighur separatist group in Xinjiang
F-14	Aircraft designator	U.S. fighter jet
F(ajr)-3	Chinese or Iranian military designator	Rocket delivered to *Hezbollah*
F(ajr)-5	Chinese or Iranian military designator	Later version of Fajr rocket
FATA	Federally Administered Tribal Areas	Pakistani territory along Afghan border
FBIS	Foreign Broadcast and Information Service	CIA's foreign media monitoring agency
FTC	Federal Trade Commission	Agency that monitors business in America
4GW	4th-Generation Warfare	War in four arenas simultaneously—martial, religious, political, & economic

GAM	*Gerakan Aceh Merdeka*	Sumatra's Free Aceh Movement, Indonesia
G-15	Organization designator	Group of seventeen developing nations
G219	Highway designator	Chinese road thru occupied Kashmir
GI	Government Issue	U.S. serviceman
HN-5	Pakistan or Iran arms designator	Chinese-made SA-7
HUJAI	*Harkat-ul Jehad-al Islami*	Militant Muslim sect active in India's far northeast and Burma
HUJI	*Harakat-ul-Jihad-i-Islami*	Militant Muslim sect based in Pakistan
HUJIBD	*Harakat-ul-Jihad-i-Islami-Bangladesh*	Bangladeshi branch of *HUJI*
ID	Identification	When associated with Caller ID, it provides the caller's telephone number
IED	Improvised Explosive Device	Remotely controlled bomb
INF	Islamic National Front	Sudanese alliance of militant groups, same as AIM
IPKF	Indian Peace Keeping Force	Indian contingent in Sri Lanka
ISI	Interservice Intelligence	Pakistani spy agency
JeI	*Jamaat-e-Islami*	Part of Bangladesh's ruling coalition
JI	*Jemaah Islamiyah*	Radical Muslim sect in Indonesia

JUI	*Jamiat Ulema-e-Islam*	Powerful Pakistani religious party
JUI/F	*Jamiat Ulema-e-Islam/Fazlur Rehman faction*	Part of *JUI* that directly supports the Afghan Taliban
JVP	*Janatha Vimukthi Perumuna*	Marxist party of Sri Lanka, now part of ruling coalition, alias People's Liberation Front
KDA	Kachin Defense Army	Militia in Burma's Northern Shan State
KOMPAK	*Komite Aksi Penanggulangan Akibat Krisis*	*JI* splinter group in Indonesian Sulawesi
LCV	Leucocrystal violet	Blood test reagent
LEJ	*Lashkar-i-Jhangvi*	Armed wing of *SSP*
LEQ	*Lashkar-e-Qahar*	Tiny Indian affiliate of *LET* that was implicated in Mumbai bombings
LET	*Lashkar-e-Toiba*	Pakistani militant group, ISI proxy, alias *Khairun Naas*
LMG	Leucomalachite green	Blood test reagent
LPRP	Communist Lao People's Revolutionary Party	Laotian political party
LSSP	*Lanka Sama Samaja Party*	Sri Lankan militant faction
LTTE	Liberation Tigers of Tamil Eelam	Bagladeshi Tamil separatists, same as Ellalan Force or Tamil Tigers

M-4	U.S. weapon designator	Barrel-shortened version of the M-16
M-16	U.S. weapon designator	Standard U.S. assault rifle
M-79	U.S. weapon designator	Vietnam vintage U.S. grenade launcher
M-203	U.S. weapon designator	Grenade launcher that can only be mounted below M-16 barrel
MCC	Maoist Communist Center	Naxalite ancestor of Communist Party of India-Maoist
MEND	Movement for the Emancipation of the Niger Delta	Non-Islamic Nigerian guerrilla movement with obvious support
MEP	*Mahajana Eksath Peramuna*	Sri Lankan militants
MILF	Moro Islamic Liberation Front	Offshoot of Filipino MNLF
MIM	Mindanao Independence Movement	Early Filipino Muslim movement
MIP	*Milat-e-Islamia Pakistan*	More recent name for *SSP*
MK-19	U.S. weapon designator	Automatic grenade thrower
MLRA	Malayan Races Liberation Army	CPM's armed wing
MMA	*Muttahida-Majlis-e Amal*	Pakistani coalition of fundamentalist Islamic parties
MMI	*Majelis Mujahidin Indonesia*	Indonesian coalition of fundamentalist Islamic parties

MNDAA	Myanmar National Democracy Alliance Army	New name for that part of Nationalist Chinese Army that fled to Burma
MNLF	Moro National Liberation Front	Filipino militant faction
MP	Military Policeman	Armed Forces law enforcement person
MSS	Ministry of State Security	Chinese spy agency
NAM	Non-Aligned Movement	Grouping of nations
NAP	National Awami Party	Bangladesh's Awami League predecessor in East Pakistan
NATO	North Atlantic Treaty Organization	European alliance
NCO	Noncommissioned Officer	Military enlisted leader
NGO	Non-Government Organization	Privately owned relief agency
NDA	New Democratic Army	Guerrilla faction in Burma's Northeast Kachin State
NDFB	National Democratic Front of Bodoland	Assamese separatist group in Bangladesh
NFIT	Unknown acronym	Assamese separatist group in Bangladesh
9/11	11 September 2001	Attack on America of this date
NIS	Naval Investigative Service	U.S. Marine Corps' external detective agency

NPA	New People's Army	Armed wing of CPP(Phil)-ML
NVA	North Vietnamese Army	Ho Chi Minh's ground forces
NWFB	Northwest Frontier Province	Pakistani region at Afghan border
NYPD	New York Police Department	New York City's law enforcement agency
OIC	Organization of Islamic Conference	Saudi-swayed alternative to Arab League (of nations)
PAIC	Popular Arab and Islamic Conference	AIM conference in Sudan in the 1990's
PBS	Public Broadcasting System	U.S. TV network
PFC	Private First Class	Second to lowest level in U.S. military rank structure
PGA	People's Guerrilla Army	Armed wing of Communist Party of India-Maoist
PKI	*Partai Komunis Indonesia*	Communist party in Indonesia
PLA	People's Liberation Army	Chinese military
PLA(P)	People's Liberation Army (of the Philippines)	Luis Taruc's Huk Communist forces
PLO	Palestinian Liberation Organization	Coalition of Palestinian groups
PRC	People's Republic of China	Mainland China
PWG	People's War Group	Naxalite ancestor of Communist Party of India-Maoist

RKK	*Runda Kumpulan Kecil*	Part of BRN-C that trained on squad tactics in Indonesia
RL	Rocket Launcher	Eastern-bloc multiple rocket launcher
RPD	Communist small-arm acronym	Automatic weapon with bipod mount
RPG	Rocket Propelled Grenade	Eastern-bloc shoulder-fired grenade launcher
RPV	Remotely Piloted Vehicle	Pilotless aircraft
RTM	Radio Television Malaysia	Malaysian regime-controlled media
SA-7	Communist missile designator	Eastern-bloc surface-to-air missile
SCO	Shanghai Cooperation Organization	Alliance of six west Asian nations
SEAL	Sea, Air, and Land	U.S. Navy commando
2GW	Second-Generation Warfare	Based on destroying enemy strongpoints
SIMI	Students Islamic Movement of India	Tiny Indian affiliate of *LET*, implicated in Mumbai bombings
SLFP	Sri Lankan Freedom Party	Part of ruling Sri Lankan coalition
SMAW	Shoulder-Fired Multipurpose Assault Weapon	Modern equivalent of American bazooka, primarily used for busting bunkers
SSP	*Sipah-i-Sahaba Pakistan*	Radical Muslim sect from Pakistan, same as *MIP*

T(aepodong)-2	Chinese missile designator	Long-range missile capable of nuclear warhead, sold to Iran by China
3GW	Third-Generation Warfare	Based on bypassing foe's strongpoints to ruin strategic assets
TMB	Tetramethylbenzidine	Blood test reagent
TV	Television	Media device
UIFO	Union of Islamic Forces and Organizations	Early Filipino Muslim movement
ULFA	United Liberation Front of Asom	Assam separatists
U.N.	United Nations	World alliance
UPFA	United People's Freedom Alliance	Ruling coalition in Sri Lanka
U.S.	United States	America
USACIDC	U.S. Army Criminal Investigations Command	Army's internal investigative unit
UW	Unconventional Warfare	Loosely shaped strife
VC	Viet Cong	Guerrilla in Vietnam
WIFJ	World Islamic Front for the Jihad against Jews and Crusaders	Osama bin Laden's alliance of militant factions
WWI	World War One	First global conflict
WWII	World War Two	Second global conflict
ZANLA	Zimbabwe African National Liberation Army	ZANU's armed wing
ZANU	Zimbabwe African National Union	Maoist party that took over Rhodesia

Bibliography

U.S. Government Publications and News Releases

"Background Note: Sri Lanka." U.S. Dept. of State, October 2006. From its website, www.state.gov.

"Bangladesh." *Library of Congress Country Studies.* Washington, D.C., 1988.

Bartley, Lt.Col. Whitman S. *Iwo Jima: Amphibious Epic.* Washington, D.C.: Hist. Branch, HQMC, 1954.

The Bear Went over the Mountain: Soviet Combat Tactics in Afghanistan. Translated and edited by Lester W. Grau, Foreign Mil. Studies Office, U.S. Dept. of Defense, Lt. Leavenworth, KS. Washington, D.C.: Nat. Defense Univ. Press, 1996. Originally published under its Russian title. Soviet Union: Frunze Mil. Acad., n.d.

Bullock, Todd. "Asia Most Likely To Shape U.S. Defense Policy, Scholars Say." U.S. Department of State's Bureau of International Information Programs, 25 September 2005. From its website, usinfo.state.gov.

CIA—The World Factbook. As updated every three months. From its website, www.odci.gov.

Country Reports on Terrorism, 2005. Washington, D.C.: U.S. Dept. of State, April 2006. From its website, www.state.gov.

Drea, Edward J. "Nomonhan: Japanese-Soviet Tactical Combat, 1939." *Leavenworth Papers No. 2.* Ft. Leavenworth, KS: Combat Studies Inst., U.S. Army Cmd. & Gen. Staff College, 1981.

"18 of Iran's 21 New Ministers Hail from Revolutionary Guards, Secret Police." Iran Report, vol. 8, no. 34. *Radio Free Europe/Radio Liberty,* 29 August 2005. From its website, www.rferl.org.

Energy Information Administration Map. From "A Natural-Gas Gang." *Time,* 16 April 2007.

Fighting on Guadalcanal. FMFRP 12-110. Washington, D.C.: U.S. War Office, 1942.

Handbook on the Chinese Communist Army. DA Pam 30-51. Washington, D.C.: Hdqts. Dept. of the Army, 1960.

Handbook on German Military Forces. TM-E 30-451. Washington, D.C.: U.S. War Dept., 1945; reprint Baton Rouge, LA: LSU Press, 1990.

Handbook on Japanese Military Forces. TM-E 30-480. Washington, D.C.: U.S. War Dept., 1944; reprint Baton Rouge, LA: LSU Press, 1991.

Huber, Thomas M. "The Battle of Manila." In CSI Home Publications Research MHIST [database on line]. Ft. Leavenworth, KS: Combat Studies Inst., U.S. Army Cmd. & Gen. Staff College, n.d. [updated 30 September 2002; cited 1 January 2003]). Available from the CSI website at www-cgsc.army.mil/csi/research/mout/mouthuber.asp.

Jalali, Ali and Lester W. Grau. *Afghan Guerrilla Warfare: In the Words of the Mujahideen Fighters*. St. Paul, MN: MBI Publishing, 2001. First published as *The Other Side of the Mountain*. Quantico, VA: Marine Corps Combat Development Cmd., 1995.

Jungle Warfare. FMFRP 12-9. Quantico, VA: Marine Corps Combat Development Cmd., 1989.

Malaysia: A Country Study. DA Pamphlet 550-45. Area Handbook Series. Washington, D.C.: Hdqts. Dept. of the Army, 1984.

Malik, Mohan. *Dragon on Terrorism: Assessing China's Tactical Gains and Strategic Losses Post-September 11*. Carlisle, PA: Strategic Studies Institute, U. S. Army War College, October 2002.

Marine Rifle Company / Platoon. FMFM 6-4. Washington, D.C.: HQMC, 17 February 1978.

National Commission on Terrorist Attacks upon the United States. Chapt. 5. of its report. As retrieved from its website that was frozen in 2004, http://www.9-11commission.gov/report/911Report_Ch5.htm. The record is now at National Archives and Records Administration and can be accessed through legislative.archives@nara.gov.

NVA-VC Small Unit Tactics & Techniques Study, Part I. U.S.A.R.V. Edited by Thomas Pike. Washington, D.C.: Archival Publishing, 1997.

"One-Point, Two-Sides Attack on Defensive Position." *Handbook on the Chinese Communist Army*. DA Pam 30-51. Washington, D.C.: Hdqts. Dept. of the Army, 1960.

Patterns of Global Terrorism, 2003 Report. Washington, D.C.: U.S. Dept. of State, April 2004. From its website.

Perl, Raphael F. "Drug Trafficking and North Korea: Issues for U.S. Policy." Congressional Research Service, Library of Congress. *Report for Congress RL32167,* 27 November 2006.

Philippines: A Country Study. DA Pamphlet 550-72. Area Handbook Series. Washington, D.C.: Hdqts. Dept. of the Army, 1983.

"State, Federal Law Enforcers Launch Sting on Business Opportunity, Work-at-Home Scams." Federal Trade Commission, Office of Public Affairs, 20 June 2002. From its website, www.ftc.gov.

Terrorist Group Profiles. U.S. Naval Postgraduate School (Dudley Knox Library), April 2006. From its website, web.nps.navy.mil.

Unrestricted Warfare. By Qiao Liang and Wang Xiangsui. Beijing: PLA Literature and Arts Publishing House, February 1999. FBIS translation over the internet.

U.S. Marines in Vietnam: Fighting the North Vietnamese in 1967. By Maj. Gary Tefler, Lt.Col. Lane Rogers, and V. Keith Fleming, Jr. Washington, D.C.: Hist. & Museums Div., HQMC, 1984.

U.S. Marines in Vietnam: The Defining Year 1968. By Lt.Col. Jack Shulimson, Leonard A. Blaisol, Charles R. Smith, and Capt. David A. Dawson. Washington, D.C.: Hist. & Museums Div., HQMC, 1998.

Civilian Publications

Analytical Studies

Ahmed, Khaled. *Pakistan: Behind the Ideological Mask*. Lahore: Vanguard, 2004.

Atwan, Abdel Bari. *The Secret History of Al-Qa'ida*. London: Abacus, an imprint of Little, Brown Book Group, 2006.

Baxter, William P. *Soviet Airland Battle Tactics*. Novato, CA: Presidio Press, 1986.

Bermudez, Joseph S., Jr. *North Korean Special Forces*. Annapolis: Naval Inst. Press, 1998.

Can, Nguyen Khac and Pham Viet Thuc. *The War 1858 - 1975 in Vietnam*. Hanoi: Nha Xuat Ban Van Hoa Dan Toc, n.d.

Chanda, Nayan. *Brother Enemy: The War after the War*. New York: Collier Books, 1986.

Chanoff, David and Doan Van Toai. *Portrait of the Enemy*. New York: Random House, 1986.

Corbett, James. *Jungle Lore*. London: Oxford Univ. Press, 1953.

Country Profiles. BBC News. From its website, bbc.co.uk.

Elford, George Robert. *Devil's Guard*. New York: Dell, 1971.

Encyclopedia of the Nations. By Thomson Gale. N.p.: Thomson Corp., 2006. From its website, www.nationsencyclopedia.com.

Esposito, John L. *Unholy War: Terror in the Name of Islam*. London: Oxford Univ. Press, 2002.

Evans, Grant and Kelvin Rowley. *Red Brotherhood at War*. London: Verso, 1984.

Dunnigan, James F. and Albert A. Nofi. *Dirty Little Secrets of the Vietnam War*. New York: Thomas Dunne Books, 1999.

Fletcher, Connie. *Every Contact Leaves a Trace*. New York: St. Martin's Press, 2006.

Fremont-Barnes, Gregory. *The Boer War: 1899-1902*. Oxford, England: Osprey, 2003.

Geberth, Vernon J. *Practical Homicide Investigation: Tactics, Procedures, and Techniques*. Fourth Edition. Boca Raton, FL: CRC Press (an imprint of Taylor & Francis), 2006.

Gertz, Bill *The China Threat*. Washington, D.C.: Regnery Publishing, 2002.

Giap, Gen. Vo Nguyen. *Dien Bien Phu*. 6th edition supplemented. Hanoi: Gioi Publishers, 1999.

Goulden, Joseph C. *Korea: The Untold Story of the War*. New York: Times Books, 1982.

Gudmundsson, Bruce I. *Stormtroop Tactics—Innovation in the German Army 1914-1918*. New York: Praeger, 1989.

Gunaratna, Rohan. *Inside al-Qaeda: Global Network of Terror*. Lahore: Vanguard, 2002.

Hammel, Eric. *Fire in the Streets: The Battle for Hue, Tet 1968*. Pacifica, CA: Pacifica Military History, 1991.

Hammer, Carl. *Tide of Terror: America, Islamic Extremism, and the War on Terror*. Boulder, CO: Paladin Press, 2003.

Hatsumi, Masaaki. *The Essence of Ninjutsu*. Chicago: Contemporary Books, 1988.

Huntington, Samuel P. *The Clash of Civilizations and the Remaking of World Order*. London: Simon & Schuster UK, 1997.

"Hypnosis." Chapter in *The Complete Manual of Physical Fitness and Well-Being*. Pleasantville, NY: The Reader's Digest Assoc., 1984.

The Jerusalem Bible. Garden City, NY: Doubleday, 1966.

John Paul II, His Holiness. *Crossing the Threshold of Hope*. New York: Alfred A. Knopf, 1995.

Kaplan, Robert D. *Soldiers of God: With Islamic Warriors in Afghanistan and Pakistan,* revised edition. New York: Vintage Books, 2001.

Katzman, Kenneth. *Warriors of Islam: Iran's Revolutionary Guard*. Boulder, CO: Westview Press, 1993.

Knox, Donald. *The Korean War: Pusan to Chosin, an Oral History*. San Diego: Harcourt Janovich, 1985.

Lanning, Michael Lee and Dan Cragg. *Inside the VC and the NVA: The Real Story of North Vietnam's Armed Forces*. New York: Ivy Books, 1992.

Levin, Nora. *The Holocaust*. New York: Thomas Y. Crowell Co., 1968.

Lung, Haha. *Nights of Darkness: Secrets of the World's Deadliest Night Fighters*. Boulder, CO: Paladin Press, 1998.

Macfarlan, Allan A. *Exploring the Outdoors with Indian Secrets*. Harrisburg, PA: Stackpole Books, 1971.

Mannes, Aaron. *Profiles in Terror: The Guide to Middle East Terror Organizations.* Lanham, MD: Rowman & Littlefield Publishers, Inc., 2004.

Mao Tse-Tung: An Anthology of His Writings. Edited by Anne Fremantle. New York: Mentor, 1962.

Mao's Generals Remember Korea, Translated and edited by Xiaobing Li, Allan R. Millet, and bin Yu. Lawrence, KS: Univ. Press of Kansas, 2001.

McCrery, Nigel. *All the King's Men.* New York: Simon & Schuster, 1999. Previously titled *The Vanished Battalion.* N.p, n.d.

McGuire, D.J. *Dragon in the Dark: How and Why Communist China Helps Our Enemies in the War on Terror.* Bloomington, IN: Authorhouse, November 2003.

Menges, Constantine. *China: The Gathering Threat.* Nashville, TN: Nelson Current, 2005.

Mir, Amir. *The True Face of Jihadis.* Lahore: Mashal Books, 2004.

Night Movements. Translated and preface by C. Burnett. Port Townsend, WA: Loompanics Unlimited, n.d. Originally released as Japanese training manual. Tokyo: Imperial Japanese Army, 1913.

Nolan, Keith William. *Operation Buffalo: USMC Fight for the DMZ.* Novato, CA: Presidio Press, 1983.

Nolan, Keith William. *Sappers in the Wire: The Life and Death of Firebase Mary Ann.* College Station, TX: Texas A&M Univ. Press, 1995.

O'Brien, Michael. *Conscripts and Regulars: With the Seventh Battalion in Vietnam.* St. Leonards, Australia: Allen & Unwin, 1995.

Poole, H. John. *The Last Hundred Yards: The NCO's Contribution to Warfare.* Emerald Isle, NC: Posterity Press, 1997.

Poole, H. John. *Militant Tricks: Battlefield Ruses of the Islamic Insurgent.* Emerald Isle, NC: Posterity Press, 2005.

Poole, H. John. *One More Bridge to Cross: Lowering the Cost of War.* Emerald Isle, NC: Posterity Press, 1999.

Poole, H. John. *Phantom Soldier: The Enemy's Answer to U.S. Firepower.* Emerald Isle, NC: Posterity Press, 2001.

Poole, H. John. *Tactics of the Crescent Moon: Militant Muslim Combat Methods.* Emerald Isle, NC: Posterity Press, 2004.

Poole, H. John. *Terrorist Trail: Backtracking the Foreign Fighter.* Emerald Isle, NC: Posterity Press, 2006.

Poole, H. John. *The Tiger's Way: A U.S. Private's Best Chance of Survival.* Emerald Isle, NC: Posterity Press, 2003.

Reid-Daly, Lt.Col. R.F. *Pamwe Chete: The Legend of the Selous Scouts.* Weltevreden Park, South Africa: Covos-Day Books, 1999.

Ross, Bill D. *Iwo Jima: Legacy of Valor.* New York: Vintage Books, 1986.

"The Second Chechen War." *P31.* Edited by Mrs. A.C. Aldis. Sandhurst, UK: Conflict Studies Research Centre, June 2000.

Smith, George W. *The Siege at Hue.* New York: Ballantine Publishing, 1999.

Smith, John F. and James R. Sheridan and Dennis F. Yurcisin. *How to Set Up and Run a Successful Law Enforcement Sting Operation.* Upper Saddle River, NJ: Prentice Hall, n.d.

Stiff, Peter. *The Silent War: South African Recce Operations, 1969-1994.* Alberton, South Africa: Galago Publishing, 1999.

Thompson, Leroy. *Dirty Wars: Elite Forces vs. the Guerrillas.* Devon, England: David & Charles, 1991.

Twentieth Century Atlas—Death Tolls. From its website, users.erols.com/mwhite28/warstat1.html.

Unmasking Terror: A Global Review of Terrorist Activities. Volumes I, II, and III. The first two edited by Christopher Heffelfinger, and the third by Jonathan Hutzley. Washington, D.C: Jamestown Foundation, 2005 through 2007.

Uris, Leon. *Mila 18.* New York: Bantam, 1983.

Warner, Philip. *Japanese Army of World War II.* London: Osprey Publishing, 1972.

Warr, Nicholas. *Phase Line Green: The Battle for Hue, 1968.* Annapolis, MD: Naval Inst. Press, 1997.

Wheeler, Keith and the editors of Time-Life Books. *The Road to Tokyo.* World War II Series. Alexandria, VA: Time-Life Books, 1979.

World Army Uniforms since 1939. London: Blandford Press Ltd., 1980.

Yousaf, Brigadier Mohammad, and Maj. Mark Adkin. *Bear Trap: Afghanistan's Untold Story.* South Yorkshire, UK: Leo Cooper, n.d. From www.afghanbooks.com.

<u>Photos, Videotapes, Movies, TV Programs, Slide Shows, and Illustrations</u>

"Aiming High." Photograph. *China Daily* (Beijing), 15 August 2007.

"All the Kings Men." *Exxon Masterpiece Theater.* BBC in conjunction with WGBH Boston. NC Public Television, 26 November 2000.

"Al-Qaeda Cornered." AP photo. From "U.S. Assists Pakistan in Battle," by Riaz Khan. *Jacksonville Daily News* (NC), 20 March 2004.

"Al-Qaeda's New Front." PBS's *Frontline.* NC Public Television, 25 January 2005.

The Battle of Dien Bien Phu. Visions of War Series, vol. 10. New Star Video, 1988. 50 min. Videocassette #4010.

"Burma Road Map." National Geographic Society, 2003. From its website.

"Chechen Ambush of an Armored Column." Illustration. *Infantry Magazine,* January-February 2004.

"Freedom and Justice." PBS's *China from the Inside.* Part IV. NC Public Television, 17 January 2007.
"Great Escape." PBS's *Nova.* NC Public Television, 5 June 2007.
"Inside America's Empire." PBS's *America at a Crossroads.* NC Public Television, 11 September 2007.
MEND photograph. In "Curse of the Black Gold: Hope and Betrayal in the Niger Delta." *National Geographic,* February 2007.
"Mujahideen Training and Operating in China ('Eastern Turkestan')." Islamist website video. As extracted by Middle East Media Research Inst. (MEMRI), 8 November 2006. From its website, memri.org.
"Mullah Omar Slept Here." Photo. From "The Strange Case of Haji Bashar Noorzai," by Bill Powell. *Time Magazine,* 19 February 2007.
"Musharraf Opposes Ex-PM's Return." By the Agencies. *China Daily* (Beijing), 13 August 2007.
"No More Tears Sister." PBS's *Point of View.* NC Public Television, 27 June 2006.
"Path to 9/11." ABC News, 10 September 2006.
"Platoon." Written and directed by Oliver Stone. Produced by Hemdale Film Corp. Metro Goldwyn Mayer Home Entertainment, 1986. 1 hour, 59:00 min. Videocassette #M208119.
"Power and the People." PBS's *China from the Inside.* Part I. NC Public Television, 10 January 2007.
"Return of the Taliban." PBS's *Frontline.* NC Public Television, 8 January 2007.
"Return with Honor." PBS's *American Experience.* NC Public Television, April 2007.
"Seoul Train." PBS's *Independent Lens.* NC Public Television, 13 June 2006.
"Violence and Repression in Myanmar." PBS's *Frontline World.* NC Public Television, 31 October 2006.
Weir, Bill. Interview in Tibet. ABC's *Good Morning America,* 9 November 2006.
"What Cameramen Saw through Their Lenses." 85:00 min. *A Tribute to WWII Combat Cameramen of Japan* series. Tokyo: Nippon Television, 3 August 1995.
"Zimbabwe: Shadows and Lies." PBS's *Frontline / World.* NC Public Television, 27 June 2006

Letters, E-Mail, and Verbal Conversations

American couple who had just traveled by train from Russia to Chongqing. In conversation with author in June 2000.
Anonymous traveler to Pyongyang, in conversation with the author on 23 August 2007.

Chinese Military Attache to the U.N. (or his representative). In unsolicited phone call to the author about 1996.
Mark Mosher (U.S. serviceman in Iraq). In e-mail to author on 13 May 2005.
New Delhi businessman. In conversation with author on 30 May 2006.
Probable CIA official (McClean address and too much international insight). In phone call to author around the middle of October 2006.
Seventy-year-old Chinese man (in Shanghai airport). In conversation with author in June 2000.
Sexton, Mark (U.S. Special Forces multi-tour returnee from Afghanistan in September 2006). In series of telephone conversations with author between 26 September 2006 and 1 February 2007.
Smith, P. C. (Marine platoon sergeant during the Vietnam War). In conversation with the author in December 2006.
Soard, Charles (experienced infantry scout and frequent visitor to Vietnam). In telephone conversation with author, 28 March 2001.
U.S. Marine Colonel (company commander with British battalion in Malaysia in 1962). In school graduation address the author attended about 1986.

Newspaper, Magazine, and Website Articles

Abuza, Zachary. "Indonesians Infiltrate Southern Thailand's Insurgency." Jamestown Foundation. *Terrorism Focus,* vol. III, issue 27, 11 July 2006. From its website, www.jamestown.org.
Abuza, Zachary. "Tentacles of Terror: Al Qaeda's Southeast Asian Network." *Contemporary Southeast Asia,* vol. 24, no. 3, 2002.
Adhikari, Dharma. "Joy and Caution in Nepal's Peace Deal." *Christian Science Monitor,* 5 December 2006.
Ahmad, Munir. Associated Press. "Pakistan President Denies Claim bin Laden Hiding inside Nation." *Jacksonville Daily News* (NC), 1 March 2007.
Ahmad, Zulfiqar. "Intra-MMA Friction Swells over NSC." *Daily Mail* (Islamabad), 30 May 2005.
"Ahmadinejad Has Been Pushing for His Own Candidate." World News in Brief. *Christian Science Monitor,* 15 November 2006.
"All Five Remaining Elections Commissioners in Bangladesh Quit." World News in Brief. *Christian Science Monitor,* 1 February 2007.
"Al Qaeda Has Drones." Agence France-Presse, 13 September 2005.
Amiuzadeh, H.E. Mu. Mohsen (Deputy Minister of External Affairs of Asia-Oceania of the Islamic Republic of Iran). Special Address to the Federation of Indian Chambers of Commerce and Industry. New Dehli, 22 July 2003. From its website, www.ficci.com.

Arnoldy, Ben and Owais Tohid. "Why Koran Is Such a Hot Button." *Christian Science Monitor,* 16 May 2005.
Avila, Jim. "Dream Team of U.S. Bashers Gathers in Cuba." *New York Times,* 11 September 2006. From the ABC News website.
Baldauf, Scott. "Al Qaeda Massing for New Fight." *Christian Science Monitor,* 9 August 2002.
Baldauf, Scott. "How Al Qaeda Seeks to Buy Chinese Arms." *Christian Science Monitor,* 23 August 2002.
"Banned Bangladeshi Group Training Indian Extremists." *Hindustan Times* (New Delhi), 1 September 2004.
Bartsch, William H. "Crucial Battle Ignored." *Marine Corps Gazette,* September 1997.
Batty, Robin and David Hoffman. "Afghanistan: Crisis of Impunity." *Human Rights Watch.* Vol. 13, no. 3(c), July 2001.
Behn, Sharon. "U.S. Targets Aid to All Militants." *Washington Times,* 11 July 2007.
Bhutto, Benazir. "The Price of Dictatorship." *The Guardian* (UK), 23 August 2006. From its website, www.guardian.co.uk. Reprinted from "Only Democracy Can Break Pakistan Terror Link," by Benazir Bhutto. *The Tribune* (Chicago), Global Viewpoint, 16 August 2006.
Blanchard, Ben. Reuters. "Hu to Seal Laos Push at Vietnam Expense." *The Standard* (China's Business Newspaper), 18 November 2006. From its website.
Blanford, Nicholas. "Hizbullah Builds New Line of Defense." *Christian Science Monitor,* 26 February 2007.
Blanford, Nicholas, and Daniel McGrory, and Stephen Farrell. "Tactics That Have Kept the Middle East's Most Powerful Army at Bay." *The Times* (UK), 10 August 2006.
Boadle, Anthony. "Absent Castro Overshadows Non-Aligned Summit." Reuters, 14 September 2006. From their website.
Breslau, Karen. "A Cold Case Warms Up." Periscope. *Newsweek,* 19 March 2007.
Brunnstrom, David. Reuters. "U.S. Says Iran May Be 'More Involved' in Afghan Fight," *Christian Science Monitor,* 19 April 2007.
"Bush Criticizes Planned Taiwan Referendum." From Associated Press. Newsmax.com, 9 December 2003.
"Cambodian PM denounces UN Envoy." BBC News, 29 March 2006. From its website, bbc.co.uk.
"Chavez's Whistlestop World Tour." BBC News, 1 September 2006. From its website, bbc.co.uk.
"China Forging Strategic Ties to Radical Islam." *China Confidential,* 22 July 2006. Through access@g2-forward.org.
"China Gives Cambodia $600m in Aid." BBC News, 8 April 2006. From its website, bbc.co.uk.

"China, Libya, and Others Investing in Sudan's Booming Economy." *The Citizen* (Khartoum), 1 June 2006.

"China Moves Forces into Afghanistan." DEBKAfile, 6 October 2001.

"China: North Korea Has No Plans for a Second Nuclear Test." From Associated Press. *Jacksonville Daily News* (NC), 25 October 2005.

"China . . . Pledged Monday." World Briefs Wire Reports (AP). *Jacksonville Daily News* (NC), 19 September 2006.

"China Pledges $12.4 Million in Aid to Cambodia." *Asian Economic News,* 12 December, 2005.

"China Praises Achievements of Sudan's National Congress Party." From Xinhua. *People's Daily* (China), 24 November 2005. From its website, english.peopledaily.com.cn.

"China Ready to Offer Aid to Build 3rd Bridge across Mekong River." *Asian Economic News,* 20 November 2006. From its website.

"China Recruits Young Volunteers to Work in Laos." *People's Daily* (China), 29 March 2002. From its website, english.peopledaily.com.cn.

"China Sending PC Priests Abroad as 'Intelligence Operatives'." *East-Asia-Intel,* 26 July 2006. Through access@g2-forward.org.

"China Winning Resources and Loyalties of Africa." *The Financial Times* (UK), 28 February 2006.

"China's 'Comprehensive Warfare' Strategy Wears Down Enemy Using Non-Military Means." *Geostrategy-Direct,* 2 August 2006.

"China's Global Reach." *Christian Science Monitor,* 30 January 2007.

"Chinese Company Gets EU Afghan Road Contract." DAWN Group of Newspapers (Pakistan), 2 December 2003. From its website, dawn.com.

"Chinese Company to Reconstruct Afghan Road." *People's Daily* (China), 28 August 2006. From its website, english.peopledaily.com.cn.

"Chinese Gunned Down in Afghanistan." CNN, 10 June 2004. From its website.

"Chinese-Made Ammo in al Qaeda Caves Confirms." *DEBKAfile,* 17 December 2001.

"Chinese Missile Aid for Indonesia." International Institute for Strategic Studies (London), vol. 6, issue 6, August 2005. From its website, www.iiss.org.

Chopra, Anuj. "Maoist Rebels Spread across Rural India." *Christian Science Monitor,* 22 August 2006.

Chopra, Anuj. "Sri Lankan Talks a Welcome Step for Weary Observers." *Christian Science Monitor,* 30 October 2006.

Cody, Edward and Molly Moore. "Analysts Attribute Hezbollah's Resilience to Zeal, Secrecy and Iranian Funding." *Washington Post,* 14 August 2006.

"The Conciliatory Approach Taken by Thailand's Military." World News in Brief. *Christian Science Monitor*, 14 February 2007.
Cooney, Daniel. Associated Press. "Military Reveals Details of Crash." *Jacksonville Daily News* (NC), 7 July 2005.
Coughlin, Con. "N. Korea Helping Iran with Nuclear Testing." *Telegraph* (Britain), 25 January 2007. From its website, telegraph.co.uk.
"Crackdown on Burmese Muslims." *Human Rights Watch Briefing Paper,* July 2002. From its website, hrw.org.
Creedon, Dan. "Standardize Police Sting Operations." HB 3162. *Oil Can, The* (n.p.), first quarter 2002.
"Crossing the Line: China's Railway to Lhasa." Internat. Campaign for Tibet, 10 July 2006. From its website, www.savetibet.org.
"A Deal That Will Bring Communist Rebels into the Government of Nepal." World News in Brief. *Christian Science Monitor,* 10 November 2006.
De Launey, Guy. "Cambodia Clamps Down on Dissent." BBC News, 7 January 2006. From its website, bbc.co.uk.
De Launey, Guy. "Cambodia's 'Out of Control' Evictions." BBC News, 29 September 2006. From its website, bbc.co.uk.
"East Turkestan Islamic Movement (ETIM)." By Seva Gunitskiy. Center for Defense Info. (Washington, D.C.), 9 December 2002. From its website, cdi.org.
"Eastern Shan State Army (ESSA), Mong Tai Army (MTA), Myanmar National Democratic Alliance Army (MNDAA), United Wa State Army (UWSA)." *FAS Intelligence Resource Program,* 5 December 1999. From its website, www.fas.org.
Elegant, Simon. "Taking the Hard Road." *Time,* Asia Edition, 23 September 2002. From its website, www.time.com.
Elliott, Michael. "The Chinese Century." *Time,* 22 January 2007.
Escobar, Pepe. "The Roving Eye." *Asia Times,* 4 October 2001. From its website, atimes.com.
"Explosive Powder Found on Chinese Ship." FOX News, 8 November 2006. Through access@g2-forward.org.
Filkins, Dexter. "In Iraq, Armed Police Carry Out Militias' Work." *International Herald Tribune,* 25 May 2006.
"40% Top Chinese Students Choose to Study Abroad." From Xinhua. *China Daily* (Beijing), 13 August 2007.
Frenkel, Jason. "New Terror Target Warning." *Herald Sun* (Australia), 16 March 2005.
Frommer, Frederick J. "Anti-Terror Laws Keeping Out Old Vietnam War Allies." *Jacksonville Daily News* (NC), 21 February 2007.
Fullbrook, David. "Beijing Pulls Laos into Its Orbit," *Asia Times,* 25 October 2006. From its website.

Fullbrook, David. “China to Europe via a New Burma Road.” *Asia Times Online,* 23 September 2004.

Gamel, Kim. “Militants Claim to Have Killed Soldiers.” *Jacksonville Daily News* (NC), 5 June 2007.

Garrastazu, Antonio and Jerry Haar. “International Terrorism: The Western Hemisphere Connection.” Organization of American States. *America's Forum North-South Center Update,* 2001. From its website, www.oas.org.

Gearan, Anne. Associated Press. “Rice Cites Progress in War against Terror despite Iraq Violence.” *Jacksonville Daily News* (NC), 2 May 2007.

Gertz Bill. “China-Made Artillery Seized in Afghanistan.” *Washington Times,* 12 April 2002.

Gertz, Bill. “China Trained Taliban and al-Qaeda Fighters Says U.S. Intel.” As posted 22 June 2002 on www.rense.com.

Gertz, Bill and Rowan Scarborough. “China-Trained Taliban.” Inside the Ring. *Washington Times,* 21 June 2002. Unedited version from www.gertzfile.com.

Gomez, Jim. Associated Press. “Terrorists Train for Seaborne Attacks.” *Seattle Post-Intelligencer,* 18 March 2005.

Graham, Stephen. Associated Press. “Latest Assault Leaves 2 Brits, Afghan Interpreter Dead.” *Jacksonville Daily News* (NC), 6 May 2004.

“Great Expectations for Indonesia.” *People's Daily* (Beijing), 17 August 2007.

Griswold, Eliza. “Waging Peace in the Philippines.” *Smithsonian,* December 2006.

Guinto, J. “President: MILF Has until June 1 to Cut Terror Links.” *Philippine Daily Inquirer,* 13 May 2003.

Hakim, Zakki. Associated Press. “Indonesian Jet Still Missing.” *Jacksonville Daily News* (NC), 3 January 2007.

Harman, Danna. “How China's Quiet Support Shields a Regime Called ‘Genocidal’.” *Christian Science Monitor,* 26 June 2007.

“Hezbollah Leader Vows Not to Give Up Weapons.” From Associated Press. *Jacksonville Daily News* (NC), 23 September 2006.

Hord, J. Mark. “Review of Terrorist Trail.” As posted at www.d-n-i.net and g2-forward.org on 31 January 2007.

Huang, Carol. “Al Qaeda in 2006.” Briefing. *Christian Science Monitor,* 1 February 2007.

“India's Naxalites: A Spectre Haunting India.” *The Economist,* 17 August 2006. From its website, economist.com.

“Indian Security Forces Stepped Up Counterinsurgency Operations.” World News in Brief. *Christian Science Monitor,* 8 January 2007.

“Indonesian Backgrounder: Jihad in Central Sulawesi.” *International Crisis Group (Brussels) Asia Report No. 74,* 3 February 2004.

Inside North Korea: Three Decades of Duplicity. Seoul: Inst. of Internal and External Affairs, 1975.

"Iran Signs $20-Billion Gas Deal with China." United Press International, 20 March 2004.

"Israel Intercepts Dual-Use Military Shipment from China to Gaza. *World Tribune,* 4 May 2006. Through access@g2-forward.org.

"Islamist Rebels Ambushed Marines Looking for a Kidnapped . . . Priest." World News in Brief. *Christian Science Monitor,* 12 July 2007.

"It Is Easy to Gulp Down but Difficult to Digest." *People's Daily* (China), 6 November 2003. From its website, english.peopledaily.com.cn.

Jelinek, Pauline. Associated Press. "New Military Chiefs Have Know-How, New Outlook." *Jacksonville Daily News* (NC), 7 January 2007.

Kahn, Joseph. "Where's Mao? Chinese Revise History Books." *New York Times*, 1 September. 2006.

"Karzai Accuses Pakistan of Backing Taliban Insurgents." News Digest Wire Reports (AP). *Jacksonville Daily News* (NC), 13 December 2006.

"Karzai Attends Starting Ceremony of Road Project." Pakistani News Service, 28 August 2006. From its website, paktribune.com.

Kate, Daniel Ten. "Thai Coup May Ease Violence in the South." *Christian Science Monitor,* 26 September 2006.

Kate, Daniel Ten. "Thai Military Reformer Takes the Helm." *Christian Science Monitor,* 2 October 2006.

Khan, Ashraf. "Voters Reverse Islamists' Rise in Pakistani Politics." *Christian Science Monitor,* 6 September 2005.

"Khmer Rouge Judges Begin Work." BBC News, 4 July 2006. From its website, bbc.co.uk.

Kim, Suzy. "Saying I Do Willingly This Time." Backstory. *Christian Science Monitor,* 16 January 2007.

Kinetz, Erika. "U.S. Congress Warms to Cambodia." *Christian Science Monitor,* 14 March 2007.

Kirk, Alejandro and Dalia Acosta. "Non-Aligned Summit Opens amidst Suspense over Castro." Inter-Press-Service News Agency, 21 September 2006.

Kirk, Donald. "New Phase as N. Korea Shuts Down Reactor." *Christian Science Monitor,* 16 July 2007.

Koster, Suzanna. "Taliban Fighters Talk Tactics While Safe in Pakistan." *Christian Science Monitor,* 9 November 2006.

Krausz, Tibor. "Cambodia's Healing History Lessons." Christian Science Monitor, 11 December 2006.

Kurlantzick, Josh. "China's Charm Offensive in Southeast Asia." *Current History,* September 2006. Republished by Carnegie Endowment for International Peace. From its website, www.carnegieendowment.org.

LaFranchi, Howard. "Pakistan: U.S. Ally, U.S. Dilemma." *Christian Science Monitor,* 29 March 2007.

LaFranchi, Howard. "U.S. Presses to Enforce N. Korea Resolution." *Christian Science Monitor,* 16 October 2006.

LaFranchi, Howard. "Will Iran, Korea Really Back Off Nukes?" *Christian Science Monitor,* 18 July 2007.

Lamb, Christina. "Britain Says Pakistan Is Hiding Taliban Chief." *The Sunday Times* (UK), 8 October 2006. From its website, www.timesonline.co.uk.

Lasseter, Tom. Knight Ridder. "Iraqi Forces May Need Years of Preparation." *Jacksonville Daily News* (NC), 28 August 2005.

Lev, Michael A. "U.S. Holds 300 Chinese Extremists, Beijing Says." *Chicago Tribune,* 28 May 2002.

Lin Biao. "Carry out the Strategy and Tactics of People's War." Marxist Internet Archive, n.d. From its website, www.marxists.org.

Llana, Sara Miller. "Nicaragua Plans a Big Dig to Rival Panama Canal." *Christian Science Monitor,* 15 November 2006.

Llana, Sara Miller. "Venezuela's Chavez Nears a Victory Fed by Free Stew." *Christian Science Monitor,* 1 December 2006.

LoBaido, Anthony. "China behind Christian Persecution in S.E. Asia." *World Net Daily,* 22 March 2000. From its website.

Lubold, Gordon. "U.S. Seeks More Info on China's Military. *Christian Science Monitor,* 29 May 2007.

Lynch, David J. "China Elevates Its Economic Profile in Africa." *USA Today,* 3 November 2006.

MacLeod, Scott. "A Date with a Dangerous Mind." *Time,* 25 September 2006.

McCawley, Tom. "Indonesia's Terrorist Hunt Bears Fruit." *Christian Science Monitor,* 15 June 2007.

McLaughlin, Kathleen E. "Centuries-Old Partnership Binds China, Iran Together." *San Francisco Chronicle,* 18 September 2006. From its website, SFGate.com.

"Militants Kill Five Afghans Involved in Opium Project." World News Wire Reports (AP). *Jacksonville Daily News* (NC), 19 May 2005.

"Military: Iran Teaching Iraqi Militia to Build Bombs." From Associated Press. *Jacksonville Daily News* (NC), 12 April 2007.

Millward, James. "Violent Separatism in Xinjiang: A Critical Assessment." East-West Center Washington. Policy Study 6, n.d. From its website, eastwestcenterwashington.org.

Montero, David. "Attacks Heat Up Afghan-Pakistani Border." *Christian Science Monitor,* 12 January 2007.

Montero, David. "The Bribe to Exit Pakistan." *Christian Science Monitor,* 30 April 2006.

Montero, David. "China, Pakistan Team Up on Energy." *Christian Science Monitor,* 13 April 2007.

Montero, David. "In Border Zone, Pakistan Backs Off from Taliban." *Christian Science Monitor,* 26 September 2006.
Montero, David. "In Talks with India, Pressure Is on Pakistan." *Christian Science Monitor,* 15 November 2006.
Montero, David. "More Evidence of Taliban Leader Hiding in Pakistan." *Christian Science Monitor,* 19 January 2007.
Montero, David. "Pakistan: Delicate Dance of a Key Ally." *Christian Science Monitor,* 26 September 2006.
Montero, David. "Quiet Bangladesh Woken by Bombs." *Christian Science Monitor,* 18 August 2006.
Montero, David. "Riots in Bangladesh May Benefit Islamists." *Christian Science Monitor,* 30 October 2006.
Montlake, Simon. "As Thai Insurgency Spreads, Government Opens Door to Dialogue." *Christian Science Monitor,* 25 April 2005.
Montlake, Simon. "In Philippines, a Renewed Bid to Drive Out Terror Factions." *Christian Science Monitor,* 14 December 2004.
Montlake, Simon. "Indonesian Terror Group Hobbled." *Christian Science Monitor,* 30 August 2005.
Montlake, Simon. "Malaysia's Ex-Leader Stays in the Game." *Christian Science Monitor,* 10 November 2006.
Montlake, Simon. "Political Killings Traced to Philippine Military." *Christian Science Monitor,* 23 February 2007.
Montlake, Simon. "Tension Grows between Thai Security Forces and Muslim Locals." *Christian Science Monitor,* 12 July 2005.
Montlake, Simon. "Thai Rebel Tactic: Divide the Faiths." *Christian Science Monitor,* 20 July 2005.
Montlake, Simon. "U.S. Troops in Philippines Defy Old Stereotype." *Christian Science Monitor,* 1 March 2007.
Montlake, Simon. "Where U.S. Is Gaining against Terror." *Christian Science Monitor,* 15 February 2007.
Moreau, Ron, and Sami Yousafzai, and Michael Hirsh. "The Rise of Jihadistan." *Newsweek,* 2 October 2007.
Munro, Ian. "Covert Police Methods Revealed" and "Lawyers Warn against Police Stings." *The Age* (Melbourne), 8 and 9 September 2004, respectively.
Mahnaimi, Uzi and Sarah Baxter. "Israelis Seized Nuclear Material in Syrian Raid." *Times on Line* (UK), 23 September 2007.
Mahnaimi, Uzi and Sarah Baxter and Michael Sheridan. "Israelis 'Blew Apart Syrian Nuclear Cache'." *Times on Line* (UK), 16 September 2007.
Myers, Lt.Col. Patrick and Patrick Poole. "Hezbollah, Illegal Immigration, and the Next 9/11." *FrontPageMagazine.com,* 28 April 2006. Through access@g2-forward.org.
Nalls, Capt. John B. "A Company Commander's Thoughts on Iraq." *Armor Magazine,* February 2004.

Navarro, Peter. "Watch Your Flanks America." Opinion Piece. *Christian Science Monitor,* 26 February 2007.

Nessman, Ravi. Associated Press. "Israelis Step Up Offensive." *Jacksonville Daily News* (NC), 10 August 2006.

"New Political Parties Banned in Thailand." World Briefs Wire Reports (AP). *Jacksonville Daily News* (NC), 22 September 2006.

"The New Prime Minister of Thailand Said. . . ." World News in Brief. *Christian Science Monitor*, 19 October 2006.

"A New Wave of Violence Erupted in Muslim-Dominated Southern Thailand. " World News in Brief. *Christian Science Monitor*, 3 February 2006.

"No Survivors, Wreckage Found in Ferry Sinking." *Asian Economic News,* 3 July 2000.

Nojumi, Neamatollah. *The Rise of the Taliban in Afghanistan: Mass Mobilization, Civil War, and the Future of the Region.* New York: Palgrave, 2002.

Nordland, Rod. "Walk through Fire." *Newsweek,* 9 April 2007.

"North Koreans Assisted Hezbollah with Tunnel Construction." Jamestown Foundation. *Terrorism Focus,* vol. III, issue 30, August 2006. From its website, www.jamestown.org.

Nyirigwa, Watts Roba Gibia. "Why 2011 Referendum Is the Only Hope for South Sudanese: Part One." *Khartoum Monitor,* 31 May 2006.

Olcott, Martha. "The Great Powers in Central Asia," Carnegie Endowment for International Peace (Moscow Center), October 2006. From its website, carnegie.ru.

Ommani, Ardeshir. "The Non-Aligned Movement Has Been an Organization of, More or Less, Deprived Nations of the Planet," *Iran Heritage,* 18 September 2006, from its website, iranian.com.

"One of the Terrorist Leaders Most Wanted by U.S. Authorities." World News in Brief. *Christian Science Monitor,* 18 January 2007.

"Osama's Secret Citadel." *DEBKA-Net-Weekly,* 28 September 2001. As posted at vbulletin.thesite.org.

"Parliament Suicide Attack Stuns India." BBC News, 13 December 2001. From its website, bbc.co.uk.

Peck, Grant. "Thailand's Military Ousts Prime Minister While He's in New York." *Jacksonville Daily News* (NC), 20 September 2006.

Pennington, Matthe. Associated Press. "Pakistan Unsure If Target Is al-Zawahri." *Jacksonville Daily News* (NC), 21 March 2004.

Peraino, Kevin, and Babak Dehghanpisheh, and Christopher Dickey. "Eye for an Eye." *Newsweek,* 14 August 2006.

Peterson, Scott. "Hostile in Public, Iran Seeks Quiet Discourse with U.S." *Christian Science Monitor,* 25 September 2003.

Peterson, Scott. "Shiites Rising—Part One." *Christian Science Monitor,* 6 June 2007.

Peterson, Scott and Nicholas Blandford. "A Gauge of Iran's Hand in Iraq." *Christian Science Monitor,* 5 July 2007.
Piore, Adam. "Cash-Strapped Cambodia Eyes Black Gold." *Christian Science Monitor,* 30 August 2006.
"Political Gatherings Were Banned in Bangladesh." World News in Brief. *Christian Science Monitor,* 20 November 2006.
Polleross, Josef. "China Competes with West in Aid to Its Neighbors." *New York Times,* 18 September 2006.
"Profile: Al-Qaeda 'Kingpin'." BBC News, 28 September 2006. From its website, bbc.co.uk.
"Profile: Hun Sen." BBC News, 15 July 2004. From its website, bbc.co.uk.
Prusher, Ilene R. "Israel Sends a 'Message' on Nukes." *Christian Science Monitor,* 19 September 2007.
Ramesh, Randeep. "Inside India's Hidden War." *The Guardian* (UK), 9 May 2006. From its website, www.guardian.co.uk.
Ramesh, Randeep. "PM Accuses Pakistan over Mumbai Bombs." *The Guardian* (UK), 14 July 2006. From its website, www.guardian.co.uk.
Rashid, Ahmed. "Losing the War on Terror: Why Militants Are Beating Technology Five Years After Sept. 11." *Washington Post,* 11 September 2006. Republished as "Slipping into the Shadows." *Maine Sunday Telegram,* 17 September 2006.
Roul, Animesh. "Trail from Mumbai Blasts Leads to Multiple Terrorist Groups." Jamestown Foundation. *Terrorism Focus,* vol. III, issue 29, 25 July 2006. From its website, www.jamestown.org.
Sangraula, Bikash. "Nepalese Hit the Streets—Again—for a Change." *Christian Science Monitor,* 27 July 2006.
Sangraula, Bikash. "Nepal's Children Forced to Fight." *Christian Science Monitor,* 28 July 2006.
Sangraula, Bikash. "Nepal's Decade of War Draws to a Close." *Christian Science Monitor,* 9 November 2006.
Sangraula, Bikash. "Popular Protests Ignite Nepal." *Christian Science Monitor,* 11 April 2006.
Sappenfield, Mark. "Bombs Fail to Ignite As Indian Imams Urge Calm." *Christian Science Monitor,* 14 September 2006.
Sappenfield, Mark and David Montero. "China Woos India and Pakistan with Nuclear Know-How." *Christian Science Monitor,* 21 November 2006.
Scarpello, Fabio. "Indonesia's Jihadist Revival." *Christian Science Monitor,* 5 February 2007.
Schearf, Daniel "China-North Korea Relations Tested as Reports Say Kim Jong Il to Visit Beijing," *VOA,* 24 August 2006.

Shichor, Yitzhah. Central Asia-Caucasus Institute. Silk Road Studies Program. "Fact and Fiction: A Chinese Documentary on Eastern Turkestan Terrorism." *China and Eurasia Forum Quarterly,* vol. 4, no. 2, 2006.

Short, Anthony. "Communism, Race and Politics in Malaysia." *Asian Survey,* vol. 10, no. 12, December 1970.

Shrader, Katherine. Associated Press. "Sanctions on North Korea." *Jacksonville Daily News* (NC), 13 October 2005.

Shrader, Katherine. "North Korean Client List Is Said to Take In Iran, Syria, 16 Others." From Associated Press. As posted on 13 October 2006 at access@g2-forward.org.

"Six Afghans Die in Rebel Ambush." World News Wire Reports (AP). *Jacksonville Daily News* (NC), 20 May 2005.

Smith, Charles R. "U.S. Bombs Chinese Network in Afghanistan, PRC Sold Taliban Advanced Air Defense System." Newsmax.com, 20 October 2001.

Spinetta, Maj. Lawrence (USAF). "Cutting China's 'String of Pearls'." *U.S. Naval Institute Proceedings,* October 2006.

"Spy plane" articles from *Washington Post*: "China Says It Will Return Disassembled U.S. Plane," 25 May 2001; "Surveillance Plane to Be Returned to U.S. in Pieces," 30 May 2001; "U.S., China Agree on Plan to Return Spy Plane: U.S. Team Arrives in China to Begin Dismantling Jet," 7 June 2001; "Disassembled Navy Plane Scheduled to Leave China Today," 3 July 2001; "China Bills U.S. Over Collision: $1 Million in Surveillance Plane Dispute Termed 'Exaggerated' ," 7 July 2001; "U.S. to Pay China $34,567 for Costs of Downed Plane," 10 August 2001.

"Sri Lanka Offers Oil Block to India in Return for Construction of Railway." *Sri Lanka Newspapers,* 30 January 2007. From its website, www.lankanewspapers.com.

Story, Ian. "China and the Philippines: Moving beyond the South China Sea Dispute." Jamestown Foundation. *China Brief,* vol. VI, issue 17, 16 August 2006. From its website, www.jamestown.org.

Straziuso, Jason. Associated Press. "Afghan Bomber Deadlier." *Jacksonville Daily News* (NC), 3 June 2007.

"Strong Chinese-Hamas Intelligence Connection." *DEBKAfile* (Israel), 19 June 2006.

"Sudan Unity Requires Secular State." *Khartoum Monitor,* 1 June 2006.

"Taiwan Election/Referendum, March 20, 2004" *Asia Media News Daily,* n.d. UCLA Asia Inst. From its website, www.asiamedia.ucla.edu.

"Taliban Forces Are Regrouping in Afghanistan." World Briefs Wire Reports (AP). *Jacksonville Daily News* (NC), 15 September 2006.

"There Will Be No Year-End Strike in Nepal." World News in Brief. *Christian Science Monitor,* 26 December 2006.

"Thousands of People Were Seeking Refuge in School Buildings." World News in Brief. *Christian Science Monitor,* 18 April 2007.

"Three Policemen Were Killed and Rail Service in Southern Thailand Was Disrupted." World Briefs Wire Reports (AP). *Jacksonville Daily News* (NC), 3 August 2006.

Timperlake, Ed. "Clues How Chinese Missile Ended Up in Hezbollah's Arsenal." As posted on 26 July 2006 at access@g2-forward.org.

"A Truck Packed with Explosives and Driven by Tamil Separatist." World News in Brief. *Christian Science Monitor,* 17 October 2006.

"2001: Suicide Attack on Indian Parliament." BBC News, 13 December 2001. From its website, bbc.co.uk.

"2002: Hindus Die in Train Fire." BBC News, 27 February 2002. From its website, bbc.co.uk.

"A Two-Week Ultimatum Was Issued by Communists." World News in Brief. *Christian Science Monitor,* 3 May 2007.

"U.S. Government Drops Vietnam from List of Worst Religious Freedom Violators." From Associated Press. *Jacksonville Daily News* (NC), 14 November 2006.

"U.S. Hopes China Will Help Moderate Havana Meeting." *China Confidential,* 11 September 2006. From its website.

Vincent, Steven. "Shiites Bring Rigid Piety to Iraq's South." *Christian Science Monitor,* 13 July 2005.

Vincent, Steven. "Switched Off in Basra." *New York Times,* 31 July 2005.

"Violence Erupts in Southern Thailand." World Briefs Wire Reports (AP). *Jacksonville Daily News* (NC), 17 July 2005.

Watanabe, Chisaki. Associated Press. "U.S., Others Concerned after China's Anti-Satellite Launch." *Jacksonville Daily News* (NC), 20 January 2007.

"Wednesday Brought Yet Another Major Transportation Accident to Indonesia." World News in Brief. *Christian Science Monitor,* 8 March 2007.

Weir, Fred. "Big Powers Jockey for Oil in Central Asia." *Christian Science Monitor*, 28 March 2007.

Zakaria, Fareed. "True or False: We Are Losing the War against Radical Islam." *Newsweek,* 2 July 2007.

About the Author

After 28 years of commissioned and noncommissioned infantry service, John Poole retired from the United States Marine Corps in April 1993. While on active duty, he studied small-unit tactics for nine years: (1) six months at the Basic School in Quantico (1966); (2) seven months as a rifle platoon commander in Vietnam (1966-67); (3) three months as a rifle company commander at Camp Pendleton (1967); (4) five months as a regimental headquarters company (and camp) commander in Vietnam (1968); (5) eight months as a rifle company commander in Vietnam (1968-69); (6) five and a half years as an instructor with the Advanced Infantry Training Company (AITC) at Camp Lejeune (1986-92); and (7) one year as the Staff Noncommissioned Officer in Charge of the 3rd Marine Division Combat Squad Leaders Course (CSLC) on Okinawa (1992-93).

While at AITC, he developed, taught, and refined courses on maneuver warfare, land navigation, fire support coordination, call for fire, adjust fire, close air support, M203 grenade launcher, movement to contact, daylight attack, night attack, infiltration, defense, offensive Military Operations in Urban Terrain (MOUT), defensive MOUT, Nuclear/Biological/Chemical (NBC) defense, and leadership. While at CSLC, he further refined the same periods of instruction and developed others on patrolling.

He has completed all of the correspondence school requirements for the Marine Corps Command and Staff College, Naval War College (1,000-hour curriculum), and Marine Corps Warfighting Skills Program. He is a graduate of the Camp Lejeune Instructional Management Course, the 2nd Marine Division Skill Leaders in Advanced Marksmanship (SLAM) Course, and the East-Coast School of Infantry Platoon Sergeants' Course.

In the 14 years since retirement, John Poole has researched the small-unit tactics of other nations and written seven other books: (1) *The Last Hundred Yards: The NCO's Contribution to Warfare,* a squad combat study based on the consensus opinions of 1,200 NCOs and casualty statistics of AITC and CSLC field trials; (2) *One More Bridge to Cross: Lowering the Cost of War*, a treatise on enemy proficiency at short range and how to match it; (3) *Phantom Soldier: The Enemy's Answer to U.S. Firepower,* an in-depth look at the highly deceptive Asian style of war; (4) *The Tiger's Way: A U.S. Private's Best Chance of Survival,* a study of how Eastern fire teams and individual soldiers fight; (5) *Tactics of the Crescent Moon: Militant Muslim*

Combat Methods, a comprehensive analysis of the insurgents' battlefield procedures in Palestine, Chechnya, Afghanistan, and Iraq; (6) *Militant Tricks: Battlefield Ruses of the Islamic Insurgent,* an honest appraisal of the so-far-undefeated *jihadist* method; and (7) *Terrorist Trail: Backtracking the Foreign Fighter,* how many of the *jihadists* in Iraq can be traced back to Africa.

As of September 2007, he had conducted multiday training sessions (on 4GW for small units) at 39 (mostly Marine) battalions, nine Marine schools, and seven special-operations units from all four U.S. service branches. He has been stationed twice each in South Vietnam and Okinawa, and has traveled twice to Communist China. He has also visited Japan, Taiwan, the Philippines, Indonesia, both Koreas, Hong Kong, Macao, northern Vietnam, Myanmar (Burma), Thailand, Cambodia, Malaysia, Singapore, Tibet, Nepal, Bangladesh, India, Pakistan, Russia, East Germany, West Germany, Morocco, Israel (to include the West Bank), Turkey, Iran, Lebanon, Egypt, and Sudan.

Between early tours in the Marine Corps (from 1969 to 1971), John Poole worked as a criminal investigator for the Illinois Bureau of Investigation (IBI). After attending the State Police Academy for several months in Springfield, he was assigned to the IBI's Chicago office.

Name Index

A

Ahmadinejad, President Mahmoud 6
Amarasinghe, Somowansa 101
Ampatuan, Governor 48
Asari, Alhaji Mujahid Dokubo 18
Azzam, Addallah Yusuf 35

B

Ba'asyir, Abu Bakar 28, 53, 59, 62
Badawi, Prime Minister Abdullah Ahmad 26, 27
Bhutto, Prime Minister Benazir 111
Bin Abas, Nasir 54
Bin Attash, Tawfiq (same as Khallad) 42
Bin Laden, Osama xxiv, 6, 18, 20, 41, 42, 54, 59, 60, 119, 120, 125, 126, 136, 137, 140, 165, 186
Boonyaratkalin, Gen. Sondhi 29
Burke, Edmund 1

C

Carlson, Brig.Gen. Evans 367, 369
Chalabi, Ahmad 194
Chater, David 120
Chavez, President Hugo 21
Chulanont, Sarayud 29
Conboy, Ken 57

D

Dahal, Pushpa Kamal (same as Pranchanda) 81, 82
Daqduq, Ali Musa 15
Daud 124
Dillinger, John 364
Downs, Capt. Michael 349
Dujana, Abu 61
Dwikarna, Agus 57

E

no entries

F

no entries

G

Galan, Jusuf 57
Gandhi, Mahatma (Mohandas Karamchand) 197
Gandhi, Prime Minister Rajiv 101
Geberth, Vernon J. 167
Gertz, Bill 10
Ghai, Yash 74
Gunaratna, Rohan 43, 53, 54, 101

H

Haddad, Najy Awaita (same as Ramzi Ahmed Yousef) 41, 42, 43
Hakim, Abdul (same as Abdul Hakim Ali Hashim Murad) 42, 43
Hambali (same as Riduan Isamuddin) 43
al-Hamzi, Nawaf 43
Haqqani, Maulvi Jalaluddin 109, 112
Hasanuddin 61
Hasina, Sheikh 85
Hekmatyar, Gulbuddin 18, 61
Hendropriyono, Abdulah Makhmud 57
Hitler, Fuhrer Adolph 192
Holmes, Sherlock 175
Hussain, Lt.Gen. Safdar 126
Hussein, President Saddam 200, 311

I

Isamuddin, Riduan (same as Hambali) 43

J

Janjalani, Khadaffy 48
Jiaboa, Premier Wen 72, 73
Jiaxuan, Tang 13
Jirapaet, Krirk-krai 76
John Paul II, Pope xxviii, 43, 161

K

Kallad (same as Tawfiq bin Attash) 41
Karzai, President Hamed 110, 111, 129, 142
Khalifa, Abdul Rahman (same as Muhammed Jamal Khalifa) 41
Khalifa, Muhammed Jamal (same as Abdul Rahman Khalifa) 41
Khamenei, Grand Ayatollah Ali 165
King, Martin Luther 197
Kumarasiri, Premalal 98
Kurlantzick, Joshua 127

L

Linder, Col. Jim 189
Locard, Edmond 166
Ludendorff, Gen. Erich 369

M

Mackerras, Colin 127
Mahsum, Hahsan 123
Mao Tse-Tung, Chairman xix, xx, xxv, xxvii, 101, 195, 282
Marcos, President Ferdinand E. 38, 40
Marshall, Gen. George C., Jr. 373

Marx, Karl xx
al-Masri, Basir 120
McCain, Sen. John S., III 283
McIntyre, James 125
Merrill, Brig.Gen. Frank 367
al-Mihdhar, Khalid 43
Miranda, Ernesto 166, 185
Mo, Nguyen Van 212
Mohammed, Khalid Shaikh 43
Mohammed, Prime Minister Mahathir 26
Mosby, John 335
Mugabe, President Robert 68, 69
Mughniyeh, Imad 7
Mujib, President Sheikh 88
Murad, Abdul Hakim Ali Hashim (same as Abdul Hakim) 42, 43
Musharraf, President Pervez 107, 108, 109, 110, 111

N

Nasrallah, Sheikh Sayyed Hassan 82, 165
Noriega, President Manuel 21

O

Omar, Mullah Mohammed 108, 110

P

Polo, Marco 136
Pontoh, Coen Hussein 57
Pot, Prime Minister Pol 65, 66, 68, 70
Prabhakaran, Velapillai 104
Pranchanda (same as Pushpa Kamal Dahal) 78, 79, 80
Premadasa, President Ranasinghe 102

Q

no entries

R

Rainsy, Sam 70
Rais, Amien 50
Rajapakse, President Mahinda 98, 104
Ranariddh, Prince Norodom 68
Riadi, Ilham 57
Rumsfeld, Donald H. 125

S

al-Sadr, Muqtada 82, 163
Sambath, Reach 69
Sen, Prime Minister Hun 66, 67, 68, 72, 73, 74
Seyam, Reda 57
Shinawatra, Prime Minister Thaksin 29
Singh, Prime Minister Manmohan 96
Singh, President Moni 88
Siregar, Parlindungan 57
Sithol, Phai 69
Suharto, President 50, 62
Sukarno, President 26
Sukarnoputri, President Megawati 62
Sulaiman, Abu 49
Sun Tzu xxiii, 19, 84, 126, 143, 194, 206, 374
Sungkar, Abdullah 28, 42, 54, 58, 59, 62

T

Taruc, Luis 38
Terzi, Lt. Joe 290, 324
Thop, Nurdin Nur (same as Noordin Mohamed Top) 58
Thucydides 370
Top, Noordin Mohamed (same as Nurdin Nur Thop) 58

U

no entries

V

no entries

W

Wahid, President Abdurrahman 50
Wickremanayake, Prime Minister Ratnasiri 98
Wijeweera, Rohana 98, 100

X

Xiansheng, Col. Meng xxv, 19
Xiaoping, Deng xx

Y

Yarkas, Imad Eddris Barakat 57
Yousaf, Brigadier Mohammad 203
Yousef, Ramzi Ahmed (same as Najy Awaita Haddad) 41, 42, 43
Yudhoyono, President Suslio Bambang 50

Z

Zawahiri, Ayman 125, 186
Zia ul-Haq, President Muhammad 110